KT-131-715

Praise for the first edition of
THE MADWOMAN IN THE ATTIC: *The Woman Writer and the Nineteenth-Century Literary Imagination*

"The authors have an encyclopedic command of literature and a particularly generous respect for their colleagues (and some 'precursors') in feminist criticism. Their summa is deeply scholarly, but it is also elegant and vigorous. I came to it expecting to be stunned by learning; I read it in a state of sustained excitement because it offered a new way of seeing."
—Frances Taliaferro, *Harper's*

"It's unlikely that anyone reading this massive, brilliantly argued and radically reinterpretive study of Jane Austen, Mary Shelley, Emily and Charlotte Brontë, George Eliot and Emily Dickinson (among others) will ever see these writers quite as they did before."—*Publishers Weekly*

"Thanks to Gilbert and Gubar, we return to the writing of these nineteenth-century women with renewed curiosity, with intimations of a discernible female imagination." —Valerie Miner, *Christian Science Monitor*

"Having (the book) at hand is like having a good friend nearby. She is enormously well read, sharp, visionary in what she sees when she reads a book. You love to talk with her. You thank her for what she shows you; you always come back to her; count on her insights; and you like her enormously."
—Louise Bernikow, *Ms.*

"[Gilbert and Gubar] have an important subject to explore. They are equipped ... with a scholarly knowledge of the period, including its obscure corners—*Frankenstein, Aurora Leigh*, Maria Edgeworth, Jane Austen's juvenilia—and they ingeniously bring in myth and fairy tale to support their arguments.... Indeed they do open up a new dimension in these works, and one will always see them differently."—Rosemary Dinnage, *New York Review of Books*

The Madwoman in the Attic

The Madwoman in the Attic

THE WOMAN WRITER AND THE NINETEENTH-CENTURY LITERARY IMAGINATION

SECOND EDITION

SANDRA M. GILBERT

and SUSAN GUBAR

YALE NOTA BENE
YALE UNIVERSITY PRESS
NEW HAVEN AND LONDON

First published as a Yale Nota Bene book in 2000.

Copyright © 1979 by Yale University.
Copyright © 1984 by Sandra M. Gilbert and Susan Gubar.
Introduction to Second Edition copyright © 2000 by Sandra M. Gilbert and Susan Gubar.
All rights reserved.
This book may not be reproduced, in whole or in part, in any form (beyond that copying
permitted by Sections 107 and 108 of the U.S. Copyright Law and except by reviewers for
the public press), without written permission from the publishers.

For information about this and other Yale University Press publications, please contact:
U. S. office   sales.press@yale.edu
Europe office   sales@yaleup.co.uk

Printed in the United States of America.

Library of Congress Cataloging-in-Publication Data
Gilbert, Sandra M.
    The madwoman in the attic : the woman writer and the nineteenth-century literary
    imagination / Sandra M. Gilbert and Susan Gubar.—2nd. ed.
        p. cm.
    Includes bibliographical references and index.
    ISBN 0-300-08458-7
    1. English literature—Women authors—History and criticism. 2. English literature—
    19th century—History and criticism. 3. Women in literature. 4. Women authors—
    Psychology. 5. English literature—Psychological aspects. I. Gubar, Susan, 1944– II. Title.

PR115.G5 2000
820.9´9287´09034—dc21   99–086038

A catalogue record for this book is available from the British Library.

Acknowledgment is made to the following for permission to reprint portions of this book,
originally published in slightly different form: Feminist Studies, for "The Genesis of
Hunger, according to Shirley" (by Susan Gubar) and "Horror's Twin: Mary Shelley's
Monstrous Eve" (by Sandra Gilbert). / Novel, for "Sane Jane and the Critics" (by Susan
Gubar) and "A Revisionary Company" (by Sandra Gilbert and Susan Gubar). / PMLA, for
"Patriarchal Poetry and Women Readers: Reflections on Milton's Bogey" (by Sandra
Gilbert). / Signs, for "Plain Jane's Progress" (by Sandra Gilbert) and "The Female
Monster in Augustan Satire" (by Susan Gubar). / The Cornell Review, for portions of "Liber
Scriptus: The Metaphor of Literary Paternity" (by Sandra Gilbert). / Indiana University
Press, for portions of "Introduction: Gender, Creativity, and the Woman Poet" (by Sandra
Gilbert and Susan Gubar), in Gilbert and Gubar, ed., Shakespeare's Sisters: Feminist Essays on
Women Poets (Indiana University Press, 1979).

Acknowledgment is made for permission to quote from the following: Thomas H.
Johnson, ed. The Poems of Emily Dickinson. Cambridge, Mass.: The Belknap Press of
Harvard University Press. Copyright 1951, 1955 by the President and Fellows of Harvard
College. By permission of the publishers and the Trustees of Amherst College. / Thomas
H. Johnson, ed. The Complete Poems of Emily Dickinson. Boston, Mass.: Little, Brown and
Company. Copyright 1914, 1935, 1942 by Martha Dickinson Bianchi. Copyright 1929,
© 1957, 1963 by Mary L. Hampson. By permission of the publishers. / Ruth Stone. Cheap.
Copyright © 1975 by Ruth Stone. By permission of Harcourt Brace Jovanovich, Inc.

10   9   8   7   6   5   4   3   2

This book is as much for Edward, Elliot, and Roger, as it is for Kathy, Molly, Sandra, Simone, Susan, and Susanna.

The strife of thought, accusing and excusing, began afresh, and gathered fierceness. The soul of Lilith lay naked to the torture of pure interpenetrating inward light. She began to moan, and sigh deep sighs, then murmur as if holding colloquy with a dividual self: her queendom was no longer whole; it was divided against itself. . . . At length she began what seemed a tale about herself, in a language so strange, and in forms so shadowy, that I could but here and there understand a little.

—George MacDonald, *Lilith*

It was not at first clear to me exactly what I was, except that I was someone who was being made to do certain things by someone else who was really the same person as myself—I have always called her Lilith. And yet the acts were mine, not Lilith's.

—Laura Riding, "Eve's Side of It"

Contents

Part V. Captivity and Consciousness in George Eliot's Fiction

Part VI. Strength in Agony: Nineteenth-Century Poetry by Women

Preface to the First Edition

This book began with a course in literature by women that we taught together at Indiana University in the fall of 1974. Reading the writing of women from Jane Austen and Charlotte Brontë to Emily Dickinson, Virginia Woolf, and Sylvia Plath, we were surprised by the coherence of theme and imagery that we encountered in the works of writers who were often geographically, historically, and psychologically distant from each other. Indeed, even when we studied women's achievements in radically different genres, we found what began to seem a distinctively female literary tradition, a tradition that had been approached and appreciated by many women readers and writers but which no one had yet defined in its entirety. Images of enclosure and escape, fantasies in which maddened doubles functioned as asocial surrogates for docile selves, metaphors of physical discomfort manifested in frozen landscapes and fiery interiors—such patterns recurred throughout this tradition, along with obsessive depictions of diseases like anorexia, agoraphobia, and claustrophobia.

Seeking to understand the anxieties out of which this tradition must have grown, we undertook a close study of the literature produced by women in the nineteenth century, for that seemed to us to be the first era in which female authorship was no longer in some sense anomalous. As we explored this literature, however, we found ourselves over and over again confronting two separate but related matters: first, the social position in which nineteenth-century women writers found themselves and, second, the reading that they themselves did. Both in life and in art, we saw, the artists we studied were literally and figuratively confined. Enclosed in the architecture of an overwhelmingly male-dominated society, these literary women were also, inevitably, trapped in the specifically literary constructs of what Gertrude Stein was to call "patriarchal poetry." For not only did a nineteenth-century woman writer have to inhabit ancestral mansions (or cottages) owned and built by men, she was also constricted and restricted by the Palaces of Art and Houses of Fiction male writers authored. We decided, therefore, that the striking coherence we noticed in literature by women could be explained by a common, female impulse to struggle free from social and literary confinement through strategic redefinitions of self, art, and society.

As our title's allusion to *Jane Eyre* suggests, we began our own definition of these redefinitions with close readings of Charlotte Brontë, who seemed to us to provide a paradigm of many distinctively female anxieties and abilities. Thus, although we have attempted to maintain a very roughly chronological ordering of authors throughout the book, this often under-appreciated nineteenth-century novelist really does occupy a central position in our study: through detailed analyses of her novels, we hope to show new ways in which all nineteenth-century works by women can be interpreted. As our table of contents indicates, however, we eventually felt that we had to branch out from Brontë, if only to understand her more fully. For in the process of researching our book we realized that, like many other feminists, we were trying to recover not only a major (and neglected) female literature but a whole (neglected) female history.

In this connection, the work of social historians like Gerda Lerner, Alice Rossi, Ann Douglas, and Martha Vicinus not only helped us but helped remind us just how much of women's history has been lost or misunderstood. Even more useful for our project, however, were the recent demonstrations by Ellen Moers and Elaine Showalter that nineteenth-century literary women *did* have both a literature and a culture of their own—that, in other words, by the nineteenth century there was a rich and clearly defined female literary subculture, a community in which women consciously read and related to each other's works. Because both Moers and Showalter have so skillfully traced the overall history of this community, we have been able here to focus closely on a number of nineteenth-century texts we consider crucial to that history; and in a future volume we plan similar readings of key twentieth-century texts. For us, such touchstones have provided models for understanding the dynamics of female literary response to male literary assertion and coercion.

That literary texts are coercive (or at least compellingly persuasive) has been one of our major observations, for just as women have been repeatedly defined by male authors, they seem in reaction to have found it necessary to act out male metaphors in their own texts, as if trying to understand their implications. Our literary methodology has therefore been based on the Bloomian premise that literary history consists of strong action and inevitable reaction. Moreover, like such phenomenological critics as Gaston Bachelard, Simone de Beauvoir, and J. Hillis Miller, we have sought to describe both the experience that generates metaphor and the metaphor that creates experience.

Reading metaphors in this experiential way, we have inevitably ended up reading our own lives as well as the texts we study, so that the process of writing this book has been as transformative for us as the process of "attempting the pen" was for so many of the women we discuss. And much of the exhilaration of writing has come from working together. Like most collaborators, we have divided our responsibilities: Sandra Gilbert drafted the section on "Milton's daughters," the essays on *The Professor* and *Jane Eyre*, and the chapters on the "Aesthetics of Renunciation" and on Emily Dickinson; Susan Gubar drafted the section on Jane Austen, the essays on *Shirley* and *Villette*, and the two chapters about George Eliot; and each of us has drafted portions of the introductory exploration of a feminist poetics. We have continually exchanged and discussed our drafts, however, so that we feel our book represents not just a dialogue but a consensus. Redefining what has so far been male-defined literary history in the same way that women writers have revised "patriarchal poetics," we have found that the process of collaboration has given us the essential support we needed to complete such an ambitious project.

Besides our own friendship, however, we were fortunate enough to have much additional help from colleagues, friends, students, husbands, and children. Useful suggestions were offered by many, including Frederic Amory, Wendy Barker, Elyse Blankley, Timothy Bovy, Moneera Doss, Robert Griffin, Dolores Gros Louis, Anne Hedin, Robert Hopkins, Kenneth Johnston, Cynthia Kinnard, U. C. Knoepflmacher, Wendy Kolmar, Richard Levin, Barbara Clarke Mossberg, Celeste Wright, and, especially, Donald Gray, whose detailed comments were often crucial. We are grateful to many others as well. The encouragement of Harold Bloom, Tillie Olsen, Robert Scholes, Catharine Stimpson, and Ruth Stone aided us in significant ways, and we are particularly grateful to Kenneth R. R. Gros Louis, whose interest in this project has enabled us to teach together several times at Indiana and whose good will has continually heartened us. In this connection, we want especially to thank our home institutions, Indiana University and the University of California at Davis, which also encouraged us by generously providing travel money, research grants, and summer fellowships when no other funding agencies would.

We must thank, too, the people connected with Yale University Press who helped make this book possible. In particular, Garrett Stewart, chosen as outside advisor by the Press, was an ideal reader, whose enthusiasm and perceptiveness were important to our work; Ellen Graham was a perfect editor, whose exemplary patience helped guide this project to completion; and Lynn Walterick was a superb and sympathetic copyeditor, whose skillful questions invariably helped us find better answers. Without Edith Lavis's dedication in preparing the manuscript, however, their efforts would have been in vain, so we must thank her as well, while we must also thank Mrs. Virginia French for devoted childcare without which even the act of composition would have been impossible, Tricia Lootens and Roger Gilbert for help in indexing, and both Eileen Frye and Alison Hilton for useful suggestions. As this book goes to press we want to note, too, that Hopewell Selby occupies a special place in our thoughts. Finally, we want most of all to acknowledge what has been profoundly important to both of us: the revisionary advice and consent of our husbands, Elliot Gilbert and Edward Gubar, and our children, Roger, Kathy, and Susanna Gilbert, and Molly and Simone Gubar, all of whom, together, have given us lives that are a joy to read.

Introduction to the Second Edition: The Madwoman in the Academy

A Note to the Reader

SMG: In the introduction to this millennial edition of *The Madwoman in the Attic*, Susan Gubar and I have departed from our usual attempt at the creation of a seamlessly "unitary" text. Instead of writing a collaborative essay, we've engaged in a dialogue that deliberately—both literally and figuratively—dramatizes the differences between our two voices, demonstrating what readers have no doubt always understood: that behind the hyphenated yet superficially monolithic authorial entity known as Gilbert-and-Gubar there are and always have been two distinct, if deeply bonded, human beings, each with her own view of the world and, more particularly, of women (mad or sane), of attics and parlors, of language, and of the arts of language.

Our current conversation covers a range of topics that we outlined together, but throughout, as we review our early years of feminist education and collaboration (in "Scenes of Instruction"), analyze the reasons for our initial focus on a particular literary period ("The Nineteenth Century and After"), consider the scholarship that has followed our own ("Beyond *The Madwoman*"), and reflect on the problems and possibilities posed by the urgent now of the new millennium ("The Present Moment"), each of us has spoken for herself.

SCENES OF INSTRUCTION

SDG: Although the elevator was going up, we were both feeling down when we noticed each other arriving for work at Ballantine Hall early that first fall semester of 1973. We had each just moved to Bloomington, Indiana, but was it Sandra or was it Susan who asked, "Do you ever get telephone calls at home that are NOT long distance?" Exchanging promises to phone each other, we admitted how uprooted, how lonely we felt in this midwestern university town.

Our discomfort had something to do with what seemed like an overwhelmingly Protestant and masculine ethos of productivity, or so it seemed to us. "Have you had a productive weekend?": the question intoned by processions of solemn colleagues hung heavy in the hall on Monday mornings. Sandra was the one who came up with the "Sassafras Tea Theory" that so bonded us, though our common origins as ex–New Yorkers and Euro-ethnics didn't hurt our evolving friendship.

"They've drunk it," she nodded, to my initial mystification. "The Sassafras Tea. It's what has infused them with gravitas." Giddy with the hilarity upon which our future friendship would be based, we probably sounded like a couple of madwomen cackling in front of the English department office. Our colleagues (overwhelmingly male) looked obligingly askance at our stubborn refusal to imbibe the professional draft that would have turned us into replicants. Even if it was only a fiction, we liked to think that our refusal to swallow the sassafras tea made us thirsty for the headier elixirs that flowed so plentifully when we eventually got our two families together for a grand Thanksgiving feast or a weekday picnic supper.

SMG: My anxiety about sassafras tea was real and serious! For my decision to come to Indiana had at that time felt quite radical. A born-and-bred New Yorker, married to somebody several steps ahead of me in his academic career, I'd had three children by the time I was twenty-seven, and although I was still working on my Columbia dissertation, the four of us had dutifully followed our head of household to California, when he accepted a job at the University of California, Davis. Elliot and I were emphatically bicoastal people. What were we and our three junior Berkeley hippies doing now, in the fall of 1973, in the heart of the heart of the country? Our map of America basically recapped the geography of the famous Steinberg cartoon: Manhattan at the center of things, California a glamorous possibility on the other side of a huge chasm known as the U.S.A., with a few mysterious squiggles in the intervening blankness. How had we ended up in Indiana, of all places?

We were an academic couple, that was why, and an academic couple at a time when such pairs were punished rather than rewarded for daring to have common interests, or perhaps, more precisely, when *wives* had to pay a steep price for wanting to work in the same fields dominated by *husbands*. Throughout graduate school I'd been paying that price—a cost that would eventually become, in the now quaint terminology of the 1970s, "consciousness raising" but that I hadn't yet altogether grasped, even when I arrived in Bloomington.

Remember the old feminist device of the mental "click" that you experience when you find yourself confronting what used to be called sexism? By the time I ran into Susan in the elevator, I'd encountered a tap-dance worth of potential clicks, without paying much attention to them. Click: what was I doing in graduate school anyway? demanded one of my professors at Columbia when he found out that my husband was teaching in Columbia College while I was enrolled in the graduate program. Click: there was absolutely no chance of my getting a job at Davis because nepotism rules were inviolable, explained one of my husband's colleagues as soon as we arrived on campus. Click: and that was only right, chimed in another, because it wouldn't be fair if there were "two salaries in one family." Click: I gave up and began teaching as a lecturer in the California State system, where a number of other University of California wives had similar jobs, with teaching loads twice their husbands', prefiguring the kind of work all too many people of both sexes do on all too many campuses today.

By the time I met Susan, click after click, most of them unheard by me, had ratcheted my particular wheel of fortune into a whole new position: in 1972, I'd applied for jobs *all over the country*, forgetting for the first time that I was just the lesser half of an academic couple, and to my delight I'd had a few offers, though none were in California, and the best of them was in, of all places, Indiana, a state so shocking to my bicoastal system that when I finally got there I began to have bad dreams about a deeply alien beverage.

Why sassafras tea? Well, settled for the first year in a large, scary, rather Gothic house we'd sublet in Bloomington, my family and I decided that as long as we were here we should drive around, look at cornfields, small towns, pastures, things people don't get to see in Queens or the Bronx. Nashville, Indiana, for instance. A charming little town, featuring grits and home-cured hams for breakfast, log cabins, and even a few illegal stills, along with soda fountains where people actually (and quite legally!) drank sassafras tea.

I ate the grits and ham with enthusiasm, failed to locate any manufacturers of moonshine, and refused, I hardly knew why, to drink the sassafras tea. Until not long after seeing *The Invasion of the Body Snatchers,* I found out *why:* I had the dream to which Susan refers, in which I discovered I'd joined a department full of Pod People (many of whom looked deceptively like pipe-smoking male professors in tweed jackets), all solemnly advising me to "Drink the Sassafras Tea"—an act that I knew, with the certainty bestowed by REM sleep, would turn me into either a Pod Person or a midwesterner.

As I hope this rather convoluted tale makes clear, the fatalities that had conspired to shape my nightmares were not unrelated to the forces that would become *the* focus of collaborative attention for me and Susan not too long after we met in the elevator.

SDG: We had decided to team-teach an accelerated senior seminar, in part so Sandra could commute more easily to California, since her family had returned to their Berkeley house in the fall of 1974. Although I was trained in the eighteenth-century novel and Sandra in twentieth-century poetry, we had found our most animated conversations circling around texts by women that neither one of us had studied in graduate school but that both of us had loved either as young adult or as more recent readers: fiction by Jane Austen, the Brontës, Louisa May Alcott, Virginia Woolf; verse all over the map, from Christina Rossetti to Sylvia Plath. So what should we call our undergraduate course? "Upstairs Downstairs," suggested Sandra, influenced by a popular television show playing at the time and the uncanonized status of most of our authors. "Vulgar," I vetoed, in my broadest Brooklyn accent. She tried again: "The Madwoman in the Attic," this time inspired by her discussions of *Jane Eyre* with her second-grade daughter, Susanna. Not a visionary by a longshot, I prevaricated: "Let's try it out on a Victorianist." So we turned to Don Gray, seated at a neighboring table in the Union cafeteria, who promptly delivered what turned out to be the first of his many affirmations of support.

For me, the most memorable event in that remarkably stimulating class was a highly paradoxical moment. Denise Levertov, invited to the Bloomington campus for a reading, had graciously accepted a request to meet our undergraduates, with whom we had previously studied many of her poems. The chairs had been arranged in a circle and the visiting dignitary placed before the desk at the front of the room, when in bustled a latecomer (was her name Dorothy?) with a soft sculpture she had created, titled "In Mind," after Levertov's poem. A prooftext for us because it so succinctly expressed the split between a modestly compliant femininity and the energies of a rebelliously wild imagination, "In Mind"—now transfigured into its colorful fabric version—sat as a sort of offering at the feet of Levertov. "That's not what I meant, not what I meant at all," she sniffed rather contemptuously, much to our astonished discomfort. "I've never considered myself a *woman* artist," she admonished her interlocutors, as (bewildered by her hostile reaction) we gazed meaningfully at our students. "Trust the tale, not the teller," we chanted at subsequent meetings of the class, praising the tactile sister arts and using the episode to instruct not only our undergraduates but ourselves as well in the vagaries of self-definition within the gender politics of a decidedly masculinist literary marketplace.

SMG: Once the scales fell from our eyes on the road to the attic, everything glowed with significance: all the parts of our lives began to rearrange themselves, as in some dazzling kaleidoscope, so that each radiated new and luminous meanings. We'd undertaken to team-teach in the first place not just to make my commuting easier (for arduous commuting was what my problematic coupledness now entailed) but also in response to our enlightened chair's call for a course in that hitherto unheard-of subject, literature by women. I think we put the syllabus together the same way we negotiated the course title that Susan just discussed: brainstorming in a cafeteria or a pizza parlor. Basically, we listed most of the women's texts we knew (and they were of course what some critic of *The Madwoman* was later to call the "old chestnuts"—or, to switch metaphors, the "Brontë mountains," the "Dickinson hills," and the like—a geography of prominence), tried to put them in some sort of order, and then read them with each other and with our students.

By the time Denise Levertov innocently arrived in Bloomington for a poetry reading, unconscious of the fevered scenes of instruction upon which she was entering, we were in a mutual state of what can only be described as revisionary transport, the same condition in which so many of the early second-wave feminists of the now too easily dismissed seventies found themselves. The personal was the political, the literary was the personal, the sexual was the textual, the feminist was the redemptive, and on and on! I don't mean, incidentally, to be sardonic about these revelations (for revelations they were). At the risk of attributing improperly logocentric authority to what some theorists might call a "moment of origin," I have to affirm: bliss *was* it to be alive in that time, at that place! And I hope that some of the bliss was portioned out, like a delicious dessert, to that first group of students who took the journey of conversion with us. Certainly the eye contact Susan mentions was electrically exciting, an epiphanic network of understanding that passed among those of us who wanted to communicate agreement that "maybe Levertov didn't herself understand what she had in mind," in *all* her mind, when she drafted "In Mind." Never trust the teller, trust the feminist analysis—at least for now.

And how transformative that analysis became for us! It was as if the clicks I was just describing had become thunderclaps. Sometimes Susan and I couldn't stop talking after class or office hours, so we'd stop by a supermarket to pick up some stuff to bring to her house, where I'd become a kind of honorary family member. Other nights we'd be on the phone trading insights into the meanings made by women's texts—*Frankenstein* and *Wuthering Heights, Jane Eyre* and the poems of Emily Dickinson, *Mrs. Dal-*

loway and *Ariel*—when they were read not separately and not in the usual graduate-school context of, say, the "Victorian novel" or "nineteenth-century American lit." but *together*, in the newly defined context of a female literary tradition.

That there emphatically was such a tradition became clearer every day. But the dynamics of its formation had still to be traced—and we knew we wanted to be among those who would do that, knew we wanted to write a book exploring what Emily Dickinson called the "Tomes of solid Witchcraft" through which literary women had spoken to one another over and across centuries dominated (as Gertrude Stein put it) by "patriarchal poetry." For as we now began to see (and as early feminist critics were beginning to say), women of letters from Anne Bradstreet to Anne Brontë and on through Gertrude Stein to Sylvia Plath *had* engaged in a complex, sometimes conspiratorial, sometimes convivial conversation that crossed national as well as temporal boundaries. And that conversation had been far more energetic, indeed far more rebellious, than we'd ever realized. Take Emily Dickinson, for instance: as we read, really *read*, her poems we now understood that she was nothing like the "prim little home-keeping person" described (in those words) by John Crowe Ransom and taught in such terms to most high school and college students. On the contrary, hers was "a Soul *at the White Heat*," her "Tomes of solid Witchcraft" produced by an imagination that had, as she herself admitted, the Vesuvian ferocity of a loaded gun.

SDG: Falling in love with Emily Dickinson had everything to do with the power of Sandra's words and the tension, then the tingling when the milk comes. The scene, oddly enough, was a conference entitled "Language and Style" at the Graduate Center of the City University of New York on April 17, 1977. I had arrived the day before to present the first paper of several that I would compose on H. D.'s long poem *Trilogy*, at an early morning session that included more people seated at the front of the room (speakers on the program) than in the (happily) small classroom. But the timing was excellent for me since it meant I could take the subway back to my mother's Upper West Side apartment in time to nurse my second daughter (then three months old). The logistics would be more complex at an afternoon panel on the seventeenth, because I was standing in for Sandra and presenting one of her first drafts of the last chapter of *The Madwoman in the Attic.* She had by this time relocated in California and was giving a poetry reading in Berkeley that same day before flying to New York so that we could work on the introductory chapters of our book.

But the crisis occurred way before the rush-hour delays that had led me to leave a supplementary bottle with my mother. Maybe because of the more humane hour, maybe because of the fame of Dickinson or (for that matter) the reputation of Sandra, whose recently published *Acts of Attention* had focused critical attention on D. H. Lawrence's poetry, many people showed up at her session, including Annette Kolodny who (as if clued into my personal situation) informed me that she had been my babysitter years ago in Brooklyn. It hardly surprised me that I began to quake and shake at the podium as Sandra's words on Dickinson spilled from my lips. What words they were, though. They stopped me and everyone in the room in our various mental tracks, because in some eerie way Sandra's prose made the verse vibrate, brought Dickinson dancing like a bomb abroad into the CUNY lecture hall. Later, when I heard Sandra read from her book of poems *Emily's Bread,* I understood it was a poet's address to her precursor that I had been allowed to mime. At the time, all I knew was the tension, then the tingling as milk soaked the front of the only dress I possessed that would cover my then (and, alas, only then) ample breasts.

SMG: Mothering, motherhood, and mothers: as I look back on the years when we were researching and writing *The Madwoman,* I realize that maternity was always somehow central to our project. Resisting "patriarchal poetry" and poetics, we struggled, like all feminist critics of our generation, to find alternative tropes for creativity. If a pen wasn't even metaphorically speaking a penis (and a penis certainly wasn't a pen!), then what was a womb, and whose aesthetic was nurtured by its Wordsworthian "wise passiveness" or for that matter by its seething and bloody energies? Of course, as soon as we started trying to figure out new ways of figuring creativity, we were accused of essentialism. When I sent a copy of our revisionary meditation on Plato's cave to an old friend who'd become a prominent activist, she responded in those precomputer days with ten single-spaced typewritten pages of vituperation. (Today her tirade might crash my email program!)

But as Susan reveals, we were literally mothering and being mothered too. In the fall of 1974, when I was living alone in Bloomington, I clamped a letter from my younger daughter, Susanna, to the door of the fridge in my tiny rental apartment. It was she who, as a second-grade novel reader, had inspired me to *re*read *Jane Eyre* so I could chat with her about it at bedtime. Now, because she guessed I was often homesick and knew for sure how much I missed her and her brother and sister, she'd sent me a consoling note, reminding me of the pleasures of friendship among women. "Remember the wonderful tea in *Jane Eyre!*" she said—as if to prove that instead of imbibing the dread sassafras tea, Susan and I had chosen to partake of the kindlier potion that Miss Temple offers Jane and Helen along with those magical slices of seed cake.

Mothered from time to time by my daughters (for my daughter Kathy, then an eleven-year-old feminist, also nurtured her mother-the-feminist), I was also supportively mothered by my feminist mother, as Susan was by hers. Both mothers lived in New York, and we almost always saw them when we were in town. Indeed, we rather solemnly referred to them as "The Mothers"— as if they shared some kind of magic with the deific presences who have so much power in Goethe's *Faust*—and we happily introduced them to each other. (They're still friends.) Although their ethnic backgrounds are very different, they are both immigrants in this country; both, indeed, had fled the pains of Europe for the possibilities of a new world.

Like so many immigrants, of course, they guarded secrets whose significance Susan and I often sought to decode. In reading the palimpsestic subtexts of women's texts, we once wondered, were we in some sense striving to decipher the submerged plots of our mothers' lives? Or were we reimagining *ourselves* as immigrants or anyway *explorers*—geographers trying to map the newly risen Atlantis of women's literature, the Herland of the female imagination? To be sure, such exalted speculations didn't occupy all that much of our time, especially once we were confronted with the startling ink-and-paper reality of a book whose completed typescript filled not one but two weighty typewriter-paper boxes and needed endless footnotes, a nightmarishly complicated index, jacket copy, and even jacket photographs!

SDG: "Howdy Doody Meets the Bride of Frankenstein": we roared with laughter, tears streaming down our cheeks, whenever we managed to negotiate the always eccentric circumstances that issued in photographs for book jackets or publicity that made Sandra look like Uncle Bob's puppet sidekick, me like the monster's mate. (Aneta Sperber's picture for the first edition of *The Madwoman* turned out to be the exception to this rule.) Once, while collaborating on the northern California coast, we made our circuitous way to a tumbled-down cabin in a remote setting where we were expecting to be shot dead but were surprised to be shot as the tiny wooden doll of the little screen, the tottering towering hulk of the big screen. Although we are not really that distinct in stature, subsequent sittings taught us that some trick in lighting or perspective invariably would turn Sandra into a grinning wired miniature, me into a mammoth mutant. Later, while brainstorming in Bloomington, we entered what looked like the Bates Motel from *Psycho* to be photographed through antique cameras that confirmed the view of another (in this case professional) photographer who had been sent by *Ms.* magazine, when, to celebrate the publication of the *Norton Anthology of Literature by Women*, the editors chose us as "Women of the Year": "You two are difficult to take together," he grumbled. A number of our friends, colleagues, and editors would have agreed with him.

SMG: If it was more than a little bizarre to see ourselves transformed into Howdy Doody and the Bride of Frankenstein by portrait photographers, it was (and sometimes still is) equally odd to encounter critiques of *The Madwoman* that faulted us, years later, for intellectual crimes whose lineaments most of us would never have recognized in that blissfully naive dawn of the 1970s. Decades after we had the conversion experiences that issued in our first attempt to define *a* (if not *the*) female literary tradition, we were being accused of sins that in those early days we knew not of—essentialism, racism, heterosexism, phallologocentrism—accused, sometimes shrilly, by sister feminists and, sometimes patronizingly, by male quasi-feminists.

In this context, the figures of Howdy Doody and the Bride of Frankenstein take on new meaning. As not one but two amiably beaming Howdy Doodys, we were cast as establishment puppets just too dumb to notice that we wrote from a position of middle-class, white, heterosexual privilege, too foolish even to realize that (as Simone de Beauvoir so famously put it) "woman is made, not born." But if we were Brides of Frankenstein, that was even worse. In that case, we were wittingly or unwittingly married to—indeed, creatures and creations of!—patriarchy itself, with our implicitly phallologocentric insistence on a monolithic "plot" underlying the writings produced by women of letters and, worse, with our evil faith in the nostalgic, politically regressive concept of the "author" as not just a language field but a living being.

To be sure, the theoretical sophistication of such charges, with their insistence on *nuance*, does tell us something about the progress feminism has made since those first starry-eyed awakenings in the late 1960s and early 1970s. But such nuance may be precisely what we couldn't afford at a time when it was enough suddenly to see that there could be a new way of seeing, to beam like Howdy Doody at the thought, to be electrified with excitement like the Bride of Frankenstein. As for our earliest hostile critics, they too lacked nuance. They were almost all men and, as my husband once noted, their attacks on the basic arguments of *The Madwoman* could be summarized by two simple and simply plaintive statements. The one: "Men suffer too." The other: "*My* wife doesn't feel that way!"

SDG: I once cautioned Sandra, "I don't believe Heathcliff is a woman." And more than once I quizzed her, "Do you *really* think we can get away with using the word 'penis' in the very first sentence?" So much for my inspirational role in the collaboration.

Our abounding conversations—on the phone; in cars and air-
planes, restaurants and hotel rooms; while team-teaching; at conferences; later through Fed Ex and email—shaped the writing
even as the writing configured the conversations. But these were
discussions that included a host of other people as well: my
daughters, Marah and Simone, whose passionate reactions to the
physical artifacts and acts related to our research (ranging from
the cover of Jane Gallop's *Thinking Through the Body* to their
mother's frequent absences—in their words—"on business
trips") always enlightened me; my ex-husband, Edward Gubar,
who facilitated our replacing the typewriter with the computer
(since *The Madwoman* was composed in the era when "cut and
paste" meant scissors and glue); and my dear friend Mary Jo
Weaver, who, along with my smart and supportive colleagues at
Indiana University, was living proof that not all midwesterners
have been or will become Pod People.

Elliot Gilbert, Sandra's late husband, most of all: his passionate
clarity taught us how to think, how to write, as he delivered spontaneous lectures on *The Magic Flute's* Queen of the Night, imper-
sonated Dickens impersonating Sykes in *Oliver Twist*, cracked
Jewish jokes, executed complex recipes, polished articles that
appeared in *PMLA,* or analyzed administrative politics at Davis.
When the scholars who organized the 1999 Dickens Project at the
University of California, Santa Cruz, decided to stage their con-
cluding panels of papers around the twentieth birthday of *The
Madwoman,* it seemed appropriate to be celebrating at an annual
conference he helped to establish.

THE NINETEENTH CENTURY AND AFTER

SMG: Like Susan, I could thank countless friends and colleagues,
as well as my children—Roger, Kathy, and Susanna—for their
encouragement and support throughout those crucial years
when we were working on *The Madwoman.* But I'd have to agree
with her about Elliot's intellectual as well as emotional centrality.
Not only was he a kind of muse and mentor, he was in fact a Victorianist—the only bona fide one in my family or Susan's at that
point. Obviously, therefore, his always invaluable advice and

counsel particularly helped facilitate my passage backward from the twentieth century (as well as, to some extent, Susan's journey forward from the eighteenth century) to that fascinatingly problematic heart of the nineteenth century known as the Victorian period. Susan and I weren't ourselves entirely without intellectual credentials for studies of that era, however, and maybe it was even useful that our training forced us to see Victorian letters somewhat "slant," in the Dickinsonian sense. Susan had combined her work in eighteenth-century literature with attention to the history of the novel and, more generally, to genre theory, while throughout graduate school I had been torn between research in modernism and studies of Romanticism; indeed, I'd consistently tried to integrate the two fields through examinations of the ways modernism was specifically shaped by many of the major legacies of Romanticism.

Beyond our personal backgrounds, though, there were clearly reasons why, like so many of feminist criticism's other newly born women, we focused our earliest intellectual energies on the nineteenth century. For one thing, most of the major texts that we now understood to have constituted us as *female* readers were in fact nineteenth-century texts—and of how many theoretically and historically "innocent" literary women could that not then have been said? The syllabus that became the basis for *The Madwoman* probably reflected a canon that lived in the mind of just about every *femme moyenne intellectuelle* who spent her girlhood avidly devouring the classics of the female imagination produced by Austen and the Brontës, Mary Shelley and George Eliot, and yes, if the girl liked poetry, Emily Dickinson. And fortunately, a context for this syllabus was being explored in the early seventies by such social historians as Carroll Smith-Rosenberg, Nancy Cott, and Martha Vicinus, along with such pioneering critics as Ellen Moers and Elaine Showalter, both of whom had begun to publish research that would eventually be included in Moers's *Literary Women* (1976) and Showalter's *A Literature of Their Own* (1977). (Indeed, Elliot had even been a reader of Elaine's dissertation on British women novelists, completed at the University of California, Davis, in the 1960s, so that as soon as I got back to California, after the scales had fallen from my eyes on the road to *The*

Madwoman, I immediately went to the library and began to study the campus copy of her bound and signed thesis.) As we noted in our 1979 preface, Susan and I saw it as a privilege that because "both Moers and Showalter [had] so skillfully traced the overall history" of a "female literary subculture" we could "focus closely on a number of nineteenth-century texts . . . crucial to that history" (xii).

To be sure, the nascent feminist critical movement had already begun a move to excavate forgotten works by women that issued at that point in the resurrection or reevaluation of key texts like "The Yellow Wallpaper," "Goblin Market," and *The Awakening;* and we certainly included such writings in the literary geography we undertook to map. Moreover, from studying what we recognized as the Great Mother of all feminist critical texts—meaning, of course, *A Room of One's Own*—we gained a special interest in half-lost but now newly found literary ladies (and I use the word "ladies" advisedly) like Anne Finch and Margaret Cavendish. But we sensed that the most powerful and empowering forces acting on our female imaginations and those of many other women readers and writers were nevertheless those four horsewomen of at least one kind of novelistic Apocalypse: Jane Austen, Charlotte Brontë, Emily Brontë, and George Eliot. And because we sensed, too, that the great women poets who were these writers' contemporaries or descendants—notably Elizabeth Barrett Browning, Emily Dickinson, and Christina Rossetti—both shared in and were shaped by the particular, often duplicitous sensibility that inhabited those novelists, we experienced these poets, too, as powerful in a richly significant female literary tradition.

That this tradition can be said to have different historical contours from the supposedly "mainstream" (i.e., male-dominated) literary history we had studied in school gave (and still gives) the nineteenth century additional resonance. As recently as 1990, Susan and I were arguing on the page and at the podium that female literary history, as it emerges not just in *The Madwoman* but in our later *Norton Anthology of Literature by Women,* is shaped very differently from male literary history—that, more specifically, the strategy of periodization through which scholars routinely struggle to make sense of fluctuations in what used to be called the zeitgeist results in very different chronological patternings for differently gendered authors. In fact, as we and others have observed, women's past is not always quite the same as men's.[1] Why, for example, do we tend to perceive a golden age of women's writing—the age of the Brontës, Eliot, Dickinson, and Rossetti, which constituted a kind of female Renaissance—not in what is ordinarily called the Renaissance but in the mid-nineteenth century?

Of course, as scholars of early modern English literature have increasingly demonstrated, there were many more women of letters flourishing in the sixteenth and seventeenth centuries than even that preternaturally knowledgeable feminist historian Virginia Woolf suspected. The table of contents of our *Norton Anthology of Literature by Women* reveals that from Mary Sidney Herbert, countess of Pembroke (1562–1621), and her niece Mary Wroth (1587?–1651/53) to Margaret Cavendish, duchess of Newcastle (1623–73), and Anne Finch, countess of Winchilsea (1661–1720), a range of highly privileged Renaissance aristocrats produced sophisticated translations and intricate sonnet sequences, along with eloquent polemics, utopias, epistolary verses, and a host of other manuscripts, some of which appeared in print but most of which were privately circulated. Perhaps even more strikingly—because against greater odds—a number of their less privileged female contemporaries also wrote and published significant work in these centuries. Artists who displayed what we would now consider a serious "professional" commitment to the craft of letters would surely include Aemelia Lanyer (1569–1645) and Katherine Philips (1632–64), but especially (of course) Anne Bradstreet (1612–72) and Aphra Behn (1640–89).

By the eighteenth century, moreover, as recent scholars have amply demonstrated, women had entered the literary marketplace in earnest. From Eliza Haywood (1693?–1756) to Charlotte Smith (1749–1806) and Ann Radcliffe (1764–1823), pioneering female novelists and poets didn't just "*attemp[t]* the pen" (as Anne Finch rather sardonically put it), they lived by the fruits of its labors.[2] And though the tradition they were slowly but surely shaping may have often been deprecated or derided by male (and even some female) readers, though it plainly didn't feel comparable in weight and strength to the mainstream tradition forged by centuries of literary masculinity, it offered possibilities of place and precedent—offered a perhaps invisibly thickening critical mass of literary *femininity*—to aspiring women of letters in the nineteenth century. "England has had many learned ladies," conceded Elizabeth Barrett Browning after all, even while, perhaps disingenuously, claiming that she knew of no ancestral "poetesses" ("I look everywhere for grandmothers and find none").[3]

What gave special urgency to the projects of nineteenth-century literary women on both sides of the Atlantic, however, was precisely the Romantic heritage of aesthetic and political rebellion that we sought to trace throughout *The Madwoman*. For from Mary Wollstonecraft's articulation of the "Rights of Woman" to the abolitionist movement and the movements for national self-determination that fueled not only the European uprisings of 1848 but also—and of crucial importance for the history of women in this period—the feminist uprising that began that same year in Seneca Falls, New York, the revolution in whose dawn Wordsworth had thought it "bliss" to be alive, evolved into another dawning revolution, the morning of newly blossoming art that inspired Barrett Browning to name her heroine *Aurora* and that Emily Dickinson, perhaps in homage to that much admired English precursor, was later in the century to label both a magical "morn by men unseen" and a "different dawn" (J.24). The radicalism of Jane Eyre's defiant assertion that "women feel just as men feel; they need exercise for their faculties and a field for their efforts as much as their brothers do" (chap. 12) was undoubtedly anticipated by the radicalism of covertly or overtly feminist women of letters, from the sixteenth-century Aemelia Lanyer to the eighteenth-century Anne Finch, but Charlotte Brontë's nineteenth-century heroine was to find herself in the company of an unprecedentedly powerful and startlingly empowering sisterhood.

The processes strengthening that sisterhood, as we argued both in *The Madwoman* and, more recently, in the *Norton*

Anthology of Literature by Women, had to be defined not only against the grain of traditional history but also against the grounds of the usual literary geography. Because until recently women only tenuously inhabited the public world whose national records separate state from state, we postulated as we worked on *The Madwoman* that the female community out of which female literary tradition is constituted crosses political and national boundaries. In particular, we speculated that for English-speaking women, there are not a number of different, nationally defined nineteenth centuries; there is only one—which contains and sustains the achievements of British and American women writers, all of whom were coming to terms in prose and poetry with the discrepancy between the Victorian ideology of femininity and the reality of Victorian women's lives.[4] And that transatlantic continuity of female imaginative enterprises has long seemed to us to create interesting incongruities. What does it mean, for instance, that Harriet Jacobs, the author of an important slave narrative, was born the same year as the author of *Wuthering Heights?* Or that Sojourner Truth was born the same year as Mary Shelley? And why—to turn to an issue of evaluation—does what one might imagine as the more exhilarating, early twentieth-century period of suffrage militancy seem to be characterized by lesser artistic voices, among poets Alice Meynell instead of Christina Rossetti, and among novelists May Sinclair instead of George Eliot?

As this question suggests, we suspect that the centrality of nineteenth-century studies for feminist criticism has still to be explored. On the one hand, the sexual ideology of the era was in many ways particularly oppressive, confining women, as Virginia Woolf long ago noted, not just to corsets but to the "Private House," with all its deprivations and discontents. But on the other hand, its aesthetic and political imperatives were especially inspiring, engendering not just a range of revolutionary movements but some of the richest productions of the female imagination. Perhaps, I sometimes speculate, one of William Butler Yeats's oddest ventures into literary periodization—the enigmatic quatrain entitled "The Nineteenth Century and After"—best summarizes a *feminist* sense of belatedness that occasionally sweeps over those of us who are the readers, scholars, and inheritors of a tradition forged by Austen and the Brontës, Barrett Browning and Dickinson, Eliot and Rossetti:

> Though the great song return no more
> There's keen delight in what we have.
> The rattle of pebbles on the shore
> Under the receding wave.[5]

Readers of the three-volume sequel to *The Madwoman,* entitled *No Man's Land: The Place of the Woman Writer in the Twentieth Century,* will know that Susan and I, often enthralled by the advances of twentieth-century women, don't truly share the ironic resignation that marks Yeats's little poem. And yet, and yet. . .

BEYOND *THE MADWOMAN*

SDG: If a brief backward glance at the early stages of feminist criticism establishes its vital origins in the Victorian period, an equally abbreviated look forward from the book's publication in 1979 proves that the nineteenth century continues to provide a lively field of activity for feminist thinking that has undergone a series of dramatic methodological transformations. Actually, what startles is the *dis*continuity of feminism's evolution as new historicism, queer theory, postcolonialism, African-American and cultural studies as well as poststructuralist approaches altered the received maps of the Romantic and Victorian periods. Although one of our colleagues greeted the 1980 publication of *The Maniac in the Cellar* with a tongue-in-cheek prophecy about a sequel to be entitled *The Lunatic on the Lawn, The Madwoman in the Attic* was not cloned by our successors in nineteenth-century literary history.

That the figure of *The Madwoman* did get recycled in quite disparate domains only underscores this point. Completely unrelated to our project, Germaine Greer's *The Madwoman's Underclothes: Essays and Occasional Writings* (1987) can stand for a host of books, none of which deal with nineteenth-century literary history: *Ou Lu Khen and the Beautiful Madwoman,* by Jessica Amanda

Salmonson (1985); *The Marshal and the Madwoman,* by Magdalen Nabb (1988); *Meeting the Madwoman: An Inner Challenge for Feminine Spirit,* by Linda Schierse Leonard (1993); *The Letters of a Victorian Madwoman,* by John S. Hughes (1993); and *The Madwoman's Reason: The Concept of the Appropriate in Ethical Thought,* by Nancy J. Holland (1998). Even a work of literary criticism like Marta Caminero-Santangelo's recent *The Madwoman Can't Speak: Or Why Insanity Is Not Subversive* (1998) switches the ground of inquiry to the twentieth century. On the Internet, too, *The Madwoman's* avatars appear in far-flung areas. Jayn Scott admits as much when she begins her fictional *Diary of a Madwoman in the Attic* by cheerfully acknowledging the allusion in her title: "I don't remember the authors—though I know I should—but I'll look it up and put it in another entry"; however, no such concession appears (or appears necessary) on other Internet pages: about Tori Amos, "the madwoman in the attic of pop music," for instance; or the "madwoman" qua "Gorgon" whom your guide shields you from "as you sneak down the hall from the Attic"; or the "Attic Chat" links to photographs of massively endowed women accompanied by "sexually oriented adult material intended for individuals 18 years of age or older."

Yet within the more inventive, if rarified, atmosphere of academic humanism, the most vigorous feminist approaches to nineteenth-century literary history refrained from replicating *The Madwoman's* lexicon, instead taking issue with it. To be sure, after its publication, a number of scholars produced studies very much attuned to the formal and thematic issues we had addressed: one thinks of stimulating books on allied subjects by Margaret Homans, Carolyn Heilbrun, Nancy K. Miller, Nina Auerbach, Barbara Christian, Patricia Yaeger, Susan Fraiman, and Cheryl Wall. However, soon the field became populated with agonistic (not to say antagonistic) players. To avoid an inevitably incomplete and tedious listing of the critics of such studies, to circumvent also an equally boring defensiveness, we shall foreground here the ways nineteenth-century feminist scholarship after 1979 questioned each of the terms in our title and subtitle. For the categories—of literature, gender, and authorship—upon which we relied have undergone extraordinary alterations during the past twenty years, transformations that shifted scholarly attention from literature to culture; from gender as a privileged lens to gender combined with sexuality, nation, race, class, religion, and a host of other designations; from authors to texts. Challenges to each of the phrases on our title page that dramatize these changes issued in stimulating new work.

The Nineteenth-Century Literary Imagination: this rubric (at the end of our subtitle) underwent a metamorphosis related primarily to issues of genre and of periodization. Although in *The Madwoman* we analyzed verse along with fiction and expository prose in order to posit a coherent female tradition, the last two decades have witnessed an exciting recovery of nineteenth-century women's poetry beyond that produced by the now canonical Christina Rossetti, Elizabeth Barrett Browning, and Emily Dickinson. In the British context, the anthology *Nineteenth-Century Women Poets* (1996), which Isobel Armstrong compiled with Joseph Bristow and Cath Sharrock, can stand as a touchstone of the considerable research of many other scholars on such figures as Charlotte Smith, Helen Maria Williams, Amelia Opie, Felicia Hemans, L. E. L., and Amy Levi. Not widely available in print before, the achievements of these literary women have been analyzed and taught during the 1980s and 1990s. In addition, the Victorian Women Writers Project has put the whole corpus of many of these poets on the Internet. As their listing here demonstrates, moreover, the productivity of previously neglected women poets appears especially evident at the beginning of the nineteenth century and has therefore given rise to the new and important area of feminist analyses of women and Romanticism.

Particularly in "Milton's Bogey" (chap. 6), we presented Victorian women writers as the inheritors of Romantic tropes of a rebellious imaginative creativity and a visionary politics that both excluded and empowered them. Inevitably, this meant conceptualizing the nineteenth century as a single historical period. However, the recent excavation not only of women's poetry but of women's writing in a variety of prose genres has shifted critical attention from the Romantic heritage of aesthetic and political rebelliousness we traced in mid- and late-nineteenth-century lit-

erature to *Romanticism and Feminism,* the title Anne K. Mellor gave
her 1988 book. Whereas the recovery of women's verse, journals,
and letters revitalized scrutiny of late-eighteenth- and early-nine-
teenth-century letters, Victorian studies was being stretched at
the other end of the century by a new historicist fascination with
law cases, theatrical venues, advertisements, paintings, early
experiments in photography, and medical as well as religious and
philosophical treatises. No longer defining their domain in terms
of literature or (for that matter) "high" or elite art forms, feminist critics of fin-de-siècle American and British culture explored
what (in volume 2 of the three-volume sequel to *The Madwoman*)
we called *Sexchanges* (1989). Such an enterprise necessarily accen-
tuates the need to understand literary women's evolution as an
ongoing dialectical interaction with their male contemporaries
within complex sexual ideologies that shaped shifting definitions
of masculinity as profoundly as they did those of femininity.

Given this reasoning, an understanding of the first words in
our subtitle—*The Woman Writer*—had to be supplemented with
analyses of male authors that were fueled by the work of gay and
lesbian thinkers. By elaborating upon the theoretical insights of
Gayle Rubin, Eve Kosofsky Sedgwick's *Between Men* (1985)
exerted a profound impact on the mapping of Victorian fiction,
moving scholarly investigators from the female character as an
object of exchange toward what that commodified gift meant to
the two men on either side of this "homosocial" transaction.[6] Just
as Sedgwick's concept of "homosexual panic" among heterosexual men generated research attending to the influence of
changing definitions of homo- and heterosexuality on men of letters, the range of women's relationships—as friends, siblings,
lovers, competitors, coworkers—received greater attention when
Adrienne Rich's "lesbian continuum" spawned discussions about
female sexuality.[7] In the process, these studies undercut any
monolithic idea of *The Woman Writer* that elided differences
among women from various geographic regions.

Increasingly influential within the humanities in its spotlight-
ing of nation, postcolonial studies contested the arguments of
our book, most dramatically in Gayatri Chakravorty Spivak's
widely circulated 1985 essay "Three Women's Texts and a

Critique of Imperialism."[8] For Spivak speculated that the "cult text" status of *Jane Eyre* in women's studies reflects an ideology of "feminist individualism in the age of imperialism" (176) that actively linked the feminist with the imperialist project. According to this postcolonial perspective, *The Attic* of our title should be identified as the site of the disenfranchised Third World female character on the borders of, or outside, Western civilization, not as that of the relatively privileged First World heroine. In other words, the coupling we hypothesized between the demure heroines and the enraged female monsters of nineteenth-century literature had to be either divorced or dismissed as a slippage produced by fictions upon which the imperial white self established its precedency. Missionary in its rhetoric, the marriage making and soul making celebrated by Charlotte Brontë in *Jane Eyre* and by *The Madwoman in the Attic* in its interpretation of the novel are therefore thought to depend upon the dehumanization of Bertha Mason Rochester, the Jamaican Creole whose racial and geographical marginality oils the mechanism by which the heathen, bestial Other could be annihilated to constitute European female subjectivity. Throughout the 1990s, a critique of imperialism undertaken by British and American scholars expanded critical comprehension of canonical nineteenth-century texts by attending to the interplay between gender and the geopolitics of race as well as place, but it also issued in efforts to bring noncanonical texts by colonized and enslaved people into scholarly inquiry and the classroom. Jennifer DeVere Brody's *Impossible Purities: Blackness, Femininity, and Victorian Culture* (1998) can stand for the incursion of black feminist theory and African-American studies into Victorian studies.

Once not only nation and race but also class economics were factored into the speculations of materialist thinkers, Anglo-American women writers needed to be comprehended less in terms of the privations they suffered and more in terms of the privileges they enjoyed and exploited. In the 1980s, American-studies scholars like Nina Baym and Jane Tompkins analyzed the cultural centrality of women in the literary marketplace and especially the commercial success of the sentimental fiction produced by nineteenth-century novelists. Their studies attempted to thwart earlier critics' propensities to use the popularity of American women of letters against them: not simply pandering to their readers, Harriet Beecher Stowe and Elizabeth Stuart Phelps were engaged in revaluing women's moral and aesthetic spheres of influence. In the 1990s, the next wave of Americanists, consisting of such feminists as Hazel Carby and Lauren Berlant, explored the relationships between sentimentality and slavery, between citizenship and the regulation of desire in nationally as well as transnationally engendered ideologies.[9] Considering English literary history, two important critics—Mary Poovey and Nancy Armstrong—emphasized the ways literary women transmuted stereotypical images of femininity into sources of strength. According to Poovey (*The Proper Lady and the Woman Writer* [1984] and *Uneven Developments* [1988]) and Armstrong (*Desire and Domestic Fiction* [1987]), domestic space constitutes neither the imprisoning attic nor the confining parlor we stressed as a source of Victorian women's rage but a feminine household economy that helped to establish the conditions for modern institutional culture.

On the one hand, scholars following the lead of Poovey and Armstrong explored the organized social movements that improved women's political and economic position in the Victorian period; on the other, they examined the ways women from various classes, ethnicities, and religions actually benefited from their contributions to the construction of domestic ideals that restricted female access to the public sphere. Why should every or any one of these enterprising nineteenth-century societal figures be dubbed *Mad*? With literary texts now supplemented by physicians' reports, legal briefs, legislative debates, and conduct books concerning divorce, child rearing, sexuality, and employment, cultural critics thickened our sense of social history to map the multiple and multiply different roles various women played in British and American social life. Accompanying such expanded definitions of nineteenth-century womanhood was a deconstruction of such categories as woman, self, and author. Needless to say, the idea that a *Madwoman* character represents Victorian women's thwarted desire for authority would be singularly uncongenial to a critical approach that repudiates the concept of selfhood and cannot, therefore, take seriously the struggle of authors or their characters toward self-sovereignty.

In the framework established by the influential books of Michel Foucault, what replaces the self as a source of power are institutional regimes whose social forces shape people laboring under the delusion of individuality. Although it deals with literary women from an earlier period than Victorian times, Catherine Gallagher's *Nobody's Story: The Vanishing Acts of Women Writers in the Marketplace, 1670–1820* (1994) views the disembodiment of women writers less as a psychosexual problem, more as a requirement of the literary marketplace that advances their careers.[10] Nineteenth-century literature repeatedly refers to the creation of the self; however, what it actually achieves—for poststructuralists—is the naturalization of this historical concept. Under the aegis of deconstruction in, for example, the writings of Mary Jacobus and Toril Moi, the attack on the paradigm of *The Madwoman* could and did go beyond the content of this particular metaphorical model (of the rebelliously diseased woman writer struggling to gain independence) to a poststructuralist rejection of *any* formulation that would lend credence either to the term "woman" or to the category "women writers," a disavowal that necessarily makes it difficult indeed to do feminist work in a literary historical context. Whether or not the tensions between poststructuralism (which made a major mark on feminist theory through the publications of Judith Butler in the 1990s) and cultural studies (with its investment in materialism) have stymied the production of groundbreaking scholarship, the influence of Jacques Lacan, Jacques Derrida, and especially Michel Foucault has led some critics to align themselves with a poststructuralist repudiation of "essentialism," which makes them less interested in individual writers as originators of meaning and more focused on textual production as a complex and powerful set of meaning-effects with political implications. Since it is language that constitutes subjectivity, not vice versa, the split between the docile Victorian heroine and her mad double pales in comparison to the myth of an autonomous subject that drives the conceptualization of both of these characters (in, say, Charlotte Brontë's fiction, but also in various chapters of *Madwoman*).

Short of admiring the sophistication of such investigations, short of exclaiming that the implications of some of the arguments embedded in them and against *The Madwoman in the Attic* have turned *us* into madwomen in the academy, what can we possible say about them? Most obviously, they demonstrate that feminist criticism in nineteenth-century studies functions as a microcosm of English in particular, the humanities in general: for good and for ill, the impact of new historicism, queer theory, postcolonialism, African-American studies, cultural studies, and poststructuralism has been felt in many other disciplines throughout contemporary scholarship.[11] But, given the history of criticism during the twentieth century's fin de siècle that we have just traced, what is the sum effect of feminist criticism's trajectory? And what does the future hold for Victorianists, for feminist critics, for humanists, for academicians?

THE PRESENT MOMENT

SMG: Clearly *The Madwoman*'s descent from the attic to the classroom has been in many ways a journey full of paradoxes. Predictably enough, "her" incendiary impulses at first encountered considerable opposition from the antifeminist thought police. Less predictably, as Susan has demonstrated, even some of her own feminist allies soon began to express suspicion about her credentials, while she met with outright hostility from a number of so-called postfeminist sisters, cousins, and aunts. Perhaps more surprisingly, she found that some parts of the academy into which she'd stepped had already been set ablaze, often by the male as well as female theorists, from deconstructionists to cultural critics, about whom Susan has been speaking.

The world in which *The Madwoman* now moves, moreover, is virtually new—and to go on being paradoxical, I mean the word *virtually* quite literally. For what has been labeled the Information Revolution fostered by the lightning rise of computer technologies will no doubt bring with it changes as enormous as those associated with the Industrial Revolution that marked the century in which she was born. What, after all, will become of those entities quaintly known as "books" in the imminent, hypertextually hypersophisticated millennium? Will there be real people who will really read, really study, and really teach what used to be called literature in the brave new world toward which we're zooming with such alarming speed?

Some of my formulations may seem extravagant, but all point to questions of serious consequence to feminist critics and, more generally, to the academy. Putting aside for the moment my hyperbole about the hypertextual, is there in this posttheoretical era a phenomenon we can still call "literature," which can be distinguished from, say, telephone directories, railway schedules, Nordstrom catalogs, and maybe even Web pages? Are there people (once known as "authors") who produce that stuff, and people (still, I guess, known as "readers") who in some way consume it? Does it make a difference that some of those people formerly known as authors are beings called "women" rather than beings called "men"? If so, how can we study and teach the effects of that difference? Further, in the hypertechnical future toward which we're zooming—no, let me correct myself, in the hyperreal future we already inhabit, with its glimmering computer screens, skeptical postmodernists, and decaying educational infrastructure—will there even be positions (once known as "jobs") in which people can study and teach those differences that shape and determine the hypothetical phenomenon once called literature?

As Susan has observed, feminist criticism today "functions as a microcosm of English in particular, the humanities in general," for the intellectual history she's recounted has both responded to and elicited a number of notable real-world effects. There are multiple explanations, for example, for our profession's move toward what we now know as theory. One of the most positive, surely, and I think a very cogent one, would locate the impulse to excavate and examine intellectual assumptions within the urge to question supposedly inevitable and timeless cultural arrangements that motivate feminism itself. But this analysis doesn't preclude a rather more cynical speculation, which would argue that the move of literary criticism toward "high" theory (note that adjective!) reflects the need for humanists to compete for funding with scientists in national and local academic arenas that are always, and no doubt always *will* be, disposed to prize "hard" scientists rather than "soft" humanists.

And note those adjectives again! From a gender studies perspective, as a number of thinkers (including Susan and me) have observed, the humanities in general and our profession in particular have lately been increasingly feminized, both literally and figuratively. Literally: the membership of the Modern Language Association is now about 50 percent women, and graduate students in many departments are overwhelmingly female. Figuratively: if the sciences are hard and we are soft, that's at least in part because we do the genteel, wifely job of acculturation and socialization on campus, while the guys in astrophysics shoot for Mars. No wonder, then, that in a world where the richly rewarded scientists speak a host of hard-to-acquire, difficult, private languages, we humble, formerly plain-speaking humanists have yearned for sole access to a similarly difficult private discourse—a jargon, as it were, of our own, which would offer acolytes in our field the same kind of linguistic mastery that bespeaks professionalism in, say, microbiologists and geologists. Along with all its exhilarating demolitions of philosophical and sociocultural clichés, "theory" has offered a "discourse" that facilitates just such professional certification, putting ordinary language "in question," substituting "subjects" or "subjectivities" for "people," and "language fields" for "books," while in the process alienating us from even the cultivated Woolfian "common readers" who used to be our off-campus constituency.

Is there any remedy for this situation, or is the hyperprofessionalism whose ills I'm describing inescapable in the hypercompetitive academic milieu of the future we already, surprisingly, inhabit? I don't have any global answers to this question, because I myself am just as conflicted as many of my feminist colleagues are these days. I obviously wouldn't want to roll back the clock in the Ivory Tower to that mythical moment when Wellek and Warren laid down the literary laws, when you had to smoke a pipe to be a professor, and when, as Rupert Brooke put it, there was "honey still for tea." On the other hand, perhaps especially as a poet but also as a common reader, writer, and teacher, I share Adrienne Rich's "dream of a common language" for criticism as well as for daily life. One of the pleasures of the text that *The Madwoman* bestowed on the authorial entity known as Gilbert-and-Gubar was the book's *popular* reception. Partly because of its historically privileged position as an early venture in feminist criticism, it was widely reviewed in countless newspapers around in the world and in magazines like *Harper's* and *The Atlantic* as well as in scholarly journals. And partly because as an early venture it just couldn't be as theoretically sophisticated and specialized as some of its granddaughters, it seems to have communicated its political aspirations to a number of readers outside our field.

Can we feminist critics continue to speak in the larger world not as stereotypical "talking heads" but as what have come to be called "public intellectuals"? And can we do such a job without losing the disciplinary sophistication and methodological savvy we've so carefully cultivated? Lately, alas, the women who represent a female (not feminist) perspective to large popular audiences tend to be called Camille Paglia, Christina Hoff Summers, and maybe at best Susan Faludi or Naomi Wolf. But if those of us who now dwell mostly in the academy can in every sense recall the blissful originatory moment I mentioned earlier—the fleeting yet fiery instant when we feminists of the seventies realized that the personal was the political, the sexual was the textual, and so forth—we may find a clue as to how we should proceed. For perhaps our challenge today is to integrate the professional with both the political *and* the personal. The recent spate of memoirs by academics representing virtually the entire political spectrum (ranging from Alvin Kernan and Frank Kermode to Nancy K. Miller, Marianna Torgovnik, Jane Tompkins, and Jane Gallop) suggests that even those of us who suspect that as "subjectivities" we're little more than conglomerations of "linguistic practices" and "cultural citations" do know how to author—and authorize—ourselves. Perhaps, then, millennial feminists need to steal a leaf from one of Elizabeth Barrett Browning's most brilliant books and, aligning ourselves with that eloquent collection of signifiers known as "Aurora Leigh," explain to the world, loudly and clearly, that we too have our

> vocation,—work to do
> . . . .
> Most serious work, most necessary work
> As any of the economists'

—or astrophysicists' or microbiologists'.

SDG: Still, the difficulties of speaking as a public intellectual seem daunting, because it remains difficult for academics to gain access to the media and because we inhabit an age of specialization. That Rich's "dream of a common language" was followed by her insistence on a "politics of location" hints how hard it will be to do Barrett Browning's "most necessary work" today.[12] Besides the electronic information explosion and the need to compete for financial support with scientists (themselves beleaguered by the skyrocketing costs of research) for financial support, we face a diversification of research not unrelated to the economic depression that has hit higher education at the end of the twentieth century (despite a booming economy in other arenas of American society). Institutionalized during a period of retrenchment (through proliferating journals, conferences, book series, professional organizations, undergraduate majors and minors, graduate programs), feminist criticism inside and outside women's studies has been regulated by the exigencies of the so-called downsizing of the humanities. Pressure to publish, lest one perish; escalating levels of productivity expected of junior faculty; competition for fewer jobs; the overvaluation of research in promotion decisions—all have contributed to an astonishing proliferation of scholarship. But as academic publishing suffers a slump, we may have more difficulty getting our criticism in print in the future. Should the job market stay depressed, we will definitely continue to face difficulties in getting our Ph.D. candidates the tenure-track positions they deserve.

If we add to all these material conditions the enormous amount of research that has already been produced in our various area studies, we might be tempted to view the hectic pace at which theoretical vocabularies and critical approaches go in and out of fashion as an index of the strenuous efforts of humanists to keep the ever more distant past of nineteenth-century women alive, to "make it new" and thus relevant to undergraduates in universities as well as to the culture at large. Perhaps, too, a sense of anxiety over mounting scholarly material focused on British and American literature has contributed to the efforts of critics to move beyond the literary sphere of novels and poems, beyond the geopolitical sphere of the First World. The recent marginal-ization of the literary and the emphasis on Third World cultures that have emphatically marked feminist criticism threaten to eliminate from our undertaking the pleasures of the aesthetic and the achievements of women before the twentieth century. Perhaps for this reason, Victorian-studies scholars, like feminist literary critics, increasingly find it difficult to produce the sort of crossover book we would like to think *The Madwoman* is.

Maybe one of the tasks facing future generations, then, should consist in an effort not to bypass methodological sophistication but to harness it to more accessible modes of critical writing. How can we purge our critical prose of the gobbledygook of stale theo-retical platitudes, of hollow political grandstanding, making it more supple and perhaps even more fun to read for specialists and general readers alike? Yet another labor might involve crit-ical self-reflection, an effort to grapple in more depth with the implications of the professional and intellectual evolution of the humanities and the women's movement over the past several decades and to direct attention to the consequences of our dis-persal. What does it mean that Victorianists now study Hollywood films and produce BBC shows? That feminists can be found in vir-tually every methodological stripe, every area study strip? A third job may entail coping more productively with generational rival-ries, inventing ways to extend the scholarly past without trashing it. Certainly part of the fun of writing *The Madwoman* derived not from our generous high-mindedness in dealing with generational rivalry but instead from the luck of what today would be called our "historical positionality"; for us, there simply were no acad-emic feminist precursors, because feminist criticism did not exist when we met and began working together on *The Madwoman in the Attic,* which accounts for our feelings of elation about being present at an originatory moment.

Precisely such a sense of exhilaration must buoy up those critics whose works have helped to found other politicized academic fields, disciplines like African-American studies or gay and lesbian studies. Just as *their* successors revel in their subsequent transformation of the field, we hope *our* successors in feminist criticism will also. For if at times we feel somewhat frayed by the attacks we have received, if at other times we worry about the obfuscatory or elitist jargon recycled theories generate, it would nevertheless be shortsighted to let the wrangling overwhelm our sense of the vitality of a feminist criticism more cantankerous but also more populous, more porous, more downright adventurous than it has ever been before. Nostalgia for originatory moments may be inevitable, but it would be a mistake to simplify their complexity or misuse them to generate complacency about or (worse yet) disengagement from the present moment: despite some successes, women's problems have *not* yet been solved either inside or outside the academy. Given the backlashes women's gains ordinarily occasion, such nostalgia may therefore threaten to place feminist successors in a diminished future that hardly accords with the important intellectual labor that will continue to be in need of doing. Neither our progeny nor our replicants but very much our confederates, younger feminists face daunting professional and scholarly tasks, which those of us who made our mark in the 1970s can undertake along with them.

Despite our occasional bouts of cynicism, our "keen delight in what we have" convinces us that "the great song" to which Yeats turned in "The Nineteenth Century and After," the tunes and tomes to which we turned in *The Madwoman*—the sage and savvy lyricism of Austen and the Brontës, Mary Shelley and Elizabeth Barrett Browning, George Eliot and Emily Dickinson—will return again and be heard in cadences that none of us can prophesy. For this reason, we are particularly pleased about the return of our book in this Yale University Press imprint slated for *The Madwoman*'s twenty-first birthday, her coming of age.

Notes

1   See, for example, Joan Kelly's classic essay "Did Women Have a Renaissance?" in *Women, History and Theory: The Essays of Joan Kelly* (Chicago: University of Chicago Press, 1986), pp. 19–50.

2   Emphasis ours; see Anne Finch, countess of Winchilsea, "The Introduction," in Sandra M. Gilbert and Susan Gubar, eds., *The Norton Anthology of Literature by Women: The Traditions in English*, 2d ed. (New York: Norton, 1996), p. 168.

3   *The Letters of Elizabeth Barrett Browning*, ed. Frederic G. Kenyon, 2 vols. in 1 (New York: Macmillan, 1899), 1:230–32.

4   To be sure, analyses of distinctly American and British female literary traditions in the nineteenth century, have been offered by such critics as Nina Baym (*Woman's Fiction: A Guide to Novels by and about Women in America, 1820–1870* [Ithaca: Cornell University Press, 1978], Cheryl Walker (*The Nightingale's Burden: Women Poets and American Culture Before 1900* [Bloomington: Indiana University Press, 1982]), Elaine Showalter (*A Literature of Their Own: British Women Novelists from Brontë to Lessing* [Princeton: Princeton University Press, 1977]), and Kathleen Hickock (*Representations of Women: Nineteenth-Century British Women's Poetry* [Westport, Conn.: Greenwood, 1984]).

5   *The Collected Poems of W. B. Yeats* (New York: Macmillan, 1956), p. 235.

6   See Gayle Rubin's "The Traffic in Women: Notes on the 'Political Economy' of Sex," in Rayna R. Reiter, ed., *Toward an Anthropology of Women* (New York: Monthly Review Press, 1975), pp. 157–210.

7   See Rich's influential "Compulsory Heterosexuality and Lesbian Existence," in Catharine R. Stimpson and Ethel Spector Person, eds., *Women, Sex, and Sexuality* (Chicago: University of Chicago Press, 1980), pp. 60–91.

8   Reprinted in Catherine Belsey and Jane Moore, eds., *The Feminist Reader: Essays in Gender and the Politics of Literary Criticism* (New York: Basil Blackwell, 1989), pp. 175–96.

9   Among others, Annette Kolodny and Judith Fetterley also produced important early texts in American Studies, while Susan Jeffords, Janice Radway, Cecilia Tichi, Valerie Smith, Ann duCille, Robyn Wiegman, and Nellie McKay are only a sample of the those who have published significant later feminist studies of American culture.

10 Gallagher's "authorial Nobodies" (Aphra Behn, Delarivier Manley, Charlotte Lennox, Frances Burney, and Maria Edgeworth) stress their femininity and dispossession in a "rhetoric of authorship" that they deploy to present themselves as merely "effects of exchange" (xix, xxi), but that paradoxically thereby gains them considerable financial advantage.

11 Amanda Anderson's recent efforts in *Tainted Souls and Painted Faces: The Rhetoric of Fallenness in Victorian Culture* (1993) to get beyond the current dilemma over the evaporation of agency and the reification of subjectivity in poststructuralist approaches to gender suggest that Victorian literary scholars will continue to play a pivotal role in the future evolution of feminist literary theorizing.

12 See Rich's "Notes toward a Politics of Location," in Myriam Diaz-Diocaretz and Iris M. Zavala, eds., *Women, Feminist Identity, and Society in the 1980s* (Amsterdam: John Benjamins, 1985), pp. 5–22.

I
Toward a Feminist Poetics

The Queen's Looking Glass: Female Creativity, Male Images of Women, and the Metaphor of Literary Paternity

And the lady of the house was seen only as she appeared in each room, according to the nature of the lord of the room. None saw the whole of her, none but herself. For the light which she was was both her mirror and her body. None could tell the whole of her, none but herself.

— Laura Riding

Alas! A woman that attempts the pen
Such an intruder on the rights of men,
Such a presumptuous Creature is esteem'd
The fault can by no vertue be redeem'd.
— Anne Finch, Countess of Winchilsea

As to all that nonsense Henry and Larry talked about, the necessity of "I am God" in order to create (I suppose they mean "I am God, I am not a woman"). . . . this "I am God," which makes creation an act of solitude and pride, this image of God alone making sky, earth, sea, it is this image which has confused woman.

— Anaïs Nin

Is a pen a metaphorical penis? Gerard Manley Hopkins seems to have thought so. In a letter to his friend R. W. Dixon in 1886 he confided a crucial feature of his theory of poetry. The artist's "most essential quality," he declared, is "masterly execution, which is a kind of male gift, and especially marks off men from women, the begetting of one's thought on paper, on verse, or whatever the matter is." In addition, he noted that "on better consideration it strikes me that the mastery I speak of is not so much in the mind as a puberty in the life of that quality. The male quality is the creative gift."[1]

Male sexuality, in other words, is not just analogically but actually the essence of literary power. The poet's pen is in some sense (even more than figuratively) a penis.

Eccentric and obscure though he was, Hopkins was articulating a concept central to that Victorian culture of which he was in this case a representative male citizen. But of course the patriarchal notion that the writer "fathers" his text just as God fathered the world is and has been all-pervasive in Western literary civilization, so much so that, as Edward Said has shown, the metaphor is built into the very word, *author*, with which writer, deity, and *pater familias* are identified. Said's miniature meditation on the word *authority* is worth quoting in full because it summarizes so much that is relevant here:

> *Authority* suggests to me a constellation of linked meanings: not only, as the OED tells us, "a power to enforce obedience," or "a derived or delegated power," or "a power to influence action," or "a power to inspire belief," or "a person whose opinion is accepted"; not only those, but a connection as well with *author*—that is, a person who originates or gives existence to something, a begetter, beginner, father, or ancestor, a person also who sets forth written statements. There is still another cluster of meanings: *author* is tied to the past participle *auctus* of the verb *augere*; therefore *auctor*, according to Eric Partridge, is literally an increaser and thus a founder. *Auctoritas* is production, invention, cause, in addition to meaning a right of possession. Finally, it means continuance, or a causing to continue. Taken together these meanings are all grounded in the following notions: (1) that of the power of an individual to initiate, institute, establish—in short, to begin; (2) that this power and its product are an increase over what had been there previously; (3) that the individual wielding this power controls its issue and what is derived therefrom; (4) that authority maintains the continuity of its course.[2]

In conclusion, Said, who is discussing "The Novel as Beginning Intention," remarks that "All four of these [last] abstractions can be used to describe the way in which narrative fiction asserts itself psychologically and aesthetically through the technical efforts of the novelist." But they can also, of course, be used to describe both the author and the authority of any literary text, a point Hopkins's sexual/aesthetic theory seems to have been designed to elaborate. Indeed, Said himself later observes that a convention of most literary texts is "that the unity or integrity of the text is maintained by a series of genealogical connections: author—text, beginning-middle-end, text—meaning, reader—interpretation, and so on. *Underneath all these is the imagery of succession, of paternity, or hierarchy*" (italics ours).[3]

There is a sense in which the very notion of paternity is itself, as Stephen Dedalus puts it in *Ulysses*, a "legal fiction,"[4] a story requiring imagination if not faith. A man cannot verify his fatherhood by either sense or reason, after all; that his child is *his* is in a sense a tale he tells himself to explain the infant's existence. Obviously, the anxiety implicit in such storytelling urgently needs not only the reassurances of male superiority that patriarchal misogyny implies, but also such compensatory fictions of the Word as those embodied in the genealogical imagery Said describes. Thus it is possible to trace the history of this compensatory, sometimes frankly stated and sometimes submerged imagery that elaborates upon what Stephen Dedalus calls the "mystical estate" of paternity[5] through the works of many literary theoreticians besides Hopkins and Said. Defining poetry as a mirror held up to nature, the mimetic aesthetic that begins with Aristotle and descends through Sidney, Shakespeare, and Johnson implies that the poet, like a lesser God, has made or engendered an alternative, mirror-universe in which he actually seems to enclose or trap shadows of reality. Similarly, Coleridge's Romantic concept of the human "imagination or esemplastic power" is of a virile, generative force which echoes "the eternal act of creation in the infinite I AM," while Ruskin's phallic-sounding "Penetrative Imagination" is a "possession-taking faculty" and a "piercing . . . mind's tongue" that seizes, cuts down, and gets at the root of experience in order "to throw up what new shoots it will."[6] In all these aesthetics the poet, like God the Father, is a paternalistic ruler of the fictive world he has created. Shelley called him a "legislator." Keats noted, speaking of writers, that "the antients [*sic*] were Emperors of vast Provinces" though "each of the moderns" is merely an "Elector of Hanover."[7]

In medieval philosophy, the network of connections among sexual, literary, and theological metaphors is equally complex: God the

Father both engenders the cosmos and, as Ernst Robert Curtius notes, writes the Book of Nature: both tropes describe a single act of creation.[8] In addition, the Heavenly Author's ultimate eschatological power is made manifest when, as the *Liber Scriptus* of the traditional requiem mass indicates, He writes the Book of Judgment. More recently, male artists like the Earl of Rochester in the seventeenth century and Auguste Renoir in the nineteenth, have frankly defined aesthetics based on male sexual delight. "I . . . never Rhym'd, but for my Pintle's [penis's] sake," declares Rochester's witty Timon,[9] and (according to the painter Bridget Riley) Renoir "is supposed to have said that he painted his paintings with his prick."[10] Clearly, both these artists believe, with Norman O. Brown, that "the penis is the head of the body," and they might both agree, too, with John Irwin's suggestion that the relationship "of the masculine self with the feminine-masculine work is also an autoerotic act . . . a kind of creative onanism in which through the use of the phallic pen on the 'pure space' of the virgin page . . . the self is continually spent and wasted. . . . "[11] No doubt it is for all these reasons, moreover, that poets have traditionally used a vocabulary derived from the patriarchal "family romance" to describe their relations with each other. As Harold Bloom has pointed out, "from the sons of Homer to the sons of Ben Jonson, poetic influence [has] been described as a filial relationship," a relationship of "*sonship*." The fierce struggle at the heart of literary history, says Bloom, is a "battle between strong equals, father and son as mighty opposites, Laius and Oedipus at the crossroads."[12]

Though many of these writers use the metaphor of literary paternity in different ways and for different purposes, all seem overwhelmingly to agree that a literary text is not only speech quite literally embodied, but also power mysteriously made manifest, made flesh. In patriarchal Western culture, therefore, the text's author is a father, a progenitor, a procreator, an aesthetic patriarch whose pen is an instrument of generative power like his penis. More, his pen's power, like his penis's power, is not just the ability to generate life but the power to create a posterity to which he lays claim, as, in Said's paraphrase of Partridge, "an increaser and thus a founder." In this respect, the pen is truly mightier than its phallic counterpart the sword, and in patriarchy more resonantly sexual. Not only does the writer respond to his muse's quasi-sexual excitation with an out-pouring of the aesthetic energy Hopkins called "the fine delight that fathers thought"—a delight poured seminally from pen to page—but as the author of an enduring text the writer engages the attention of the future in exactly the same way that a king (or father) "owns" the homage of the present. No sword-wielding general could rule so long or possess so vast a kingdom.

Finally, that such a notion of "ownership" or possession is embedded in the metaphor of paternity leads to yet another implication of this complex metaphor. For if the author/father is owner of his text and of his reader's attention, he is also, of course, owner/possessor of the subjects of his text, that is to say of those figures, scenes, and events—those brain children—he has both incarnated in black and white and "bound" in cloth or leather. Thus, because he is an *author*, a "man of letters" is simultaneously, like his divine counterpart, a father, a master or ruler, and an owner: the spiritual type of a patriarch, as we understand that term in Western society.

Where does such an implicitly or explicitly patriarchal theory of literature leave literary women? If the pen is a metaphorical penis, with what organ can females generate texts? The question may seem frivolous, but as our epigraph from Anaïs Nin indicates, both the patriarchal etiology that defines a solitary Father God as the only creator of all things, and the male metaphors of literary creation that depend upon such an etiology, have long "confused" literary women, readers and writers alike. For what if such a proudly masculine cosmic Author is the sole legitimate model for all earthly authors? Or worse, what if the male generative power is not just the only legitimate power but the only power there is? That literary theoreticians from Aristotle to Hopkins seemed to believe this was so no doubt prevented many women from ever "attempting the pen"—to use Anne Finch's phrase—and caused enormous anxiety in generations of those women who were "presumptuous" enough to dare such an attempt. Jane Austen's Anne Elliot understates the case when she decorously observes, toward the end of *Persuasion*, that "men have had every advantage of us in telling their story. Education has been theirs in so much higher a degree; the pen has been in their hands" (II, chap. 11).[13] For, as Anne Finch's complaint suggests, the pen has been defined as not just accidentally but essentially a male "tool," and therefore not only inappropriate but actually alien to women. Lacking Austen's demure irony, Finch's passionate protest goes almost as far toward the center of the metaphor of literary paternity as Hopkins's letter to Canon Dixon. Not only is "a woman that attempts the pen" an intrusive and "presumptuous Creature," she is absolutely unredeemable: no virtue can outweigh the "fault" of her presumption because she has grotesquely crossed boundaries dictated by Nature:

> They tell us, we mistake our sex and way;
> Good breeding, fassion, dancing, dressing, play
> Are the accomplishments we shou'd desire;
> To write, or read, or think, or to enquire
> Wou'd cloud our beauty, and exaust our time,
> And interrupt the conquests of our prime;
> Whilst the dull mannage, of a servile house
> Is held by some, our outmost art and use.[14]

Because they are by definition male activities, this passage implies, writing, reading, and thinking are not only alien but also inimical to "female" characteristics. One hundred years later, in a famous letter to Charlotte Brontë, Robert Southey rephrased the same notion: "Literature is not the business of a woman's life, and it cannot be."[15] It cannot be, the metaphor of literary paternity implies, because it is physiologically as well as sociologically impossible. If male sexuality is integrally associated with the assertive presence of literary power, female sexuality is associated with the absence of such power, with the idea—expressed by the nineteenth-century thinker Otto Weininger—that "woman has no share in ontological reality." As we shall see, a further implication of the paternity/creativity metaphor is the notion (implicit both in Weininger and in Southey's letter) that women exist only to be acted on by men, both as literary and as sensual objects. Again one of Anne Finch's poems explores the assumptions submerged in so many literary theories. Addressing three male poets, she exclaims:

> Happy you three! happy the Race of Men!
> Born to inform or to correct the Pen
> To proffitts pleasures freedom and command

> Whilst we beside you but as Cyphers stand
> T' increase your Numbers and to swell th' account
> Of your delights which from our charms amount
> And sadly are by this distinction taught
> That since the Fall (by our seducement wrought)
> Our is the greater losse as ours the greater fault.[16]

Since Eve's daughters have fallen so much lower than Adam's sons, this passage says, *all* females are "Cyphers"—nullities, vacancies—existing merely and punningly to increase male "Numbers" (either poems or persons) by pleasuring either men's bodies or their minds, their penises or their pens.

In that case, however, devoid of what Richard Chase once called "the masculine *élan*," and implicitly rejecting even the slavish consolations of her "femininity," a literary woman is doubly a "Cypher," for she is really a "eunuch," to use the striking figure Germaine Greer applied to all women in patriarchal society. Thus Anthony Burgess recently declared that Jane Austen's novels fail because her writing "lacks a strong male thrust," and William Gass lamented that literary women "lack that blood congested genital drive which energizes every great style."[17] The assumptions that underlie their statements were articulated more than a century ago by the nineteenth-century editor-critic Rufus Griswold. Introducing an anthology entitled *The Female Poets of America*, Griswold outlined a theory of literary sex roles which builds upon, and clarifies, these grim implications of the metaphor of literary paternity.

> It is less easy to be assured of the genuineness of literary ability in women than in men. The moral nature of women, in its finest and richest development, partakes of some of the qualities of genius; it assumes, at least, the similitude of that which in men is the characteristic or accompaniment of the highest grade of mental inspiration. We are in danger, therefore, of mistaking for the efflorescent energy of creative intelligence, that which is only the exuberance of personal "feelings unemployed." . . . The most exquisite susceptibility of the spirit, and the capacity to mirror in dazzling variety the effects which circumstances or surrounding minds work upon it, may be accompanied by *no power to originate, nor even, in any proper sense, to reproduce.* [Italics ours][18]

Since Griswold has actually compiled a collection of poems by women,
he plainly does not believe that all women lack reproductive or
generative literary power all the time. His gender-definitions imply,
however, that when such creative energy appears in a woman it
may be anomalous, freakish, because as a "male" characteristic it
is essentially "unfeminine."

The converse of these explicit and implicit definitions of "femininity" may also be true for those who develop literary theories
based upon the "mystical estate" of fatherhood: if a woman lacks
generative literary power, then a man who loses or abuses such power
becomes like a eunuch—or like a woman. When the imprisoned
Marquis de Sade was denied "any use of pencil, ink, pen, and paper,"
declares Roland Barthes, he was figuratively emasculated, for "the
scriptural sperm" could flow no longer, and "without exercise, without a pen, Sade [become] *bloated*, [became] a eunuch." Similarly,
when Hopkins wanted to explain to R. W. Dixon the aesthetic
consequences of a *lack* of male mastery, he seized upon an explanation
which developed the implicit parallel between women and eunuchs,
declaring that "if the life" is not "conveyed into the work and . . .
displayed there . . . the product is one of those *hens' eggs* that are good
to eat and look just like live ones but never hatch" (italics ours).[19]
And when, late in his life, he tried to define his own sense of sterility,
his thickening writer's block, he described himself (in the sonnet
"The Fine Delight That Fathers Thought") both as a eunuch and
as a woman, specifically a woman deserted by male power: "the widow
of an insight lost," surviving in a diminished "winter world" that
entirely lacks "the roll, the rise, the carol, the creation" of male
generative power, whose "strong / Spur" is phallically "live and
lancing like the blow pipe flame." And once again some lines from
one of Anne Finch's plaintive protests against male literary hegemony
seem to support Hopkins's image of the powerless and sterile woman
artist. Remarking in the conclusion of her "Introduction" to her
Poems that women are "to be dull / Expected and dessigned" she
does not repudiate such expectations, but on the contrary admonishes
herself, with bitter irony, to *be* dull:

> Be caution'd then my Muse, and still retir'd;
> Nor be dispis'd, aiming to be admir'd;

> Conscious of wants, still with contracted wing,
> To some few friends, and to thy sorrows sing;
> For groves of Lawrell, thou wert never meant;
> Be dark enough thy shades, and be thou there content.[20]

Cut off from generative energy, in a dark and wintry world, Finch seems to be defining herself here not only as a "Cypher" but as "the widow of an insight lost."

Finch's despairing (if ironic) acceptance of male expectations and designs summarizes in a single episode the coercive power not only of cultural constraints but of the literary texts which incarnate them. For it is as much from literature as from "life" that literate women learn they are "to be dull / Expected and dessigned." As Leo Bersani puts it, written "language doesn't merely describe identity but actually produces moral and perhaps even physical identity. . . . We have to allow for a kind of dissolution or at least elasticity of being induced by an immersion in literature."[21] A century and a half earlier, Jane Austen had Anne Elliot's interlocutor, Captain Harville, make a related point in *Persuasion*. Arguing women's inconstancy over Anne's heated objections, he notes that "all histories are against you—all stories, prose, and verse. . . . I could bring you fifty quotations in a moment on my side the argument, and I do not think I ever opened a book in my life which had not something to say upon woman's inconstancy" (II, chap. 11). To this Anne responds, as we have seen, that the pen has been in male hands. In the context of Harville's speech, her remark implies that women have not only been excluded from authorship but in addition they have been subjust to (and subjects of) male authority. With Chaucer's astute Wife of Bath, therefore, Anne might demand, "Who peynted the leoun, tel me who?" And, like the Wife's, her own answer to her own rhetorical question would emphasize our culture's historical confusion of literary authorship with patriarchal authority:

> By God, if wommen hadde writen stories,
> As clerkes han withinne hir oratories,
> They wolde han writen of men more wikednesse
> Than all the mark of Adam may redresse.

In other words, what Bersani, Austen, and Chaucer all imply is that, precisely because a writer "fathers" his text, his literary creations (as we pointed out earlier) are his possession, his property. Having defined them in language and thus generated them, he owns them, controls them, and encloses them on the printed page. Describing his earliest sense of vocation as a writer, Jean-Paul Sartre recalled in *Les Mots* his childhood belief that "to write was to engrave new beings upon [the infinite Tables of the Word] or ... to catch living things in the trap of phrases." [22] Naive as such a notion may seem on the face of it, it is not "wholly an illusion, for it is his [Sartre's] truth," as one commentator observes[23]—and indeed it is every writer's "truth," a truth which has traditionally led male authors to assume patriarchal rights of ownership over the female "characters" they engrave upon "the infinite Tables of the Word."

Male authors have also, of course, generated male characters over whom they would seem to have had similar rights of ownership. But further implicit in the metaphor of literary paternity is the idea that each man, arriving at what Hopkins called the "puberty" of his creative gift, has the ability, even perhaps the obligation, to talk back to other men by generating alternative fictions of his own. Lacking the pen/penis which would enable them similarly to refute one fiction by another, women in patriarchal societies have historically been reduced to *mere* properties, to characters and images imprisoned in male texts because generated solely, as Anne Elliot and Anne Finch observe, by male expectations and designs.

Like the metaphor of literary paternity itself, this corollary notion that the chief creature man has generated is woman has a long and complex history. From Eve, Minerva, Sophia, and Galatea onward, after all, patriarchal mythology defines women as created by, from, and for men, the children of male brains, ribs, and ingenuity. For Blake the eternal female was at her best an Emanation of the male creative principle. For Shelley she was an epi-psyche, a soul out of the poet's soul, whose inception paralleled on a spiritual plane the solider births of Eve and Minerva. Throughout the history of Western culture, moreover, male-engendered female figures as superficially disparate as Milton's Sin, Swift's Chloe, and Yeats's Crazy Jane have incarnated men's ambivalence not only toward female sexuality but toward their own (male) physicality. At the same time, male texts, continually elaborating the metaphor of literary paternity, have continually proclaimed that, in Honoré de Balzac's ambiguous words, "woman's virtue is man's greatest invention."[24] A characteristically condensed and oracular comment by Norman O. Brown perfectly summarizes the assumptions on which all such texts are based:

> Poetry, the creative act, the act of life, the archetypal sexual act. Sexuality is poetry. The lady is our creation, or Pygmalion's statue. The lady is the poem; [Petrarch's] Laura is, really, poetry.[25]

No doubt this complex of metaphors and etiologies simply reflects not just the fiercely patriarchal structure of Western society but also the underpinning of misogyny upon which that severe patriarchy has stood. The roots of "authority" tell us, after all, that if woman is man's property then he must have authored her, just as surely as they tell us that if he authored her she must be his property. As a creation "penned" by man, moreover, woman has been "penned up" or "penned in." As a sort of "sentence" man has spoken, she has herself been "sentenced": fated, jailed, for he has both "indited" her and "indicted" her. As a thought he has "framed," she has been both "framed" (enclosed) in his texts, glyphs, graphics, and "framed up" (found guilty, found wanting) in his cosmologies. For as Humpty Dumpty tells Alice in *Through the Looking Glass*, the "master" of words, utterances, phrases, literary properties, "can manage the whole lot of them!"[26] The etymology and etiology of masculine authority are, it seems, almost necessarily identical. However, for women who felt themselves to be more than, in every sense, the properties of literary texts, the problem posed by such authority was neither metaphysical nor philological, but (as the pain expressed by Anne Finch and Anne Elliot indicates) psychological. Since both patriarchy and its texts subordinate and imprison women, before women can even attempt that pen which is so rigorously kept from them they must escape just those male texts which, defining them as "Cyphers," deny them the autonomy to formulate alternatives to the authority that has imprisoned them and kept them from attempting the pen.

The vicious circularity of this problem helps explain the curious passivity with which Finch responded (or pretended to respond) to male expectations and designs, and it helps explain, too, the centuries-long silence of so many women who must have had talents comparable to Finch's. A final paradox of the metaphor of literary paternity is the fact that in the same way an author both generates and imprisons his fictive creatures, he silences them by depriving them of autonomy (that is, of the power of independent speech) even as he gives them life. He silences them and, as Keats's "Ode on a Grecian Urn" suggests, he stills them, or—embedding them in the marble of his art—kills them. As Albert Gelpi neatly puts it, "the artist kills experience into art, for temporal experience can only escape death by dying into the 'immortality' of artistic form. The fixity of 'life' in art and the fluidity of 'life' in nature are incompatible." [27] The pen, therefore, is not only mightier than the sword, it is also *like* the sword in its power—its need, even—to kill. And this last attribute of the pen once again seems to be associatively linked with its metaphorical maleness. Simone de Beauvoir has commented that the human male's "transcendence" of nature is symbolized by his ability to hunt and kill, just as the human female's identification with nature, her role as a symbol of immanence, is expressed by her central involvement in that life-giving but involuntary birth process which perpetuates the species. Thus, superiority—or authority—"has been accorded in humanity not to the sex that brings forth but to that which kills." [28] In D. H. Lawrence's words, "the Lords of Life are the Masters of Death"—and therefore, patriarchal poetics implies, they are the masters of art. [29]

Commentators on female subordination from Freud and Horney to de Beauvoir, Wolfgang Lederer, and most recently, Dorothy Dinnerstein, have of course explored other aspects of the relationship between the sexes that also lead men to want figuratively to "kill" women. What Horney called male "dread" of the female is a phenomenon to which Lederer has devoted a long and scholarly book. [30] Elaborating on de Beauvoir's assertion that as mother of life "woman's first lie, her first treason [seems to be] that of life itself—life which, though clothed in the most attractive forms, is always infested by the ferments of age and death," Lederer remarks upon woman's own tendency to "kill" *herself* into art in order "to appeal to man":

> From the Paleolithic on, we have evidence that woman, through careful coiffure, through adornment and makeup, tried to stress

the eternal type rather than the mortal self. Such makeup, in Africa or Japan, may reach the, to us, somewhat estranging degree of a lifeless mask—and yet that is precisely the purpose of it: where nothing is lifelike, nothing speaks of death.[31]

For yet another reason, then, it is no wonder that women have historically hesitated to attempt the pen. Authored by a male God and by a godlike male, killed into a "perfect" image of herself, the woman writer's self-contemplation may be said to have begun with a searching glance into the mirror of the male-inscribed literary text. There she would see at first only those eternal lineaments fixed on her like a mask to conceal her dreadful and bloody link to nature. But looking long enough, looking hard enough, she would see—like the speaker of Mary Elizabeth Coleridge's "The Other Side of the Mirror"—an enraged prisoner: herself. The poem describing this vision is central to the feminist poetics we are trying to construct:

> I sat before my glass one day,
>   And conjured up a vision bare,
> Unlike the aspects glad and gay,
>   That erst were found reflected there—
> The vision of a woman, wild
>   With more than womanly despair.
>
> Her hair stood back on either side
>   A face bereft of loveliness.
> It had no envy now to hide
>   What once no man on earth could guess.
> It formed the thorny aureole
>   Of hard unsanctified distress.
>
> Her lips were open—not a sound
>   Came through the parted lines of red.
> Whate'er it was, the hideous wound
>   In silence and in secret bled.
> No sigh relieved her speechless woe,
>   She had no voice to speak her dread.
>
> And in her lurid eyes there shone
>   The dying flame of life's desire,
> Made mad because its hope was gone,

> And kindled at the leaping fire
> Of jealousy, and fierce revenge,
>   And strength that could not change nor tire.
>
> Shade of a shadow in the glass,
>   O set the crystal surface free!
> Pass—as the fairer visions pass—
>   Nor ever more return, to be
> The ghost of a distracted hour,
> That heard me whisper, 'I am she!' [32]

What this poem suggests is that, although the woman who is the prisoner of the mirror/text's images has "no voice to speak her dread," although "no sigh" interrupts "her speechless woe," she has an invincible sense of her own autonomy, her own interiority; she has a sense, to paraphrase Chaucer's Wife of Bath, of the authority of her own experience.[33] The power of metaphor, says Mary Elizabeth Coleridge's poem, can only extend so far. Finally, no human creature can be completely silenced by a text or by an image. Just as stories notoriously have a habit of "getting away" from their authors, human beings since Eden have had a habit of defying authority, both divine and literary.[34]

Once more the debate in which Austen's Anne Elliot and her Captain Harville engage is relevant here, for it is surely no accident that the question these two characters are discussing is woman's "inconstancy"—her refusal, that is, to be fixed or "killed" by an author/owner, her stubborn insistence on her own way. That male authors berate her for this refusal even while they themselves generate female characters who (as we shall see) perversely display "monstrous" autonomy is one of the ironies of literary art. From a female perspective, however, such "inconstancy" can only be encouraging, for—implying duplicity—it suggests that women themselves have the power to create themselves as characters, even perhaps the power to reach toward the woman trapped on the other side of the mirror/text and help her to climb out.

Before the woman writer can journey through the looking glass toward literary autonomy, however, she must come to terms with the images on the surface of the glass, with, that is, those mythic masks male artists have fastened over her human face both to lessen their dread of her "inconstancy" and—by identifying her with the "eternal types" they have themselves invented—to possess her more thoroughly. Specifically, as we will try to show here, a woman writer must examine, assimilate, and transcend the extreme images of "angel" and "monster" which male authors have generated for her. Before we women can write, declared Virginia Woolf, we must "kill" the "angel in the house."[35] In other words, women must kill the aesthetic ideal through which they themselves have been "killed" into art. And similarly, all women writers must kill the angel's necessary opposite and double, the "monster" in the house, whose Medusa-face also kills female creativity. For us as feminist critics, however, the Woolfian act of "killing" both angels and monsters must here begin with an understanding of the nature and origin of these images. At this point in our construction of a feminist poetics, then, we really must dissect in order to murder. And we must particularly do this in order to understand literature by women because, as we shall show, the images of "angel" and "monster" have been so ubiquitous throughout literature by men that they have also pervaded women's writing to such an extent that few women have definitively "killed" either figure. Rather, the female imagination has perceived itself, as it were, through a glass darkly: until quite recently the woman writer has had (if only unconsciously) to define herself as a mysterious creature who resides behind the angel or monster or angel/monster image that lives on what Mary Elizabeth Coleridge called "the crystal surface."

For all literary artists, of course, self-definition necessarily precedes self-assertion: the creative "I AM" cannot be uttered if the "I" knows not what it is. But for the female artist the essential process of self-definition is complicated by all those patriarchal definitions that intervene between herself and herself. From Anne Finch's Ardelia, who struggles to escape the male designs in which she feels herself enmeshed, to Sylvia Plath's "Lady Lazarus," who tells "Herr Doktor . . . Herr Enemy" that "I am your opus, / I am your valuable,"[36] the woman writer acknowledges with pain, confusion, and anger that what she sees in the mirror is usually a male construct, the "pure gold baby" of male brains, a glittering and wholly artificial

child. With Christina Rossetti, moreover, she realizes that the male
artist often "feeds" upon his female subject's face "not as she is but
as she fills his dreams."[37] Finally, as "A Woman's Poem" of 1859
simply puts it, the woman writer insists that "You [men] make the
worlds wherein you move.... Our world (alas you make that too!)"
—and in its narrow confines, "shut in four blank walls ... we act
our parts."[38]

Though the highly stylized women's roles to which this last poem
alludes are all ultimately variations upon the roles of angel and
monster, they seem on the surface quite varied, because so many
masks, reflecting such an elaborate typology, have been invented
for women. A crucial passage from Elizabeth Barrett Browning's
Aurora Leigh suggests both the mystifying deathliness and the mysterious variety female artists perceive in male imagery of women.
Contemplating a portrait of her mother which, significantly, was
made after its subject was dead (so that it is a kind of death mask,
an image of a woman metaphorically killed into art) the young
Aurora broods on the work's iconography. Noting that her mother's
chambermaid had insisted upon having her dead mistress painted
in "the red stiff silk" of her court dress rather than in an "English-
fashioned shroud," she remarks that the effect of this unlikely costume
was "very strange." As the child stared at the painting, her mother's
"swan-like supernatural white life" seemed to mingle with "whatever
I last read, or heard, or dreamed," and thus in its charismatic beauty,
her mother's image became

> by turns
> Ghost, fiend, and angel, fairy, witch, and sprite;
> A dauntless Muse who eyes a dreadful Fate;
> A loving Psyche who loses sight of Love;
> A still Medusa with mild milky brows,
> All curdled and all clothed upon with snakes
> Whose slime falls fast as sweat will; or anon
> Our Lady of the Passion, stabbed with swords
> Where the Babe sucked; or Lamia in her first
> Moonlighted pallor, ere she shrunk and blinked,
> And shuddering wriggled down to the unclean;
> Or my own mother, leaving her last smile

> In her last kiss upon the baby-mouth
> My father pushed down on the bed for that;
> Or my dead mother, without smile or kiss,
> Buried at Florence.[39]

The female forms Aurora sees in her dead mother's picture are extreme, melodramatic, gothic—"Ghost, fiend, and angel, fairy, witch, and sprite"—specifically, as she tells us, because her reading merges with her seeing. What this implies, however, is not only that she herself is fated to inhabit male-defined masks and costumes, as her mother did, but that male-defined masks and costumes inevitably inhabit *her*, altering her vision. Aurora's self-development as a poet is the central concern of Barrett Browning's *Bildungsroman* in verse, but if she is to be a poet she must deconstruct the dead self that is a male "opus" and discover a living, "inconstant" self. She must, in other words, replace the "copy" with the "individuality," as Barrett Browning once said she thought she herself had done in her mature art.[40] Significantly, however, the "copy" selves depicted in Aurora's mother's portrait ultimately represent, once again, the moral extremes of angel ("angel," "fairy," and perhaps "sprite") and monster ("ghost," "witch," "fiend").

In her brilliant and influential analysis of the question "Is Female to Male as Nature Is to Culture?" the anthropologist Sherry Ortner notes that in every society "the psychic mode associated with women seems to stand at both the bottom and the top of the scale of human modes of relating." Attempting to account for this "symbolic ambiguity," Ortner explains "both the subversive feminine symbols (witches, evil eye, menstrual pollution, castrating mothers) and the feminine symbols of transcendence (mother goddesses, merciful dispensers of salvation, female symbols of justice)" by pointing out that women "can appear from certain points of view to stand both under and over (but really simply outside of) the sphere of culture's hegemony."[41] That is, precisely because a woman is denied the autonomy—the subjectivity—that the pen represents, she is not only excluded from culture (whose emblem might well be the pen) but she also becomes herself an embodiment of just those extremes of mysterious and intransigent Otherness which culture confronts with worship or fear, love or loathing. As "Ghost, fiend, and angel, fairy,

witch, and sprite," she mediates between the male artist and the
Unknown, simultaneously teaching him purity and instructing him
in degradation. But what of her own artistic growth? Because that
growth has for so long been radically qualified by the angel- and
monster-imagery the literary woman sees in the looking glass of the
male-authored text, some understanding of such imagery is an
essential preliminary to any study of literature by women. As Joan
Didion recently noted, "writing is an aggression" precisely because
it is "an imposition ... an invasion of someone else's most private
space."[42] Like Leo Bersani's observation that an "elasticity of being
[is] induced by an immersion in literature," her remark has special
significance in this connection. A thorough study of those male constructs which have invaded the "most private space" of countless
literate women would require hundreds of pages—indeed, a number
of excellent books have been devoted to the subject[43]—but we will
attempt here a brief review of the fundamental extremes of angel
and monster, in order to demonstrate the severity of the male text's
"imposition" upon women.

The ideal woman that male authors dream of generating is always
an angel, as Norman O. Brown's comment about Laura/poetry
suggested. At the same time, from Virginia Woolf's point of view,
the "angel in the house" is the most pernicious image male authors
have ever imposed upon literary women. Where and how did this
ambiguous image originate, particularly the trivialized Victorian
angel in the house that so disturbed Woolf? In the Middle Ages, of
course, mankind's great teacher of purity was the Virgin Mary, a
mother goddess who perfectly fitted the female role Ortner defines
as "merciful dispenser of salvation." For the more secular nineteenth
century, however, the eternal type of female purity was represented
not by a madonna in heaven but by an angel in the house. Nevertheless, there is a clear line of literary descent from divine Virgin to
domestic angel, passing through (among many others) Dante, Milton,
and Goethe.

Like most Renaissance neo-Platonists, Dante claimed to know God
and His Virgin handmaid by knowing the Virgin's virgin attendant,

Beatrice. Similarly, Milton, despite his undeniable misogyny (which we shall examine later), speaks of having been granted a vision of "my late espoused saint," who

> Came vested all in white, pure as her mind.
> Her face was veiled, yet to my fancied sight,
> Love sweetness goodness, in her person shined
> So clear, as in no face with more delight.

In death, in other words, Milton's human wife has taken on both the celestial brightness of Mary and (since she has been "washed from spot of childbed taint") the virginal purity of Beatrice. In fact, if she could be resurrected in the flesh she might now be an angel in the house, interpreting heaven's luminous mysteries to her wondering husband.

The famous vision of the "Eternal Feminine" (*Das Ewig-Weibliche*) with which Goethe's *Faust* concludes presents women from penitent prostitutes to angelic virgins in just this role of interpreters or intermediaries between the divine Father and his human sons. The German of *Faust's* "Chorus Mysticus" is extraordinarily difficult to translate in verse, but Hans Eichner's English paraphrase easily suggests the ways in which Goethe's image of female intercessors seems almost to be a revision of Milton's "late espoused saint": "All that is transitory is merely symbolical; here (that is to say, in the scene before you) the inaccessible is (symbolically) portrayed and the inexpressible is (symbolically) made manifest. The eternal feminine (i.e. the eternal principle symbolized by woman) draws us to higher spheres." Meditating on the exact nature of this eternal feminine, moreover, Eichner comments that for Goethe the "ideal of contemplative purity" is always feminine while "the ideal of significant action is masculine."[44] Once again, therefore, it is just because women are defined as wholly passive, completely void of generative power (like "Cyphers") that they become numinous to male artists. For in the metaphysical emptiness their "purity" signifies they are, of course, *self-less*, with all the moral and psychological implications that word suggests.

Elaborating further on Goethe's eternal feminine, Eichner gives an example of the culmination of Goethe's "chain of representatives of the 'noblest femininity'": Makarie, in the late novel *Wilhelm Meister's Travels*. His description of her usefully summarizes the philosophical background of the angel in the house:

> She ... leads a life of almost pure contemplation.... in considerable isolation on a country estate ... a life without external events—a life whose story cannot be told as there is no story. Her existence is not useless. On the contrary ... she shines like a beacon in a dark world, like a motionless lighthouse by which others, the travellers whose lives do have a story, can set their course. When those involved in feeling and action turn to her in their need, they are never dismissed without advice and consolation. She is an ideal, a model of selflessness and of purity of heart.[45]

She has no story of her own but gives "advice and consolation" to others, listens, smiles, sympathizes: such characteristics show that Makarie is not only the descendent of Western culture's cloistered virgins but also the direct ancestress of Coventry Patmore's angel in the house, the eponymous heroine of what may have been the middle nineteenth century's most popular book of poems.

Dedicated to "the memory of her by whom and for whom I became a poet," Patmore's *The Angel in the House* is a verse-sequence which hymns the praises and narrates the courtship and marriage of Honoria, one of the three daughters of a country Dean, a girl whose unselfish grace, gentleness, simplicity, and nobility reveal that she is not only a pattern Victorian lady but almost literally an angel on earth. Certainly her spirituality interprets the divine for her poet-husband, so that

> No happier post than this I ask,
>   To live her laureate all my life.
> On wings of love uplifted free,
>   And by her gentleness made great,
> I'll teach how noble man should be
>   To match with such a lovely mate.[46]

Honoria's essential virtue, in other words, is that her virtue makes her *man* "great." In and of herself, she is neither great nor extraordinary. Indeed, Patmore adduces many details to stress the almost pathetic ordinariness of her life: she picks violets, loses her gloves, feeds her birds, waters her rose plot, and journeys to London on a train with her father the Dean, carrying in her lap a volume of Petrarch borrowed from her lover but entirely ignorant that the book is, as he tells us, "worth its weight in gold." In short, like Goethe's Makarie, Honoria has no story except a sort of anti-story of selfless innocence based on the notion that "Man must be pleased; but him to please / Is woman's pleasure." [47]

Significantly, when the young poet-lover first visits the Deanery where his Honoria awaits him like Sleeping Beauty or Snow White, one of her sisters asks him if, since leaving Cambridge, he has "outgrown" Kant and Goethe. But if his paean of praise to the *Ewig-Weibliche* in rural England suggests that he has not, at any rate, outgrown the latter of these, that is because for Victorian men of letters Goethe represented not collegiate immaturity but moral maturity. After all, the climactic words of *Sartor Resartus*, that most influential masterpiece of Victorian sagacity, were "Close thy *Byron;* open thy *Goethe*," [48] and though Carlyle was not specifically thinking of what came to be called "the woman question," his canonization of Goethe meant, among other things, a new emphasis on the eternal feminine, the angel woman Patmore describes in his verses, Aurora Leigh perceives in her mother's picture, and Virginia Woolf shudders to remember.

Of course, from the eighteenth century on, conduct books for ladies had proliferated, enjoining young girls to submissiveness, modesty, self-lessness; reminding all women that they should be angelic. There is a long and crowded road from *The Booke of Curtesye* (1477) to the columns of "Dear Abby," but social historians have fully explored its part in the creation of those "eternal feminine" virtues of modesty, gracefulness, purity, delicacy, civility, compliancy, reticence, chastity, affability, politeness—all of which are modes of mannerliness that contributed to Honoria's angelic innocence. Ladies were assured by the writers of such conduct books that "There are Rules for all our Actions, even down to Sleeping with a good Grace," and they were told that this good Grace was a woman's duty to her husband because "if Woman owes her Being to the Comfort and Profit of man, 'tis highly reasonable that she should be careful and diligent to content and please him." [49]

The arts of pleasing men, in other words, are not only angelic characteristics; in more worldly terms, they are the proper acts of a lady. "What shall I do to gratify myself or to be admired?" is not the question a lady asks on arising, declared Mrs. Sarah Ellis, Victorian England's foremost preceptress of female morals and manners, in 1844. No, because she is "the least engaged of any member of the household," a woman of right feeling should devote herself to the good of others.[50] And she should do this silently, without calling attention to her exertions because "all that would tend to draw away her thoughts from others and fix them on herself, ought to be avoided as an evil to her."[51] Similarly, John Ruskin affirmed in 1865 that the woman's "power is not for rule, not for battle, and her intellect is not for invention or creation, but for sweet orderings" of domesticity.[52] Plainly, both writers meant that, enshrined within her home, a Victorian angel-woman should become her husband's holy refuge from the blood and sweat that inevitably accompanies a "life of significant action," as well as, in her "contemplative purity," a living *memento* of the otherness of the divine.

At times, however, in the severity of her selflessness, as well as in the extremity of her alienation from ordinary fleshly life, this nineteenth-century angel-woman becomes not just a memento of otherness but actually a *memento mori* or, as Alexander Welsh has noted, an "Angel of Death." Discussing Dickens's heroines in particular and what he calls Victorian "angelology" in general, Welsh analyzes the ways in which a spiritualized heroine like Florence Dombey "assists in the translation of the dying to a future state," not only by officiating at the sickbed but also by maternally welcoming the sufferer "from the other side of death."[53] But if the angel-woman in some curious way simultaneously inhabits both this world and the next, then there is a sense in which, besides ministering to the dying, she is herself already dead. Welsh muses on "the apparent reversibility of the heroine's role, whereby the acts of dying and of saving someone from death seem confused," and he points out that Dickens actually describes Florence Dombey as having the unearthly serenity of one who is dead.[54] A spiritual messenger, an interpreter of mysteries to wondering and devoted men, the *Ewig-Weibliche* angel becomes, finally, a messenger of the mystical otherness of death.

As Ann Douglas has recently shown, the nineteenth-century cult of such death-angels as Harriet Beecher Stowe's little Eva or Dickens's little Nell resulted in a veritable "domestication of death," producing both a conventionalized iconography and a stylized hagiography of dying women and children.[55] Like Dickens's dead-alive Florence Dombey, for instance, Louisa May Alcott's dying Beth March is a household saint, and the deathbed at which she surrenders herself to heaven is the ultimate shrine of the angel-woman's mysteries. At the same time, moreover, the aesthetic cult of ladylike fragility and delicate beauty—no doubt associated with the moral cult of the angel-woman—obliged "genteel" women to "kill" themselves (as Lederer observed) into art objects: slim, pale, passive beings whose "charms" eerily recalled the snowy, porcelain immobility of the dead. Tight-lacing, fasting, vinegar-drinking, and similar cosmetic or dietary excesses were all parts of a physical regimen that helped women either to feign morbid weakness or actually to "decline" into real illness. Beth March's beautiful ladylike sister Amy is thus, in her artful way, as pale and frail as her consumptive sibling, and together these two heroines constitute complementary halves of the emblematic "beautiful woman" whose *death*, thought Edgar Allan Poe, "is unquestionably the most poetical topic in the world."[56]

Whether she becomes an *objet d'art* or a saint, however, it is the surrender of her self—of her personal comfort, her personal desires, or both—that is the beautiful angel-woman's key act, while it is precisely this sacrifice which dooms her both to death and to heaven. For to be selfless is not only to be noble, it is to be dead. A life that has no story, like the life of Goethe's Makarie, is really a life of death, a death-in-life. The ideal of "contemplative purity" evokes, finally, both heaven and the grave. To return to Aurora Leigh's catalogue, then—her vision of "Ghost, fiend, and angel, fairy, witch, and sprite" in her mother's portrait—there is a sense in which as a celestial "angel" Aurora's mother is also a somewhat sinister "ghost," because she wears the face of the spiritualized Victorian woman who, having died to her own desires, her own self, her own life, leads a posthumous existence in her own lifetime.

As Douglas reminds us too, though, the Victorian domestication of death represents not just an acquiescence in death by the selfless, but also a secret striving for power by the powerless. "The tombstone," she notes, "is the sacred emblem in the cult of the overlooked."[57]

Exorcised from public life, denied the pleasures (though not the pains) of sensual existence, the Victorian angel in the house was allowed to hold sway over at least one realm beyond her own household: the kingdom of the dead. But if, as nurse and comforter, spirit-guide and mystical messenger, a woman ruled the dying and the dead, might not even her admirers sometimes fear that, besides dying or easing death, she could *bring* death? As Welsh puts it, "the power of an angel to save implies, even while it denies, the power of death." Speaking of angelic Agnes Wickfield (in *David Copperfield*), he adds a sinister but witty question: "Who, in the language of detective fiction, was the last person to see Dora Copperfield alive?" [58]

Neither Welsh nor Dickens does more than hint at the angel-woman's pernicious potential. But in this context a word to the wise is enough, for such a hint helps explain the fluid metamorphoses that the figure of Aurora's mother undergoes. Her images of "Ghost, fiend, and angel, fairy, witch and sprite," we begin to see, are inextricably linked, one to another, each to its opposite. Certainly, imprisoned in the coffinlike shape of a death angel, a woman might long demonically for escape. In addition, if as death angel the woman suggests a providentially selfless mother, delivering the male soul from one realm to another, the same woman's maternal power implies, too, the fearful bondage of mortality into which every mother delivers her children. Finally, the fact that the angel woman manipulates her domestic/mystical sphere in order to ensure the well-being of those entrusted to her care reveals that she *can* manipulate; she can scheme; she can plot—stories as well as strategies.

The Victorian angel's scheming, her mortal fleshliness, and her repressed (but therefore all the more frightening) capacity for explosive rage are often subtly acknowledged, even in the most glowing texts of male "angelographers." Patmore's Honoria, for instance, proves to be considerably more duplicitous than at first she seemed. "To the sweet folly of the dove," her poet-lover admits, "She joins the cunning of the snake." To be sure, the speaker shows that her wiliness is exercised in a "good" cause: "to rivet and exalt his love." Nevertheless,

> Her mode of candour is deceit;
> And what she thinks from what she'll say

> (Although I'll never call her cheat)
> Lies far as Scotland from Cathay.[59]

Clearly, the poet is here acknowledging his beloved's potential for what Austen's Captain Harville called "inconstancy"—that is, her stubborn autonomy and unknowable subjectivity, meaning the ineradicable selfishness that underlies even her angelic renunciation of self.

Similarly, exploring analogous tensions between flesh and spirit in yet another version of the angel-woman, Dante Gabriel Rossetti places his "Blessed Damozel" behind "golden barriers" in heaven, but then observes that she is still humanly embodied. The bars she leans on are oddly warm; her voice, her hair, her tears are weirdly real and sensual, perhaps to emphasize the impossibility of complete spirituality for any woman. This "damozel's" life-in-death, at any rate, is still in some sense physical and therefore (paradoxically) emblematic of mortality. But though Rossetti wrote "The Blessed Damozel" in 1846, sixteen years before the suicide of his wife and model Elizabeth Siddal, the secret anxieties such imagery expressed came to the surface long after Lizzie's death. In 1869, to retrieve a poetry manuscript he had sentimentally buried with this beloved woman whose face "fill[ed] his dreams"—buried as if woman and artwork were necessarily inseparable—Rossetti had Lizzie's coffin exhumed, and literary London buzzed with rumors that her hair had "continued to grow after her death, to grow so long, so beautiful, so luxuriantly as to fill the coffin with its gold!"[60] As if symbolizing the indomitable earthliness that no woman, however angelic, could entirely renounce, Lizzie Siddal Rossetti's hair leaps like a metaphor for monstrous female sexual energies from the literal and figurative coffins in which her artist-husband enclosed her. To Rossetti, its assertive radiance made the dead Lizzie seem both terrifyingly physical and fiercely supernatural. "'Mid change the changeless night environeth, / Lies all that golden hair undimmed in death," he wrote.[61]

If we define a woman like Rossetti's dead wife as indomitably earthly yet somehow supernatural, we are defining her as a witch or monster, a magical creature of the lower world who is a kind of antithetical mirror image of an angel. As such, she still stands, in Sherry Ortner's words, "both under and over (but really simply outside of) the sphere of culture's hegemony." But now, as a representative of otherness, she incarnates the damning otherness of the flesh rather than the inspiring otherness of the spirit, expressing what—to use Anne Finch's words—men consider her own "presumptuous" desires rather than the angelic humility and "dullness" for which she was designed. Indeed, if we return to the literary definitions of "authority" with which we began this discussion, we will see that the monster-woman, threatening to replace her angelic sister, embodies intransigent female autonomy and thus represents both the author's power to allay "his" anxieties by calling their source bad names (witch, bitch, fiend, monster) and, simultaneously, the mysterious power of the character who refuses to stay in her textually ordained "place" and thus generates a story that "gets away" from its author.

Because, as Dorothy Dinnerstein has proposed, male anxieties about female autonomy probably go as deep as everyone's mother-dominated infancy, patriarchal texts have traditionally suggested that every angelically selfless Snow White must be hunted, if not haunted, by a wickedly assertive Stepmother: for every glowing portrait of submissive women enshrined in domesticity, there exists an equally important negative image that embodies the sacrilegious fiendishness of what William Blake called the "Female Will." Thus, while male writers traditionally praise the simplicity of the dove, they invariably castigate the cunning of the serpent—at least when that cunning is exercised in her own behalf. Similarly, assertiveness, aggressiveness—all characteristics of a male life of "significant action"—are "monstrous" in women precisely because "unfeminine" and therefore unsuited to a gentle life of "contemplative purity." Musing on "The Daughter of Eve," Patmore's poet-speaker remarks, significantly, that

> The woman's gentle mood o'erstept
>   Withers my love, that lightly scans
> The rest, and does in her accept
>   All her own faults, but none of man's.[62]

Luckily, his Honoria has no such vicious defects; her serpentine cunning, as we noted earlier, is concentrated entirely on pleasing her lover. But repeatedly, throughout most male literature, a sweet heroine inside the house (like Honoria) is opposed to a vicious bitch outside.

Behind Thackeray's angelically submissive Amelia Sedley, for instance—an Honoria whose career is traced in gloomier detail than that of Patmore's angel—lurks *Vanity Fair*'s stubbornly autonomous Becky Sharp, an independent "charmer" whom the novelist at one point actually describes as a monstrous and snaky sorceress:

> In describing this siren, singing and smiling, coaxing and cajoling, the author, with modest pride, asks his readers all around, has he once forgotten the laws of politeness, and showed the monster's hideous tail above water? No! Those who like may peep down under waves that are pretty transparent, and see it writhing and twirling, diabolically hideous and slimy, flapping amongst bones, or curling around corpses; but above the water line, I ask, has not everything been proper, agreeable, and decorous. . . . [63]

As this extraordinary passage suggests, the monster may not only be concealed *behind* the angel, she may actually turn out to reside *within* (or in the lower half of) the angel. Thus, Thackeray implies, every angel in the house—"proper, agreeable, and decorous," "coaxing and cajoling" hapless men—is really, perhaps, a monster, "diabolically hideous and slimy."

"A woman in the shape of a monster," Adrienne Rich observes in "Planetarium," "a monster in the shape of a woman / the skies are full of them."[64] Because the skies *are* full of them, even if we focus only on those female monsters who are directly related to Thackeray's serpentine siren, we will find that such monsters have long inhabited male texts. Emblems of filthy materiality, committed only to their own private ends, these women are accidents of nature, deformities meant to repel, but in their very freakishness they possess unhealthy energies, powerful and dangerous arts. Moreover, to the extent that they incarnate male dread of women and, specifically, male scorn of female creativity, such characters have drastically affected the self-images of women writers, negatively reinforcing those messages of submissiveness conveyed by their angelic sisters.

The first book of Spenser's *The Faerie Queene* introduces a female monster who serves as a prototype of the entire line. *Errour* is half woman, half serpent, "Most lothsom, filthie, foule, and full of vile disdaine" (1.1.126). She breeds in a dark den where her young suck on her poisonous dugs or creep back into her mouth at the sight of hated light, and in battle against the noble Red-crosse Knight, she spews out a flood of books and papers, frogs and toads. Symbolizing the dangerous effect of misdirected and undigested learning, her filthiness adumbrates that of two other powerful females in book 1, Duessa and Lucifera. But because these other women can create false appearances to hide their vile natures, they are even more dangerous.

Like Errour, Duessa is deformed below the waist, as if to foreshadow *Lear*'s "But to the girdle do the Gods inherit, Beneath is all the fiend's." When, like all witches, she must do penance at the time of the new moon by bathing with herbs traditionally used by such other witches as Scylla, Circe, and Medea, her "neather parts" are revealed as "misshapen, monstruous."[65] But significantly, Duessa deceives and ensnares men by assuming the shape of Una, the beautiful and angelic heroine who represents Christianity, charity, docility. Similarly, Lucifera lives in what seems to be a lovely mansion, a cunningly constructed House of Pride whose weak foundation and ruinous rear quarters are carefully concealed. Both women use their arts of deception to entrap and destroy men, and the secret, shameful ugliness of both is closely associated with their hidden genitals—that is, with their femaleness.

Descending from Patristic misogynists like Tertullian and St. Augustine through Renaissance and Restoration literature—through Sidney's Cecropia, Shakespeare's Lady Macbeth and his Goneril and Regan, Milton's Sin (and even, as we shall see, his Eve)—the female monster populates the works of the satirists of the eighteenth century, a company of male artists whose virulent visions must have been particularly alarming to feminine readers in an age when women had just begun to "attempt the pen." These authors attacked literary women on two fronts. First, and most obviously, through the construction of cartoon figures like Sheridan's Mrs. Malaprop and

Fielding's Mrs. Slipslop, and Smollett's Tabitha Bramble, they implied that language itself was almost literally alien to the female tongue. In the mouths of women, vocabulary loses meaning, sentences dissolve, literary messages are distorted or destroyed. At the same time, more subtly but perhaps for that reason even more significantly, such authors devised elaborate anti-romances to show that the female "angel" was really a female "fiend," the ladylike paragon really an unladylike monster. Thus while the "Bluestocking" Anne Finch would find herself directly caricatured (as she was by Pope and Gay) as a character afflicted with the "poetical Itch" like Phoebe Clinket in *Three Hours After Marriage*,[66] she might well feel herself to be indirectly but even more profoundly attacked by Johnson's famous observation that a woman preacher was like a dog standing on its hind legs, or by the suggestion—embedded in works by Swift, Pope, Gay, and others—that *all* women were inexorably and inescapably monstrous, in the flesh as well as in the spirit. Finally, in a comment like Horace Walpole's remark that Mary Wollstonecraft was "a hyena in petticoats," the two kinds of misogynistic attacks definitively merged.[67]

It is significant, then, that Jonathan Swift's disgust with the monstrous females who populate so many of his verses seems to have been caused specifically by the inexorable failure of female art. Like disgusted Gulliver, who returns to England only to prefer the stable to the parlor, his horses to his wife, Swift projects his horror of time, his dread of physicality, on to another stinking creature—the degenerate woman. Probably the most famous instance of this projection occurs in his so-called dirty poems. In these works, we peer behind the facade of the angel woman to discover that, say, the idealized "Caelia, Caelia, Caelia, shits!" We discover that the seemingly unblemished Chloe must "either void or burst," and that the female "inner space" of the "Queen of Love" is like a foul chamber pot.[68] Though some critics have suggested that the misogyny implied by Swift's characterizations of these women is merely ironic, what emerges from his most furious poems in this vein is a horror of female flesh and a revulsion at the inability—the powerlessness—of female arts to redeem or to transform the flesh. Thus for Swift female sexuality is consistently equated with degeneration, disease, and death, while female arts are trivial attempts to forestall an inevitable end.

Significantly, as if defining the tradition of duplicity in which even Patmore's uxorious speaker placed his heroine, Swift devotes many poems to an examination of the role deception plays in the creation of a saving but inadequate fiction of femininity. In "A Beautiful Young Nymph," a battered prostitute removes her wig, her crystal eye, her teeth, and her padding at bedtime, so that the next morning she must employ all her "Arts" to reconstruct her "scatter'd Parts."[69] Such as they are, however, her arts only contribute to her own suffering or that of others, and the same thing is true of Diana in "The Progress of Beauty," who awakes as a mingled mass of dirt and sweat, with cracked lips, foul teeth, and gummy eyes, to spend four hours artfully reconstructing herself. Because she is inexorably rotting away, however, Swift declares that eventually all forms will fail, for "Art no longer can prevayl / When the Materialls all are gone."[70] The strategies of Chloe, Caelia, Corinna, and Diana—artists manqué all—have no success, Swift shows, except in temporarily staving off dissolution, for like Pope's "S... of Queens," Swift's females are composed of what Pope called "Matter too soft," and their arts are thus always inadequate.[71]

No wonder, then, that the Augustan satirist attacks the female scribbler so virulently, reinforcing Anne Finch's doleful sense that for a woman to attempt the pen is monstrous and "presumptuous," for she is "to be dull / Expected and dessigned." At least in part reflecting male artists' anxieties about the adequacy of their *own* arts, female writers are maligned as failures in eighteenth-century satire precisely because they cannot transcend their female bodily limitations: they cannot *conceive* of themselves in any but reproductive terms. Poor Phoebe Clinket, for instance, is both a caricature of Finch herself and a prototype of the female dunce who proves that literary creativity in women is merely the result of sexual frustration. Lovingly nurturing the unworthy "issue" of her muse because it attests to the "Fertility and Readiness" of her imagination, Phoebe is as sensual and indiscriminate in her poetic strainings as Lady Townley is in her insatiable erotic longings.[72] Like mothers of illegitimate or misshapen offspring, female writers are not producing what they ought, the satirists declare, so that a loose lady novelist is, appropriately enough, the first prize in *The Dunciad*'s urinary contest, while a chamberpot is awarded to the runner-up.

For the most part, eighteenth-century satirists limited their depiction of the female monster to low mimetic equivalents like Phoebe Clinket or Swift's corroding coquettes. But there were several important avatars of the monster woman who retained the allegorical anatomy of their more fantastic precursors. In *The Battle of the Books*, for instance, Swift's "Goddess Criticism" clearly symbolizes the demise of wit and learning. Devouring numberless volumes in a den as dark as Errour's, she is surrounded by relatives like Ignorance, Pride, Opinion, Noise, Impudence, and Pedantry, and she herself is as allegorically deformed as any of Spenser's females.

> The Goddess herself had claws like a Cat; her Head, and Ears, and Voice, resembled those of an Ass; Her Teeth fallen out before; Her Eyes turned inward, as if she lookt only upon Herself; Her diet was the overflowing of her own Gall: Her Spleen was so large, as to stand prominent like a Dug of the first Rate, nor wanted Excrescencies in forms of Teats, at which a Crew of ugly Monsters were greedily sucking; and what is wonderful to conceive, the bulk of Spleen increased faster than the Sucking could diminish it.[73]

Like Spenser's Errour and Milton's Sin, Criticism is linked by her processes of eternal breeding, eating, spewing, feeding, and redevouring to biological cycles all three poets view as destructive to transcendent, intellectual life. More, since all the creations of each monstrous mother are her excretions, and since all her excretions are both her food and her weaponry, each mother forms with her brood a self-enclosed system, cannibalistic and solipsistic: the creativity of the world made flesh is annihilating. At the same time, Swift's spleen-producing and splenetic Goddess cannot be far removed from the Goddess of Spleen in Pope's *The Rape of the Lock*, and—because she is a mother Goddess—she also has much in common with the Goddess of Dullness who appears in Pope's *Dunciad*. The parent of "Vapours and Female Wit," the "*Hysteric* or *Poetic* fit," the Queen of Spleen rules over all women between the ages of fifteen and fifty, and thus, as a sort of patroness of the female sexual cycle, she is associated with the same anti-creation that characterizes Errour, Sin, and Criticism.[74] Similarly, the Goddess of Dullness, a nursing mother worshipped by a society of dunces, symbolizes the failure of culture, the failure of art, and the death of the satirist. The huge daughter of Chaos and Night, she rocks the laureate in her ample lap while handing out rewards and intoxicating drinks to her dull sons. A Queen of Ooze, whose inertia comments on idealized Queens of Love, she nods and all of Nature falls asleep, its light destroyed by the stupor that spreads throughout the land in the milk of her "kindness." [75]

In all these incarnations—from Errour to Dullness, from Goneril and Regan to Chloe and Caelia—the female monster is a striking illustration of Simone de Beauvoir's thesis that woman has been made to represent all of man's ambivalent feelings about his own inability to control his own physical existence, his own birth and death. As the Other, woman comes to represent the contingency of life, life that is made to be destroyed. "It is the horror of his own carnal contingence," de Beauvoir notes, "which [man] projects upon [woman]." [76] In addition, as Karen Horney and Dorothy Dinnerstein have shown, male dread of women, and specifically the infantile dread of maternal autonomy, has historically objectified itself in vilification of women, while male ambivalence about female "charms" underlies the traditional images of such terrible sorceress-goddesses as the Sphinx, Medusa, Circe, Kali, Delilah, and Salome, all of whom possess duplicitous arts that allow them both to seduce and to steal male generative energy. [77]

The sexual nausea associated with all these monster women helps explain why so many real women have for so long expressed loathing of (or at least anxiety about) their own, inexorably female bodies. The "killing" of oneself into an art object—the pruning and preening, the mirror madness, and concern with odors and aging, with hair which is invariably too curly or too lank, with bodies too thin or too thick—all this testifies to the efforts women have expended not just trying to be angels but trying *not* to become female monsters. More significantly for our purposes, however, the female freak is and has been a powerfully coercive and monitory image for women secretly desiring to attempt the pen, an image that helped enforce the injunctions to silence implicit also in the concept of the *Ewig-Weibliche*. If becoming an *author* meant mistaking one's "sex and way," if it meant becoming an "unsexed" or perversely sexed female, then it meant becoming a monster or freak, a vile Errour, a grotesque

Lady Macbeth, a disgusting goddess of Dullness, or (to name a few later witches) a murderous Lamia, a sinister Geraldine. Perhaps, then, the "presumptuous" effort should not be made at all. Certainly the story of Lilith, one more monster woman—indeed, according to Hebrew mythology, both the first woman *and* the first monster— specifically connects poetic presumption with madness, freakishness, monstrosity.

Created not from Adam's rib but, like him, from the dust, Lilith was Adam's first wife, according to apocryphal Jewish lore. Because she considered herself his equal, she objected to lying beneath him, so that when he tried to force her submission, she became enraged and, speaking the Ineffable Name, flew away to the edge of the Red Sea to reside with demons. Threatened by God's angelic emissaries, told that she must return or daily lose a hundred of her demon children to death, Lilith preferred punishment to patriarchal marriage, and she took her revenge against both God and Adam by injuring babies— especially male babies, who were traditionally thought to be more vulnerable to her attacks. What her history suggests is that in patri- archal culture, female speech and female "presumption"—that is, angry revolt against male domination—are inextricably linked and inevitably daemonic. Excluded from the human community, even from the semidivine communal chronicles of the Bible, the figure of Lilith represents the price women have been told they must pay for attempting to define themselves. And it is a terrible price: cursed both because she is a character who "got away" and because she dared to usurp the essentially literary authority implied by the act of naming, Lilith is locked into a vengeance (child-killing) which can only bring her more suffering (the killing of her own children). And even the nature of her one-woman revolution emphasizes her helplessness and her isolation, for her protest takes the form of a refusal and a departure, a flight of escape rather than an active rebellion like, say, Satan's. As a paradigm of both the "witch" and the "fiend" of Aurora Leigh's "Ghost, fiend, and angel, fairy, witch and sprite," Lilith reveals, then, just how difficult it is for women even to attempt the pen. And from George MacDonald, the Victorian fantasist who portrayed her in his astonishing *Lilith* as a paradigm of the self-tormenting assertive woman, to Laura Riding, who depicted her in "Eve's Side of It" as an archetypal woman Creator, the problem Lilith represents has been associated with the problems of female authorship and female authority.[78] Even if they had not studied her legend, literary women like Anne Finch, bemoaning the double bind in which the mutually dependent images of angel and monster had left them, must have gotten the message Lilith incarnates: a life of feminine submission, of "contemplative purity," is a life of silence, a life that has no pen and no story, while a life of female rebellion, of "significant action," is a life that must be silenced, a life whose monstrous pen tells a terrible story. Either way, the images on the surface of the looking glass, into which the female artist peers in search of her *self*, warn her that she is or must be a "Cypher," framed and framed up, indited and indicted.

As the legend of Lilith shows, and as psychoanalysts from Freud and Jung onward have observed, myths and fairy tales often both state and enforce culture's sentences with greater accuracy than more sophisticated literary texts. If Lilith's story summarizes the genesis of the female monster in a single useful parable, the Grimm tale of "Little Snow White" dramatizes the essential but equivocal relationship between the angel-woman and the monster-woman, a relationship that is also implicit in Aurora Leigh's bewildered speculations about her dead mother. "Little Snow White," which Walt Disney entitled "Snow White and the Seven Dwarves," should really be called Snow White and Her Wicked Stepmother, for the central action of the tale—indeed, its only real action—arises from the relationship between these two women: the one fair, young, pale, the other just as fair, but older, fiercer; the one a daughter, the other a mother; the one sweet, ignorant, passive, the other both artful and active; the one a sort of angel, the other an undeniable witch.

Significantly, the conflict between these two women is fought out largely in the transparent enclosures into which, like all the other images of women we have been discussing here, both have been locked: a magic looking glass, an enchanted and enchanting glass coffin. Here, wielding as weapons the tools patriarchy suggests that women use to kill themselves into art, the two women literally try to kill each other with art. Shadow fights shadow, image destroys image in the crystal prison, as if the "fiend" of Aurora's mother's portrait should plot to destroy the "angel" who is another one of her selves.

The story begins in midwinter, with a Queen sitting and sewing, framed by a window. As in so many fairy tales, she pricks her finger, bleeds, and is thereby assumed into the cycle of sexuality William Blake called the realm of "generation," giving birth "soon after" to a daughter "as white as snow, as red as blood, and as black as the wood of the window frame."[79] All the motifs introduced in this prefatory first paragraph—sewing, snow, blood, enclosure—are associated with key themes in female lives (hence in female writing), and they are thus themes we shall be studying throughout this book. But for our purposes here the tale's opening *is* merely prefatory. The real story begins when the Queen, having become a mother, metamorphoses also into a witch—that is, into a wicked "step" mother: " . . . when the child was born, the Queen died," and "After a year had passed the King took to himself another wife."

When we first encounter this "new" wife, she is framed in a magic looking glass, just as her predecessor—that is, her earlier self—had been framed in a window. To be caught and trapped in a mirror rather than a window, however, is to be driven inward, obsessively studying self-images as if seeking a viable self. The first Queen seems still to have had prospects; not yet fallen into sexuality, she looked outward, if only upon the snow. The second Queen is doomed to the inward search that psychoanalysts like Bruno Bettelheim censoriously define as "narcissism,"[80] but which (as Mary Elizabeth Coleridge's "The Other Side of the Mirror" suggested) is necessitated by a state from which all outward prospects have been removed.

That outward prospects *have* been removed—or lost or dissolved away—is suggested not only by the Queen's mirror obsession but by the absence of the King from the story as it is related in the Grimm version. The Queen's husband and Snow White's father (for whose attentions, according to Bettelheim, the two women are battling in a feminized Oedipal struggle) never actually appears in this story at all, a fact that emphasizes the almost stifling intensity with which the tale concentrates on the conflict in the mirror between mother and daughter, woman and woman, self and self. At the same time, though, there is clearly at least one way in which the King *is* present.

His, surely, is the voice of the looking glass, the patriarchal voice of judgment that rules the Queen's—and every woman's—self-evaluation. He it is who decides, first, that his consort is "the fairest of all," and then, as she becomes maddened, rebellious, witchlike, that she must be replaced by his angelically innocent and dutiful daughter, a girl who is therefore defined as "more beautiful still" than the Queen. To the extent, then, that the King, and only the King, constituted the first Queen's prospects, he need no longer appear in the story because, having assimilated the meaning of her own sexuality (and having, thus, become the second Queen) the woman has internalized the King's rules: his voice resides now in her own mirror, her own mind.

But if Snow White is "really" the daughter of the second as well as of the first Queen (i.e., if the two Queens are identical), why does the Queen hate her so much? The traditional explanation—that the mother is as threatened by her daughter's "budding sexuality" as the daughter is by the mother's "possession" of the father—is helpful but does not seem entirely adequate, considering the depth and ferocity of the Queen's rage. It is true, of course, that in the patriarchal Kingdom of the text these women inhabit the Queen's life can be literally imperiled by her daughter's beauty, and true (as we shall see throughout this study) that, given the female vulnerability such perils imply, female bonding is extraordinarily difficult in patriarchy: women almost inevitably turn against women because the voice of the looking glass sets them against each other. But, beyond all this, it seems as if there is a sense in which the intense desperation with which the Queen enacts her rituals of self-absorption causes (or is caused by) her hatred of Snow White. Innocent, passive, and self-lessly free of the mirror madness that consumes the Queen, Snow White represents the ideal of renunciation that the Queen has already renounced at the beginning of the story. Thus Snow White is destined to replace the Queen *because* the Queen hates her, rather than vice versa. The Queen's hatred of Snow White, in other words, exists before the looking glass has provided an obvious reason for hatred.

For the Queen, as we come to see more clearly in the course of the story, is a plotter, a plot-maker, a schemer, a witch, an artist, an impersonator, a woman of almost infinite creative energy, witty, wily, and self-absorbed as all artists traditionally are. On the other hand, in her absolute chastity, her frozen innocence, her sweet nullity, Snow White represents precisely the ideal of "contemplative purity" we have already discussed, an ideal that could quite literally kill the Queen. An angel in the house of myth, Snow White is not only a child but (as female angels always are) childlike, docile, submissive, the heroine of a life that *has no story*. But the Queen, adult and demonic, plainly wants a life of "significant action," by definition an "unfeminine" life of stories and story-telling. And therefore, to the extent that Snow White, as her daughter, is a part of herself, she wants to kill the Snow White *in herself*, the angel who would keep deeds and dramas out of her own house.

The first death plot the Queen invents is a naively straightforward murder story: she commands one of her huntsmen to kill Snow White. But, as Bruno Bettelheim has shown, the huntsman is really a surrogate for the King, a parental—or, more specifically, patriarchal—figure "who dominates, controls, and subdues wild ferocious beasts" and who thus "represents the subjugation of the animal, asocial, violent tendencies in man."[81] In a sense, then, the Queen has foolishly asked her patriarchal master to act for her in doing the subversive deed she wants to do in part to retain power over him and in part to steal his power from him. Obviously, he will not do this. As patriarchy's angelic daughter, Snow White is, after all, *his* child, and he must save her, not kill her. Hence he kills a wild boar in her stead, and brings its lung and liver to the Queen as proof that he has murdered the child. Thinking that she is devouring her ice-pure enemy, therefore, the Queen consumes, instead, the wild boar's organs; that is, symbolically speaking, she devours her own beastly rage, and becomes (of course) even more enraged.

When she learns that her first plot has failed, then, the Queen's story-telling becomes angrier as well as more inventive, more sophisticated, more subversive. Significantly, each of the three "tales" she tells—that is, each of the three plots she invents—depends on a poisonous or parodic use of a distinctively female device as a murder weapon, and in each case she reinforces the sardonic commentary on "femininity" that such weaponry makes by impersonating a "wise" woman, a "good" mother, or, as Ellen Moers would put it, an "educating heroine."[82] As a "kind" old pedlar woman, she offers to lace Snow White "properly" for once—then suffocates her with a very Victorian set of tight laces. As another wise old expert in female beauty, she promises to comb Snow White's hair "properly," then assaults her with a poisonous comb. Finally, as a wholesome farmer's wife, she gives Snow White a "very poisonous apple," which she has made in "a quite secret, lonely room, where no one ever came." The girl finally falls, killed, so it seems, by the female arts of cosmetology and cookery. Paradoxically, however, even though the Queen has been using such feminine wiles as the sirens' comb and Eve's apple subversively, to destroy angelic Snow White so that she (the Queen) can assert and aggrandize herself, these arts have had on her daughter an opposite effect from those she intended. Strengthening the chaste maiden in her passivity, they have made her into precisely the eternally beautiful, inanimate *objet d'art* patriarchal aesthetics want a girl to be. From the point of view of the mad, self-assertive Queen, conventional female arts *kill*. But from the point of view of the docile and selfless princess, such arts, even while they kill, confer the only measure of power available to a woman in a patriarchal culture.

Certainly when the kindly huntsman-father saved her life by abandoning her in the forest at the edge of his kingdom, Snow White discovered her own powerlessness. Though she had been allowed to live because she was a "good" girl, she had to find her own devious way of resisting the onslaughts of the maddened Queen, both inside and outside her self. In this connection, the seven dwarves probably represent her own dwarfed powers, her stunted selfhood, for, as Bettelheim points out, they can do little to help save the girl from the Queen. At the same time, however, her life with them is an important part of her education in submissive femininity, for in serving them she learns essential lessons of service, of selflessness, of domesticity. Finally, that at this point Snow White is a housekeeping angel in a *tiny* house conveys the story's attitude toward "woman's world and woman's work": the realm of domesticity is a miniaturized kingdom in which the best of women is not only like a dwarf but like a dwarf's servant.

Does the irony and bitterness consequent upon such a perception lead to Snow White's few small acts of disobedience? Or would Snow White ultimately have rebelled anyway, precisely because she *is* the Queen's true daughter? The story does not, of course, answer such questions, but it does seem to imply them, since its turning point comes from Snow White's significant willingness to be tempted by the Queen's "gifts," despite the dwarves' admonitions. Indeed, the only hint of self-interest that Snow White displays throughout the whole story comes in her "narcissistic" desire for the stay-laces, the comb, and the apple that the disguised murderess offers. As Bettelheim remarks, this "suggests how close the stepmother's temptations are to Snow White's inner desires."[83] Indeed, it suggests that, as we have already noted, the Queen and Snow White are in some sense one: while the Queen struggles to free herself from the passive Snow White in herself, Snow White must struggle to repress the assertive Queen in herself. That both women eat from the same deadly apple in the third temptation episode merely clarifies and dramatizes this point. The Queen's lonely art has enabled her to contrive a two-faced fruit—one white and one red "cheek"—that represents her ambiguous relationship to this angelic girl who is both her daughter and her enemy, her self and her opposite. Her intention is that the girl will die of the apple's poisoned red half—red with her sexual energy, her assertive desire for deeds of blood and triumph—while she herself will be unharmed by the passivity of the white half.

But though at first this seems to have happened, the apple's effect is, finally, of course, quite different. After the Queen's artfulness has killed Snow White into art, the girl becomes if anything even more dangerous to her "step" mother's autonomy than she was before, because even more opposed to it in both mind and body. For, dead and self-less in her glass coffin, she is an object, to be displayed and desired, patriarchy's marble "opus," the decorative and decorous Galatea with whom every ruler would like to grace his parlor. Thus, when the Prince first sees Snow White in her coffin, he begs the dwarves to give "it" to him as a gift, "for I cannot live without seeing Snow White. I will honor and prize her as my dearest possession". An "it," a possession, Snow White has become an idealized image of herself, a woman in a portrait like Aurora Leigh's mother, and as such she has definitively proven herself to be patriarchy's ideal woman, the perfect candidate for Queen. At this point, therefore, she regurgitates the poison apple (whose madness had stuck in her throat) and rises from her coffin. The fairest in the land, she will marry the most powerful in the land; bidden to their wedding, the egotistically assertive, plotting Queen will become a former Queen, dancing herself to death in red-hot iron shoes.

What does the future hold for Snow White, however? When her Prince becomes a King and she becomes a Queen, what will her life be like? Trained to domesticity by her dwarf instructors, will she sit in the window, gazing out on the wild forest of her past, and sigh, and sew, and prick her finger, and conceive a child white as snow, red as blood, black as ebony wood? Surely, fairest of them all, Snow White has exchanged one glass coffin for another, delivered from the prison where the Queen put her only to be imprisoned in the looking glass from which the King's voice speaks daily. There is, after all, no female model for her in this tale except the "good" (dead) mother and her living avatar the "bad" mother. And if Snow White escaped her first glass coffin by her goodness, her passivity and docility, her only escape from her second glass coffin, the imprisoning mirror, must evidently be through "badness," through plots and stories, duplicitous schemes, wild dreams, fierce fictions, mad impersonations. The cycle of her fate seems inexorable. Renouncing "contemplative purity," she must now embark on that life of "significant action" which, for a woman, is defined as a witch's life because it is so monstrous, so unnatural. Grotesque as Errour, Duessa, Lucifera, she will practice false arts in her secret, lonely room. Suicidal as Lilith and Medea, she will become a murderess bent on the self-slaughter implicit in her murderous attempts against the life of her own child. Finally, in fiery shoes that parody the costumes of femininity as surely as the comb and stays she herself contrived, she will do a silent terrible death-dance out of the story, the looking glass, the transparent coffin of her own image. Her only deed, this death will imply, can be a deed of death, her only action the pernicious action of self-destruction.

In this connection, it seems especially significant that the Queen's dance of death is a silent one. In "The Juniper Tree," a version of "Little Snow White" in which a *boy's* mother tries to kill him (for different reasons, of course) the dead boy is transformed not into a silent art object but into a furious golden bird who sings a song of vengeance against his murderess and finally crushes her to death with a millstone.[84] The male child's progress toward adulthood is a growth toward both self-assertion and self-articulation, "The Juniper Tree" implies, a development of the *powers* of speech. But the girl child must learn the arts of silence either as herself a silent image invented and defined by the magic looking glass of the male-authored text, or as a silent dancer of her own woes, a dancer who enacts rather than articulates. From the abused Procne to the reclusive Lady of Shallott, therefore, women have been told that their art, like the witch's dance in "Little Snow White," is an art of silence. Procne must record her sufferings with what Geoffrey Hartman calls "the voice of the shuttle" because when she was raped her tongue was cut out.[85] The Lady of Shallott must weave her story because she is imprisoned in a tower as adamantine as any glass coffin, doomed to escape only through the self-annihilating madness of romantic love (just as the Queen is doomed to escape only through the self-annihilating madness of her death dance), and her last work of art is her own dead body floating downstream in a boat. And even when such maddened or grotesque female artists make sounds, they are for the most part, say patriarchal theorists, absurd or grotesque or pitiful. Procne's sister Philomel, for instance, speaks with an unintelligible bird's voice (unlike the voice of the hero of "The Juniper Tree"). And when Gerard Manley Hopkins, with whom we began this meditation on pens and penises and kings and queens, wrote of her in an epigram "On a Poetess," he wrote as follows:

> Miss M. 's a nightingale. 'Tis well
>   Your simile I keep.
> It is the way with Philomel
>   To sing while others sleep.[86]

Even Matthew Arnold's more sympathetically conceived Philomel speaks "a wild, unquenched, deep-sunken, old-world pain" that arises from the stirrings of a "bewildered brain."[87]

Yet, as Mary Elizabeth Coleridge's yearning toward that sane and serious self concealed on the other side of the mirror suggested —and as Anne Finch's complaint and Anne Elliot's protest told us too—women writers, longing to attempt the pen, have longed to escape from the many-faceted glass coffins of the patriarchal texts whose properties male authors insisted that they are. Reaching a hand to the stern, self-determining self behind the looking-glass portrait of her mother, reaching past those grotesque and obstructive images of "Ghost, fiend, and angel, fairy, witch, and sprite," Aurora Leigh, like all the women artists whose careers we will trace in this book, tries to excavate the real self buried beneath the "copy" selves. Similarly, Mary Elizabeth Coleridge, staring into a mirror where her own mouth appears as a "hideous wound" bleeding "in silence and in secret," strives for a "voice to speak her dread."

In their attempts at the escape that the female pen offers from the prison of the male text, women like Aurora Leigh and Mary Elizabeth Coleridge begin, as we shall see, by alternately defining themselves as angel-women or as monster-women. Like Snow White and the wicked Queen, their earliest impulses, as we shall also see, are ambivalent. Either they are inclined to immobilize themselves with suffocating tight-laces in the glass coffins of patriarchy, or they are tempted to destroy themselves by doing fiery and suicidal tarantellas out of the looking glass. Yet, despite the obstacles presented by those twin images of angel and monster, despite the fears of sterility and the anxieties of authorship from which women have suffered, generations of texts *have* been possible for female writers. By the end of the eighteenth century—and here is the most important phenomenon we will see throughout this volume—women were not only writing, they were conceiving fictional worlds in which patriarchal images and conventions were severely, radically revised. And as self-conceiving women from Anne Finch and Anne Elliot to Emily Brontë and Emily Dickinson rose from the glass coffin of the male-authored text, as they exploded out of the Queen's looking glass, the old silent dance of death became a dance of triumph, a dance into speech, a dance of authority.

Infection in the Sentence:
The Woman Writer and the Anxiety
of Authorship

2

The man who does not know sick women does not know women.
—S. Weir Mitchell

I try to describe this long limitation, hoping that with such power
as is now mine, and such use of language as is within that power,
this will convince any one who cares about it that this "living" of
mine had been done under a heavy handicap. . . .
—Charlotte Perkins Gilman

A Word dropped careless on a Page
May stimulate an eye
When folded in perpetual seam
The Wrinkled Maker lie

Infection in the sentence breeds
We may inhale Despair
At distances of Centuries
From the Malaria—
—Emily Dickinson

I stand in the ring
in the dead city
and tie on the red shoes
. . . .
They are not mine,
they are my mother's,
her mother's before,
handed down like an heirloom
but hidden like shameful letters.
—Anne Sexton

What does it mean to be a woman writer in a culture whose fundamental definitions of literary authority are, as we have seen, both

45

overtly and covertly patriarchal? If the vexed and vexing polarities of angel and monster, sweet dumb Snow White and fierce mad Queen, are major images literary tradition offers women, how does such imagery influence the ways in which women attempt the pen? If the Queen's looking glass speaks with the King's voice, how do its perpetual kingly admonitions affect the Queen's own voice? Since his is the chief voice she hears, does the Queen try to sound like the King, imitating his tone, his inflections, his phrasing, his point of view? Or does she "talk back" to him in her own vocabulary, her own timbre, insisting on her own viewpoint? We believe these are basic questions feminist literary criticism—both theoretical and practical—must answer, and consequently they are questions to which we shall turn again and again, not only in this chapter but in all our readings of nineteenth-century literature by women.

That writers assimilate and then consciously or unconsciously affirm or deny the achievements of their predecessors is, of course, a central fact of literary history, a fact whose aesthetic and metaphysical implications have been discussed in detail by theorists as diverse as T. S. Eliot, M. H. Abrams, Erich Auerbach, and Frank Kermode.[1] More recently, some literary theorists have begun to explore what we might call the psychology of literary history—the tensions and anxieties, hostilities and inadequacies writers feel when they confront not only the achievements of their predecessors but the traditions of genre, style, and metaphor that they inherit from such "forefathers." Increasingly, these critics study the ways in which, as J. Hillis Miller has put it, a literary text "is inhabited . . . by a long chain of parasitical presences, echoes, allusions, guests, ghosts of previous texts."[2]

As Miller himself also notes, the first and foremost student of such literary psychohistory has been Harold Bloom. Applying Freudian structures to literary genealogies, Bloom has postulated that the dynamics of literary history arise from the artist's "anxiety of influence," his fear that he is not his own creator and that the works of his predecessors, existing before and beyond him, assume essential priority over his own writings. In fact, as we pointed out in our discussion of the metaphor of literary paternity, Bloom's paradigm of the sequential historical relationship between literary artists is the relationship of father and son, specifically that relationship as it was defined by Freud. Thus Bloom explains that a "strong poet" must engage in heroic warfare with his "precursor," for, involved as he is in a literary Oedipal struggle, a man can only become a poet by somehow invalidating his poetic father.

Bloom's model of literary history is intensely (even exclusively) male, and necessarily patriarchal. For this reason it has seemed, and no doubt will continue to seem, offensively sexist to some feminist critics. Not only, after all, does Bloom describe literary history as the crucial warfare of fathers and sons, he sees Milton's fiercely masculine fallen Satan as *the* type of the poet in our culture, and he metaphorically defines the poetic process as a sexual encounter between a male poet and his female muse. Where, then, does the female poet fit in? Does she want to annihilate a "forefather" or a "foremother"? What if she can find no models, no precursors? Does she have a muse, and what is its sex? Such questions are inevitable in any female consideration of Bloomian poetics.[3] And yet, from a feminist perspective, their inevitability may be just the point; it may, that is, call our attention not to what is wrong about Bloom's conceptualization of the dynamics of Western literary history, but to what is right (or at least suggestive) about his theory.

For Western literary history *is* overwhelmingly male—or, more accurately, patriarchal—and Bloom analyzes and explains this fact, while other theorists have ignored it, precisely, one supposes, because they assumed literature had to be male. Like Freud, whose psychoanalytic postulates permeate Bloom's literary psychoanalyses of the "anxiety of influence," Bloom has defined processes of interaction that his predecessors did not bother to consider because, among other reasons, they were themselves so caught up in such processes. Like Freud, too, Bloom has insisted on bringing to consciousness assumptions readers and writers do not ordinarily examine. In doing so, he has clarified the implications of the psychosexual and sociosexual con-texts by which every literary text is surrounded, and thus the meanings of the "guests" and "ghosts" which inhabit texts themselves. Speaking of Freud, the feminist theorist Juliet Mitchell has remarked that "psychoanalysis is not a recommendation *for* a patriarchal society, but an analysis of one."[4] The same sort of statement could be made about Bloom's model of literary history, which is not a recommendation for but an analysis of the patriarchal poetics (and attendant anxieties) which underlie our culture's chief literary movements.

For our purposes here, however, Bloom's historical construct is useful not only because it helps identify and define the patriarchal psychosexual context in which so much Western literature was authored, but also because it can help us distinguish the anxieties and achievements of female writers from those of male writers. If we return to the question we asked earlier—where does a woman writer "fit in" to the overwhelmingly and essentially male literary history Bloom describes?—we find we have to answer that a woman writer does *not* "fit in." At first glance, indeed, she seems to be anomalous, indefinable, alienated, a freakish outsider. Just as in Freud's theories of male and female psychosexual development there is no symmetry between a boy's growth and a girl's (with, say, the male "Oedipus complex" balanced by a female "Electra complex") so Bloom's male-oriented theory of the "anxiety of influence" cannot be simply reversed or inverted in order to account for the situation of the woman writer.

Certainly if we acquiesce in the patriarchal Bloomian model, we can be sure that the female poet does not experience the "anxiety of influence" in the same way that her male counterpart would, for the simple reason that she must confront precursors who are almost exclusively male, and therefore significantly different from her. Not only do these precursors incarnate patriarchal authority (as our discussion of the metaphor of literary paternity argued), they attempt to enclose her in definitions of her person and her potential which, by reducing her to extreme stereotypes (angel, monster) drastically conflict with her own sense of her self—that is, of her subjectivity, her autonomy, her creativity. On the one hand, therefore, the woman writer's male precursors symbolize authority; on the other hand, despite their authority, they fail to define the ways in which she experiences her own identity as a writer. More, the masculine authority with which they construct their literary personae, as well as the fierce power struggles in which they engage in their efforts of self-creation, seem to the woman writer directly to contradict the terms of her own gender definition. Thus the "anxiety of influence" that a male poet experiences is felt by a female poet as an even more primary "anxiety of authorship"—a radical fear that she cannot create, that because she can never become a "precursor" the act of writing will isolate or destroy her.

This anxiety is, of course, exacerbated by her fear that not only can she not fight a male precursor on "his" terms and win, she cannot "beget" art upon the (female) body of the muse. As Juliet Mitchell notes, in a concise summary of the implications Freud's theory of psychosexual development has for women, both a boy and a girl, "as they learn to speak and live within society, want to take the father's [in Bloom's terminology the precursor's] place, and *only the boy will one day be allowed to do so*. Furthermore both sexes are born into the desire of the mother, and as, through cultural heritage, what the mother desires is the phallus-turned-baby, *both* children desire to be the phallus for the mother. Again, *only the boy can fully recognize himself in his mother's desire*. Thus *both* sexes repudiate the implications of femininity," but the girl learns (in relation to her father) "that her subjugation to the law of the father entails her becoming the representative of 'nature' and 'sexuality,' a chaos of spontaneous, intuitive creativity."[5]

Unlike her male counterpart, then, the female artist must first struggle against the effects of a socialization which makes conflict with the will of her (male) precursors seem inexpressibly absurd, futile, or even—as in the case of the Queen in "Little Snow White"—self-annihilating. And just as the male artist's struggle against his precursor takes the form of what Bloom calls revisionary swerves, flights, misreadings, so the female writer's battle for self-creation involves her in a revisionary process. Her battle, however, is not against her (male) precursor's reading of the world but against his reading of *her*. In order to define herself as an author she must redefine the terms of her socialization. Her revisionary struggle, therefore, often becomes a struggle for what Adrienne Rich has called "Re-vision—the act of looking back, of seeing with fresh eyes, of entering an old text from a new critical direction . . . an act of survival."[6] Frequently, moreover, she can begin such a struggle only by actively seeking a *female* precursor who, far from representing a threatening force to be denied or killed, proves by example that a revolt against patriarchal literary authority is possible.

For this reason, as well as for the sound psychoanalytic reasons

Mitchell and others give, it would be foolish to lock the woman artist into an Electra pattern matching the Oedipal structure Bloom proposes for male writers. The woman writer—and we shall see women doing this over and over again—searches for a female model not because she wants dutifully to comply with male definitions of her "femininity" but because she must legitimize her own rebellious endeavors. At the same time, like most women in patriarchal society, the woman writer does experience her gender as a painful obstacle, or even a debilitating inadequacy; like most patriarchally conditioned women, in other words, she is victimized by what Mitchell calls "the inferiorized and 'alternative' (second sex) psychology of women under patriarchy."[7] Thus the loneliness of the female artist, her feelings of alienation from male predecessors coupled with her need for sisterly precursors and successors, her urgent sense of her need for a female audience together with her fear of the antagonism of male readers, her culturally conditioned timidity about self-dramatization, her dread of the patriarchal authority of art, her anxiety about the impropriety of female invention—all these phenomena of "inferiorization" mark the woman writer's struggle for artistic self-definition and differentiate her efforts at self-creation from those of her male counterpart.

As we shall see, such sociosexual differentiation means that, as Elaine Showalter has suggested, women writers participate in a quite different literary subculture from that inhabited by male writers, a subculture which has its own distinctive literary traditions, even—though it defines itself *in relation to* the "main," male-dominated, literary culture—a distinctive history.[8] At best, the separateness of this female subculture has been exhilarating for women. In recent years, for instance, while male writers seem increasingly to have felt exhausted by the need for revisionism which Bloom's theory of the "anxiety of influence" accurately describes, women writers have seen themselves as pioneers in a creativity so intense that their male counterparts have probably not experienced its analog since the Renaissance, or at least since the Romantic era. The son of many fathers, today's male writer feels hopelessly belated; the daughter of too few mothers, today's female writer feels that she is helping to create a viable tradition which is at last definitively emerging.

There is a darker side of this female literary subculture, however, especially when women's struggles for literary self-creation are seen in the psychosexual context described by Bloom's Freudian theories of patrilineal literary inheritance. As we noted above, for an "anxiety of influence" the woman writer substitutes what we have called an "anxiety of authorship," an anxiety built from complex and often only barely conscious fears of that authority which seems to the female artist to be by definition inappropriate to her sex. Because it is based on the woman's socially determined sense of her own biology, this anxiety of authorship is quite distinct from the anxiety about creativity that could be traced in such male writers as Hawthorne or Dostoevsky. Indeed, to the extent that it forms one of the unique bonds that link women in what we might call the secret sisterhood of their literary subculture, such anxiety in itself constitutes a crucial mark of that subculture.

In comparison to the "male" tradition of strong, father-son combat, however, this female anxiety of authorship is profoundly debilitating. Handed down not from one woman to another but from the stern literary "fathers" of patriarchy to all their "inferiorized" female descendants, it is in many ways the germ of a dis-ease or, at any rate, a disaffection, a disturbance, a distrust, that spreads like a stain throughout the style and structure of much literature by women, especially—as we shall see in this study—throughout literature by women before the twentieth century. For if contemporary women do now attempt the pen with energy and authority, they are able to do so only because their eighteenth- and nineteenth-century foremothers struggled in isolation that felt like illness, alienation that felt like madness, obscurity that felt like paralysis to overcome the anxiety of authorship that was endemic to their literary subculture. Thus, while the recent feminist emphasis on positive role models has undoubtedly helped many women, it should not keep us from realizing the terrible odds against which a creative female subculture was established. Far from reinforcing socially oppressive sexual stereotyping, only a full consideration of such problems can reveal the extraordinary strength of women's literary accomplishments in the eighteenth and nineteenth centuries.

Emily Dickinson's acute observations about "infection in the sentence," quoted in our epigraphs, resonate in a number of different ways, then, for women writers, given the literary woman's special concept of her place in literary psychohistory. To begin with, the words seem to indicate Dickinson's keen consciousness that, in the purest Bloomian or Millerian sense, pernicious "guests" and "ghosts" inhabit all literary texts. For any reader, but especially for a reader who is also a writer, every text can become a "sentence" or weapon in a kind of metaphorical germ warfare. Beyond this, however, the fact that "infection in the sentence *breeds*" suggests Dickinson's recognition that literary texts are coercive, imprisoning, fever-inducing; that, since literature usurps a reader's interiority, it is an invasion of privacy. Moreover, given Dickinson's own gender definition, the sexual ambiguity of her poem's "Wrinkled Maker" is significant. For while, on the one hand, "we" (meaning especially women writers) "may inhale Despair" from all those patriarchal texts which seek to deny female autonomy and authority, on the other hand "we" (meaning especially women writers) "may inhale Despair" from all those "foremothers" who have both overtly and covertly conveyed their traditional authorship anxiety to their bewildered female descendants. Finally, such traditional, metaphorically matrilineal anxiety ensures that even the maker of a text, when she is a woman, may feel imprisoned within texts—folded and "wrinkled" by their pages and thus trapped in their "perpetual seam[s]" which perpetually tell her how she *seems*.

Although contemporary women writers are relatively free of the infection of this "Despair" Dickinson defines (at least in comparison to their nineteenth-century precursors), an anecdote recently related by the American poet and essayist Annie Gottlieb summarizes our point about the ways in which, for all women, "Infection in the sentence breeds":

> When I began to enjoy my powers as a writer, I dreamt that my mother had me sterilized! (Even in dreams we still blame our mothers for the punitive choices our culture forces on us.) I went after the mother-figure in my dream, brandishing a large knife; on its blade was writing. I cried, "Do you know what you are doing? You are destroying my femaleness, my *female power*, which is important to me *because of you*!"[9]

Seeking motherly precursors, says Gottlieb, as if echoing Dickinson, the woman writer may find only infection, debilitation. Yet still she must seek, not seek to subvert, her *"female power*, which is important" to her because of her lost literary matrilineage. In this connection, Dickinson's own words about mothers are revealing, for she alternately claimed that "I never had a mother," that "I always ran Home to Awe as a child. . . . He was an awful Mother but I liked him better than none," and that "a mother [was] a miracle." [10] Yet, as we shall see, her own anxiety of authorship was a "Despair" inhaled not only from the infections suffered by her own ailing physical mother, and her many tormented literary mothers, but from the literary fathers who spoke to her—even "lied" to her—sometimes near at hand, sometimes "at distances of Centuries," from the censorious looking glasses of literary texts.

It is debilitating to be *any* woman in a society where women are warned that if they do not behave like angels they must be monsters. Recently, in fact, social scientists and social historians like Jessie Bernard, Phyllis Chesler, Naomi Weisstein, and Pauline Bart have begun to study the ways in which patriarchal socialization literally makes women sick, both physically and mentally. [11] Hysteria, the disease with which Freud so famously began his investigations into the dynamic connections between *psyche* and *soma*, is by definition a "female disease," not so much because it takes its name from the Greek word for womb, *hyster* (the organ which was in the nineteenth century supposed to "cause" this emotional disturbance), but because hysteria did occur mainly among women in turn-of-the-century Vienna, and because throughout the nineteenth century this mental illness, like many other nervous disorders, was thought to be caused by the female reproductive system, as if to elaborate upon Aristotle's notion that femaleness was in and of itself a deformity. [12] And, indeed, such diseases of maladjustment to the physical and social environment as anorexia and agoraphobia did and do strike a disproportionate number of women. Sufferers from anorexia—loss of appetite, self-starvation—are primarily adolescent girls. Sufferers from agoraphobia—fear of open or "public" places—are usually female, most frequently middle-aged housewives, as are sufferers from crippling rheumatoid arthritis. [13]

Such diseases are caused by patriarchal socialization in several ways. Most obviously, of course, any young girl, but especially a lively or imaginative one, is likely to experience her education in docility, submissiveness, self-lessness as in some sense sickening. To be trained in renunciation is almost necessarily to be trained to ill health, since the human animal's first and strongest urge is to his/her *own* survival, pleasure, assertion. In addition, each of the "subjects" in which a young girl is educated may be sickening in a specific way. Learning to become a beautiful object, the girl learns anxiety about—perhaps even loathing of—her own flesh. Peering obsessively into the real as well as metaphoric looking glasses that surround her, she desires literally to "reduce" her own body. In the nineteenth century, as we noted earlier, this desire to be beautiful and "frail" led to tight-lacing and vinegar-drinking. In our own era it has spawned in-numerable diets and "controlled" fasts, as well as the extraordinary phenomenon of teenage anorexia.[14] Similarly, it seems inevitable that women reared for, and conditioned to, lives of privacy, reticence, domesticity, might develop pathological fears of public places and unconfined spaces. Like the comb, stay-laces, and apple which the Queen in "Little Snow White" uses as weapons against her hated stepdaughter, such afflictions as anorexia and agoraphobia simply carry patriarchal definitions of "femininity" to absurd extremes, and thus function as essential or at least inescapable parodies of social prescriptions.

In the nineteenth century, however, the complex of social prescrip-tions these diseases parody did not merely urge women to act in ways which would cause them to become ill; nineteenth-century culture seems to have actually admonished women to *be* ill. In other words, the "female diseases" from which Victorian women suffered were not always byproducts of their training in femininity; they were the goals of such training. As Barbara Ehrenreich and Deirdre English have shown, throughout much of the nineteenth century "Upper-and upper-middle-class women were [defined as] 'sick' [frail, ill]; working-class women were [defined as] 'sickening' [infectious, dis-eased]." Speaking of the "lady," they go on to point out that "Society agreed that she was frail and sickly," and consequently a "cult of female invalidism" developed in England and America. For the products of such a cult, it was, as Dr. Mary Putnam Jacobi wrote in 1895, "considered natural and almost laudable to break down under all conceivable varieties of strain—a winter dissipation, a houseful of servants, a quarrel with a female friend, not to speak of more legitimate reasons. . . . Constantly considering their nerves, urged to consider them by well-intentioned but short-sighted advisors, [women] pretty soon become nothing but a bundle of nerves."[15]

Given this socially conditioned epidemic of female illness, it is not surprising to find that the angel in the house of literature frequently suffered not just from fear and trembling but from literal and figurative sicknesses unto death. Although her hyperactive stepmother dances herself into the grave, after all, beautiful Snow White has just barely recovered from a catatonic trance in her glass coffin. And if we return to Goethe's Makarie, the "good" woman of *Wilhelm Meister's Travels* whom Hans Eichner has described as incarnating her author's ideal of "contemplative purity," we find that this "model of selflessness and of purity of heart . . . this embodiment of *das Ewig-Weibliche*, suffers from migraine headaches."[16] Implying ruthless self-suppression, does the "eternal feminine" necessarily imply illness? If so, we may have found yet another meaning for Dickinson's assertion that "Infection in the sentence breeds." The despair we "inhale" even "at distances of centuries" may be the despair of a life like Makarie's, a life that "*has no story.*"

At the same time, however, the despair of the monster-woman is also real, undeniable, and infectious. The Queen's mad tarantella is plainly unhealthy and metaphorically the result of too much storytelling. As the Romantic poets feared, too much imagination may be dangerous to anyone, male or female, but for women in particular patriarchal culture has always assumed mental exercises would have dire consequences. In 1645 John Winthrop, the governor of the Massachusetts Bay Colony, noted in his journal that Anne Hopkins "has fallen into a sad infirmity, the loss of her understanding and reason, which had been growing upon her divers years, by occasion of her giving herself wholly to reading and writing, and had written many books," adding that "if she had attended her household affairs, and such things as belong to women . . . she had kept her wits."[17] And as Wendy Martin has noted

in the nineteenth century this fear of the intellectual woman
became so intense that the phenomenon ... was recorded in
medical annals. A thinking woman was considered such a
breach of nature that a Harvard doctor reported during his
autopsy on a Radcliffe graduate he discovered that her uterus
had shrivelled to the size of a pea.[18]

If, then, as Anne Sexton suggests (in a poem parts of which we
have also used here as an epigraph), the red shoes passed furtively
down from woman to woman are the shoes of art, the Queen's
dancing shoes, it is as sickening to be a Queen who wears them as
it is to be an angelic Makarie who repudiates them. Several passages
in Sexton's verse express what we have defined as "anxiety of authorship" in the form of a feverish dread of the suicidal tarantella of
female creativity:

> All those girls
> who wore red shoes,
> each boarded a train that would not stop.
> . . . .
> They tore off their ears like safety pins.
> Their arms fell off them and became hats.
> Their heads rolled off and sang down the street.
> And their feet—oh God, their feet in the market place—
> . . . the feet went on.
> The feet could not stop.
> . . . .
> They could not listen.
> They could not stop.
> What they did was the death dance.
>
> What they did would do them in.

Certainly infection breeds in these sentences, and despair: female
art, Sexton suggests, has a "hidden" but crucial tradition of uncontrollable madness. Perhaps it was her semi-conscious perception
of this tradition that gave Sexton herself "a secret fear" of being "a
reincarnation" of Edna Millay, whose reputation seemed based on
romance. In a letter to DeWitt Snodgrass she confessed that she had
"a fear of writing as a woman writes," adding, "I wish I were a man

—I would rather write the way a man writes."[19] After all, dancing the death dance, "all those girls / who wore the red shoes" dismantle their own bodies, like anorexics renouncing the guilty weight of their female flesh. But if their arms, ears, and heads fall off, perhaps their wombs, too, will "shrivel" to "the size of a pea"?

In this connection, a passage from Margaret Atwood's *Lady Oracle* acts almost as a gloss on the conflict between creativity and "femininity" which Sexton's violent imagery embodies (or dis-embodies). Significantly, the protagonist of Atwood's novel is a writer of the sort of fiction that has recently been called "female gothic," and even more significantly she too projects her anxieties of authorship into the fairy-tale metaphor of the red shoes. Stepping in glass, she sees blood on her feet, and suddenly feels that she has discovered

> The real red shoes, the feet punished for dancing. You could dance, or you could have the love of a good man. But you were afraid to dance, because you had this unnatural fear that if you danced they'd cut your feet off so you wouldn't be able to dance. . . . Finally you overcame your fear and danced, and they cut your feet off. The good man went away too, because you wanted to dance.[20]

Whether she is a passive angel or an active monster, in other words, the woman writer feels herself to be literally or figuratively crippled by the debilitating alternatives her culture offers her, and the crippling effects of her conditioning sometimes seem to "breed" like sentences of death in the bloody shoes she inherits from her literary foremothers.

Surrounded as she is by images of disease, traditions of disease, and invitations both to disease and to dis-ease, it is no wonder that the woman writer has held many mirrors up to the discomforts of her own nature. As we shall see, the notion that "Infection in the sentence breeds" has been so central a truth for literary women that the great artistic achievements of nineteenth-century novelists and poets from Austen and Shelley to Dickinson and Barrett Browning are often both literally and figuratively concerned with disease, as if to emphasize the effort with which health and wholeness were won from the infectious "vapors" of despair and fragmentation. Rejecting the poisoned apples her culture offers her, the woman writer often becomes in some sense anorexic, resolutely closing her mouth on silence (since—in the words of Jane Austen's Henry Tilney—"a woman's only power is the power of refusal"[21]), even while she complains of starvation. Thus both Charlotte and Emily Brontë depict the travails of starved or starving anorexic heroines, while Emily Dickinson declares in one breath that she "had been hungry, all the Years," and in another opts for "Sumptuous Destitution." Similarly, Christina Rossetti represents her own anxiety of authorship in the split between one heroine who longs to "suck and suck" on goblin fruit and another who locks her lips fiercely together in a gesture of silent and passionate renunciation. In addition, many of these literary women become in one way or another agoraphobic. Trained to reticence, they fear the vertiginous openness of the literary marketplace and rationalize with Emily Dickinson that "Publication—is the Auction / Of the Mind of Man" or, worse, punningly confess that "Creation seemed a mighty Crack— / To make me visible."[22]

As we shall also see, other diseases and dis-eases accompany the two classic symptoms of anorexia and agoraphobia. Claustrophobia, for instance, agoraphobia's parallel and complementary opposite, is a disturbance we shall encounter again and again in women's writing throughout the nineteenth century. Eye "troubles," moreover, seem to abound in the lives and works of literary women, with Dickinson matter-of-factly noting that her eye got "put out," George Eliot describing patriarchal Rome as "a disease of the retina," Jane Eyre and Aurora Leigh marrying blind men, Charlotte Brontë deliberately writing with her eyes closed, and Mary Elizabeth Coleridge writing about "Blindness" that came because "Absolute and bright, / The Sun's rays smote me till they masked the Sun."[23] Finally, aphasia and amnesia—two illnesses which symbolically represent (and parody) the sort of intellectual incapacity patriarchal culture has traditionally required of women—appear and reappear in women's writings in frankly stated or disguised forms. "Foolish" women characters in Jane Austen's novels (Miss Bates in *Emma*, for instance) express Malapropish confusion about language, while Mary Shelley's monster has to learn language from scratch and Emily Dickinson herself childishly questions the meanings of the most basic English words: "Will there really be a 'Morning'? / Is there such a thing as 'Day'?"[24] At the same time, many women writers manage to imply that the reason for such ignorance of language—as well as the reason for their deep sense of alienation and inescapable feeling of anomie—is that they have *forgotten* something. Deprived of the power that even their pens don't seem to confer, these women resemble Doris Lessing's heroines, who have to fight their internalization of patriarchal strictures for even a faint trace memory of what they might have become.

"Where are the songs I used to know, / Where are the notes I used to sing?" writes Christina Rossetti in "The Key-Note," a poem whose title indicates its significance for her. "I have forgotten everything / I used to know so long ago."[25] As if to make the same point, Charlotte Brontë's Lucy Snowe conveniently "forgets" her own history and even, so it seems, the Christian name of one of the central characters in her story, while Brontë's orphaned Jane Eyre seems to have lost (or symbolically "forgotten") her family heritage. Similarly, too, Emily Brontë's Heathcliff "forgets" or is made to forget who and what he was; Mary Shelley's monster is "born" without either a memory or a family history; and Elizabeth Barrett Browning's Aurora Leigh is early separated from—and thus induced to "forget"—her "mother land" of Italy. As this last example suggests, however, what all these characters and their authors really fear they have forgotten is precisely that aspect of their lives which has been kept from them by patriarchal poetics: their matrilineal heritage of literary strength, their "female power" which, as Annie Gottlieb wrote, is important to them *because of* (not in spite of) their mothers. In order, then, not only to understand the ways in which "Infection in the sentence breeds" for women but also to learn how women have won through disease to artistic health we must begin by redefining Bloom's seminal definitions of the revisionary "anxiety of influence." In doing so, we will have to trace the difficult paths by which nineteenth-century women overcame their "anxiety of authorship," repudiated debilitating patriarchal prescriptions, and recovered or remembered the lost foremothers who could help them find their distinctive female power.

To begin with, those women who were among the first of their sex to attempt the pen were evidently infected or sickened by just the feelings of self-doubt, inadequacy, and inferiority that their education in "femininity" almost seems to have been designed to induce. The necessary converse of the metaphor of literary paternity, as we noted in our discussion of that phenomenon, was a belief in female literary sterility, a belief that caused literary women like Anne Finch to consider with deep anxiety the possibility that they might be "Cyphers," powerless intellectual eunuchs. In addition, such women were profoundly affected by the sort of assumptions that underly an assertion like Rufus Griswold's statement that in reading women's writing "We are in danger . . . of mistaking for the efflorescent energy of creative intelligence, that which is only the exuberance of personal 'feelings unemployed.'"[26] Even if it was not absurd for a woman to try to write, this remark implies, perhaps it was somehow sick or what we would today call "neurotic." "We live at home, quiet, confined, and our feelings prey upon us," says Austen's Anne Elliot to Captain Harville, not long before they embark upon the debate about the male pen and its depiction of female "inconstancy" which we discussed earlier. She speaks in what Austen describes as "a low, feeling voice," and her remarks as well as her manner suggest both her own and her author's acquiescence in the notion that women may be more vulnerable than men to the dangers and diseases of "feelings unemployed."[27]

It is not surprising, then, that one of Finch's best and most passionate poems is an ambitious Pindaric ode entitled "The Spleen." Here, in what might almost be a response to Pope's characterization of the Queen of Spleen in *The Rape of the Lock*, Finch confesses and explores her own anxiety about the "vaporous" illness whose force, she feared, ruled her life and art. Her self-examination is particularly interesting not only because of its rigorous honesty, but because that honesty compels her to reveal just how severely she herself has been influenced by the kinds of misogynistic strictures about women's "feelings unemployed" that Pope had embedded in *his* poem. Thus Pope insists that the "wayward Queen" of Spleen rules "the sex to fifty from fifteen"—rules women, that is, throughout their "prime" of female sexuality—and is therefore the "parent" of both hysteria and (female) poetry, and Finch seems at least in part to agree, for she notes that "In the Imperious *Wife* thou Vapours art." That is, insubordinate women are merely, as Pope himself would have thought, neurotic women. "Lordly *Man* [is] born to Imperial Sway," says Finch, but he is defeated by splenetic woman; he "Compounds for Peace . . . And *Woman*, arm'd with *Spleen*, do's servilely Obey." At the same time, however, Finch admits that she feels the most pernicious effects of Spleen within herself, and specifically within herself *as an artist*, and she complains of these effects quite movingly, without the self-censure that would seem to have followed from her earlier vision of female insubordination. Addressing Spleen, she writes that

> O'er me alas! thou dost too much prevail:
> I feel thy Force, whilst I against thee rail;
> I feel my Verse decay, and my crampt Numbers fail.
> Thro' thy black Jaundice I all Objects see,
>   As Dark, and Terrible as Thee,
> My Lines decry'd, and my Employme. t thought
> An useless Folly, or presumptuous Fault.[28]

Is it crazy, neurotic, splenetic, to want to be a writer? In "The Spleen" Finch admits that she fears it is, suggesting, therefore, that Pope's portrayal of her as the foolish and neurotic Phoebe Clinket had—not surprisingly—driven her into a Cave of Spleen in her own mind.

When seventeenth- and eighteenth-century women writers—and even some nineteenth-century literary women—did not confess that they thought it might actually be mad of them to want to attempt the pen, they did usually indicate that they felt in some sense apologetic about such a "presumptuous" pastime. As we saw earlier, Finch herself admonished her muse to be cautious "and still retir'd," adding that the most she could hope to do as a writer was "still with contracted wing, / To some few friends, and to thy sorrows sing." Though her self-effacing admonition is riddled with irony, it is also serious and practical. As Elaine Showalter has shown, until the end of the nineteenth century the woman writer really was supposed to take second place to her literary brothers and fathers.[29] If she refused to be modest, self-deprecating, subservient, refused to present her artistic productions as mere trifles designed to divert and distract readers in moments of idleness, she could expect to be ignored or (sometimes scurrilously) attacked. Anne Killigrew, who ambitiously implored the "Queen of Verse" to warm her soul with "poetic fire," was rewarded for her overreaching with charges of plagiarism. "I writ, and the judicious praised my pen: / Could any doubt ensuing glory then?" she notes, recounting as part of the story of her humiliation expectations that would be reasonable enough in a male artist. But instead "What ought t'have brought me honour, brought me shame."[30] Her American contemporary, Anne Bradstreet, echoes the frustration and annoyance expressed here in a discussion of the reception she could expect *her* published poems to receive:

> I am obnoxious to each carping tongue
> Who says my hand a needle better fits,
> A poet's pen all scorn I should thus wrong,
> For such despite they cast on female wits:
> If what I do prove well, it won't advance,
> They'll say it's stol'n, or else it was by chance.[31]

There is such a weary and worldly accuracy in this analysis that plainly, especially in the context of Killigrew's experience, no sensible woman writer could overlook the warning implied: be modest or else! Be dark enough thy shades, and be thou there content!

Accordingly, Bradstreet herself, eschewing Apollo's manly "bays," asks only for a "thyme or parsley wreath," suavely assuring her male readers that "This mean and unrefined ore of mine / Will make your glist'ring gold but more to shine." And though once again, as with Finch's self-admonitions, bitter irony permeates this modesty, the very pose of modesty necessarily has its ill effects, both on the poet's self-definition and on her art. Just as Finch feels her "Crampt Numbers" crippled by the gloomy disease of female Spleen, Bradstreet confesses that she has a "foolish, broken, blemished Muse" whose defects cannot be mended, since "nature made it so irreparable." After all, she adds—as if to cement the connection between femaleness and madness, or at least mental deformity—"a weak or wounded brain admits no cure." Similarly, Margaret Cavendish, the Duchess of Newcastle, whose literary activities actually inspired her contemporaries to call her "Mad Madge," seems to have tried to transcend her own "madness" by deploying the kind of modest, "sensible," and self-deprecatory misogyny that characterizes Bradstreet's *apologia pro vita sua.* "It cannot be expected," Cavendish avers, that "I should write so wisely or wittily as men, being of the effeminate sex, whose brains nature has mixed with the coldest and softest elements." Men and women, she goes on to declare, "may be compared to the blackbirds, where the hen can never sing with so strong and loud a voice, nor so clear and perfect notes as the cock; her breast is not made with that strength to strain so high."[32] But finally the contradictions between her attitude toward her gender and her sense of her own vocation seem really to have made her in some sense "mad." It may have been in a fleeting moment of despair and self-confrontation that she wrote, "Women live like Bats or Owls, labour like Beasts, and die like Worms." But eventually, as Virginia Woolf puts it, "the people crowded round her coach when she issued out," for "the crazy Duchess became a bogey to frighten clever girls with."[33]

As Woolf's comments imply, women who did *not* apologize for their literary efforts were defined as mad and monstrous: freakish because "unsexed" or freakish because sexually "fallen." If Cavendish's extraordinary intellectual ambitions made her seem like an aberration of nature, and Finch's writing caused her to be defined as a fool, an absolutely immodest, unapologetic rebel like Aphra Behn—the first really "professional" literary woman in England—was and is always considered a somewhat "shady lady," no doubt promiscuous, probably self-indulgent, and certainly "indecent." "What has poor woman done, that she must be / Debarred from sense and sacred poetry?" Behn frankly asked, and she seems just as frankly to have lived the life of a Restoration rake.[34] In consequence, like some real-life Duessa, she was gradually but inexorably excluded (even exorcized) not only from the canon of serious literature but from the parlors and libraries of respectability.

By the beginning of the bourgeois nineteenth century, however, both money and "morality" had become so important that no serious writer could afford either psychologically or economically to risk Behn's kind of "shadiness." Thus we find Jane Austen decorously protesting in 1816 that she is constitutionally unable to join "manly, spirited Sketches" to the "little bit (two Inches wide) of Ivory," on which, figuratively speaking, she claimed to inscribe her novels, and Charlotte Brontë assuring Robert Southey in 1837 that "I have

endeavored . . . to observe all the duties a woman ought to fulfil."
Confessing with shame that "I don't always succeed, for sometimes
when I'm teaching or sewing, I would rather be reading or writing,"
she dutifully adds that "I try to deny myself; and my father's approbation amply reward[s] me for the privation."[35] Similarly, in
1862 we discover Emily Dickinson telling Thomas Wentworth
Higginson that publication is as "foreign to my thought, as Fir-
mament to Fin," implying that she is *generically* unsuited to such
self-advertisement,[36] while in 1869 we see Louisa May Alcott's Jo
March learning to write moral homilies for children instead of
ambitious gothic thrillers. Clearly there is conscious or semiconscious
irony in all these choices of the apparently miniature over the
assuredly major, of the domestic over the dramatic, of the private
over the public, of obscurity over glory. But just as clearly the very
need to make such choices emphasizes the sickening anxiety of
authorship inherent in the situation of almost every woman writer
in England and America until quite recently.

What the lives and lines and choices of all these women tell us,
in short, is that the literary woman has always faced equally degrading options when she had to define her public presence in the
world. If she did not suppress her work entirely or publish it pseud-
onymously or anonymously, she could modestly confess her female
"limitations" and concentrate on the "lesser" subjects reserved for
ladies as becoming to their inferior powers. If the latter alternative
seemed an admission of failure, she could rebel, accepting the ostracism that must have seemed inevitable. Thus, as Virginia Woolf
observed, the woman writer seemed locked into a disconcerting
double bind: she had to choose between admitting she was "only a
woman" or protesting that she was "as good as a man."[37] Inevitably,
as we shall see, the literature produced by women confronted with
such anxiety-inducing choices has been strongly marked not only
by an obsessive interest in these limited options but also by obsessive
imagery of confinement that reveals the ways in which female artists
feel trapped and sickened both by suffocating alternatives and by
the culture that created them. Goethe's fictional Makarie was not,
after all, the only angelic woman to suffer from terrible headaches.
George Eliot (like Virginia Woolf) had them too, and perhaps we
can begin to understand why.

To consider the afflictions of George Eliot, however, is to bring to mind another strategy the insubordinate woman writer eventually developed for dealing with her socially prescribed subordination. Where women like Finch and Bradstreet apologized for their supposed inadequacies while women like Behn and Cavendish flaunted their freakishness, the most rebellious of their nineteenth-century descendants attempted to solve the literary problem of being female by presenting themselves as *male*. In effect, such writers protested not that they were "as good as" men but that, as writers, they *were* men. George Sand and (following her) George Eliot most famously used a kind of male-impersonation to gain male acceptance of their intellectual seriousness. But the three Brontë sisters, too, concealed their troublesome femaleness behind the masks of Currer, Ellis, and Acton Bell, names which Charlotte Brontë disingenuously insisted they had chosen for their androgynous neutrality but which most of their earliest readers assumed were male. For all these women, the cloak of maleness was obviously a practical-seeming refuge from those claustrophobic double binds of "femininity" which had given so much pain to writers like Bradstreet, Finch, and Cavendish.

Disguised as a man, after all, a woman writer could move vigorously away from the "lesser subjects" and "lesser lives" which had constrained her foremothers. Like the nineteenth-century French painter Rosa Bonheur, who wore male clothes so she could visit slaughterhouses and racecourses to study the animals she depicted, the "male-identified" woman writer felt that, dressed in the male "costume" of her pseudonym, she could walk more freely about the provinces of literature that were ordinarily forbidden to ladies. With Bonheur, therefore, she could boast that "My trousers have been my great protectors. . . . Many times I have congratulated myself for having dared to break with traditions which would have forced me to abstain from certain kinds of work, due to the obligation to drag my skirts everywhere."[38]

Yet though the metaphorical trousers of women like Sand and Eliot and the Brontës enabled them to maneuver for position in an overwhelmingly male literary tradition, such costumes also proved to be as problematical if not as debilitating as any of the more modest and ladylike garments writers like Finch and Bradstreet might be said to have adopted. For a woman artist is, after all, a woman—that is her "problem"—and if she denies her own gender she inevitably confronts an identity crisis as severe as the anxiety of authorship she is trying to surmount. There is a hint of such a crisis in Bonheur's discussion of her trousers. "I had no alternative but to realize that the garments of my own sex were a total nuisance," she explains. "But the costume I am wearing is my working outfit, nothing else. [And] if you are the slightest bit put off, I am completely prepared to put on a skirt, especially since all I have to do is to open a closet to find a whole assortment of feminine outfits."[39] Literal or figurative male impersonation seems to bring with it a nervous compulsion toward "feminine protest," along with a resurgence of the same fear of freakishness or monstrosity that necessitated male mimicry in the first place. As most literary women would have remembered, after all, it is Lady Macbeth—one of Shakespeare's most unsavory heroines —who asks the gods to "unsex" her in the cause of ambition.

Inalterably female in a culture where creativity is defined purely in male terms, almost every woman writer must have experienced the kinds of gender-conflicts that Aphra Behn expressed when she spoke of "my masculine part, the poet in me."[40] But for the nineteenth-century woman who tried to transcend her own anxiety of authorship and achieve patriarchal authority through metaphorical transvestism or male impersonation, even more radical psychic confusion must have been inevitable. Elizabeth Barrett Browning's two striking sonnets on George Sand define and analyze the problem such a woman faced. In the first of these pieces ("To George Sand, A Desire") Barrett Browning describes the French writer, whom she passionately admired, as a self-created freak, a "large-brained woman and large-hearted man / Self-called George Sand," and she declares her hope that "to woman's claim / And man's" Sand might join an "angel's grace," the redeeming strength "of a pure genius sanctified from blame." The implication is that, since Sand has crossed into forbidden and anomalous sociosexual territory, she desperately needs "purification"—sexual, spiritual, and social. On the other hand, in the second sonnet ("To George Sand, A Recognition") Barrett Browning insists that no matter what Sand does she is still inalterably female, and thus inexorably agonized.

> True genius, but true woman, dost deny
> The woman's nature with a manly scorn,
> And break away the gauds and armlets worn
> By weaker women in captivity?
> Ah, vain denial! that revolted cry
> Is sobbed in by a woman's voice forlorn.
> Thy woman's hair, my sister, all unshorn,
> Floats back dishevelled strength in agony,
> Disproving thy man's name.... [41]

In fact, Barrett Browning declares, only in death will Sand be able to transcend the constrictions of her gender. Then *God* will "unsex" her "on the heavenly shore." But until then, she must acquiesce in her inescapable femaleness, manifested by her "woman-heart's" terrible beating "in a poet fire."

Barrett Browning's imagery is drastic, melodramatic, even grotesque, but there are strong reasons for the intensity with which she characterizes Sand's representative identity crisis. As her own passionate involvement suggests, the problem Barrett Browning is really confronting in the Sand sonnets goes beyond the contradictions between vocation and gender that induced such anxiety in all these women, to include what we might call contradictions of genre and gender. Most Western literary genres are, after all, essentially male—devised by male authors to tell male stories about the world.

In its original form, for instance, the novel traditionally traces what patriarchal society has always thought of as a masculine pattern: the rise of a middle-class hero past dramatically depicted social and economic obstacles to a higher and more suitable position in the world. (Significantly, indeed, when a heroine rises—as in *Pamela*—she usually does so through the offices of a hero.) Similarly, our great paradigmatic tragedies, from *Oedipus* to *Faust*, tend to focus on a male "overreacher" whose virile will to dominate or rebel (or both) makes him simultaneously noble and vulnerable. From the rake-rogue to his modern counterpart the traveling salesman, moreover, our comic heroes are quintessentially male in their escapades and conquests, while from the epic to the historical novel, the detective story to the "western," European and American narrative literature has concentrated much of its attention on male characters who

occupy powerful public roles from which women have almost always
been excluded.

Verse genres have been even more thoroughly male than fictional
ones. The sonnet, beginning with Petrarch's celebrations of "his"
Laura, took shape as a poem in praise of the poet's mistress (who,
we saw in Norman O. Brown's comment, can never herself be a poet
because she "is" *poetry*). The "Great Ode" encourages the poet to
define himself as a priestlike bard. The satiric epistle is usually written
when a writer's manly rage transforms "his" pen into a figurative
sword. And the pastoral elegy—beginning with Moscus's "Lament
for Bion"—traditionally expresses a poet's grief over the death of a
brother-poet, through whose untimely loss he faces and resolves the
cosmic questions of death and rebirth.

It is true, of course, that even beyond what we might call the *Pamela*
plot, some stories have been imagined for women, by male poets as
well as male novelists. As we have seen, however, most of these stories
tend to perpetuate extreme and debilitating images of women as
angels or monsters. Thus the genres associated with such plot paradigms present just as many difficulties to the woman writer as those
works of literature which focus primarily on men. If she identifies
with a snow-white heroine, the glass coffin of romance "feels" like
a deathbed to the female novelist, as Mary Shelley trenchantly shows
in *Frankenstein*, while the grim exorcism from society of such a female
"overreacher" as "Snow White's" Queen has always been a source
of anxiety to literary women rather than the inspiration for a tale
of tragic grandeur. It is Macbeth, after all, who is noble; Lady
Macbeth is a monster. Similarly, Oedipus is a heroic figure while
Medea is merely a witch, and Lear's madness is gloriously universal
while Ophelia's is just pathetic. Yet to the extent that the structure of
tragedy reflects the structure of patriarchy—to the extent, that is,
that tragedy must be about the "fall" of a character who is "high"—
the genre of tragedy, rather than simply *employing* such stories, itself
necessitates them.[42]

To be sure, there is no real reason why a woman writer cannot tell
traditional kinds of stories, even if they are about male heroes and
even if they inevitably fit into male-devised generic structures. As
Joyce Carol Oates has observed, critics often "fail to see how the
creative artist shares to varying degrees the personalities of all his

characters, even those whom he appears to detest—perhaps, at times, it is these characters he is really closest to."[43] It is significant, however, that this statement was made by a woman, for the remark suggests the extent to which a female artist in particular is keenly aware that she must inevitably project herself into a number of uncongenial characters and situations. It suggests, too, the degree of anxiety a literary woman may feel about such a splitting or distribution of her identity, as well as the self-dislike she may experience in feeling that she is "really closest to" those characters she "appears to detest." Perhaps this dis-ease, which we might almost call "schizophrenia of authorship," is one to which a woman writer is especially susceptible because she herself secretly realizes that her employment of (and participation in) patriarchal plots and genres inevitably involves her in duplicity or bad faith.

If a female novelist uses the *Pamela* plot, for instance, she is exploiting a story that implies women cannot and should not do what she is herself accomplishing in writing her book. Ambitious to rise by her own literary exertions, she is implicitly admonishing her female readers that they can hope to rise only through male intervention. At the same time, as Joanna Russ has pointed out, if a woman writer "abandon[s] female protagonists altogether and stick[s] to male myths with male protagonists . . . she falsifies herself and much of her own experience."[44] For though writers (as Oates implies) do use masks and disguises in most of their work, though what Keats called "the poetical Character" in some sense has "no self" because it *is* so many selves,[45] the continual use of male models inevitably involves the female artist in a dangerous form of psychological self-denial that goes far beyond the metaphysical self-lessness Keats was contemplating. As Barrett Browning's Sand sonnets suggest, such self-denial may precipitate severe identity crises because the male impersonator begins to see herself as freakish—not wholesomely androgynous but unhealthily hermaphroditic. In addition, such self-denial may become even more than self-destructive when the female author finds herself creating works of fiction that subordinate other women by perpetuating a morality that sanctifies or vilifies all women into submission. When Harriet Beecher Stowe, in "My Wife and I," assumes the persona of an avuncular patriarch educating females in their domestic duties, we resent the duplicity and compromise involved, as well as Stowe's betrayal of her own sex.[46] Similarly, when in *Little Women* Louisa May Alcott "teaches" Jo March to renounce gothic thrillers, we cannot help feeling that it is hypocritical of her to continue writing such tales herself. And inevitably, of course, such duplicity, compromise, and hypocrisy take their greatest toll on the artist who practices them: if a writer cannot be accurate and consistent in her art, how can her work be true to its own ideas?

Finally, even when male mimicry does not entail moral or aesthetic compromises of the kind we have been discussing, the use of male devised plots, genres, and conventions may involve a female writer in uncomfortable contradictions and tensions. When Elizabeth Barrett Browning writes "An Essay on Mind," a long meditative-philosophic poem of a kind previously composed mainly by men (with Pope's "Essay on Man" a representative work in the genre), she catalogues all the world's "great" poets, and all are male; the women she describes are muses. When in the same work, moreover, she describes the joys of intellectual discovery she herself must have felt as a girl, she writes about a schoolboy and *his* exultant response to the classics. Significantly, the "Essay on Mind" is specifically the poem Barrett Browning was discussing when she noted that her early writing was done by a "copy" self. Yet even as a mature poet she included only one woman in "A Vision of Poets"—Sappho—and remarked of her, as she did of George Sand, that the contradictions between her vocation and her gender were so dangerous that they might lead to complete self-destruction.[47]

Similarly, as we shall see, Charlotte Brontë disguised herself as a man in order to narrate her first novel, *The Professor*, and devoted a good deal of space in the book to "objective" analyses of the flaws and failings of young women her own age, as if trying to distance herself as much as possible from the female sex. The result, as with Barrett Browning's "Essay on Mind," is a "copy" work which exemplifies the aesthetic tensions and moral contradictions that threaten the woman writer who tries to transcend her own female anxiety of authorship by pretending she is male. Speaking of the Brontës' desire "to throw the color of masculinity into their writing," their great admirer Mrs. Gaskell once remarked that, despite the spiritual sincerity of the sisters, at times "this desire to appear male" made their work "technically false," even "[made] their writing squint."[48]

That Gaskell used a metaphor of physical discomfort—"squinting"—is significant, for the phenomenon of male mimicry is itself a sign of female dis-ease, a sign that infection, or at least headaches, "in the sentence" breed.

Yet the attempted cure is as problematical as the disease, a point we shall consider in greater detail in our discussions both of *The Professor* and of George Eliot. For as the literary difficulties of male-impersonations show, the female genius who denies her femaleness engages in what Barrett Browning herself called a "vain denial." Her "revolted cry / Is sobbed in by a woman's voice forlorn," and her "woman's hair" reveals her "dishevelled strength in agony," all too often disproving, contradicting, and subverting whatever practical advantages she gets from her "man's name." At the same time, however, the woman who squarely confronts both her own femaleness and the patriarchal nature of the plots and poetics available to her as an artist may feel herself struck dumb by what seem to be irreconcileable contradictions of genre and gender. An entry in Margaret Fuller's journal beautifully summarizes this problem:

> For all the tides of life that flow within me, I am dumb and ineffectual, when it comes to casting my thought into a form. No old one suits me. If I could invent one, it seems to me the pleasure of creation would make it possible for me to write. . . . I love best to be a woman; but womanhood is at present too straitly-bounded to give me scope. At hours, I live truly as a woman; at others, I should stifle; as, on the other hand, I should palsy, when I play the artist.[49]

Dis-eased and infected by the sentences of patriarchy, yet unable to deny the urgency of that "poet-fire" she felt within herself, what strategies did the woman writer develop for overcoming her anxiety of authorship? How did she dance out of the looking glass of the male text into a tradition that enabled her to create her own authority? Denied the economic, social, and psychological status ordinarily essential to creativity; denied the right, skill, and education to tell their own stories with confidence, women who did not retreat into angelic silence seem at first to have had very limited options. On the one hand, they could accept the "parsley wreath" of self-denial, writing in "lesser" genres—children's books, letters, diaries—or limiting their readership to "mere" women like themselves and producing what George Eliot called "Silly Novels by Lady Novelists."[60] On the other hand, they could become males *manqués*, mimics who disguised their identities and, denying themselves, produced most frequently a literature of bad faith and inauthenticity. Given such weak solutions to what appears to have been an overwhelming problem, how could there be a great tradition of literature by women? Yet, as we shall show, there is just such a tradition, a tradition especially encompassing the works of nineteenth-century women writers who found viable ways of circumventing the problematic strategies we have just outlined.

Inappropriate as male-devised genres must always have seemed, some women have always managed to work seriously in them. Indeed, when we examine the great works written by nineteenth-century women poets and novelists, we soon notice two striking facts. First, an extraordinary number of literary women either eschewed or grew beyond both female "modesty" and male mimicry. From Austen to Dickinson, these female artists all dealt with central female experiences from a specifically female perspective. But this distinctively feminine aspect of their art has been generally ignored by critics because the most successful women writers often seem to have channeled their female concerns into secret or at least obscure corners. In effect, such women have created submerged meanings, meanings hidden within or behind the more accessible, "public" content of their works, so that their literature could be read and appreciated even when its vital concern with female dispossession and disease was ignored. Second, the writing of these women often seems "odd" in relation to the predominantly male literary history defined by the standards of what we have called patriarchal poetics. Neither Augustans nor Romantics, neither Victorian sages nor Pre-Raphaelite sensualists, many of the most distinguished late eighteenth-century and nineteenth-century English and American women writers do not seem to "fit" into any of those categories to which our literary historians have accustomed us. Indeed, to many critics and scholars, some of these literary women look like isolated eccentrics.

We may legitimately wonder, however, if the second striking fact about nineteenth-century literature by women may not in some sense be a function of the first. Could the "oddity" of this work be associated with women's secret but insistent struggle to transcend their anxiety of authorship? Could the "isolation" and apparent "eccentricity" of these women really represent their common female struggle to solve the problem of what Anne Finch called the literary woman's "fall," as well as their common female search for an aesthetic that would yield a healthy space in an overwhelmingly male "Palace of Art"? Certainly when we consider the "oddity" of women's writing in relation to its submerged content, it begins to seem that when women did not turn into male mimics or accept the "parsley wreath" they may have attempted to transcend their anxiety of authorship by *revising* male genres, using them to record their own dreams and their own stories *in disguise*. Such writers, therefore, both participated in and—to use one of Harold Bloom's key terms—"swerved" from the central sequences of male literary history, enacting a uniquely female process of revision and redefinition that necessarily caused them to seem "odd." At the same time, while they achieved essential authority by telling their own stories, these writers allayed their distinctively female anxieties of authorship by following Emily Dickinson's famous (and characteristically female) advice to "Tell all the Truth but tell it slant—."[51] In short, like the twentieth-century American poet H. D., who declared her aesthetic strategy by entitling one of her novels *Palimpsest*, women from Jane Austen and Mary Shelley to Emily Brontë and Emily Dickinson produced literary works that are in some sense palimpsestic, works whose surface designs conceal or obscure deeper, less accessible (and less socially acceptable) levels of meaning. Thus these authors managed the difficult task of achieving true female literary authority by simultaneously conforming to and subverting patriarchal literary standards.

Of course, as the allegorical figure of Duessa suggests, men have always accused women of the duplicity that is essential to the literary strategies we are describing here. In part, at least, such accusations are well founded, both in life and in art. As in the white-black relationship, the dominant group in the male-female relationship rightly fears and suspects that the docility of the subordinate caste masks rebellious passions. Moreover, just as blacks did in the master-slave relationships of the American South, women in patriarchy have traditionally cultivated accents of acquiescence in order to gain freedom to live their lives on their own terms, if only in the privacy of their own thoughts. Interestingly, indeed, several feminist critics have recently used Frantz Fanon's model of colonialism to describe the relationship between male (parent) culture and female (colonized) literature.[52] But with only one language at their disposal, women writers in England and America had to be even more adept at doubletalk than their colonized counterparts. We shall see, therefore, that in publicly presenting acceptable facades for private and dangerous visions women writers have long used a wide range of tactics to obscure but not obliterate their most subversive impulses. Along with the twentieth-century American painter Judy Chicago, any one of these artists might have noted that "formal issues" were often "something that my content had to be hidden behind in order for my work to be taken seriously." And with Judy Chicago, too, any one of these women might have confessed that "Because of this duplicity, there always appeared to be something 'not quite right' about my pieces according to the prevailing aesthetic."[53]

To be sure, male writers also "swerve" from their predecessors, and they too produce literary texts whose revolutionary messages are concealed behind stylized facades. The most original male writers, moreover, sometimes seem "not quite right" to those readers we have recently come to call "establishment" critics. As Bloom's theory of the anxiety of influence implies, however, and as our analysis of the metaphor of literary paternity also suggests, there are powerful paradigms of male intellectual struggle which enable the male writer to explain his rebelliousness, his "swerving," and his "originality" both to himself and to the world, no matter how many readers think him "not quite right." In a sense, therefore, he conceals his revolutionary energies only so that he may more powerfully reveal them, and swerves or rebels so that he may triumph by founding a new order, since his struggle against his precursor is a "battle of strong equals."

For the woman writer, however, concealment is not a military gesture but a strategy born of fear and dis-ease. Similarly, a literary "swerve" is not a motion by which the writer prepares for a victorious accession to power but a necessary evasion. Locked into structures created by and for men, eighteenth- and nineteenth-century women writers did not so much rebel against the prevailing aesthetic as feel guilty about their inability to conform to it. With little sense of a viable female culture, such women were plainly much troubled by the fact that they needed to communicate truths which other (i.e. male) writers apparently never felt or expressed. Conditioned to doubt their own authority anyway, women writers who wanted to describe what, in Dickinson's phrase, is "not brayed of tongue"[54] would find it easier to doubt themselves than the censorious voices of society. The evasions and concealments of their art are therefore far more elaborate than those of most male writers. For, given the patriarchal biases of nineteenth-century literary culture, the literary woman did have something crucial to hide.

Because so many of the lost or concealed truths of female culture have recently been retrieved by feminist scholars, women readers in particular have lately become aware that nineteenth-century literary women felt they had things to hide. Many feminist critics, therefore, have begun to write about these phenomena of evasion and concealment in women's writing. In *The Female Imagination*, for instance, Patricia Meyer Spacks repeatedly describes the ways in which women's novels are marked by "subterranean challenges" to truths that the writers of such works appear on the surface to accept. Similarly, Carolyn Heilbrun and Catharine Stimpson discuss "the presence of absence" in literature by women, the "hollows, centers, caverns within the work—places where activity that one might expect is missing. . . or deceptively coded." Perhaps most trenchantly, Elaine Showalter has recently pointed out that feminist criticism, with its emphasis on the woman writer's inevitable consciousness of her own gender, has allowed us to "see meaning in what has previously been empty space. The orthodox plot recedes, and another plot, hitherto submerged in the anonymity of the background, stands out in bold relief like a thumbprint."[55]

But what is this other plot? Is there any *one* other plot? What is the secret message of literature by women, if there is a single secret message? What, in other words, have women got to hide? Most obviously, of course, if we return to the angelic figure of Makarie—that ideal of "contemplative purity" who no doubt had headaches precisely because her author inflicted upon her a life that seemed to have "no story"—what literary women have hidden or disguised is

what each writer knows is in some sense her own story. Because, as
Simone de Beauvoir puts it, women "still dream through the dreams
of men," internalizing the strictures that the Queen's looking glass
utters in its kingly voice, the message or story that has been hidden
is "merely," in Carolyn Kizer's bitter words, "the private lives of
one half of humanity."[56] More specifically, however, the one plot
that seems to be concealed in most of the nineteenth-century literature
by women which will concern us here is in some sense a story of the
woman writer's quest for her own story; it is the story, in other words,
of the woman's quest for self-definition. Like the speaker of Mary
Elizabeth Coleridge's "The Other Side of a Mirror," the literary
woman frequently finds herself staring with horror at a fearful image
of herself that has been mysteriously inscribed on the surface of the
glass, and she tries to guess the truth that cannot be uttered by the
wounded and bleeding mouth, the truth behind the "leaping fire / Of
jealousy and fierce revenge," the truth "of hard unsanctified distress."
Uneasily aware that, like Sylvia Plath, she is "inhabited by a cry,"
she secretly seeks to unify herself by coming to terms with her own
fragmentation. Yet even though, with Mary Elizabeth Coleridge,
she strives to "set the crystal surface" of the mirror free from frightful
images, she continually feels, as May Sarton puts it, that she has
been "broken in two / By sheer definition."[57] The story "no man
may guess," therefore, is the story of her attempt to make herself
whole by healing her own infections and diseases.

To heal herself, however, the woman writer must exorcise the
sentences which bred her infection in the first place; she must overtly
or covertly free herself of the despair she inhaled from some "Wrinkled
Maker," and she can only do this by revising the Maker's texts. Or,
to put the matter in terms of a different metaphor, to "set the crystal
surface free" a literary woman must shatter the mirror that has so
long reflected what every woman was supposed to be. For these
reasons, then, women writers in England and America, throughout
the nineteenth century and on into the twentieth, have been especially
concerned with assaulting and revising, deconstructing and reconstructing those images of women inherited from male literature,
especially, as we noted in our discussion of the Queen's looking glass,
the paradigmatic polarities of angel and monster. Examining and
attacking such images, however, literary women have inevitably had

consciously or unconsciously to reject the values and assumptions of the society that created these fearsome paradigms. Thus, even when they do not overtly criticize patriarchal institutions or conventions (and most of the nineteenth-century women we shall be studying do *not* overtly do so), these writers almost obsessively create characters who enact their own, covert authorial anger. With Charlotte Brontë, they may feel that there are "evils" of which it is advisable "not too often to think." With George Eliot, they may declare that the "woman question" seems "to overhang abysses, of which even prostitution is not the worst."[58] But over and over again they project what seems to be the energy of their own despair into passionate, even melodramatic characters who act out the subversive impulses every woman inevitably feels when she contemplates the "deep-rooted" evils of patriarchy.

It is significant, then, that when the speaker of "The Other Side of a Mirror" looks into her glass the woman that she sees is a madwoman, "wild / With more than womanly despair," the monster that she fears she really is rather than the angel she has pretended to be. What the heroine of George Eliot's verse-drama *Armgart* calls "basely feigned content, the placid mask / Of woman's misery" *is* merely a mask, and Mary Elizabeth Coleridge, like so many of her contemporaries, records the emergence from behind the mask of a figure whose rage "once no man on earth could guess."[59] Repudiating "basely feigned content," this figure arises like a bad dream, bloody, envious, enraged, as if the very process of writing had itself liberated a madwoman, a crazy and angry woman, from a silence in which neither she nor her author can continue to acquiesce. Thus although Coleridge's mirrored madwoman is an emblem of "speechless woe" because she has "no voice to speak her dread," the poet ultimately speaks *for* her when she whispers "I am she!" More, she speaks for her in writing the poem that narrates her emergence from behind the placid mask, "the aspects glad and gay, / That erst were found reflected there."

As we explore nineteenth-century literature, we will find that this madwoman emerges over and over again from the mirrors women writers hold up both to their own natures and to their own visions of nature. Even the most apparently conservative and decorous women writers obsessively create fiercely independent characters who

seek to destroy all the patriarchal structures which both their authors
and their authors' submissive heroines seem to accept as inevitable. Of
course, by projecting their rebellious impulses not into their heroines
but into mad or monstrous women (who are suitably punished in
the course of the novel or poem), female authors dramatize their own
self-division, their desire both to accept the strictures of patriarchal
society and to reject them. What this means, however, is that the
madwoman in literature by women is not merely, as she might be
in male literature, an antagonist or foil to the heroine. Rather, she
is usually in some sense the *author's* double, an image of her own
anxiety and rage. Indeed, much of the poetry and fiction written
by women conjures up this mad creature so that female authors can
come to terms with their own uniquely female feelings of fragmentation, their own keen sense of the discrepancies between what they
are and what they are supposed to be.

We shall see, then, that the mad double is as crucial to the aggressively sane novels of Jane Austen and George Eliot as she is in the
more obviously rebellious stories told by Charlotte and Emily Brontë.
Both gothic and anti-gothic writers represent themselves as split like
Emily Dickinson between the elected nun and the damned witch,
or like Mary Shelley between the noble, censorious scientist and his
enraged, childish monster. In fact, so important is this female schizophrenia of authorship that, as we hope to show, it links these nineteenth-century writers with such twentieth-century descendants as
Virginia Woolf (who projects herself into both ladylike Mrs. Dalloway
and crazed Septimus Warren Smith), Doris Lessing (who divides
herself between sane Martha Hesse and mad Lynda Coldridge), and
Sylvia Plath (who sees herself as both a plaster saint and a dangerous
"old yellow" monster).

To be sure, in the works of all these artists—both nineteenth- and
twentieth-century—the mad character is sometimes created only to
be destroyed: Septimus Warren Smith and Bertha Mason Rochester
are both good examples of such characters, as is Victor Frankenstein's
monster. Yet even when a figure of rage seems to function only as a
monitory image, her (or his) fury must be acknowledged not only
by the angelic protagonist to whom s/he is opposed, but, significantly,
by the reader as well. With his usual perceptiveness, Geoffrey Chaucer
anticipated the dynamics of this situation in the *Canterbury Tales.*

When he gave the Wife of Bath a tale of her own, he portrayed her projecting her subversive vision of patriarchal institutions into the story of a furious hag who demands supreme power over her own life and that of her husband: only when she gains his complete acceptance of her authority does this witch transform herself into a modest and docile beauty. Five centuries later, the threat of the hag, the monster, the witch, the madwoman, still lurks behind the compliant paragon of women's stories.

To mention witches, however, is to be reminded once again of the traditional (patriarchally defined) association between creative women and monsters. In projecting their anger and dis-ease into dreadful figures, creating dark doubles for themselves and their heroines, women writers are both identifying with and revising the self-definitions patriarchal culture has imposed on them. All the nineteenth- and twentieth-century literary women who evoke the female monster in their novels and poems alter her meaning by virtue of their own identification with her. For it is usually because she is in some sense imbued with interiority that the witch-monster-madwoman becomes so crucial an avatar of the writer's own self. From a male point of view, women who reject the submissive silences of domesticity have been seen as terrible objects—Gorgons, Sirens, Scyllas, serpent-Lamias, Mothers of Death or Goddesses of Night. But from a female point of view the monster woman is simply a woman who seeks the power of self-articulation, and therefore, like Mary Shelley giving the first-person story of a monster who seemed to his creator to be merely a "filthy mass that moves and talks," she presents this figure for the first time from the inside out. Such a radical misreading of patriarchal poetics frees the woman artist to imply her criticism of the literary conventions she has inherited even as it allows her to express her ambiguous relationship to a culture that has not only defined her gender but shaped her mind. In a sense, as a famous poem by Muriel Rukeyser implies, all these women ultimately embrace the role of that most mythic of female monsters, the Sphinx, whose indecipherable message is the key to existence, because they know that the secret wisdom so long hidden from men is precisely *their* point of view.[60]

There is a sense, then, in which the female literary tradition we have been defining participates on all levels in the same duality or

duplicity that necessitates the generation of such doubles as monster
characters who shadow angelic authors and mad anti-heroines who
complicate the lives of sane heroines. Parody, for instance, is another
one of the key strategies through which this female duplicity reveals
itself. As we have noted, nineteenth-century women writers frequently
both use and misuse (or subvert) a common male tradition or genre.
Consequently, we shall see over and over again that a "complex
vibration" occurs between stylized generic gestures and unexpected
deviations from such obvious gestures, a vibration that undercuts
and ridicules the genre being employed. Some of the best-known
recent poetry by women openly uses such parody in the cause of
feminism: traditional figures of patriarchal mythology like Circe,
Leda, Cassandra, Medusa, Helen, and Persephone have all lately
been reinvented in the images of their female creators, and each
poem devoted to one of these figures is a reading that reinvents her
original story.[61] But though nineteenth-century women did not
employ this kind of parody so openly and angrily, they too deployed
it to give contextual force to their revisionary attempts at self-
definition. Jane Austen's novels of sense and sensibility, for instance,
suggest a revolt against both those standards of female excellence.
Similarly, Charlotte Brontë's critical revision of *Pilgrim's Progress*
questions the patriarchal ideal of female submissiveness by substituting a questing Everywoman for Bunyan's questing Christian.
In addition, as we shall show in detail in later chapters, Mary Shelley,
Emily Brontë, and George Eliot covertly reappraise and repudiate
the misogyny implicit in Milton's mythology by misreading and
revising Milton's story of woman's fall. Parodic, duplicitous, extraordinarily sophisticated, all this female writing is both revisionary
and revolutionary, even when it is produced by writers we usually
think of as models of angelic resignation.

To summarize this point, it is helpful to examine a work by
the woman who seems to be the most modest and gentle of the three
Brontë sisters. Anne Brontë's *The Tenant of Wildfell Hall* (1848) is
generally considered conservative in its espousal of Christian values,
but it tells what is in fact a story of woman's liberation. Specifically,
it describes a woman's escape from the prisonhouse of a bad marriage,
and her subsequent attempts to achieve independence by establishing
herself in a career as an artist. Since Helen Graham, the novel's

protagonist, must remain incognito in order to elude her husband, she signs with false initials the landscapes she produces when she becomes a professional artist, and she titles the works in such a way as to hide her whereabouts. In short, she uses her art both to express and to camouflage herself. But this functionally ambiguous aesthetic is not merely a result of her flight from home and husband. For even earlier in the novel, when we encounter Helen before her marriage, her use of art is duplicitous. Her painting and drawing seem at first simply to be genteel social accomplishments, but when she shows one of her paintings to her future husband, he discovers a pencil sketch of his own face on the back of the canvas. Helen has been using the reverse side of her paintings to express her secret desires, and although she has remembered to rub out all the other sketches, this one remains, eventually calling his attention to the dim traces on the backs of all the others.

In the figure of Helen Graham, Anne Brontë has given us a wonderfully useful paradigm of the female artist. Whether Helen covertly uses a supposedly modest young lady's "accomplishments" for unladylike self-expression or publicly flaunts her professionalism and independence, she must in some sense deny or conceal her own art, or at least deny the self-assertion implicit in her art. In other words, there is an essential ambiguity involved in her career as an artist. When, as a girl, she draws on the backs of her paintings, she must make the paintings themselves work as public masks to hide her private dreams, and only behind such masks does she feel free to choose her own subjects. Thus she produces a public art which she herself rejects as inadequate but which she secretly uses to discover a new aesthetic space for herself. In addition, she subverts her genteelly "feminine" works with personal representations which endure only in tracings, since her guilt about the impropriety of self-expression has caused her to efface her private drawings just as it has led her to efface herself.

It is significant, moreover, that the sketch on the other side of Helen's canvas depicts the face of the Byronically brooding, sensual Arthur Huntingdon, the man she finally decides to marry. Fatally attracted by the energy and freedom that she desires as an escape from the constraints of her own life, Helen pays for her initial attraction by watching her husband metamorphose from a fallen angel into a fiend, as he relentlessly and self-destructively pursues a diabolical career of gaming, whoring, and drinking. In this respect, too, Helen is prototypical, since we shall see that women artists are repeatedly attracted to the Satanic/Byronic hero even while they try to resist the sexual submission exacted by this oppressive younger son who seems, at first, so like a brother or a double. From Jane Austen, who almost obsessively rejected this figure, to Mary Shelley, the Brontës, and George Eliot, all of whom identified with his fierce presumption, women writers develop a subversive tradition that has a unique relationship to the Romantic ethos of revolt.

What distinguishes Helen Graham (and all the women authors who resemble her) from male Romantics, however, is precisely her anxiety about her own artistry, together with the duplicity that anxiety necessitates. Even when she becomes a professional artist, Helen continues to fear the social implications of her vocation. Associating female creativity with freedom from male domination, and dreading the misogynistic censure of her community, she produces art that at least partly hides her experience of her actual place in the world. Because her audience potentially includes the man from whom she is trying to escape, she must balance her need to paint her own condition against her need to circumvent detection. Her strained relationship to her art is thus determined almost entirely by her gender, so that from both her anxieties and her strategies for overcoming them we can extrapolate a number of the crucial ways in which women's art has been radically qualified by their femaleness.

As we shall see, Anne Brontë's sister Charlotte depicts similar anxieties and similar strategies for overcoming anxiety in the careers of all the female artists who appear in her novels. From timid Frances Henri to demure Jane Eyre, from mysterious Lucia to flamboyant Vashti, Brontë's women artists withdraw behind their art even while they assert themselves through it, as if deliberately adopting Helen Graham's duplicitous techniques of self-expression. For the great women writers of the past two centuries are linked by the ingenuity with which all, while no one was really looking, danced out of the debilitating looking glass of the male text into the health of female authority. Tracing subversive pictures behind socially acceptable facades, they managed to appear to dissociate themselves from their own revolutionary impulses even while passionately enacting such impulses. Articulating the "private lives of one half of humanity," their fiction and poetry both records and transcends the struggle of what Marge Piercy has called "Unlearning to not speak."[62]

We must not forget, however, that to hide behind the facade of art, even for so crucial a process as "Unlearning to not speak," is still to be hidden, to be confined: to be secret is to be secreted. In a poignant and perceptive poem to Emily Dickinson, Adrienne Rich has noted that in her "half-cracked way" Dickinson chose "silence for entertainment, / chose to have it out at last / on [her] own premises."[63] This is what Jane Austen, too, chose to do when she ironically defined her work-space as two inches of ivory, what Emily Brontë chose to do when she hid her poems in kitchen cabinets (and perhaps destroyed her Gondal stories), what Christina Rossetti chose when she elected an art that glorified the religious constrictions of the "convent threshold." Rich's crucial pun on the word *premises* returns us, therefore, to the confinement of these women, a confinement that was inescapable for them even at their moments of greatest triumph, a confinement that was implicit in their secretness. This confinement was both literal and figurative. Literally, women like Dickinson, Brontë, and Rossetti were imprisoned in their homes, their father's houses; indeed, almost all nineteenth-century women were in some sense imprisoned in men's houses. Figuratively, such women were, as we have seen, locked into male texts, texts from which they could escape only through ingenuity and indirection. It is not surprising, then, that spatial imagery of enclosure and escape, elaborated with what frequently becomes obsessive intensity, characterizes much of their writing.

In fact, anxieties about space sometimes seem to dominate the literature of both nineteenth-century women and their twentieth-century descendants. In the genre Ellen Moers has recently called "female Gothic,"[64] for instance, heroines who characteristically inhabit mysteriously intricate or uncomfortably stifling houses are often seen as captured, fettered, trapped, even buried alive. But other kinds of works by women—novels of manners, domestic tales, lyric poems—also show the same concern with spatial constrictions. From Ann Radcliffe's melodramatic dungeons to Jane Austen's mirrored parlors, from Charlotte Brontë's haunted garrets to Emily Brontë's coffin-shaped beds, imagery of enclosure reflects the woman writer's own discomfort, her sense of powerlessness, her fear that she inhabits alien and incomprehensible places. Indeed, it reflects her growing suspicion that what the nineteenth century called "woman's place" is itself irrational and strange. Moreover, from Emily Dickinson's haunted chambers to H. D.'s tightly shut sea-shells and Sylvia Plath's grave-caves, imagery of entrapment expresses the woman writer's sense that she has been dispossessed precisely because she is so thoroughly possessed—and possessed in every sense of the word.

The opening stanzas of Charlotte Perkins Gilman's punningly titled "In Duty Bound" show how inevitable it was for a female artist to translate into spatial terms her despair at the spiritual constrictions of what Gilman ironically called "home comfort."

> In duty bound, a life hemmed in,
>   Whichever way the spirit turns to look;
> No chance of breaking out, except by sin;
>   Not even room to shirk—
>   Simply to live, and work.
>
> An obligation preimposed, unsought,
>   Yet binding with the force of natural law;
> The pressure of antagonistic thought;
>   Aching within, each hour,
>   A sense of wasting power.
>
> A house with roof so darkly low
>   The heavy rafters shut the sunlight out;
> One cannot stand erect without a blow;
>   Until the soul inside
>   Cries for a grave—more wide.[65]

Literally confined to the house, figuratively confined to a single "place," enclosed in parlors and encased in texts, imprisoned in kitchens and enshrined in stanzas, women artists naturally found themselves describing dark interiors and confusing their sense that they were house-bound with their rebellion against being duty bound. The same connections Gilman's poem made in the nineteenth century had after all been made by Anne Finch in the eighteenth, when she complained that women who wanted to write poetry were scornfully told that "the dull mannage of a servile house" was their "outmost art and use." Inevitably, then, since they were trapped in so many ways in the architecture—both the houses and the institutions—of patriarchy, women expressed their anxiety of authorship by comparing their "presumptuous" literary ambitions with the domestic accomplishments that had been prescribed for them. Inevitably, too, they expressed their claustrophobic rage by enacting rebellious escapes.

Dramatizations of imprisonment and escape are so all-pervasive in nineteenth-century literature by women that we believe they represent a uniquely female tradition in this period. Interestingly, though works in this tradition generally begin by using houses as primary symbols of female imprisonment, they also use much of the other paraphernalia of "woman's place" to enact their central symbolic drama of enclosure and escape. Ladylike veils and costumes, mirrors, paintings, statues, locked cabinets, drawers, trunks, strongboxes, and other domestic furnishing appear and reappear in female novels and poems throughout the nineteenth century and on into the twentieth to signify the woman writer's sense that, as Emily Dickinson put it, her "life" has been "shaven and fitted to a frame," a confinement she can only tolerate by believing that "the soul has moments of escape / When bursting all the doors / She dances like a bomb abroad."[66] Significantly, too, the explosive violence of these "moments of escape" that women writers continually imagine for themselves returns us to the phenomenon of the mad double so many of these women have projected into their works. For it is, after all, through the violence of the double that the female author enacts her own raging desire to escape male houses and male texts, while at the same time it is through the double's violence that this anxious author articulates for herself the costly destructiveness of anger repressed until it can no longer be contained.

As we shall see, therefore, infection continually breeds in the sentences of women whose writing obsessively enacts this drama of enclosure and escape. Specifically, what we have called the distinctively female diseases of anorexia and agoraphobia are closely associated with this dramatic/thematic pattern. Defining themselves as prisoners of their own gender, for instance, women frequently create characters who attempt to escape, if only into nothingness, through the suicidal self-starvation of anorexia. Similarly, in a metaphorical elaboration of bulimia, the disease of overeating which is anorexia's complement and mirror-image (as Marlene Boskind-Lodahl has recently shown),[67] women writers often envision an "outbreak" that transforms their characters into huge and powerful monsters. More obviously, agoraphobia and its complementary opposite, claustrophobia, are by definition associated with the spatial imagery through which these poets and novelists express their feelings of social confinement and their yearning for spiritual escape. The paradigmatic female story, therefore—the story such angels in the house of literature as Goethe's Makarie and Patmore's Honoria were in effect "forbidden" to tell—is frequently an arrangement of the elements most readers will readily remember from Charlotte Brontë's *Jane Eyre*. Examining the psychosocial implications of a "haunted" ancestral mansion, such a tale explores the tension between parlor and attic, the psychic split between the lady who submits to male dicta and the lunatic who rebels. But in examining these matters the paradigmatic female story inevitably considers also the equally uncomfortable spatial options of expulsion into the cold outside or suffocation in the hot indoors, and in addition it often embodies an obsessive anxiety both about starvation to the point of disappearance and about monstrous inhabitation.

Many nineteenth-century male writers also, of course, used imagery of enclosure and escape to make deeply felt points about the relationship of the individual and society. Dickens and Poe, for instance, on opposite sides of the Atlantic, wrote of prisons, cages, tombs, and cellars in similar ways and for similar reasons. Still, the male writer is so much more comfortable with his literary role that he can usually elaborate upon his visionary theme more consciously and objectively than the female writer can. The distinction between male and female images of imprisonment is—and always has been— a distinction between, on the one hand, that which is both meta-physical and metaphorical, and on the other hand, that which is social and actual. Sleeping in his coffin, the seventeenth-century poet John Donne was piously rehearsing the constraints of the grave in advance, but the nineteenth-century poet Emily Dickinson, in purdah in her white dress, was anxiously living those constraints in the present.

Imagining himself buried alive in tombs and cellars, Edgar Allan Poe was letting his mind poetically wander into the deepest recesses of his own psyche, but Dickinson, reporting that "I do not cross my Father's ground to any house in town," was recording a real, self-willed, self-burial. Similarly, when Byron's Prisoner of Chillon notes that "my very chains and I grew friends," the poet himself is making an epistemological point about the nature of the human mind, as well as a political point about the tyranny of the state. But when Rose Yorke in *Shirley* describes Caroline Helstone as living the life of a toad enclosed in a block of marble, Charlotte Brontë is speaking through her about her own deprived and constricted life, and its real conditions.[68]

Thus, though most male metaphors of imprisonment have obvious implications in common (and many can be traced back to traditional images used by, say, Shakespeare and Plato), such metaphors may have very different aesthetic functions and philosophical messages in different male literary works. Wordsworth's prison-house in the "Intimations" ode serves a purpose quite unlike that served by the jails in Dickens's novels. Coleridge's twice-five miles of visionary greenery ought not to be confused with Keats's vale of soul-making, and the escape of Tennyson's Art from her Palace should not be identified with the resurrection of Poe's Ligeia. Women authors, however, reflect the literal reality of their own confinement in the constraints they depict, and so all at least begin with the same unconscious or conscious purpose in employing such spatial imagery. Recording their own distinctively female experience, they are secretly working through and within the conventions of literary texts to define their own lives.

While some male authors also use such imagery for implicitly or explicitly confessional projects, women seem forced to live more intimately with the metaphors they have created to solve the "problem" of their fall. At least one critic does deal not only with such images but with their psychological meaning as they accrue around houses. Noting in *The Poetics of Space* that "the house image would appear to have become the topography of our inmost being," Gaston Bachelard shows the ways in which houses, nests, shells, and wardrobes are in us as much as we are in them.[69] What is significant from our point of view, however, is the extraordinary discrepancy between the almost consistently "felicitous space" he discusses and the negative space we have found. Clearly, for Bachelard the protective asylum of the house is closely associated with its maternal features, and to this extent he is following the work done on dream symbolism by Freud and on female inner space by Erikson. It seems clear too, however, that such symbolism must inevitably have very different implications for male critics and for female authors.

Women themselves have often, of course, been described or imagined as houses. Most recently Erik Erikson advanced his controversial theory of female "inner space" in an effort to account for little girls' interest in domestic enclosures. But in medieval times, as if to anticipate Erikson, statues of the Madonna were made to open up and reveal the holy family hidden in the Virgin's inner space. The female womb has certainly, always and everywhere, been a child's first and most satisfying house, a source of food and dark security, and therefore a mythic paradise imaged over and over again in sacred caves, secret shrines, consecrated huts. Yet for many a woman writer these ancient associations of house and self seem mainly to have strengthened the anxiety about enclosure which she projected into her art. Disturbed by the real physiological prospect of enclosing an unknown part of herself that is somehow also not herself, the female artist may, like Mary Shelley, conflate anxieties about maternity with anxieties about literary creativity. Alternatively, troubled by the anatomical "emptiness" of spinsterhood, she may, like Emily Dickinson, fear the inhabitations of nothingness and death, the transformation of womb into tomb. Moreover, conditioned to believe that as a house she is herself owned (and ought to be inhabited) by a man, she may once again but for yet another reason see herself as inescapably an object. In other words, even if she does not experience her womb as a kind of tomb or perceive her child's occupation of her house/body as depersonalizing, she may recognize that in an essential way she has been defined simply by her purely biological usefulness to her species.

To become literally a house, after all, is to be denied the hope of that spiritual transcendence of the body which, as Simone de Beauvoir has argued, is what makes humanity distinctively human. Thus, to be confined in childbirth (and significantly "confinement" was the key nineteenth-century term for what we would now, just as significantly, call "delivery") is in a way just as problematical as to be confined in a house or prison. Indeed, it might well seem to the literary woman that, just as ontogeny may be said to recapitulate phylogeny, the confinement of pregnancy replicates the confinement of society. For even if she is only metaphorically denied transcendence, the woman writer who perceives the implications of the house/body equation must unconsciously realize that such a trope does not just "place" her in a glass coffin, it transforms her into a version of the glass coffin herself. There is a sense, therefore, in which, confined in such a network of metaphors, what Adrienne Rich has called a "thinking woman" might inevitably feel that now she has been imprisoned within her own alien and loathsome body.[70] Once again, in other words, she has become not only a prisoner but a monster.

As if to comment on the unity of all these points—on, that is, the anxiety-inducing connections between what women writers tend to see as their parallel confinements in texts, houses, and maternal female bodies—Charlotte Perkins Gilman brought them all together in 1890 in a striking story of female confinement and escape, a paradigmatic tale which (like *Jane Eyre*) seems to tell *the* story that all literary women would tell if they could speak their "speechless woe." "The Yellow Wallpaper," which Gilman herself called "a description of a case of nervous breakdown," recounts in the first person the experiences of a woman who is evidently suffering from a severe postpartum psychosis.[71] Her husband, a censorious and paternalistic physician, is treating her according to methods by which S. Weir Mitchell, a famous "nerve specialist," treated Gilman herself for a similar problem. He has confined her to a large garret room in an "ancestral hall" he has rented, and he has forbidden her to touch pen to paper until she is well again, for he feels, says the narrator, "that with my imaginative power and habit of story-making, a nervous weakness like mine is sure to lead to all manner of excited fancies, and that I ought to use my will and good sense to check the tendency" (15–16).

The cure, of course, is worse than the disease, for the sick woman's mental condition deteriorates rapidly. "I think sometimes that if I were only well enough to write a little it would relieve the press of ideas and rest me," she remarks, but literally confined in a room she thinks is a one-time nursery because it has "rings and things" in the walls, she is literally locked away from creativity. The "rings and things," although reminiscent of children's gymnastic equipment, are really the paraphernalia of confinement, like the gate at the head of the stairs, instruments that definitively indicate her imprisonment Even more tormenting, however, is the room's wallpaper: a sulphurous yellow paper, torn off in spots, and patterned with "lame uncertain curves" that "plunge off at outrageous angles" and "destroy themselves in unheard of contradictions." Ancient, smoldering, "unclean" as the oppressive structures of the society in which she finds herself, this paper surrounds the narrator like an inexplicable text, censorious and overwhelming as her physician husband, haunting as the "hereditary estate" in which she is trying to survive. Inevitably she studies its suicidal implications—and inevitably, because of her "imaginative power and habit of story-making," she revises it, projecting her own passion for escape into its otherwise incomprehensible hieroglyphics. "This wall-paper," she decides, at a key point in her story,

> has a kind of sub-pattern in a different shade, a particularly irritating one, for you can only see it in certain lights, and not clearly then.
>
> But in the places where it isn't faded and where the sun is just so—I can see a strange, provoking, formless sort of figure, that seems to skulk about behind that silly and conspicuous front design. [18]

As time passes, this figure concealed behind what corresponds (in terms of what we have been discussing) to the facade of the patriarchal text becomes clearer and clearer. By moonlight the pattern of the wallpaper "becomes bars! The outside pattern I mean, and the woman behind it is as plain as can be." And eventually, as the narrator sinks more deeply into what the world calls madness, the terrifying implications of both the paper and the figure imprisoned behind the paper begin to permeate—that is, to *haunt*—the rented ancestral mansion in which she and her husband are immured. The "yellow smell" of the paper "creeps all over the house," drenching every room in its subtle aroma of decay. And the woman creeps too— through the house, in the house, and out of the house, in the garden and "on that long road under the trees." Sometimes, indeed, the

narrator confesses, "I think there are a great many women" both
behind the paper and creeping in the garden,

> and sometimes only one, and she crawls around fast, and her
> crawling shakes [the paper] all over. . . . And she is all the time
> trying to climb through. But nobody could climb through that
> pattern—it strangles so; I think that is why it has so many
> heads. [30]

Eventually it becomes obvious to both reader and narrator that
the figure creeping through and behind the wallpaper is both the
narrator and the narrator's double. By the end of the story, moreover,
the narrator has enabled this double to escape from her textual/archi-
tectural confinement: "I pulled and she shook, I shook and she
pulled, and before morning we had peeled off yards of that paper."
Is the message of the tale's conclusion mere madness? Certainly the
righteous Doctor John—whose name links him to the anti-hero of
Charlotte Brontë's *Villette*—has been temporarily defeated, or at
least momentarily stunned. "Now why should that man have
fainted?" the narrator ironically asks as she creeps around her attic.
But John's unmasculine swoon of surprise is the least of the triumphs
Gilman imagines for her madwoman. More significant are the
madwoman's own imaginings and creations, mirages of health and
freedom with which her author endows her like a fairy godmother
showering gold on a sleeping heroine. The woman from behind the
wallpaper creeps away, for instance, creeps fast and far on the long
road, in broad daylight. "I have watched her sometimes away off
in the open country," says the narrator, "creeping as fast as a cloud
shadow in a high wind."

Indistinct and yet rapid, barely perceptible but inexorable, the
progress of that cloud shadow is not unlike the progress of nineteenth-
century literary women out of the texts defined by patriarchal poetics
into the open spaces of their own authority. That such an escape from
the numb world behind the patterned walls of the text was a flight
from dis-ease into health was quite clear to Gilman herself. When
"The Yellow Wallpaper" was published she sent it to Weir Mitchell,
whose strictures had kept her from attempting the pen during her
own breakdown, thereby aggravating her illness, and she was delighted to learn, years later, that "he had changed his treatment of

nervous prostration since reading" her story. "If that is a fact," she declared, "I have not lived in vain."[72] Because she was a rebellious feminist besides being a medical iconoclast, we can be sure that Gilman did not think of this triumph of hers in narrowly therapeutic terms. Because she knew, with Emily Dickinson, that "Infection in the sentence breeds," she knew that the cure for female despair must be spiritual as well as physical, aesthetic as well as social. What "The Yellow Wallpaper" shows she knew, too, is that even when a supposedly "mad" woman has been sentenced to imprisonment in the "infected" house of her own body, she may discover that, as Sylvia Plath was to put it seventy years later, she has "a self to recover, a queen."[73]

3 The Parables of the Cave

"Next then," I said, "take the following parable of education and ignorance as a picture of the condition of our nature. Imagine mankind as dwelling in an underground cave ... "

—Plato

Where are the songs I used to know,
  Where are the notes I used to sing?
I have forgotten everything
  I used to know so long ago.
        —Christina Rossetti

... there came upon me an overshadowing bright Cloud, and in the midst of it the figure of a Woman, most richly adorned with transparent Gold, her Hair hanging down, and her Face as the terrible Crystal for brightness [and] immediately this Voice came, saying, Behold I am God's Eternal Virgin-Wisdom ... I am to unseal the Treasures of God's deep Wisdom unto thee, and will be as Rebecca was unto Jacob, a true Natural Mother; for out of my Womb thou shalt be brought forth after the manner of a Spirit, Conceived and Born again.

—Jane Lead

Although Plato does not seem to have thought much about this point, a cave is—as Freud pointed out—a female place, a womb-shaped enclosure, a house of earth, secret and often sacred.[1] To this shrine the initiate comes to hear the voices of darkness, the wisdom of inwardness. In this prison the slave is immured, the virgin sacrificed, the priestess abandoned. "We have put her living in the tomb!" Poe's paradigmatic exclamation of horror, with its shadow of solipsism, summarizes the Victorian shudder of disgust at the thought of cavern confrontations and the evils they might reveal—the suffocation, the "black bat airs," the vampirism, the chaos of what Victor Frankenstein calls "filthy creation." But despite its melodrama, Poe's remark summarizes too (even if unintentionally) the plight of the woman in patriarchal culture, the woman whose cave-shaped anatomy is her destiny. Not just, like Plato's cave-dweller, a prisoner of Nature, this woman is a prisoner of her own nature, a prisoner in the "grave cave" of immanence which she transforms into a vaporous Cave of Spleen.[2]

In this regard, an anecdote of Simone de Beauvoir's forms a sort of counter-parable to Plato's:

> I recall seeing in a primitive village of Tunisia a subterranean cavern in which four women were squatting: the old one-eyed and toothless wife, her face horribly devastated, was cooking dough on a small brazier in the midst of an acrid smoke; two wives somewhat younger, but almost as disfigured, were lulling children in their arms—one was giving suck; seated before a loom, a young idol magnificently decked out in silk, gold, and silver was knotting threads of wool. As I left this gloomy cave— kingdom of immanence, womb, and tomb—in the corridor leading upward toward the light of day I passed the male, dressed in white, well groomed, smiling, sunny. He was returning from the marketplace, where he had discussed world affairs with other men; he would pass some hours in this retreat of his at the heart of the vast universe to which he belonged, from which he was not separated. For the withered old women, for the young wife doomed to the same rapid decay, there was no universe other than the smoky cave, whence they emerged only at night, silent and veiled.[3]

Destroyed by traditional female activities—cooking, nursing, needling, knotting—which ought to have given them life as they themselves give life to men, the women of this underground harem are obviously buried in (and by) patriarchal definitions of their sexuality. Here is immanence with no hope of transcendence, nature seduced and betrayed by culture, enclosure without any possibility of escape. Or so it would seem.

Yet the womb-shaped cave is also the place of female power, the *umbilicus mundi*, one of the great antechambers of the mysteries of transformation. As herself a kind of cave, every woman might seem to have the cave's metaphorical power of annihilation, the power—as de Beauvoir puts it elsewhere—of "night in the entrails of the earth," for "in many a legend," she notes, "we see the hero lost forever as he falls back into the maternal shadows—cave, abyss, hell."[4] At the same time, as herself a fated inhabitant of that earth-cave of immanence in which de Beauvoir's Tunisian women were trapped, every woman might seem to have metaphorical access to the dark knowledge buried in caves. Summarizing the characteristics of those female "great weavers" who determine destiny—Norns, Fates, priestesses of Demeter, prophetesses of Gaea—Helen Diner points out that "all knowledge of Fate comes from the female depths; none of the surface powers knows it. Whoever wants to know about Fate must go down to the woman," meaning the Great Mother, the Weaver Woman who weaves "the world tapestry out of genesis and demise" in her cave of power. Yet individual women are imprisoned in, not empowered by, such caves, like Blake's symbolic worms, "Weaving to Dreams the Sexual strife/And weeping over the Web of life."[5] How, therefore, does any woman—but especially a literary woman, who thinks in images—reconcile the cave's negative meta-phoric potential with its positive mythic possibilities? Immobilized and half-blinded in Plato's cave, how does such a woman distinguish what she is from what she sees, her real creative essence from the unreal cutpaper shadows the cavern-master claims as reality?

In a fictionalized "Author's Introduction" to *The Last Man* (1826) Mary Shelley tells another story about a cave, a story which implicitly answers these questions and which, therefore, constitutes yet a third parable of the cave. In 1818, she begins, she and "a friend" visited what was said to be "the gloomy cavern of the Cumaean Sibyl." Entering a mysterious, almost inaccessible chamber, they found "piles of leaves, fragments of bark, and a white filmy substance resembling the inner part of the green hood which shelters the grain of the unripe Indian corn." At first, Shelley confesses, she and her male companion (Percy Shelley) were baffled by this discovery, but "At length, my friend ... exclaimed 'This *is* the Sibyl's cave; these are sibylline leaves!' " Her account continues as follows.

On examination, we found that all the leaves, bark, and other substances were traced with written characters. What appeared to us more astonishing, was that these writings were expressed in various languages: some unknown to my companion . . . some . . . in modern dialects. . . . We could make out little by the dim light, but they seemed to contain prophecies, detailed relations of events but lately passed; names . . . and often exclamations of exultation or woe . . . were traced on their thin scant pages. . . . We made a hasty selection of such of the leaves, whose writing one, at least of us could understand, and then . . . bade adieu to the dim hypaethric cavern. . . . Since that period . . . I have been employed in deciphering these sacred remains. . . . I present the public with my latest discoveries in the slight Sibylline pages. Scattered and unconnected as they were, I have been obliged to . . . model the work into a consistent form. But the main substance rests on the divine intuitions which the Cumaean damsel obtained from heaven.[6]

Every feature of this cave journey is significant, especially for the feminist critic who seeks to understand the meaning not just of male but also of female parables of the cave.

To begin with, the sad fact that not Mary Shelley but her male companion is able to recognize the Sibyl's cave and readily to decipher some of the difficult languages in which the sibylline leaves are written suggests the woman writer's own anxieties about her equivocal position in a patriarchal literary culture which often seems to her to enact strange rituals and speak in unknown tongues. The woman may *be* the cave, but—so Mary Shelley's hesitant response suggests—it is the man who knows the cave, who analyzes its meaning, who (like Plato) authors its primary parables, and who even interprets its language, as Gerard Manley Hopkins, that apostle of aesthetic virility, was to do more than half a century after the publication of *The Last Man*, in his sonnet "Spelt from Sibyl's Leaves."

Yet the cave is a female space and it belonged to a female hierophant, the lost Sibyl, the prophetess who inscribed her "divine intuitions" on tender leaves and fragments of delicate bark. For Mary Shelley, therefore, it is intimately connected with both her own artistic authority and her own power of self-creation. A male poet or instructor may guide her to this place, but, as she herself realizes, she and she alone can effectively reconstruct the scattered truth of the Sibyl's leaves. Literally the daughter of a dead and dishonored mother—the powerful feminist Mary Wollstonecraft—Mary Shelley portrays herself in this parable as figuratively the daughter of the vanished Sybil, the primordial prophetess who mythically conceived all women artists.

That the Sibyl's leaves are now scattered, fragmented, barely comprehensible is thus the central problem Shelley faces in her own art. Earlier in her introduction, she notes that finding the cave was a preliminary problem. She and her companion were misled and misdirected by native guides, she tells us; left alone in one chamber while the guides went for new torches, they "lost" their way in the darkness; ascending in the "wrong" direction, they accidentally stumbled upon the true cave. But the difficulty of this initial discovery merely foreshadows the difficulty of the crucial task of reconstruction, as Shelley shows. For just as the path to the Sibyl's cave has been forgotten, the coherent truth of her leaves has been shattered and scattered, the body of her art dismembered, and, like Anne Finch, she has become a sort of "Cypher," powerless and enigmatic. But while the way to the cave can be "remembered" by accident, the whole meaning of the sibylline leaves can only be re-membered through painstaking labor: translation, transcription, and stitchery, re-vision and re-creation.

The specifically sexual texture of these sibylline documents, these scattered leaves and leavings, adds to their profound importance for women. Working on leaves, bark, and "a white filmy substance," the Sibyl literally wrote, and wrote *upon*, the Book of Nature. She had, in other words, a goddess's power of maternal creativity, the sexual/artistic strength that is the female equivalent of the male potential for literary paternity. In her "dim hypaethric cavern"—a dim sea-cave that was nevertheless *open* to the sky—she received her "divine intuitions" through "an aperture" in the "arched dome-like roof" which "let in the light of heaven." On her "raised seat of stone, about the size of a Grecian couch," she *conceived* her art, inscribing it on leaves and bark from the green world outside. And so fierce are her verses, so truthful her "poetic rhapsodies," that even in deciphering them Shelley exclaims that she feels herself "taken . . . out

of a world, which has averted its once benignant face from me, to
one glowing with imagination and power." For in recovering and
reconstructing the Sibyl's scattered artistic/sexual energy, Shelley
comes to recognize that she is discovering *and creating*   literally
de ciphering—her own creative power. "Sometimes I have thought,"
she modestly confesses, "that, obscure and chaotic as they are, [these
translations from the Sibyl's leaves] owe their present form to me,
their decipherer. As if we should give to another artist, the painted
fragments which form the mosaic copy of Raphael's Transfiguration
in St. Peter's; he would put them together in a form, whose mode
would be fashioned by his own peculiar mind and talent."[7]

Given all these implications and overtones, it seems to us that the
submerged message of Shelley's parable of the cave forms in itself a
fourth parable in the series we have been discussing. This last parable
is the story of the woman artist who enters the cavern of her own
mind and finds there the scattered leaves not only of her own power
but of the tradition which might have generated that power. The
body of her precursor's art, and thus the body of her own art, lies
in pieces around her, dismembered, dis-remembered, disintegrated.
How can she remember it and become a member of it, join it and
rejoin it, integrate it and in doing so achieve her own integrity, her
own selfhood? Surrounded by the ruins of her own tradition, the
leavings and unleavings of her spiritual mother's art, she feels—as
we noted earlier—like someone suffering from amnesia. Not only
did she fail to recognize—that is, to remember—the cavern itself,
she no longer knows its languages, its messages, its forms. With
Christina Rossetti, she wonders once again "Where are the songs I
used to know, / Where are the notes I used to sing?" Bewildered by
the incoherence of the fragments she confronts, she cannot help
deciding that "I have forgotten everything / I used to know so long
ago."

But it is possible, as Mary Shelley's introduction tells us, for the
woman poet to reconstruct the shattered tradition that is her matrilineal heritage. Her trip into the cavern of her own mind, despite
(or perhaps because of) its falls in darkness, its stumblings, its anxious
wanderings, begins the process of re-membering. Even her dialogue
with the Romantic poet who guides her (in Mary Shelley's version
of the parable) proves useful, for, as Northrop Frye has argued, a

revolutionary "mother-goddess myth" which allows power and dignity to women—a myth which is anti-hierarchical, a myth which would liberate the energy of all living creatures—"gained ground" in the Romantic period.[8] Finally, the sibylline messages themselves speak to her, and in speaking to her they both enable her to speak for herself and empower her to speak for the Sibyl. Going "down to the woman" of Fate whom Helen Diner describes, the woman writer recovers herself as a woman of art. Thus, where the traditional male hero makes his "night sea journey" to the center of the earth, the bottom of the mere, the belly of the whale, to slay or be slain by the dragons of darkness, the female artist makes her journey into what Adrienne Rich has called "the cratered night of female memory" to revitalize the darkness, to retrieve what has been lost, to regenerate, reconceive, and give birth.[9]

What she gives birth to is in a sense her own mother goddess and her own mother land. In this parable of the cave it is not the male god Osiris who has been torn apart but his sister, Isis, who has been dismembered and destroyed. Similarly, it is not the male poet Orpheus whose catastrophe we are confronting but his lost bride, Eurydice, whom we find abandoned in the labyrinthine caverns of Hades. Or to put the point another way, this parable suggests that (as the poet H. D. knew) the traditional figure of Isis in search of Osiris is really a figure of Isis in search of herself, and the betrayed Eurydice is really (like Virginia Woolf's "Judith Shakespeare") the woman poet who never arose from the prison of her "grave cave." Reconstructing Isis and Eurydice, then, the woman artist redefines and recovers the lost Atlantis of her literary heritage, the sunken continent whose wholeness once encompassed and explained all those figures on the horizon who now seem "odd," fragmentary, incomplete—the novelists historians call "singular anomalies," the poets critics call "poetesses," the revolutionary artists patriarchal poets see as "unsexed," monstrous, grotesque. Remembered by the community of which they are and were members, such figures gain their full authority, and their visions begin to seem like conceptions as powerful as the Sibyl's were. Emily Brontë's passionate A. G. A., Jane Lead's Sophia, H. D.'s *bona dea* all have a place in this risen Atlantis which is their mother country, and Jane Eyre's friendship for Diana and Mary Rivers, Aurora Leigh's love of her Italian mother land together with her dream of a new Jerusalem, Emily Dickinson's "mystic green" where women "live aloud," and George Eliot's concept of sisterhood—all these visions and re-visions help define the utopian boundaries of the resurrected continent.

That women have translated their yearnings for motherly or sisterly precursors into visions of such a land is as clear as it is certain that this metaphoric land, like the Sibyl's leaves and the woman writer's power, has been shattered and scattered. Emily Dickinson, a woman artist whose own carefully sewn together "packets" of poetry were—ironically enough—to be fragmented by male editors and female heirs, projected her yearning for this lost female home into the figure of a caged (and female) leopard. Her visionary nostalgia demonstrates that at times the memory of this Atlantis could be as painful for women writers as amnesia about it often was. "Civilization—spurns—the Leopard!" she noted, commenting that "Deserts—never rebuked her Satin—. . . [for] This was the Leopard's nature—Signor—/Need—a keeper—frown?" and adding, poignantly, that we should

> Pity—the Pard—that left her Asia—
> Memories—of Palm—
> Cannot be stifled—with Narcotic—
> Nor suppressed—with Balm—[10]

Similarly, though she was ostensibly using the symbolism of traditional religion, Christina Rossetti described her pained yearning for a lost, visionary continent like Dickinson's "Asia" in a poem whose title—"Mother Country"—openly acknowledges the real subject:

> Oh what is that country
>   And where can it be
> Not mine own country,
>   But dearer far to me?
>
> Yet mine own country,
>   If I one day may see
> Its spices and cedars,
>   Its gold and ivory.
>
> As I lie dreaming
>   It rises, that land;

> There rises before me
>   Its green golden strand,
> With the bowing cedars
>   And the shining sand;
> It sparkles and flashes
>   Like a shaken brand.[11]

The ambiguities with which Rossetti describes her own relationship to this land ("Not mine own . . . But dearer far") reflect the uncertainty of the self-definition upon which her vision depends. Is a woman's *mother* country her "own"? Has Mary Shelley a "right" to the Sibyl's leaves? Through what structure of definitions and qualifications can the female artist claim her matrilineal heritage, her birthright of that power which, as Annie Gottlieb's dream asserted, is important to her *because of* her mother? Despite these implicit questions, Rossetti admits that "As I lie dreaming / It rises that land"—rises, significantly, glittering and flashing "like a shaken brand," rises from "the cratered night of female memory," setting fire to the darkness, dispersing the shadows of the cavern, destroying the archaic structures which enclosed it in silence and gloom.

There is a sense in which, for us, this book is a dream of the rising of Christina Rossetti's "mother country." And there is a sense in which it is an attempt at reconstructing the Sibyl's leaves, leaves which haunt us with the possibility that if we can piece together their fragments the parts will form a whole that tells the story of the career of a single woman artist, a "mother of us all," as Gertrude Stein would put it, a woman whom patriarchal poetics dismembered and whom we have tried to remember. Detached from herself, silenced, subdued, this woman artist tried in the beginning, as we shall see, to write like an angel in the house of fiction: with Jane Austen and Maria Edgeworth, she concealed her own truth behind a decorous and ladylike facade, scattering her real wishes to the winds or translating them into incomprehensible hieroglyphics. But as time passed and her cave-prison became more constricted, more claustrophobic, she "fell" into the gothic/Satanic mode and, with the Brontës and Mary Shelley, she planned mad or monstrous escapes, then dizzily withdrew—with George Eliot and Emily Dickinson—from those open spaces where the scorching presence of the

patriarchal sun, whom Dickinson called "the man of noon," emphasized her vulnerability. Since "Creation seemed a mighty Crack" to
make her "visible," she took refuge again in the safety of the "dim
hypaethric cavern" where she could be alone with herself, with a
truth that was hers even in its fragmentation.[12]

Yet through all these stages of her history this mythic woman artist
dreamed, like her sibylline ancestress, of a visionary future, a utopian
land in which she could be whole and energetic. As tense with
longing as the giant "korl woman," a metal sculpture the man named
Wolfe carves from flesh-colored pig "refuse" in Rebecca Harding
Davis's *Life in the Iron Mills*, she turned with a "wild, eager face,"
with "the mad, half-despairing gesture of drowning," toward her
half-conscious imagination of that future. Eventually she was to
realize, with Adrienne Rich, that she was "reading the Parable of
the Cave / while living in the cave"; with Sylvia Plath she was to
decide that "I am a miner" surrounded by "tears / The earthen
womb / Exudes from its dead boredom"; and like Plath she was to
hang her cave "with roses," transfiguring it—as the Sibyl did—with
artful foliage.[13] But her vision of self-creation was consistently the
same vision of connection and resurrection. Like the rebirth of the
drowned Atlantans in Ursula Le Guin's utopian "The New Atlantis,"
this vision often began with an awakening in darkness, a dim awareness of "the whispering thunder from below," and a sense that even
if "we could not answer, we knew because we heard, because we
felt, because we wept, we knew that we were; and we remembered
other voices."[14] Like Mary Shelley's piecing together of the Sibyl's
leaves, the vision often entailed a subversive transfiguration of those
female arts to which de Beauvoir's cave-dwelling seamstresses were
condemned into the powerful arts of the underground Weaver
Woman, who uses her magical loom to weave a distinctively female
"Tapestr[y] of Paradise."[15] And the fact that the cave is and was
a place where such visions were possible is itself a sign of the power
of the cave and a crucial message of the parable of the cave, a message
to remind us that the cave is not just the place from which the past
is retrieved but the place where the future is conceived, the "earthen
womb"—or, as in Willa Cather's *My Antonia*, the "fruit cave"—from
which the new land rises.[16]

Elizabeth Barrett Browning expressed this final point for the later nineteenth century, as if to carry Mary Shelley's allegorical narrative one step further. Describing a utopian island paradise in which all creatures are "glad and safe. . . . No guns nor springs in my dream," she populated this peaceful land with visionary poets who have withdrawn to a life in dim sea caves—"I repair / To live within the caves: / And near me two or three may dwell, / Whom dreams fantastic please as well," she wrote, and then described her paradise more specifically:

> Long winding caverns, glittering far
>   Into a crystal distance!
> Through clefts of which, shall many a star
>   Shine clear without resistance!
> And carry down its rays the smell
> Of flowers above invisible.[17]

Here, she declared, her poets—implicitly female or at least matriarchal rather than patriarchal, worshipers of the Romantic mother goddess Frye describes—would create their own literary tradition through a re-vision of the high themes their famous "masculinist" counterparts had celebrated.

> . . . often, by the joy without
>   And in us overcome,
> We, through our musing, shall let float
>   Such poems—sitting dumb—
> As Pindar might have writ if he
>   Had tended sheep in Arcady;
> Or Aeschylus—the pleasant fields
>   He died in, longer knowing;
> Or Homer, had men's sins and shields
>   Been lost in Meles flowing;
> Or poet Plato, had the undim
> Unsetting Godlight broke on him.

Poet Plato revised by a shining woman of noon, a magical woman like Jane Lead's "Eternal Virgin-Wisdom," with "her Face as the terrible Crystal for brightness!" In a sense that re-vision is the major subject of our book, just as it was the theme of Barrett Browning's earnest, female prayer:

> Choose me the cave most worthy choice,
>   To make a place for prayer,
> And I will choose a praying voice
>   To pour our spirits there.

And the answer to Barrett Browning's prayer might have been given by the sibylline voice of Jane Lead's Virgin-Wisdom, or Sophia, the true goddess of the cave: "for out of my Womb thou shalt be brought forth after the manner of a Spirit, Conceived and Born again."

II
Inside the House of Fiction: Jane Austen's Tenants of Possibility

4

Shut Up in Prose:
Gender and Genre in Austen's
Juvenilia

"Run mad as often as you chuse; but do not faint—"
—Sophia to Laura, *Love and Freindship*

They shut me up in Prose—
As when a little Girl
They put me in the Closet—
Because they liked me "still"—
—Emily Dickinson

Can you be more confusing by laughing. Do say yes.
We are extra. We have the reasonableness of a
woman and we say we do not like a room. We wish
we were married.

—Gertrude Stein

She is twelve years old and already her story is written in the heavens.
She will discover it day after day without ever making it; she is
curious but frightened when she contemplates this life, every stage
of which is foreseen and toward which every day moves irresistibly.
—Simone de Beauvoir

Not a few of Jane Austen's personal acquaintances might have echoed
Sir Samuel Egerton Brydges, who noticed that "she was fair and
handsome, slight and elegant, but with cheeks a little too full," while
"never suspect[ing] she was an authoress."[1] For this novelist whose
personal obscurity was more complete than that of any other famous
writer was always quick to insist either on complete anonymity or on
the propriety of her limited craft, her delight in delineating just "3
or 4 Families in a Country Village."[2] With her self-deprecatory remarks about her inability to join "strong manly, spirited sketches,
full of Variety and Glow" with her "little bit (two Inches wide) of

Ivory,"[3] Jane Austen perpetuated the belief among her friends that
her art was just an accomplishment "by a lady," if anything "rather
too light and bright and sparkling."[4] In this respect she resembled
one of her favorite contemporaries, Mary Brunton, who would rather
have "glid[ed] through the world unknown" than been "suspected
of literary airs—to be shunned, as literary women are, by the more
pretending of their own sex, and abhorred, as literary women are,
by the more pretending of the other!—my dear, I would sooner
exhibit as a ropedancer."[5]

Yet, decorous though they might first seem, Austen's self-effacing
anonymity and her modest description of her miniaturist art also
imply a criticism, even a rejection, of the world at large. For, as
Gaston Bachelard explains, the miniature "allows us to be world
conscious at slight risk."[6] While the creators of satirically conceived
diminutive landscapes seem to see everything as small because they
are themselves so grand, Austen's analogy for her art—her "little
bit (two Inches wide) of Ivory"—suggests a fragility that reminds
us of the risk and instability outside the fictional space. Besides seeing
her art metaphorically, as her critics would too, in relation to female
arts severely devalued until quite recently[7] (for painting on ivory was
traditionally a "ladylike" occupation), Austen attempted through
self-imposed novelistic limitations to define a secure place, even as
she seemed to admit the impossibility of actually inhabiting such a
small space with any degree of comfort. And always, for Austen, it
is women—because they are too vulnerable in the world at large—
who must acquiesce in their own confinement, no matter how stifling
it may be.

But it is precisely to the limits of her art that Austen's most vocal
critics have always responded, with both praise and blame. The tone
is set by the curiously backhanded compliments of Sir Walter Scott,
who compares her novels to "cornfields and cottages and meadows,"
as opposed to "highly adorned grounds" or "the rugged sublimities
of a mountain landscape." The pleasure of such fiction is, he explains,
such that "the youthful wanderer may return from his promenade
to the ordinary business of life, without any chance of having his
head turned by the recollection of the scene through which he has
been wandering."[8] In other words, the novels are so unassuming that
they can be easily forgotten. Mundane (like cornfields) and small

(like cottages) and tame (like meadows), they wear the "common-place face" Charlotte Brontë found in *Pride and Prejudice*, a novel Brontë scornfully describes as "a carefully fenced, highly cultivated garden, with neat borders and delicate flowers; but no glance of a bright, vivid physiognomy, no open country, no fresh air, no blue hill, no bonny beck." [9]

Spatial images of boundary and enclosure seem to proliferate when-ever we find writers coming to terms with Jane Austen, as if they were displaying their own anxieties about what she represents. Edward Fitzgerald's comment—"She is capital as far as she goes: but she never goes out of the Parlour"—is a classic in this respect, as is Elizabeth Barrett Browning's breezy characterization of the novels as "perfect as far as they go—that's certain. Only they don't go far, I think." [10] It is hardly surprising that Emerson is "at a loss to understand why people hold Miss Austen's novels at so high a rate," horrified as he is by what he considers the trivializing domes-ticity and diminution of her fiction:

> ... vulgar in tone, sterile in artistic invention, imprisoned in the wretched conventions of English society, without genius, wit, or knowledge of the world. Never was life so pinched and narrow. The one problem in the mind of the writer in both the stories I have read, *Persuasion*, and *Pride and Prejudice*, is marriage-ableness. All that interests in any character introduced is still this one, Has he or (she) the money to marry with, and conditions, conforming? 'Tis "the nympholepsy of a fond despair," say, rather, of an English boarding-house. Suicide is more respect-able. [11]

But the conventionally masculine judgment of Austen's triviality is probably best illustrated by Mark Twain, who cannot even bring himself to spell her name correctly in a letter to Howells, her staunch-est American defender: Poe's "prose," he notes, "is unreadable—like Jane Austin's," adding that there is one difference: "I could read his prose on salary, but not Jane's. Jane is entirely impossible. It seems a great pity that they allowed her to die a natural death." [12] Certainly D. H. Lawrence expresses similar hostility for the lady writer in his attack on Austen as "this old maid" who "typifies 'personality' instead of character, the sharp knowing in apartness instead of knowing in togetherness, and she is, to my feeling, thoroughly unpleasant, English in the bad, mean, snobbish sense of the word."[13]

Repeatedly, in other words, Austen was placed in the double bind she would so convincingly dramatize in her novels, for when not rejected as artificial and convention-bound, she was condemned as natural and therefore a writer almost in spite of herself. Imagining her as "the brown thrush who tells his story from the garden bough," Henry James describes Austen's "light felicity," her "extraordinary grace," as a sign of "her unconsciousness":

> ... as if ... she sometimes, over her work basket, her tapestry flowers, in the spare, cool drawing-room of other days, fell a-musing, lapsed too metaphorically, as one may say, into wool gathering, and her dropped stitches, of these pardonable, of these precious moments, were afterwards picked up as little touches of human truth, little glimpses of steady vision, little master-strokes of imagination.[14]

A stereotypical "lady" author, Austen is here diminished into a small personage whose domestic productions result in artistic creation not through the exacting craft by which the male author weaves the intricate figures in his own carpets, but through fortuitous forgetfulness on the part of the lady (who drops her stitches unthinkingly) and through the presumably male critical establishment that picks them up afterwards to view them as charming miniatures of imaginative activity. The entire passage radiates James's anxiety at his own indebtedness to this "little" female precursor who, to his embarrassment, taught him so much of his presumably masterful art. Indeed, in a story that examines Austen's curious effect on men and her usefulness in male culture, Rudyard Kipling has one of his more pugnacious characters insist that Jane Austen "did leave lawful issue in the shape o' one son; an' 'is name was 'Enery James."[15]

In "The Janeites" Kipling presents several veterans from World War I listening to a shell-shocked ex-Garrison Artillery man, Humberstall, recount his experiences on the Somme Front, where he had unexpectedly discovered a secret unit of Austen fans who call themselves the Society of the Janeites. Despite the seeming discrepancy between Austen's decorously "feminine" parlor and the violent, "masculine" war, the officers analyze the significance of their restricting ranks and roles much as Austen analyzes the meaning of her characters' limiting social positions. Not only does Humberstall discover that Austen's characters are "only just like people you'd run across any day," he also knows that "They're all on the make, in a quiet way, in Jane." He is not surprised, therefore, when the whole company is blown to pieces by one man's addlepated adherence to a code: as his naming of the guns after Austen's "heavies" demonstrates, the ego that creates all the problems for her characters is the same ego that shoots Kipling's guns. Paradoxically, moreover, the firings of "General Tilney" and "The Lady Catherine de Bugg" also seem to point our attention to the explosive anger behind the decorous surfaces of Austen's novels, although the men in the trenches find in the Austen guns the symbol of what they think they are fighting for.

Using Austen the same way American servicemen might have exploited pin-up girls, the Society of Janeites transforms their heroine into a nostalgic symbol of order, culture, England, in an apocalyptic world where all the old gods have failed or disappeared. But Austen is adapted when adopted for use by masculine society, and she functions to perpetrate the male bonding and violence she would herself have deplored. Clearly Kipling is involved in ridiculing the formation of religious sects or cults, specifically the historical Janeites who sanctified Austen into the apotheosis of propriety and elegance, of what Ann Douglas has called in a somewhat different context the "feminization" of culture. But Kipling implies that so-called feminization is a male-dominated process inflicted upon women. And in this respect he illustrates how Austen has herself become a victim of the fictionalizing process we will see her acknowledging as women's basic problem in her own fiction.

Not only a parody of what male culture has made of the cult of Jane, however, "The Janeites" is also a tribute to Austen, who justifies her deification as the patron saint of the officers by furnishing Humberstall with what turns out to be a password that literally saves his life by getting him a place on a hospital train. By pronouncing the name "Miss Bates," Humberstall miraculously survives circumstances as inauspicious as those endured by Miss Bates herself, a spinster in *Emma* whose physical, economic, and social confinement is only mitigated by her good humor. Certainly Humberstall's special fondness for *Persuasion*—which celebrates Captain Harville's "ingenious contrivances and nice arrangements . . . to turn the actual space to the best possible account"[16]—is not unrelated to his appreciation of Austen herself: "There's no one to touch Jane when you're in a tight place." From Austen, then, Humberstall and his companions have gained not only an analysis of social conventions that helps make sense of their own constricted lives, but also an example of how to inhabit a small space with grace and intelligence.

It is eminently appropriate that the Army Janeites try to survive by making the best of a bad situation, accepting their tight place and digging in behind the camouflage-screens they have constructed around their trenches. While their position is finally given away, their attitude is worthy of the writer who concerns herself almost exclusively with characters inhabiting the common sitting room. Critical disparagement of the triviality of this place is related to values that find war or business somehow qualitatively more "real" or "significant" than, for example, the politics of the family.[17] But critics who patronize or castigate Austen for her acceptance of limits and boundaries are overlooking a subversive strain in even her earliest stories: Austen's courageous "grace under pressure" is not only a refuge from a dangerous reality, it is also a comment on it, as W. H. Auden implied:

> You could not shock her more than she shocks me;
>> Beside her Joyce seems innocent as grass.
> It makes me most uncomfortable to see
>> An English spinster of the middle class
>> Describe the amorous effects of "brass,"
> Reveal so frankly and with such sobriety
> The economic basis of society.[18]

Although she has become a symbol of culture, it *is* shocking how persistently Austen demonstrates her discomfort with her cultural inheritance, specifically her dissatisfaction with the tight place assigned women in patriarchy and her analysis of the economics of sexual exploitation. At the same time, however, she knows from the beginning of her career that there is no other place for her but a tight one, and her parodic strategy is itself a testimony to her struggle with inadequate but inescapable structures. If, like Scott and Brontë,

Emerson and James, we continue to see her world as narrow or trivial, perhaps we can learn from Humberstall that "there's no one to touch Jane when you're in a tight place." Since this tight place is both literary and social, we will begin with the parodic juvenilia and then consider "the amorous effects of 'brass'" in *Northanger Abbey* to trace how and why Austen is centrally concerned with the impossibility of women escaping the conventions and categories that, in every sense, belittle them.

Jane Austen has always been famous for fireside scenes in which several characters comfortably and quietly discuss options so seemingly trivial that it is astonishing when they are transformed into important ethical dilemmas. There is always a feeling, too, that we owe to her narrator's art the significance with which such scenes are invested: she seemed to know about the burdens of banality and the resulting pressure to subject even the smallest gestures to close analysis. A family in *Love and Freindship* (1790) sit by the fireplace in their "cot" when they hear a knock on the door:

> My Father started—"What noise is that," (said he.) "It sounds like a loud rapping at the door"—(replied my Mother.) "it does indeed." (cried I.) "I am of your opinion; (said my Father) it certainly does appear to proceed from some uncommon violence exerted against our unoffending door." "Yes (exclaimed I) I cannot help thinking it must be somebody who knocks for admittance."
>
> "That is another point (replied he;) We must not pretend to determine on what motive the person may knock—tho' that someone *does* rap at the door, I am partly convinced." [19]

Clearly this discursive speculation on the knocking at the door ridicules the propensity of sentimental novelists to record even the most exasperatingly trivial events, but it simultaneously demonstrates the common female ennui at having to maintain polite conversation while waiting for a prince to come. In other words, such juvenilia is important not only because in this early work Austen ridicules the false literary conventions that debase expression, thereby dangerously falsifying expectations, especially for female readers, but also because she reveals here her awareness that such conventions have inalterably shaped women's lives. For Jane Austen's parody of extravagant literary conventions turns on the culture that makes women continually vulnerable to such fantasies.

Laura of *Love and Freindship* is understandably frustrated by the banal confinement of the fireside scene. "Alas," she laments, "how am I to avoid those evils I shall never be exposed to?" Because she is allowed to pursue those evils with indecorous abandon, *Love and Freindship* is a good place to begin to understand attitudes more fully dramatized there than elsewhere in Austen's fiction. With a singular lack of the "infallible discretion"[20] for which it would later become famous, Austen's adolescent fiction includes a larger "slice of life" than we might at first expect: thievery and drunkenness, matricide and patricide, adultery and madness are common subjects. Moreover, the parodic melodrama of this fiction unfolds through hectic geographical maneuverings, particularly through female escapes and escapades quite unlike those that appear in the mature novels.

Laura, for instance, elopes with a stranger upon whom, she immediately decides, the happiness or misery of her future life depends. From her humble cottage in the vale of Uske, she travels to visit Edward's aunt in Middlesex, but she must leave immediately after Edward boasts to his father of his pride in provoking that parent's displeasure by marrying without his consent. Running off in Edward's father's carriage, the happy couple meet up with Sophia and Augustus at "M," but they are forced to remove themselves quickly when Augustus is arrested for having "gracefully purloined" his father's money. Alone in the world, after taking turns fainting on the sofa, the two girls set out for London but end up in Scotland, where they successfully encourage a young female relative to elope to Gretna Green. Thrown out in punishment for this bad advice, Laura and Sophia meet up with their dying husbands, naturally in a phaeton crash. Sophia is fittingly taken off by a galloping consumption, while Laura proceeds by a stagecoach in which she is reunited with her husband's long-lost family who have been traveling back and forth from Sterling to Edinburgh for reasons that are far too complicated and ridiculous to relate here.

Of course her contrivance of such a zany picaresque does not contradict Austen's later insistence on the limits of her artistic province, since the point of her parody is precisely to illustrate the dangerous delusiveness of fiction which seriously presents heroines like Laura (and stories like *Love and Freindship*) as models of reality. While ridiculing ludicrous literary conventions, Austen also implies that romantic stories create absurd misconceptions. Such novelistic clichés as love at first sight, the primacy of passion over all other emotions and/ or duties, the chivalric exploits of the hero, the vulnerable sensitivity of the heroine, the lovers' proclaimed indifference to financial considerations, and the cruel crudity of parents are all shown to be at best improbable; at worst they are shown to provide manipulative roles and hypocritical jargon which mask materialistic and libidinal egoism.

Living lives regulated by the rules provided by popular fiction, these characters prove only how very bankrupt that fiction is. For while Laura and Sophia proclaim their delicate feelings, tender sentiments, and refined sensibilities, they are in fact having a delightful time gratifying their desires at the expense of everyone else's. Austen's critique of the ethical effects of such literature is matched by her insistence on its basic falsity: adventure, intrigue, crime, passion, and death arrive with such intensity, in such abundance, and with such rapidity that they lose all reality. Surely they are just the hectic daydreams of an imagination infected by too many Emmelines and Emilias.[21] The extensive itinerary of a heroine like Laura is the most dramatic clue that her story is mere wish-fulfillment, one especially attractive to women who live at home confined to the domestic sphere, as do such heroines of Austen's nonparodic juvenilia as Emma Watson of *The Watsons* and Catharine of the early fiction "Catharine."

Significantly, however, Emma Watson and Catharine are both avid readers of romance, just as Austen herself was clearly one of those young women whose imagination had, in fact, been inalterably affected by all the escapist literature provided them, then as now. Not the least of the curious effects of *Love and Freindship* results from the contradiction between the narrator's insistent ridicule of her heroines and their liveliness, their general willingness to get on with it and catch the next coach. Laura and Sophia are really quite attractive in their exuberant assertiveness, their exploration and exploitation of the world, their curiously honest expression of their needs, their rebellious rejection of their fathers' advice, their demands for autonomy, their sense of the significance and drama of their lives and adventures, their gullible delight in playing out the plots they have admired. The girls' rebellion against familial restraints seems to have so fascinated Austen that she reiterates it almost obsessively in *Love and Freindship*, and again in a hilarious letter when she takes on the persona of an anonymous female correspondent who cheerfully explains, "I murdered my Father at a very early period of my Life, I have since murdered my Mother, and I am now going to murder my Sister."[22] The matricides and patricides make such characters seem much more exuberantly alive than their sensible, slow-witted, dying parents. It is this covert counterpoint that makes suspicious the overt "moral" of *Love and Freindship*, suggesting that though Austen appears to be operating in a repressive tradition, many of her generic moral signals are merely convenient camouflage.

At first glance, Sophia and Laura seem related to a common type in eighteenth-century literature. Like Biddy Tipkins of Steele's *The Tender Husband*, Coleman's *Polly Honeycombe*, and Lydia Languish of Sheridan's *The Rivals*, for instance, these girls are filled with outlandish fancies derived from their readings in the circulating library. Illustrating the dangers of feminine lawlessness and the necessity of female submission, female quixotes of eighteenth-century fiction typically exemplify the evils of romantic fiction and female assertion. The abundance of such heroines in her juvenilia would seem to place Austen in precisely the tradition Ellen Moers has recently explored, that of the educating heroine who preaches the necessity of dutiful restraint to female readers, cautioning them especially against the snares of romance. But Austen did not admire the prototypical Madame de Genlis; she was "disgusted" with her brand of didacticism[23] and with the evangelic fervor of novelists who considered themselves primarily moralists.[24]

Far from modeling herself on conservative conduct writers like Hannah Moore or Dr. Gregory or Mrs. Chapone,[25] Austen repeatedly demonstrates her alienation from the aggressively patriarchal tradition that constitutes her Augustan inheritance, as well as her agreement with Mary Wollstonecraft that these authors helped "render women more artificial, weak characters, than they would otherwise have been."[26] A writer who could parody *An Essay on Man* to read

"*Ride where you may*, Be Candid where you can" [italics ours] is not about to vindicate the ways of God to man.[27] Nor is she about to justify the ways of Pope to women. One suspects that Austen, like Marianne Dashwood, appreciates Pope no more than is proper.[28] Even Dr. Johnson, whom she obviously does value, has his oracular rhetorical style parodied, first in the empty abstractions and antitheses that abound in the juvenilia,[29] and later in the mouth of *Pride and Prejudice's* Mary Bennet, a girl who prides herself on pompous platitudes. Finally, Austen attacks *The Spectator* repeatedly, at least in part for its condescension toward female readers. The Regency, as well as her own private perspective as a woman, inalterably separates Austen from the Augustan context in which she is so frequently placed. Like her most mature heroine, Anne Elliot of *Persuasion*, she sometimes advised young readers to reflect on the wisdom of essayists who sought to "rouse and fortify the mind by the highest precepts, and the strongest examples of moral and religious endurance," but she too is "eloquent on a point in which her own conduct would ill bear examination" (*P*, I, chap. 11).

If Austen rejects the romantic traditions of her culture in a parody like *Love and Freindship*, she does so not by way of the attack on feminine flightiness so common in conduct literature, or, at least, she uses this motif to mask a somewhat different point. *Love and Freindship* is the first hint of the depth of her alienation from her culture, especially as that culture defined and circumscribed women. Far from being the usual appeal for female sobriety and submission to domestic restraints so common in anti-romantic eighteenth-century literature, *Love and Freindship* attacks a society that trivializes female assertion by channeling it into the most ridiculous and unproductive forms of behavior. With nothing to do in the world, Sophia and Laura become addicts of feeling. Like all the other heroines of Austen's parodic juvenilia, they make an identity out of passivity, as if foreshadowing the bored girls described by Simone de Beauvoir, who "give themselves up to gloomy and romantic daydreams":

> Neglected, "misunderstood," they seek consolation in narcissistic fancies: they view themselves as romantic heroines of fiction, with self-admiration and self-pity. Quite naturally they become coquettish and stagy, these defects becoming more conspicuous

at puberty. Their malaise shows itself in impatience, tantrums, tears; they enjoy crying—a taste that many women retain in later years—largely because they like to play the part of victims. , , Little girls sometimes watch themselves cry in a mirror, to double the pleasure.[30]

Sophia and Laura do make a cult of passivity, fainting and languishing dramatically on sofas, defining their virtues and beauty in terms of their physical weakness and their susceptibility to overwhelming passions.

In this way, and more overtly by constantly scrutinizing their own physical perfections, they dramatize de Beauvoir's point that women, in typical victim fashion, become narcissistic out of their fear of facing reality. And because they pride themselves not only on their frailty but also on those very "accomplishments" that insure it, their narcissism is inextricably linked to masochism, for they have been successfully socialized into believing that their subordinate status in society is precisely the fulfillment they crave. Austen is very clear on the reasons for their obsessive fancies: Sophia and Laura are the victims of what Karen Horney has recently identified as the "overvaluation of love" and in this respect, according to Austen, they typify their sex.[31] Encouraged to know and care only about the love of men, Laura and Sophia are compulsive and indiscriminate in satisfying their insatiable need for being loved, while they are themselves incapable of authentic feeling. They would and do go to any lengths to "catch" men, but they must feign ignorance, modesty, and indifference to amatory passion. Austen shows how popular romantic fiction contributes to the traditional notion that women have no other legitimate aim but to love men and how this assumption is at the root of "female" narcissism, masochism, and deceit. She could hardly have set out to create a more heretical challenge to societal definitions of the feminine.

Furthermore, *Love and Freindship* displays Austen's concern with the rhetorical effect of fiction, not in terms of the moral issues raised by Dr. Johnson in his influential essay "On Fiction," but in terms of the psychological destruction such extravagant role models and illusory plots can wreak. De Beauvoir writes of "stagy" girls who "view themselves as romantic heroines of fiction"; and at least one of the reasons Laura and Sophia seem so grotesque is that they are living out predetermined plots: as readers who have accepted, even embraced, their status as characters, they epitomize the ways in which women have been tempted to forfeit interiority and the freedom of self-definition for literary roles. For if, as we might infer from Kipling, Austen herself was destined to become a sanctified symbol, her characters are no less circumscribed by fictional stereotypes and plots that seem to transform them into manic puppets. Like Anne Elliot, who explains that she will "not allow books to prove anything" because "men have had every advantage of us in telling their own story," Austen retains her suspicions about the effect of literary images of both sexes, and she repeatedly resorts to parodic strategies to discredit such images, deconstructing, for example, Richardson's influential ideas of heroism and heroinism.

Refusing to appreciate such angelic paragons as Clarissa or Pamela, Austen criticizes the morally pernicious equation of female virtue with passivity, or masculinity with aggression. From *Lady Susan* to *Sanditon*, she rejects stories in which women simply defend their virtue against male sexual advances. Most of her heroines resemble Charlotte Heywood, who picks up a copy of *Camilla* only to put it down again because "She had not *Camilla's* Youth, & had no intention of having her Distress."[32] Similarly, Austen criticizes the Richardsonian rake by implying that sentimental fiction legitimizes the role of the seducer-rapist, thereby encouraging men to act out their most predatory impulses. Sir Edward of *Sanditon* is only the last of the false suitors who models himself on Lovelace, his life's primary objective being seduction. For Austen, the libertine is a relative of the Byronic hero, and she is quite sure that his dangerous attractions are best defused through ridicule: "I have read the *Corsair*, mended my petticoat, & have nothing else to do," she writes in a letter that probably best illustrates the technique.[33] Because she realizes that writers like Richardson and Byron have truthfully represented the power struggle between the sexes, however, she does seek a way of telling their story without perpetuating it. In each of her novels, a seduced-and-abandoned plot is embedded in the form of an interpolated tale told to the heroine as a monitory image of her own more problematic story.

For all her ladylike discretion, then, Austen is rigorous in her revolt against the conventions she inherited. But she expresses her dissent under the cover of parodic strategies that had been legitimized by the most conservative writers of her time and that therefore were then (and remain now) radically ambiguous. Informing her recurrent use of parody is her belief that the inherited literary structures which are not directly degrading to her sex are patently irrelevant. Therefore, when she begins *Sense and Sensibility* with a retelling of *King Lear*, her reversals imply that male traditions need to be evaluated and reinterpreted from a female perspective: instead of the evil daughter castrating the old king by whittling away at his retinue of knights ("what need one?"), Austen represents the male heir and his wife persuading themselves to cheat their already unjustly deprived sisters of a rightful share of the patrimony ("Altogether, they will have five hundred a-year amongst them, and what on earth can four women want for more than that?" [*SS*, I, chap. 2]). When Maria Bertram echoes the caged bird of Sterne's *A Sentimental Journey*, complaining that the locked gates of her future husband's grounds are too confining—"I cannot get out, as the starling said"[34]—she reflects on the dangers of the romantic celebration of personal liberty and self-expression for women who will be severely punished if they insist on getting out.

Whether here, or in her parodies of Fanny Burney and Sir Samuel Egerton Brydges in *Pride and Prejudice*, Austen dramatizes how damaging it has been for women to inhabit a culture created by and for men, confirming perhaps more than any of her sisterly successors the truth of Mary Ellmann's contention that

> for women writers, as for Negro, what others have said bears down on whatever they can say themselves. Both are like people looking for their own bodies under razed buildings, having to clear away debris. In their every effort to formulate a new point of view, one feels the refutation of previous points of view—a weight which must impede spontaneity.[35]

Austen demystifies the literature she has read neither because she believes it misrepresents reality, as Mary Lascelles argues, nor out of obsessive fear of emotional contact, as Marvin Mudrick claims, nor because she is writing Tory propaganda against the Jacobins, as Marilyn Butler speculates,[36] but because she seeks to illustrate how such fictions are the alien creations of writers who contribute to the enfeebling of women.

But though Ellmann's image is generally helpful for an understanding of the female artist, in Austen's case it is a simplification. Austen's culture is not a destroyed rubble around her corpse. On the contrary, it is a healthy and powerful architecture which she must learn to inhabit. Far from looking under razed buildings or (even more radically) razing buildings herself, Austen admits the limits and discomforts of the paternal roof, but learns to live beneath it. As we have seen, however, she begins by laughing at its construction, pointing out exactly how much of that construction actually depends on the subjugation of women. If she wishes to be an architect herself, however, she needs to make use of the only available building materials—the language and genres, conventions and stereotypes at her disposal. She does not reject these, she reinvents them. For one thing, she has herself admired and enjoyed the literature of such sister novelists as Maria Edgeworth, Mrs. Radcliffe, Charlotte Lennox, Mary Brunton, and Fanny Burney. For another, as we have seen, regardless of how damaging they have been, the conventions of romantic fiction have been internalized by the women of her culture and so they do describe the psychology of growing up female. Finally, these are the only available stories she has. Austen makes a virtue of her own confinement, as her heroines will do also. By exploiting the very conventions she exposes as inadequate, she demonstrates the power of patriarchy as well as the ambivalence and confinement of the female writer. She also discovers an effective subterfuge for a severe critique of her culture. For even as she dramatizes her own alienation from a society she cannot evade or transcend, she subverts the conventions of popular fiction to describe the lonely vulnerability of girls whose lives, if more mundane, are just as thwarted as those they read about so obsessively. For all their hilarious exaggeration, then, the incidents and characters of the juvenilia reappear in the later novels, where they portray the bewilderment of heroines whose guides are as inadequate as the author's in her search for a way of telling their story.

Just as Laura languishes in the Vale of Uske at the beginning of *Love and Freindship*, for example, the later heroines are confined to homes noteworthy for their suffocating atmosphere. The heroine of "Catharine" is limited to the company of an aunt who fears that all contact with society will engage the girl's heart imprudently. Living in her aunt's inexorably ordered house, Catharine has nothing to do but retreat to a romantically constructed bower, a place of adolescent illusions. Boredom is also a major affliction for Catherine Morland and Charlotte Heywood, who are involved in the drudgery of educating younger siblings in secluded areas offering few potential friends, as it is for the seemingly more privileged Emma, who suffers from intellectual loneliness, as well as the blazing fires, closed windows, and locked doors of her father's house. The Dashwood sisters move into a cottage with parlors too small for parties, and Fanny Price only manages to remove herself from her suffocatingly cramped home in Portsmouth to the little white attic which all the other occupants of Mansfield Park have outgrown. When the parental house is not downright uncomfortable because of its inadequate space, it is still a place with no privacy. Thus the only person able to retreat from the relentlessly trivial bustle at the Bennets is the father, who has his own library. Furthermore, as Nina Auerbach has shown, all the girls inhabit houses that are never endowed with the physical concreteness and comfort that specificity supplies.[37] The absence of details suggests how empty and unreal such family life feels, and a character like Anne Elliot, for example, faces the sterile elegance of her father's estate confined and confused by one of the few details the reader is provided, the mirrors in her father's private dressing room.

One reason why the adventures of the later heroines seem to supply such small relief to girls "doomed to waste [their] Days of Youth and Beauty in a humble Cottage in the Vale" is that most, like Laura, can only wait for an unpredictable and unreliable knock on the door. What characterizes the excursions of all these heroines is their total dependency on the whim of wealthier family or friends. None has the power to produce her own itinerary and none knows until the very last moment whether or not she will be taken on a trip upon which her happiness often depends. All the heroines of Austen's fiction very much want to experience the wider world outside their parents' province; each, though, must wait until lucky enough to be asked to accompany a chaperone who frequently only mars the pleasure of the adventure. Although in her earliest writing Austen ridicules the rapidity and improbability of coincidence in second-rate fiction, not a few of her own plots save the heroines from stagnation by means of the overtly literary device of an introduction to an older person who is so pleased with the heroine that "at parting she declares her sole *ambition* was to have her accompany them the next morning to Bath, whither they were going for some weeks."[38]

It is probably for this reason that, from the juvenilia to the posthumously published fragments, there is a recurrent interest in the horse and carriage. It is not surprising in the juvenilia to find a young woman marrying a man she loathes because he has promised her a new chaise, with a silver border and a saddle horse, in return for her not expecting to go to any public place for three years.[39] Indeed, not a few of the heroines recall the plight of two characters in the juvenilia who go on a walking tour through Wales with only one pony, ridden by their mother: not only do their sketches suffer, being "not such exact resemblances as might be wished, from their being taken as [they] ran along," so do their feet as they find themselves hopping home from Hereford.[40] Still, they are delighted with their excursion, and their passion for travel reminds us of the runaways who abound in Austen's novels, young women whose imaginations are tainted by romantic notions which fuel their excessive materialism or sexuality, and who would do anything with anyone in order to escape their families: Eliza Brandon, Julia and Maria Bertram, Lydia Bennet, Lucy Steele, and Georgianna Darcy are all "prepared for matrimony by an hatred of home, restraint, and tranquillity" (*MP*, II, chap. 3). Provided with only the naive clichés of sentimental literature, they insist on acting out those very plots Austen would—but therefore cannot—exorcise from her own fiction.

But hopping home from Hereford also recalls Marianne Dashwood who, like Fanny Price, is vitally concerned with her want of a horse: this pleasure and exercise is not at these girls' disposal primarily because of its expense and impropriety. Emma Woodhouse is subjected to the unwelcome proposals of Mr. Elton because she cannot avoid a ride in his carriage, and Jane Bennet becomes seriously ill at a time when her parents' horses cannot be spared. Similarly, Catherine Morland and Mrs. Parker are both victimized by male escorts whose recklessness hazards their health, if not their lives. It is no small testimony of her regard for their reciprocal partnership that Anne Elliot sees the lively and mutually self-regulating style of the Crofts' driving of their one-horse chaise as a good representation of their marriage. Coaches, barouche-landaus, and curricles are the crucial factors that will determine who goes where with whom on the expeditions to places like Northanger, Pemberly, Donwell Abbey, Southerton, and Lyme.

Every trivial social occasion, each of the many visits and calls endured if not enjoyed by the heroines, reminds us that women are dependent on fathers or brothers for even this most limited form of movement, when they are not indebted to wealthy widows who censure and criticize officiously.[41] Not possessing or controlling the means of transportation, each heroine is defined as different from the poorest men of her neighborhood, all of whom can convey themselves wherever they want or need to go. Indeed, what distinguishes the heroines from their brothers is invariably their lack of liberty: while Austen describes how younger brothers are as financially circumscribed as their sisters, for instance in their choosing of a mate, she always insists that the caste of gender takes precedence over the dictates of class; as poor a dependent as William Price is far more mobile than both his indigent sisters and his wealthy female cousins. For Austen, the domestic confinement of women is not a metaphor so much as a literal fact of life, enforced by all those elaborate rules of etiquette governing even the trivial morning calls that affect the females of each of the novels. The fact that "he is to purvey, and she to smile"[42] is what must have enraged and repelled readers like Brontë and Barrett Browning. As Anne Elliot explains, "We live at home, quiet, confined and our feelings prey upon us" (*P*, II, chap. 11).

According to popular moralists of Austen's day, what would be needed for a satisfied life in such uncongenial circumstances would be "inner resources." Yet these are what most of the young women in her novels lack, precisely because of the inadequate upbringing with which they have been provided by absent or ineffectual mothers. In fact, though Austen's juvenilia often ridicules fiction that portrays the heroine as an orphan or foundling or neglected stepdaughter, the mature novelist does not herself supply her female protagonists with very different family situations. In *A Vindication of the Rights of*

Woman Mary Wollstonecraft explained that "woman . . . a slave in every situation to prejudice, seldom exerts enlightened maternal affection; for she either neglects her children, or spoils them by improper indulgences."[43] Austen would agree, although she focuses specifically on mothers who fail in their nurturing of daughters. Emma Woodhouse, Emma Watson, Catharine, and Anne Elliot are literally motherless, as are such minor characters as Clara Brereton, Jane Fairfax, the Steele sisters, Miss Tilney, Georgianna Darcy, the Miss Bingleys, Mary Crawford, and Harriet Smith. But those girls who have living mothers are nonetheless neglected or overindulged by the absence of enlightened maternal affection.

Fanny Price "might scruple to make use of the words, but she must and did feel that her mother was a partial, ill-judging parent, a dawdle, a slattern, who neither taught nor restrained her children, whose house was the scene of mismanagement and discomfort . . . who had no talent, no conversation, no affection toward herself" (*MP*, III, chap. 8). Mrs. Price, however, is not much different from Mrs. Dashwood and Mrs. Bennet, who are as immature and silly as their youngest daughters, and who are therefore unable to guide young women into maturity. Women like Lady Bertram, Mrs. Musgrove, and Mrs. Bates are a burden on their children because their ignorance, indolence, and folly, resulting as they do in neglect, seem no better than the smothering love of those women whose officiousness spoils by improper indulgence. Fanny Dashwood and Lady Middleton of *Sense and Sensibility*, for example, are cruelly indifferent to the needs of all but their children, who are therefore transformed by such inauspicious attention into noisy, bothersome monsters. Lady Catherine de Bourgh proves conclusively that authoritative management of a daughter's life cannot be identified with nurturing love: coldly administering all aspects of her daughter's growth, overbearing Lady Catherine produces a girl who "was pale and sickly; her features, though not plain, were insignificant; and she spoke very little, except in a low voice."[44]

Because they are literally or figuratively motherless, the daughters in Austen's fiction are easily persuaded that they must look to men for security. Although their mothers' example proves how debilitating marriage can be, they seek husbands in order to escape from home. What feminists have recently called matrophobia—fear of becoming one's mother[45]—supplies one more motive to flee the parental house, as does the financial necessity of competing for male protection which their mothers really cannot supply. The parodic portrait in "Jack and Alice" of the competition between drunken Alice Johnson and the accomplished tailor's daughter, Lucy, for the incomparable Charles Adams (who was "so dazzling a Beauty that none but Eagles could look him in the Face") is thus not so different from the rivalry Emma Woodhouse feels toward Harriet Smith or Jane Fairfax over Mr. Knightley. And it is hardly surprising when in the juvenilia Austen pushes this fierce female rivalry to its fitting conclusion, describing how poor Lucy falls a victim to the envy of a female companion "who jealous of her superiour charms took her by poison from an admiring World at the age of seventeen."[46]

Austen ridicules the easy violence that embellishes melodrama even as she explores hostility between young women who feel they have no alternative but to compete on the marriage market. Like Charlotte Lucas, many an Austen heroine, "without thinking highly either of men or of matrimony," considers marriage "the only honourable provision for well-educated young women of small fortune, their pleasantest preservation from want" (*PP*, I, chap. 22). And so, at the beginning of *The Watsons*, one sister has to warn another about a third that, "There is nothing she would not do to get married. . . . Do not trust her with any secrets of your own, take warning by me, do not trust her." Because such females would rather marry a man they dislike than teach school or enter the governess "slave-trade,"[47] they fight ferociously for the few eligible men who do seem attractive. The rivalries between Miss Bingley and Miss Bennet, between Miss Dashwood and Miss Steele, between Julia and Maria Bertram for Henry Crawford, between the Musgrove sisters for Captain Wentworth are only the most obvious examples of fierce female competition where female anger is deflected from powerful male to powerless female targets.

Throughout the juvenilia, most hilariously in "Frederic and Elfrida," Austen ridicules the idea, promulgated by romantic fiction, that the only events worth recording are marriage proposals, marriage ceremonies, engagements made or broken, preparations for dances where lovers are expected, amatory disappointments, and elopements.

But her own fiction is essentially limited to just such topics. The implication is clear: marriage is crucial because it is the only accessible form of self-definition for girls in her society. Indeed, Austen's silence on all other subjects becomes itself a kind of statement, for the absences in her fiction prove how deficient are the lives of girls and women, even as they testify to her own deprivation as a woman writer. Yet Austen actually uses her self-proclaimed and celebrated acceptance of the limits of her art to mask a subversive critique of the forms of self-expression available to her both as an artist and as a woman, for her ridicule of inane literary structures helps her articulate her alienation from equally inadequate societal strictures.

Austen was indisputably fascinated by double-talk, by conversations that imply the opposite of what they intend, narrative statements that can only confuse, and descriptions that are linguistically sound, but indecipherable or tautological. We can see her concern for such matters in "Jack and Alice," where dictatorial Lady Williams is adamant in giving her friend unintelligible advice about a proposed trip to Bath:

> "What say you to accompanying these Ladies: I shall be miserable without you—t'will be a most pleasant tour to you—I hope you'll go; if you do I am sure t'will be the Death of me—pray be persuaded." [48]

Almost as if she were taking on the persona of Mrs. Slipslop or Mrs. Malaprop (that wonderful "queen of the dictionary") or Tabitha Bramble, Austen engages here in the same kind of playful nonsense that occurs in the narrator's introduction to the story of "Frederic and Elfrida" ("The Uncle of Elfrida was the Father of Frederic; in other words, they were first cousins by the Father's side") or in "Lesley Castle" ("We are handsome, my dear Charlotte, very handsome and the greatest of our Perfections is, that, we are entirely insensible of them ourselves"). Characteristically, in Austen's juvenilia one girl explains, "if a book is well written, I always find it too short," and discovers that her friend agrees: "So do I, only I get tired of it before it is finished." [49] What is so wonderful about these sentences is the "ladylike" way in which they quietly subvert the conventions of language, while managing to sound perfectly accept-able, even grammatically elegant and decorous.

With its insistent evocation of two generic frameworks, the *Bildungsroman* and the burlesque, *Northanger Abbey* (1818) supplies one reason for Austen's fascination with coding, concealing, or just plain not saying what she means, because this apparently amusing and inoffensive novel finally expresses an indictment of patriarchy that could hardly be considered proper or even permissible in Austen's day. Indeed, when this early work was published post-humously—because its author could not find a publisher who would print it during her lifetime—it was the harsh portrayal of the patriarch that most disturbed reviewers.[50] Since we have already seen that Austen tends to enact her own ambivalent relationship to her literary predecessors as she describes her heroines' vulnerability in masculine society, it is hardly surprising to find that she describes Catherine Morland's initiation into the fashionable life of Bath, balls, and marriage settlements by trying to come to terms with the complex and ambiguous relationship between women and the novel.

Northanger Abbey begins with a sentence that resonates as the novel progresses: "No one who had ever seen Catherine Morland in her infancy, would have supposed her born to be an heroine." And certainly what we see of the young Catherine is her unromantic physical exuberance and health. We are told, moreover, that she was "fond of all boys' plays, and greatly preferred cricket not merely to dolls, but to the more heroic enjoyments of infancy, nursing a dormouse, feeding a canary-bird, or watering a rose-bush" (I, chap. 1). Inattentive to books, uninterested in music or drawing, she was "noisy and wild, hated confinement and cleanliness, and loved nothing so well in the world as rolling down the green slope at the back of the house" (I, chap. 1). But at fifteen Catherine began to curl her hair and read, and "from fifteen to seventeen she was in training for a heroine" (I, chap. 1). Indeed her actual "training for a heroine" is documented in the rest of the novel, although, as we shall see, it is hard to imagine a more uncongenial or unnatural course of instruction for her or for any other spirited girl.

Puzzled, confused, anxious to please, and above else innocent and curious, Catherine wonders as she wanders up and down the two traditional settings for female initiation, the dance hall at Bath and the passageways of a gothic abbey. But Austen keeps on reminding us that Catherine is typical because she is *not* born to be a heroine: burdened with parents who were "not in the least addicted to locking up ... daughters", Catherine could "not write sonnets" and had "no notion of drawing" (I, chap. 1). There is "not one lord" in her neighborhood—"not even a baronet" (I, chap. 2)—and on her journey to Bath, "neither robbers nor tempests befriend" her (I, chap. 2). When she enters the Upper Rooms in Bath, "not one" gentleman starts with wonder on beholding her, "no whisper of eager inquiry ran round the room, nor was she once called a divinity by anybody" (I, chap. 2). Her room at the Abbey is "by no means unreasonably large, and contained neither tapestry nor velvets" (II, chap. 6). Austen dramatizes all the ways in which Catherine is unable to live up to the rather unbelievable accomplishments of Charlotte Smith's and Mrs. Radcliffe's popular paragons. Heroines, it seems, are not born like people, but manufactured like monsters, and also like monsters they seem fated to self-destruct. Thus *Northanger Abbey* describes exactly how a girl in search of her life story finds herself entrapped in a series of monstrous fictions which deprive her of primacy.

To begin with, we see this fictionalizing process most clearly in the first section at Bath. Sitting in the crowded, noisy Upper Rooms, awaiting a suitable partner, Catherine is uncomfortably situated between Mrs. Thorpe, who talks only of her children, and Mrs. Allen, who is a monomaniac on the subject of gowns, hats, muslins, and ribbons. Fit representatives not only of fashionable life but also of the state of female maturity in an aristocratic and patriarchal society, they are a constant source of irritation to Catherine, who is happy to be liberated from their ridiculous refrains by Isabella and John Thorpe. Yet if Mrs. Allen and Mrs. Thorpe are grotesque, the young Thorpes are equally absurd, for in them we see what it means to be a fashionable young lady or gentleman. Isabella is a heroine with a vengeance: flirting and feigning, she is a sister of the earlier Sophia and Laura who runs after men with a single-minded determination not even barely disguised by her protestations of sisterly affection for Catherine. Contorted "with smiles of most exquisite misery, and the laughing eye of utter despondency" (I, chap. 9), Isabella is continually acting out a script that makes her ridiculous. At the same time, her brother, as trapped in the stereotypes of masculinity as she is in femininity, continually contradicts himself, even while he constantly boasts about his skill as a hunter, his great gig, his incomparable drinking capacity, and the boldness of his riding. Not only, then, do the Thorpes represent a nightmarish version of what it means to see oneself as a hero or heroine, they also make Catherine's life miserable by preying on her gullibility and vulnerability.

What both the Thorpes do is lie *to* her and *about* her until she is entrapped in a series of coercive fictions of their making. Catherine becomes the pawn in Isabella's plot, specifically the self-consciously dramatic romance with James Morland in which Catherine is supposed to play the role of sisterly intimate to a swooning, blushing Isabella: Isabella continually gives Catherine clues that she ought to be soliciting her friend's confessions of love or eliciting her anxieties about separating from her lover, clues which Catherine never follows because she never quite catches their meaning. Similarly, John Thorpe constructs a series of fictions in which Catherine is first the object of his own amorous designs and then a wealthy heiress whom General Tilney can further fictionalize. Catherine becomes extremely uncomfortable as he manipulates all these stories about her, and only her ignorance serves to save her from the humiliating realization that her invitation to Northanger depends on General Tilney's illusive image of her.

When Henry Tilney points out to Catherine that "man has the advantage of choice, woman only the power of refusal" (I, chap. 10), he echoes a truth articulated (in a far more tragic circumstance) by Clarissa, who would give up choice if she could but preserve "the liberty of *refusal*, which belongs to my Sex."[51] But in Austen's parodic text, Henry makes a point that is as much about fiction as it is about marriage and dancing, his purported subjects: Catherine is as confined by the clichéd stories of the other characters as Austen is by her need to reject inherited stories of what it means to be a heroine. Unlike her author, however, Catherine "cannot speak well enough to be unintelligible" (II, chap. 1), so she lapses into silence when the Thorpes' version of reality contradicts her own, for instance when Isabella seats herself near a door that commands a good view of everybody entering because "it is so out of the way" (II, chap. 3), or when, in spite of John Thorpe's warnings about the violence of his horses, his carriage proceeds at a safe speed. Repeatedly, she does not understand "how to reconcile two such very different accounts of the same thing" (I, chap. 9). Enmeshed in the Thorpes' misinterpretations, Catherine can only feebly deflect Isabella's assertion that her rejection of John Thorpe represents the cooling of her first feelings: "You are describing what never happened" (II, chap. 3). While Catherine only sporadically and confusedly glimpses the discrepancies between Isabella's stated hatred of men and her continual coquetry, or John Thorpe's assertion that he saw the Tilneys driving up the Lansdown Road and her own discovery of them walking down the street, Austen is clearly quite conscious of the lies which John and his sister use to falsify Catherine's sense of reality, just as she is aware of the source of these lies in the popular fiction of her day.

Yet, despite her distaste for the falsity of fictional conventions, Austen insists quite early in the novel that she will not reject the practitioners of her own art: "I will not adopt that ungenerous and impolitic custom so common with novel-writers, of degrading by their contemptuous censure the very performances, to the number of which they are themselves adding" (I, chap. 5). In an extraordinary attack on critics of the novel, Austen makes it quite clear that she realizes male anthologists of Goldsmith, Milton, Pope, Prior, Addison, Steele, and Sterne are customarily praised ahead of the female creators of works like *Cecelia*, *Camilla*, or *Belinda*, although the work of such men is neither original nor literary. Indeed, as if to substantiate her feeling that prejudice against the novel is widespread, she shows how even an addicted reader of romances (who has been forced, like so many girls, to substitute novel reading for a formal education) needs to express disdain for the genre. In the important expedition to Beechen Cliff, we find Catherine claiming to despise the form. Novels, she says, are "not clever enough" for Henry Tilney because "gentlemen read better books" (I, chap. 14). But her censure is really, of course, a form of self-deprecation.

The novel is a status-deprived genre, Austen implies, because it is closely associated with a status-deprived gender. Catherine considers novels an inferior kind of literature precisely because they had already become the province of women writers and of a rapidly expanding female audience. Again and again we see the kind of miseducation novels confer on Catherine, teaching her to talk in inflated and stilted clichés, training her to expect impossibly villainous or virtuous behavior from people whose motives are more complex than she suspects, blinding her to the mundane selfishness of her contemporaries. Yet Austen declares that novel writers have been an "injured body," and she explicitly sets out to defend this species of composition that has been so unfairly decried out of "pride, ignorance, or fashion" (I, chap. 5).

Her passionate defense of the novel is not as out of place as it might first seem, for if *Northanger Abbey* is a parody of novelistic clichés, it also resembles the rest of the juvenilia in· its tendency to rely on these very conventions for its own shape. Austen is writing a romance as conventional in its ways as those she criticizes: Catherine Morland's most endearing quality is her inexperience, and her adventures result from the Allens' gratuitous decision to take her as a companion on their trip to Bath, where she is actually introduced to Henry Tilney by the Master of Ceremonies, and where a lucky mistake causes his father to invite her to visit, appropriately enough, his gothic mansion. Like so many of Pamela's daughters, Catherine marries the man of her dreams and is thereby elevated to his rank. In other words, she succeeds in doing what Isabella is so mercilessly punished for wanting to do, making a good match. Finally, in true heroine style, Catherine rejects the false suitor for the true one[52] and is rescued for felicity by an ending no less aggressively engineered than that of most sentimental novels.

As if justifying both her spirited defense of sister novelists and the romantic shape of her heroine's story, Austen has Catherine admit a fierce animosity for the sober pages of history. Catherine tells Henry Tilney and his sister that history "tells [her] nothing that does not either vex or weary [her]. The quarrels of popes and kings, with wars or pestilences, in every page; *the men all so good for nothing, and hardly any women at all*—it is very tiresome" [italics ours] (I, chap. 14). She is severely criticized for this view; but she is, after all, correct, for the knowledge conferred by historians does seem irrelevant to the private lives of most women. Furthermore, Austen had already explored this fact in her only attempt at history, a parody of Goldsmith's *History of England*, written in her youth and signed as the work of "a partial, prejudiced, and ignorant Historian."[53] What is conveyed in this early joke is precisely Catherine's sense of the irrationality, cruelty, and irrelevance of history, as well as the partisan spleen of most so-called objective historians. Until she can place herself, and two friends, in the company of Mary Queen of Scots, historical events seem as absurdly distant from Austen's common concerns as they do to Charlotte Brontë in *Shirley*, George Eliot in *Middlemarch*, or Virginia Woolf in *The Years*, writers who self-consciously display the ways in which history and historical narration only indirectly affect women because they deal with public events never experienced at first hand in the privatized lives of women.

Even quite late in Austen's career, when she was approached to write a history of the august House of Cobourg, she refused to take historical "reality" seriously, declaring that she could no more write a historical romance than an epic poem, "and if it were indispensable for me to keep it up and never relax into laughing at myself or other people, I am sure I should be hung before I had finished the first chapter."[54] While in this letter she could defend her "pictures of domestic life in country villages" with a sure sense of her own province as a writer, Austen's sympathy and identification with Catherine Morland's ignorance is evident elsewhere in her protestation that certain topics are entirely unknown to her. She cannot portray a clergyman sketched by a correspondent because

> Such a man's conversation must at times be on subjects of science and philosophy, of which I know nothing; or at least be occasionally abundant in quotations and allusions which a woman who, like me, knows only her own mother tongue, and has read very little in that, would be totally without the power of giving. A classical education, or at any rate a very extensive acquaintance with English literature, ancient and modern, appears to me quite indispensible for the person who would do justice to your clergyman; and I think I may boast myself to be, with all possible vanity, the most unlearned and uninformed female who ever dared to be an authoress.[55]

Like Fanny Burney, who refused Dr. Johnson's offer of Latin lessons because she could not "devote so much time to acquire something I shall always dread to have known,"[56] Austen seems to have felt the need to maintain a degree of ladylike ignorance.

Yet not only does Austen write about women's miseducation, not only does she feel herself to be a victim of it; in *Northanger Abbey* she angrily attacks their culturally conditioned ignorance, for she is clearly infuriated that "A woman especially, if she have the misfortunate of knowing anything, should conceal it as well as she can" (I, chap. 14). Though "imbecility in females is a great enhancement of their personal charms," Austen sarcastically admits that some men are "too reasonable and too well informed themselves to desire any thing more in woman than ignorance" (I, chap. 14). When at Beechen Cliff Henry Tilney moves from the subject of the natural landscape to a discussion of politics, the narrator, like Catherine, keeps still. Etiquette, it seems, would forbid such discussions (for character and author alike), even if ignorance did not make them impossible. At the same time, however, both Catherine and Austen realize that history and politics, which have been completely beyond the reach of women's experience, are far from sanctified by such a divorce. "What in the midst of that mighty drama [of history] are girls and their blind visions?" Austen might have asked, as George Eliot would in *Daniel Deronda*. And she might have answered similarly that in these "delicate vessels is borne onward through the ages the treasures of human affection."[57] Ignoring the political and economic activity of men throughout history, Austen implies that history may very well be a uniform drama of masculine posturing that is no less a fiction (and a potentially pernicious one) than gothic romance. She suggests, too, that this fiction of history is finally a matter of indifference to women, who never participate in it and who are almost completely absent from its pages. Austen thus anticipates a question Virginia Woolf would angrily pose in *Three Guineas*: "what does 'patriotism' mean to [the educated man's sister]? Has she the same reasons for being proud of England, for loving England, for defending England?"[58] For, like Woolf, Austen asserts that women see male-dominated history from the disillusioned and disaffected perspective of the outsider.

At the same time, the issue of women's reasons for "being proud of England, for loving England, for defending England" is crucial to the revision of gothic fiction we find in *Northanger Abbey*. Rather than rejecting the gothic conventions she burlesques, Austen is very clearly criticizing female gothic in order to reinvest it with authority. As A. Walton Litz has demonstrated, Austen disapproves of Mrs. Radcliffe's exotic locales because such settings imply a discrepancy between the heroine's danger and the reader's security.[59] Austen's heroine is defined as a reader, and in her narrative she blunders on more significant, if less melodramatic, truths, as potentially destructive as any in Mrs. Radcliffe's fiction. Catherine discovers in the old-fashioned black cabinet something just as awful as a lost manuscript detailing a nun's story. Could Austen be pointing at the real threat to women's happiness when she describes her heroine finding *a laundry list*? Moreover, while Catherine reveals her own naive delusions when she expects to find Mrs. Tilney shut up and receiving from her husband's pitiless hands "a nightly supply of coarse food" (II, chap. 8), she does discover that "in suspecting General Tilney of either murdering or shutting up his wife, she had scarcely sinned against his character, or magnified his cruelty" (II, chap. 15).

Using the conventions of gothic even as she transforms them into a subversive critique of patriarchy, Austen shows her heroine penetrating to the secret of the Abbey, the hidden truth of the ancestral mansion, to learn the complete and arbitrary power of the owner of the house, the father, the General. In a book not unfittingly pronounced *North/Anger*, Austen rewrites the gothic not because she disagrees with her sister novelists about the confinement of women, but because she believes women have been imprisoned more effectively by miseducation than by walls and more by financial dependency, which is the authentic ancestral curse, than by any verbal oath or warning. Austen's gothic novel is set in England because— even while it ridicules and repudiates patriarchal politics (or perhaps *because* it does so)—it is, as Robert Hopkins has shown, the most political of Jane Austen's novels. Hopkins's analysis of the political allusions in *Northanger Abbey* reveals not only the mercenary General's "callous lack of concern for the commonweal," but also his role "as an inquisitor surveying possibly seditious pamphlets." This means that Henry Tilney's eulogy of an England where gothic atrocities can presumably never occur because "every man is surrounded by a neighborhood of voluntary spies" (II, chap. 9) refers ironically to the political paranoia and repression of the General, whose role as a modern inquisitor reflects Austen's sense of "the nightmarish political world of the 1790s and very early 1800s." [60] The writers of romance, Austen implies, were not so much wrong as simplistic in their descriptions of female vulnerability. In spite of her professed or actual ignorance, then, Austen brilliantly relocates the villain of the exotic, faraway gothic locale here, now, in England.

It is significant, then, that General Tilney drives Catherine from his house without sufficient funds, without an escort for the seventy-mile journey, because she has no fortune of her own. Ellen Moers may exaggerate in her claim that "money and its making were characteristically female rather than male subjects in English fiction," [61] but Austen does characteristically explore the specific ways in which patriarchal control of women depends on women being denied the right to earn or even inherit their own money. From *Sense and Sensibility*, where a male heir deprives his sisters of their home, to *Pride and Prejudice*, where the male entail threatens the Bennet girls with marriages of convenience, from *Emma*, where Jane Fairfax must become a governess if she cannot engage herself to a wealthy husband, to *Persuasion*, where the widowed Mrs. Smith struggles ineffectually against poverty, Austen reminds her readers that the laws and customs of England may, as Henry Tilney glowingly announces, insure against wife-murder (II, chap. 10), but they do not offer much more than this minimal security for a wife not beloved, or a woman not a wife: as Austen explains in a letter to her favorite niece, "single women have a dreadful propensity for being poor." [62] Thus, in all her novels Austen examines the female powerlessness that underlies monetary pressure to marry, the injustice of inheritance laws, the ignorance of women denied formal education, the psychological vulnerability of the heiress or widow, the exploited dependency of the spinster, the boredom of the lady provided with no vocation. And the powerlessness implicit in all these situations is also a part of the secret behind the graceful and even elegant surfaces of English society that Catherine manages to penetrate. Like Austen's other heroines, she comes to realize that most women resemble her friend Eleanor Tilney, who is only "a nominal mistress of [the house]"; her "real power is nothing" (II, chap. 13).

Catherine's realization that the family, as represented by the

Tilneys, is a bankrupt and coercive institution matches the discoveries of many of Austen's other heroines. Specifically, her realization that General Tilney controls the household despite his lack of honor and feeling matches Elizabeth Bennet's recognition that her father's withdrawal into his library is destructive and selfish, or Emma Woodhouse's recognition that her valetudinarian father has strengthened her egotism out of *his* selfish need for her undivided attention. More than the discoveries of the others, though, Catherine's realization of General Tilney's greed and coercion resembles Fanny Price's recognition that the head of the Bertram family is not only fallible and inflexible in his judgment but mercenary in his motives. In a sense, then, all of Austen's later heroines resemble Catherine Morland in their discovery of the failure of the father, the emptiness of the patriarchal hierarchy, and, as Mary Burgan has shown, the inadequacy of the family as the basic psychological and economic unit of society.[63]

Significantly, all these fathers who control the finances of the house are in their various ways incapable of sustaining their children. Mr. Woodhouse quite literally tries to starve his family and guests, while Sir Walter Elliot is too cheap to provide dinners for his daughters, and Sir Thomas Bertram is so concerned with the elegance of his repast that his children only seek to escape his well-stocked table. As an exacting gourmet, General Tilney looks upon a "tolerably large eating-room as one of the necessities of life" (II, chap. 6), but his own appetite is not a little alarming, and the meals over which he presides are invariably a testimony to his childrens' and his guest's deprivation. Continually oppressed at the General's table with his incessant attentions, "perverse as it seemed, [Catherine] doubted whether she might not have felt less, had she been less attended to" [II, chap. 5]. What continues to mystify her about the General is "why he should say one thing so positively, and mean another all the while" (II, chap. 11). In fact, Austen redefines the gothic in yet another way in *Northanger Abbey* by showing that Catherine Morland is trapped, not inside the General's Abbey, but inside his fiction, a tale in which she figures as an heiress and thus a suitable bride for his second son. Moreover, though it may be less obvious, Catherine is also trapped by the interpretations of the General's children.

Even before Beechen Cliff Elinor Tilney is "not at home" to Catherine, who then sees her leaving the house with her father (I, chap. 12). And on Beechen Cliff, Catherine finds that her own language is not understood. While all the critics seem to side with Henry Tilney's "corrections" of her "mistakes," it is clear from Catherine's defense of herself that her language quite accurately reflects her own perspective. She uses the word *torment*, for example, in place of *instruct* because she knows what Henry Tilney has never experienced:

> "You think me foolish to call instruction a torment, but if you had been as much used as myself to hear poor little children first learning their letters and then learning to spell, if you had ever seen how stupid they can be for a whole morning together, and how tired my poor mother is at the end of it, as I am in the habit of seeing almost every day of my life at home, you would allow that to *torment* and to *instruct* might sometimes be used as synonymous words." [I, chap. 14]

Immediately following this linguistic debate, Catherine watches the Tilneys' "viewing the country with the eyes of persons accustomed to drawing," and hears them talking "in phrases which conveyed scarcely any idea to her" (I, chap. 14). She is convinced moreover that "the little which she could understand ... appeared to contradict the very few notions she had entertained on the matter before." Surely instruction which causes her to doubt the evidence of her own eyes and understanding *is* a kind of torment. And she is further victimized by the process of depersonalization begun in Bath when she wholeheartedly adopts Henry's view and even entertains the belief "that Henry Tilney could never be wrong" (I, chap. 14).

While the Tilneys are certainly neither as hypocritical nor as coercive as the Thorpes, they do contribute to Catherine's confused anxiety over the validity of her own interpretations. Whenever Henry talks with her, he mockingly treats her like a "heroine," thereby surrounding her with clichéd language and clichéd plots. When they meet at a dance in Bath, he claims to worry about the poor figure he will make in her journal, and while his ridicule is no doubt meant for the sentimental novels in which every girl covers reams of paper with the most mundane details of her less than heroic life, such ridicule gratuitously misinterprets (and confuses) Catherine. At Northanger, when she confides to Henry that his sister has taught her how to love a hyacinth, he responds with approbation: "a taste for flowers is always desirable in your sex, as a means of getting you out of doors, and tempting you to more frequent exercise than you would otherwise take!" This, although we know that Catherine has always been happy outdoors; she is left quietly to protest that "Mamma says I am never within" (II, chap. 7). Furthermore, as Katrin Ristkok Burlin has noticed, it is Henry who provides Catherine with the plot that really threatens to overwhelm her in the Abbey.[64] While General Tilney resembles the fathers of Austen's mature fiction in his attempts to watch and control his children as an author would "his" characters—witness the narcissistic Sir Walter and the witty Mr. Bennet—it is Henry Tilney who teaches Catherine at Beechen Cliff to view nature aesthetically, and it is he, as his father's son, who authors the gothic story that entraps Catherine in the sliding panels, ancient tapestries, gloomy passageways, funereal beds, and haunted halls of Northanger.

Of course, though Austen's portrait of the artist as a young man stresses the dangers of literary manipulation, Henry's miniature gothic *is* clearly a burlesque, and no one except the gullible Catherine would ever be taken in for a minute. Indeed, many critics are uncomfortable with this aspect of the novel, finding that it splits here into two parts. But the two sections are not differentiated so much by the realism of the Bath section and the burlesque of the Abbey scenes as by a crucial shift in Catherine, who seems at the Abbey finally to fall into literacy, to be confined in prose. The girl who originally preferred cricket, baseball, and horseback riding to books becomes fascinated with Henry Tilney's plot because it is the culminating step in her training to become a heroine, which has progressed from her early perusal of Gray and Pope to her shutting herself up in Bath with Isabella to read novels and her purchasing a new writing desk which she takes with her in the chaise to Northanger. Indeed, what seems to attract Catherine to Henry Tilney is his lively literariness, for he is very closely associated with books. He has read "hundreds and hundreds" of novels (I, chap. 14), all of which furnish him with misogynistic stereotypes for her. This man whose room at Northanger is littered with books, guns, and great-coats is a specialist in "young ladies' ways."

"Everybody allows that the talent of writing agreeable letters is peculiarly female," Henry explains, and that female style is faultless except for "a general deficiency in subject, a total inattention to stops, and a very frequent ignorance of grammar" (I, chap. 3). Proving himself a man, he says, "no less by the generosity of my soul, than the clearness of my head" (I, chap. 14), Henry has "no patience with such of my sex as disdain to let themselves sometimes down to the comprehension of yours." He feels, moreover, that "perhaps the abilities of women are neither sound nor acute—neither vigorous nor keen. Perhaps they want observation, discernment, judgment, fire, genius and wit" (I, chap. 14). For all his charming vivacity, then, Henry Tilney's misogyny is closely identified with his literary authority so that, when his tale of Northanger sounds "just like a book" to Catherine (II, chap. 5), she is bound to be shut up inside this "horrid" novel by finally acquiescing to her status as a character.

Yet Catherine is one of the first examples we have of a character who gets away from her author, since her imagination runs away with the plot and role Henry has supplied her. Significantly, the story that Catherine enacts involves her in a series of terrifying, gothic adventures. Shaking and sweating through a succession of sleepless nights, she becomes obsessed with broken handles on chests that suggest "premature violence" to her, and "strange ciphers" that promise to disclose "hidden secrets" (II, chap. 6). Searching for clues to some impending evil or doom, she finds herself terrified when a cabinet will not open, only to discover in the morning that she had locked it herself; and, worse, she becomes convinced of Mrs. Tilney's confinement and finds herself weeping before the monument to the dead woman's memory. The monument notwithstanding, however, she is unconvinced of Mrs. Tilney's decease because she knows that a waxen figure might have been introduced and substituted in the family vault. Indeed, when she does not find a lost manuscript to document the General's iniquity, Catherine is only further assured that this villain has too much wit to leave clues that would lead to his detection.

Most simply, of course, this section of *Northanger Abbey* testifies to the delusions created when girls internalize the ridiculous expectations and standards of gothic fiction. But the anxiety Catherine experiences just at the point when she has truly come like a heroine to the home of the man of her dreams seems also to express feelings of confusion that are more than understandable if we remember how constantly she has been beset with alien visions of herself and with incomprehensible and contradictory standards for behavior. Since heroines are not born but made, the making of a heroine seems to imply an unnatural acquiescence in all these incomprehensible fictions: indeed, Austen seems to be implying that the girl who becomes a heroine will become ill, if not mad. Here is the natural consequence of a young lady's sentimental education in preening, reading, shopping, and dreaming. Already, in Bath, caught between the contradictory claims of friends and relatives, Catherine meditates "by turns, on broken promises and broken arches, phaetons and false hangings, Tilneys and trap-doors" (I, chap. 11), as if she inhabits Pope's mad Cave of Spleen. Later, however, wandering through the Abbey at night, Catherine could be said to be searching finally for her own true story, seeking to unearth the past fate of a lost female who will somehow unlock the secret of her own future. Aspiring to become the next Mrs. Tilney, Catherine is understandably obsessed with the figure of the last Mrs. Tilney, and if we take her fantasy seriously, in spite of the heavy parodic tone here, we can see why, for Mrs. Tilney is an image of herself. Feeling confined and constrained in the General's house, but not understanding why, Catherine projects her own feelings of victimization into her imaginings of the General's wife, whose mild countenance is fitted to a frame in death, as presumably in life, and whose painting finds no more favor in the Abbey than her person did. Like Mary Elizabeth Coleridge in "The Other Side of a Mirror," Catherine confronts the image of this imprisoned, silenced woman only to realize "I am she!" Significantly, this story of the female prisoner is Catherine's *only* independent fiction, and it is a story that she must immediately renounce as a "voluntary, self-created delusion" (II, chap. 10) which can earn only her self-hatred.

If General Tilney is a monster of manipulation, then, Catherine Morland, as George Levine has shown, is also "an incipient monster," not very different from the monsters that haunt Austen's contemporary, Mary Shelley.[65] But Catherine's monstrosity is not just, as Levine claims, the result of social climbing at odds with the limits imposed by the social and moral order; it is also the result of her search for a story of her own. Imaginative and sensitive, Catherine genuinely believes that she can become the heroine of her own life story, that she can author herself, and thereby define and control reality. But, like Mary Shelley's monster, she must finally come to terms with herself as a creature of someone else's making, a character trapped inside an uncongenial plot. In fact, like Mary Shelley's monster, Catherine cannot make sense of the signs of her culture, and her frustration is at least partially reflected in her fiction of the starving, suffering Mrs. Tilney. That she sees herself liberating this female prisoner is thus only part of her delusion, because Catherine is destined to fall not just from what Ellen Moers calls "heroinism" but even from authorship and authority: she is fated to be taught the indelicacy of her own attempt at fiction-making. Searching to understand the literary problems that persistently tease her, seeking to find the hidden origin of her own discomfort, we shall see that Catherine is motivated by a curiosity that links her not only to Mary Shelley's monster, but also to such rebellious, dissatisfied inquirers as Catherine Earnshaw, Jane Eyre, and Dorothea Brooke.

Mystified first by the Thorpes, then by the Tilneys, Catherine Morland is understandably filled with a sense of her own otherness, and the story of the imprisoned wife fully reveals both her anger and her self-pity. But her gravest loss of power comes when she is fully "awakened" and "the visions of romance were over" (II, chap. 10). Forced to renounce her story-telling, Catherine matures when "the anxieties of common life began soon to succeed to the alarms of romance" (II, chap. 10). First, her double, Isabella, who has been "all for ambition" (II, chap. 10), must be completely punished and revealed in all her monstrous aspiration. Henry Tilney is joking when he exclaims that Catherine must feel "that in losing Isabella, you lose half yourself" (II, chap. 10); but he is at least partially correct, since Isabella represents the distillation of Catherine's ambition to author herself as a heroine. For this reason, the conversations about Isabella's want of fortune and the difficulty this places in the way of her marrying Captain Tilney raise Catherine's alarms about herself because, as Catherine admits, "she was as insignificant, and perhaps as portionless, as Isabella" (II, chap. 11).

Isabella's last verbal attempt to revise reality is extremely unsuccessful; its inconsistencies and artificialities strike even Catherine as false. "Ashamed of Isabella, and ashamed of having ever loved her" (II, chap. 12), Catherine therefore begins to awaken to the anxieties of common life, and her own fall follows close upon Isabella's. Driven from the General's house, she now experiences agitations "mournfully superior in reality and substance" to her earlier imaginings (II, chap. 13). Catherine had been convinced by Henry of the "absurdity of her curiosity and her fears," but now she discovers that he erred not only in his sense of Isabella's story ("you little thought of its ending so" [II, chap. 10]), but also in his sense of hers. Not the least of Catherine's agitations must involve the realization that she has submitted to Henry's estimate that her fears of the General were "only" imaginary, when all along she had been right.

This is why *Northanger Abbey* is, finally, a gothic story as frightening as any told by Mrs. Radcliffe, for the evil it describes is the horror described by writers as dissimilar as Charlotte Perkins Gilman, Phyllis Chesler, and Sylvia Plath, the terror and self-loathing that results when a woman is made to disregard her personal sense of danger, to accept as real what contradicts her perception of her own situation. More dramatic, if not more debilitating, examples can be cited to illustrate Catherine's confusion when she realizes she has replaced her own interiority or authenticity with Henry's inadequate judgments. For the process of being brainwashed that almost fatally confuses Catherine has always painfully humiliated women subjected to a maddening process that Florence Rush, in an allusion to the famous Ingrid Bergman movie about a woman so driven insane, has recently called "gaslighting."[66]

While "a heroine returning, at the close of her career, to her native village, in all the triumph of recovered reputation" would be "a delight" for writer and reader alike, Austen admits, "I bring my heroine to her home in solitude and disgrace" (II, chap. 14). Catherine has nothing else to do but "to be silent and alone" (II, chap. 14). Having relinquished her attempt to gain a story or even a point of view, she composes a letter to Elinor that will not pain her if Henry should chance to read it. Like so many heroines, from Snow White to Kate Brown, who stands waiting for the kettle to boil at the beginning of *Summer Before the Dark*, Catherine is left with nothing to do but wait:

> She could neither sit still, nor employ herself for ten minutes together, walking round the garden and orchard again and again, as if nothing but motion was voluntary; and it seemed as if she could even walk about the house rather than remain fixed for any time in the parlour. [II, chap. 15]

Her mother gives her a book of moral essays entitled *The Mirror*, which is what must now supplant the romances, for it tells stories appropriate to her "silence and sadness" (II, chap. 15). From this glass coffin she is rescued by the prince whose "affection originated in nothing better than gratitude" for her partiality toward him (II, chap. 15).

In spite of Henry's faults and the inevitable coercion of his authority over her, his parsonage will of course be a more pleasant dwelling than either the General's Abbey or the parental cot. Within its well-proportioned rooms, the girl who so enjoyed rolling down green slopes can at least gain a glimpse through the windows of luxuriant green meadows; in other words, Catherine's future home holds out the promise that women can find comfortable spaces to inhabit in their society. Austen even removes Elinor Tilney from "the evils of such a home as Northanger" (II, chap. 16), if only by marrying her to the gentleman whose servant left behind the laundry list. Yet the happy ending is the result of neither woman's education since, Austen implies, each continues to find the secret of the Abbey perplexing. We shall see that in this respect Catherine's fate foreshadows that of the later heroines, most of whom are also "saved" when they relinquish their subjectivity through the manipulations of a narrator who calls attention to her own exertions and thereby makes us wonder whether the lives of women not so benevolently protected would have turned out quite so well.

At the same time, even if the marriage of the past Mrs. Tilney makes us wonder about the future Mrs. Tilney's prospects for happiness, Austen has successfully balanced her own artistic commitment to an inherited literary structure that idealizes feminine submission against her rebellious imaginative sympathies. With a heavy reliance on characters who are readers, all of Austen's early parodies point us, then, to the important subject of female imagination in her mature novels. But it is in *Northanger Abbey* that this novelist most forcefully indicates her consciousness of what Harold Bloom might call her "belatedness," a belatedness inextricably related to her definition of herself as female and therefore secondary. Just as Catherine Morland remains a reader, Austen presents herself as a "mere" interpreter and critic of prior fictions, and thereby quite modestly demonstrates her willingness to inhabit a house of fiction not of her own making.

5 Jane Austen's Cover Story (and Its Secret Agents)

> I am like the needy knife-grinder—I have no story to tell.
> —Maria Edgeworth

> I dwell in Possibility—
> A fairer House than Prose—
> More numerous of Windows—
> Superior—for Doors—
> —Emily Dickinson

> ... the modes of fainting should be all as different as possible and
> may be made very diverting.
> —*The Girls' Book of Diversions* (ca. 1840)

> From Sappho to myself, consider the fate of women.
> How unwomanly to discuss it!
> —Carolyn Kizer

Jane Austen was not alone in experiencing the tensions inherent in being a "lady" writer, a fact that she herself seemed to stress when, in *Northanger Abbey*, she gently admonished literary women like Maria Edgeworth for being embarrassed about their status as novelists. Interestingly, Austen came close to analyzing a central problem for Edgeworth, who constantly judged and depreciated her own "feminine" fiction in terms of her father's commitment to pedagogically sound moral instruction. Indeed, as our first epigraph is meant to suggest, Maria Edgeworth's persistent belief that she had no story of her own reflects Catherine Morland's initiation into her fallen female state as a person without a history, without a name of her own, without a story of significance which she could herself author. Yet, because Edgeworth's image of herself as a needy knife-grinder suggests a potential for cutting remarks not dissimilar from what Virginia Woolf called Austen's delight in slicing her characters' heads off,[1] and because her reaction against General Tilney—"quite outrageously out of drawing and out of nature"[2]—reflects Austen's own discretion about male power in her later books, Maria Edgeworth's career is worth considering as a preface to the achievement of Austen's maturity.

Although she was possibly one of the most popular and influential novelists of her time, Maria Edgeworth's personal reticence and modesty matched Austen's, causing Byron, among others, to observe, "One would never have guessed she could write *her name*; whereas her father talked, *not* as if he could write nothing else, but as if nothing else was worth writing."[3] Even to her most recent biographer, the name Edgeworth still means Richard Lovell Edgeworth, the father whose overbearing egotism amused or annoyed many of the people he met. And while Marilyn Butler explains that Richard Edgeworth must not be viewed as an unscrupulous Svengali operating on an unsuspecting child,[4] she does not seem to realize that his daughter's voluntary devotion could also inhibit and circumscribe her talent, creating perhaps an even more complex problem for the emerging author than outright coercion would have spawned. The portrait of Richard Edgeworth as a scientific inventor and Enlightenment theorist who practiced his pedagogy at home for the greater intellectual development of his family must be balanced against his Rousseauistic experiment with his first son (whose erratic and uncontrollable spirits convinced him that Rousseau was wrong) and his fathering twenty-two children by four wives, more than one of whom was an object of his profound indifference.

As the third of twenty-two and the daughter of the wife most completely neglected, Maria Edgeworth seems to have used her writing to gain the attention and approval of her father. From the beginning of her career, by their common consent, he became the impresario and narrator of her life. He first set her to work on censorious Madame de Genlis's *Adèle et Théodore*, the work that would have launched her career, if his friend Thomas Day had not congratulated him when Maria's translation was cancelled by the publishers. While Maria wrote her *Letters for Literary Ladies* (1795) as a response to the ensuing correspondence between Day and Richard Lovell Edgeworth about the issue of female authorship, it can hardly be viewed as an act of literary assertion.

For, far from defending female authority, this manuscript, which she described as "disfigured by all manner of crooked marks of papa's critical indignation, besides various abusive marginal notes,"[5] actually contains an attack on female flightiness and self-dramatization (in "Letters of Julia and Caroline") and a satiric essay implying that feminine arguments for even the most minor sorts of self-determination are manipulative, hypocritical, self-congratulatory, and irrational ("Essay on the Noble Science of Self-Justification"). She does include an exchange of letters between a misogynist (presumably modelled on Day) who argues that "female prodigies . . . are scarcely less offensive to my taste than monsters" and a defender of female learning (presumably her father) who claims that

> considering that the pen was to women a new instrument, I think they have made at least as good a use of it as learned men did of the needle some centuries ago, when they set themselves to determine how many spirits could stand upon its point, and were ready to tear one another to pieces in the discussion of this sublime question.[6]

But this "defense," which argues that women are no sillier than medieval theologians, is hardly a compliment, coming—as it does—from an enlightened philosopher, nor is the subsequent proposition that education is necessary to make women better wives and mothers, two roles Maria Edgeworth herself never undertook. Written for an audience composed of Days and Edgeworths, *Letters for Literary Ladies* helps us understand why Maria Edgeworth could not become an author without turning herself into a literary lady, a creature of her father's imagination who was understandably anxious for and about her father's control.

"Where should I be without my father? I should sink into that nothing from which he has raised me,"[7] Maria Edgeworth worried in an eerie adumbration of the fears expressed by George Eliot and a host of other dutiful daughter-writers. Because Richard Lovell Edgeworth "pointed out" to her that "to be a mere writer of pretty stories and novellettes would be unworthy of his partner, pupil &

daughter,"[8] Maria soon stopped writing the books which her early talent seemed to make so successful—not before, however, she wrote one novel without either his aid or his knowledge. Not only was *Castle Rackrent* (1800) one of her earliest and most popular productions, it contains a subversive critique of patriarchy surprisingly similar to what we found in *Northanger Abbey*.

As narrated by the trusty servant Thady Quirk, this history of an Irish ancestral mansion is told in terms of the succession of its owners, Irish aristocrats best characterized by their indolence, improvidence, and love for litigation, alcohol, and women. Sir Tallyhoos, Sir Patrick, Sir Murtagh, Sir Kit, and Sir Condy are praised and served by their loyal retainer, who nevertheless reveals their irresponsible abuse of their position in Irish society. *Castle Rackrent* also includes a particularly interesting episode about an imprisoned wife that further links it to the secret we discovered in the overlooked passageways of Northanger. All of the Rackrent landlords marry for money, but one of them, Sir Kit, brings back to Ireland a Jewish heiress as his wife. While Thady ostensibly bemoans what "this heretic Blackamore"[9] will bring down on the head of the estate, he actually describes the pathetic ignorance and vulnerability of the wealthy foreigner, who is completely at the mercy of her cruelly capricious husband. Her helplessness is dramatized, characteristically, in an argument over the food for their table, since Sir Kit insists on irritating her with the presence of sausages, bacon, and pork at every meal. Refusing to feed on forbidden, foreign foods, as so many later heroines will, she responds by shutting herself up in her room, a dangerous solution since Sir Kit then locks her up. "We none of us ever saw or heard her speak for seven years after that" (29), Thady calmly explains.

As if aware of the potential impact of this episode, the author affixes a long explanatory footnote attesting to the historical accuracy of what "can scarcely be thought credible" by citing "the celebrated Lady Cathcart's conjugal imprisonment," a case that might also have reminded Maria Edgeworth of the story of George I's wife, who was shut up in Hanover when he left to ascend to the English throne, and who escaped only through her death thirty-two years later.[10] Sir Kit is shown to follow the example of Lady Cathcart's husband when he drinks Lady Rackrent's good health with his table companions, sending a servant on a sham errand to ask if "there was anything at table he might send her," and accepting the sham answer returned by his servant that "she did not wish for anything, but drank the company's health" (30–31). Starving inside the ancestral mansion, the literally imprisoned wife is also figuratively imprisoned within her husband's fictions. Meanwhile, Thady loyally proclaims that Sir Kit was never cured of the gaming tricks that mortgaged his estate, but that this "was the only fault he had, God bless him!" (32).

When, after her husband's death, Lady Rackrent recovers, fires the cook, and departs the country, Thady decides that "it was a shame for her, being his wife, not to show more duty," specifically not to have saved him from financial ruin. But clearly the lady's escape is a triumph that goes far in explaining why *Castle Rackrent* was scribbled fast, in secret, almost the only work of fiction Maria Edgeworth wrote without her father's help. Indeed she insisted that the story spontaneously came to her when she heard an old steward's voice, and that she simply recorded it. We will see other instances of such "trance" writing, especially with regard to the Brontës, but here it clearly helps explain why *Castle Rackrent* remained *her* book, why she steadily resisted her father's encouragement to add "corrections" to it.[11]

Certainly, when viewed as a woman's creation, *Castle Rackrent* must be considered a critique of patriarchy, for the male aristocratic line is criticized because it exploits Ireland, that traditional old sow, leaving a peasantry starved and dispossessed. Rackrent means destructive rental, and *Castle Rackrent* is a protest against exploitative landlords. Furthermore, Thady Quirk enacts the typically powerless role of housekeeper with the same ambivalence that characterizes women like Elinor Tilney in *Northanger Abbey* and Nelly Dean in *Wuthering Heights*, both of whom identify with the male owner and enforce his will, although they see it as arbitrary and coercive. Yet, like Maria Edgeworth, the needy knifegrinder, even while Thady pretends to be of use by telling not his own story but his providers', his words are damaging, for he reveals the depravity of the very masters he seems to praise so loyally. And this steward who appears to serve his lords with such docility actually benefits from their decline, sets into motion the machinery that finishes them off, and even contributes to the demise of their last representative. Whether consciously or unconsciously,[12] this "faithful family retainer" manages to get the big house. Exploiting the dissembling tactics of the powerless, Thady is an effective antagonist, and, at the end of the story, although he claims to despise him, it is his own son who has inherited the power of the Rackrent family.

Pursuing her career in her father's sitting room and writing primarily to please him, Maria Edgeworth managed in this early fiction to evade her father's control by dramatizing the retaliatory revenge of the seemingly dutiful and the apparently weak. But in spite of its success and the good reception accorded her romance *Belinda*, she turned away from her own "pretty stories and novellettes" as "unworthy" of her father's "partner, pupil & daughter," deciding to pursue instead her father's projects, for example his *Professional Education*, a study of vocational education for boys. Devoted until his death to writing Irish tales and children's stories which serve as a gloss on his political and educational theories, Maria Edgeworth went as far as she could in seeing herself and presenting herself as her father's secretary: "I have only repeated the same opinions [Edgeworth's] in other forms," she explained; "A certain quantity of bullion was given to me and I coined it into as many pieces as I thought would be convenient for popular use."[13] Admitting frequently that her "acting and most kind literary partner" made all the final decisions, she explained that "it was to please my father I first exerted myself to write, to please him I continued." But if "the first stone was thrown the first motion given by him," she understandably believed that "when there is no similar moving power the beauteous circles vanish and the water stagnates."[14]

Although she was clearly troubled that without her author she would cease to exist or create, Maria Edgeworth solved the problem of what we have been calling "the anxiety of female authorship" by writing as if she were her father's pen. Like so many of her successors—Mrs. Gaskell, Geraldine Jewsbury, George Eliot, Olive Schreiner—she was plagued by headaches that might have reflected the strain of this solution. She was also convinced that her father's skill in cutting, his criticism, and invention alone allowed her to write by relieving her from the vacillation and anxiety to which she was so much subject.[15] In this respect Maria Edgeworth resembles

Dorothea Brooke of *Middlemarch*, for "if she had written a book she must have done it as Saint Theresa did, under the command of an authority that constrained her conscience" (chap. 10). Certainly we sense the strain in her biography, for example in the incident at Richard Lovell Edgeworth's deathbed: the day before he died, Marilyn Butler explains, Richard Edgeworth dictated to his daughter a letter for his publisher explaining that she would add 200 pages to his 480-page memoir within a month after his death. In the margin his secretary wrote what she apparently could not find the courage to say: "I never promised." [16] Like Dorothea Casaubon, who finally never promises to complete Casaubon's book and instead writes silently a message on his notes explaining why she cannot, Maria Edgeworth must have struggled with the conflict between her desire to fulfill her father's wishes by living out his plots and her need to assert her own talents. Unlike Dorothea, however, she finally wrote her father's book in spite of the pain doing so must have entailed.

Literally writing her father's book, however, was doing little more than what she did throughout her career when she wrote stories illustrating his theories and portraying the wise benevolence of male authority figures. At least one critic believes that she did manage to balance her father's standards with her personal allegiances. But even if she did covertly express her dissent from her father's values—by sustaining a dialogue in her fiction between moral surface and symbolic resistence[17]—what this rather schizophrenic solution earned her on the domestic front was her father's patronizing inscription on her writing desk:

> On this humble desk were written all the numerous works of my daughter, Maria Edgeworth, in the common sitting-room of my family. In these works which were chiefly written to please me, she has never attacked the personal character of any human being or interfered with the opinions of any sect or party, religious or political; ... she improved and amused her own mind, and gratified her heart, which I do believe is better than her head.[18]

Even as *Castle Rackrent* displays the same critique of patriarchy we traced in *Northanger Abbey*, then, Mr. Edgeworth's condescending praise of *his* daughter's desk in *his* sitting room reminds us that

Austen also worked in such a decorous space. Likewise, just as Richard Lovell Edgeworth perceives this space as a sign of Maria's ladylike submission to his domestic control, Virginia Woolf suggests that such a writing place can serve as an emblem of the confinement of the "lady" novelist:

> If a woman wrote, she would have to write in the common sitting-room .... She was always interrupted.... Jane Austen wrote like that to the end of her days. "How she was able to effect all this," her nephew writes in his Memoir, "is surprising, for she had no separate study to repair to, and most of the work must have been done in the general sitting-room subject to all kinds of casual interruptions. She was careful that her occupation should not be suspected by servants or visitors or any persons beyond her own family party." Jane Austen hid her manuscripts or covered them with a piece of blotting-paper. ... [She] was glad that a hinge creaked, so that she might hide her manuscript before any one came in.[19]

Despite the odd contradiction we sense between Woolf's repeated assertions elsewhere in *A Room of One's Own* that Austen was unimpeded by her sex and her clear-sighted recognition in this passage of the limits placed on Austen because of it, the image of the lady writing in the common sitting room is especially useful in helping us understand both Austen's confinement and the fictional strategies she developed for coping with it. We have already seen that even in the juvenilia (which many critics consider her most conservative work) there are clues that Austen is hiding a distinctly unladylike outlook behind the "cover" or "blotter" of parody. But the blotting paper poised in anticipation of a forewarning creak can serve as an emblem of a far more organic camouflage existing within the mature novels, even as it calls to our attention the anxiety that authorship entailed for Austen.

We can see Austen struggling after *Northanger Abbey* to combine her implicitly rebellious vision with an explicitly decorous form as she follows Miss Edgeworth's example and writes in order to make herself useful, justifying her presumptuous attempts at the pen by inspiring other women with respect for the moral and social responsibilities of their domestic duties, and thereby allowing her surviving relatives to make the same claims as Mr. Edgeworth. Yet the repressive implications of the story she tells—a story, invariably, of the need for women to renounce their claims to stories of their own—paradoxically allow her to escape the imprisonment she defines and defends as her heroines' fate so that, like Emily Dickinson, Austen herself can finally be said to "dwell in Possibility—/A fairer House than Prose—" (J. 657).

Austen's propriety is most apparent in the overt lesson she sets out to teach in all of her mature novels. Aware that male superiority is far more than a fiction, she always defers to the economic, social, and political power of men as she dramatizes how and why female survival depends on gaining male approval and protection. All the heroines who reject inadequate fathers are engaged in a search for better, more sensitive men who are, nevertheless, still the representatives of authority. As in *Northanger Abbey*, the happy ending of an Austen novel occurs when the girl becomes a daughter to her husband, an older and wiser man who has been her teacher and her advisor, whose house can provide her with shelter and sustenance and at least derived status, reflected glory. Whether it be parsonage or ancestral mansion, the man's house is where the heroine can retreat from both her parents' inadequacies and the perils of the outside world: like Henry Tilney's Woodston, Delaford, Pemberley, Donwell, and Thornton Lacy are spacious, beautiful places almost always supplied with the loveliest fruit trees and the prettiest prospects. Whereas becoming a man means proving or testing oneself or earning a vocation, becoming a woman means relinquishing achievement and accommodating oneself to men and the spaces they provide.

Dramatizing the necessity of female submission for female survival, Austen's story is especially flattering to male readers because it describes the taming not just of any woman but specifically of a rebellious, imaginative girl who is amorously mastered by a sensible man. No less than the blotter literally held over the manuscript on her writing desk, Austen's cover story of the necessity for silence and submission reinforces women's subordinate position in patriarchal culture. Interestingly, what common law called "coverture" at this time actually defined the married woman's status as suspended or "covered": "the very being or legal existence of the woman is suspended during the marriage," wrote Sir William Blackstone, "or at least is incorporated and consolidated into that of the husband: under whose wing, protection and cover, she performs everything."[20] The happiest ending envisioned by Austen, at least until her very last novel, accepts the necessity of protection and cover for heroines who wish to perform anything at all.

At the same time, however, we shall see that Austen herself "performs everything" under this cover story. As Virginia Woolf noted, for all her "infallible discretion," Austen always stimulates her readers "to supply what is not there."[21] A story as sexist as that of the taming of the shrew, for example, provides her with a "blotter" or socially acceptable cover for expressing her own self-division. Undoubtedly a useful acknowledgment of her own ladylike submission and her acquiescence to masculine values, this plot also allows Austen to consider her own anxiety about female assertion and expression, to dramatize her doubts about the possibility of being both a woman and a writer. She describes both her own dilemma and, by extension, that of all women who experience themselves as divided, caught in the contradiction between their status as human beings and their vocation as females.

The impropriety of female creativity first emerges as a problem in *Lady Susan*, where Austen seems divided between her delight in the vitality of a talented libertine lady and her simultaneous rejection of the sexuality and selfishness of her heroine's plots. In this first version of the taming of the shrew, Austen exposes the wicked wilfulness of Lady Susan, who gets her own way because of her "artful" (Letters 4, 13, and 17), "bewitching powers" (Letter 4), powers intimately related to her "clever" and "happy command of language" (Letter 8). Using "deep arts," Lady Susan always has a "design" (Letter 4) or "artifice" that testifies to her great "talent" (Letters 16 and 36) as a "Mistress of Deceit" (Letter 23) who knows how to play a number of parts quite convincingly. She is the first of a series of heroines, of varying degrees of attractiveness, whose lively wit and energetic imagination make them both fascinating and frightening to their creator.

Several critics have explored how Lady Susan's London ways are contrasted to her daughter's love of the country, how the mother's talkative liveliness and sexuality are balanced against the daughter's silence and chastity, how art is opposed to nature.[22] But, if Lady Susan is energetic in her pursuit of pleasure, her daughter is quite vapid and weak; indeed, she seems far more socialized into passivity than a fit representative of nature would be. Actually she is only necessary to emphasize Lady Susan's unattractiveness—her cruelty to her daughter—which can best be viewed as Austen's reflex to suppress her interest in such wilful sorts of women. For the relationship between Lady Susan and Frederica is not unlike that between the crafty Queen and her angelic step daughter, Snow White: Lady Susan seems almost obsessed with hatred of her daughter, who represents an extension of her own self, a projection of her own inescapable femininity which she tries to destroy or transcend even at the risk of the social ostracism she must inevitably incur at the end of the novel. These two, mother and daughter, reappear transformed in the mature novels into sisters, sometimes because Austen wishes to consider how they embody available options that are in some ways equally attractive yet mutually exclusive, sometimes because she seeks to illustrate how these two divided aspects of the self can be integrated.

In *Sense and Sensibility* (1811), as most readers of the novel have noted, Marianne Dashwood's sensibility links her to the Romantic imagination. Repeatedly described as fanciful, imaginative, emotionally responsive, and receptive to the natural beauty of trees and the aesthetic beauties of Cowper, Marianne is extremely sensitive to language, repelled by clichés, and impatient with the polite lies of civility. Although quite different from Lady Susan, she too allows her lively affections to involve her in an improper amorous involvement, and her indiscreet behavior is contrasted with that of her sister Elinor, who is silent, reserved, and eminently proper. If the imagination is linked with Machiavellian evil in *Lady Susan*, it is closely associated with self-destruction in *Sense and Sensibility*: when Elinor and Marianne have to confront the same painful situation— betrayal by the men they deemed future husbands—Elinor's stoical self-restraint is the strength born of her good sense while Marianne's indulgence in sensibility almost causes her own death, the unfettered play of her imagination seeming to result in a terrible fever that represents how imaginative women are infected and sickened by their dreams.

Marianne's youthful enthusiasm is very attractive, and the reader, like Colonel Brandon, is tempted to find "something so amiable in the prejudices of a young mind, that one is sorry to see them give way to the reception of more general opinions" (I, chap. 11). But give way they apparently must and evidently do. Eagerness of fancy is a passion like any other, perhaps more imprudent because it is not recognized as such. As delightful as it might first seem, moreover, it is always shown to be a sign of immaturity, of a refusal to submit. Finally this is unbecoming and unproductive in women, who must exert their inner resources for pliancy, elasticity of spirit, and accommodation. *Sense and Sensibility* is an especially painful novel to read because Austen herself seems caught between her attraction to Marianne's sincerity and spontaneity, while at the same identifying with the civil falsehoods and the reserved, polite silences of Elinor, whose art is fittingly portrayed as the painting of screens.

Pride and Prejudice (1813) continues to associate the perils of the imagination with the pitfalls of selfhood, sexuality, and assertion. Elizabeth Bennet is her father's favorite daughter because she has inherited his wit. She is talkative, satirical, quick at interpreting appearances and articulating her judgments, and so she too is contrasted to a sensible silent sister, Jane, who is quiet, unwilling to express her needs or desires, supportive of all and critical of none. While moral Jane remains an invalid, captive at the Bingleys, her satirical sister Elizabeth walks two miles along muddy roads to help nurse her. While Jane visits the Gardners only to remain inside their house waiting hopelessly for the visitors she wishes to receive, Elizabeth travels to the Collins' establishment where she visits Lady Catherine. While Jane remains at home, lovesick but uncomplaining, Elizabeth accompanies the Gardeners on a walking tour of Derbyshire. Jane's docility, gentleness, and benevolence are remarkable, for she suffers silently throughout the entire plot, until she is finally set free by her Prince Charming. In these respects, she adumbrates Jane Fairfax of Austen's *Emma* (1816), another Jane who is totally passive and quiet, despite the fact that she is repeatedly humiliated by her lover. Indeed, although Jane Fairfax is eventually driven to a gesture of revolt—the pathetic decision to endure the "slave-trade" of becoming a governess rather than wait for Frank Churchill to become her husband—she is a paragon of submissive politeness and patience throughout her ordeal, so much so that, "wrapped up in a cloak of politeness," she was to Emma and even to Mr Knightley "disgustingly . . . suspiciously, reserved" (II, chap. 2).

Just as Jane Bennet forecasts the role and character of Jane Fairfax, Elizabeth Bennet shares much with Emma who, perhaps more than all the others, demonstrates Austen's ambivalence about her imaginative powers, since she created in Emma a heroine whom she suspected no one but herself would like.[23] A player of word games, a painter of portraits and a spinner of tales, Emma is clearly an avatar of Austen the artist. And more than all the other playful, lively girls, Emma reminds us that the witty woman is responding to her own confining situation with words that become her weapon, a defense against banality, a way of at least *seeming* to control her life. Like Austen, Emma has at her disposal worn-out, hackneyed stories of romance that she is smart enough to resist in her own life. If Emma is an artist who manipulates people as if they were characters in her own stories, Austen emphasizes not only the immorality of this activity, but its cause or motivation: except for placating her father, Emma has nothing to do. Given her intelligence and imagination, her impatient attempts to transform a mundane reality are completely understandable.

Emma and her friends believe her capable of answering questions which puzzle less quick and assured girls, an ability shown to be necessary in a world of professions and falsehoods, puzzles, charades, and riddles. But word games deceive especially those players who think they have discovered the hidden meanings, and Emma misinterprets every riddle. Most of the letters in the novel contain "nothing but truth, though there might be some truths not told" (II, chap. 2). Because readiness to talk frequently masks reticence to communicate, the vast majority of conversations involve characters who not only remain unaffected by dialogue, but barely hear each other talking: Isabella, Miss Bates and Mr. Woodhouse, Mrs. Elton and Mr. Weston are participating in simultaneous soliloquies. The civil falsehoods that keep society running make each character a riddle to the others, a polite puzzle. With professions of openness Frank Churchill has been keeping a secret that threatens to embarrass and pain both Emma and Jane Fairfax. Emma discovers the ambiguous nature of discourse that mystifies, withholds, coerces, and lies as much as it reveals.

Yet Austen could not punish her more thoroughly than she does, and in this respect too Emma resembles the other imaginative girls. For all these heroines are mortified, humiliated, even bullied into sense. Austen's heavy attack on Emma, for instance, depends on the abject failure of the girl's wit. The very brilliant and assertive playfulness that initially marks her as a heroine is finally criticized on the grounds that it is self-deluding. Unable to imagine her visions into reality, she finds that she has all along been manipulated as a character in someone else's fiction. Through Emma, Austen is confronting the inadequacy of fiction and the pain of the "imaginist" who encounters the relentless recalcitrance of the world in which she lives, but she is also exposing the vulnerable delusions that Emma shares with Catherine Morland before the latter learns that she has no story to tell. Not only does the female artist fail, then, her efforts are condemned as tyrannical and coercive. Emma feels great self-loathing when she discovers how blind she has been: she is "ashamed of every sensation but the one revealed to her—her affection for Mr. Knightley—Every other part of her mind was disgusting" (III, chap. 2).

Although Emma is the center of Austen's fiction, what she has to learn is her commonality with Jane Fairfax, her vulnerability as a female. Like the antithetical sisters we have discussed, Jane Fairfax and Emma are doubles. Since they are the most accomplished girls in Highbury, exactly the same age, suitable companions, the fact that they are not friends is in itself quite significant. Emma even believes at times that her dislike for Jane is caused by her seeing in Jane "the really accomplished young woman which she wanted to be thought herself" (II, chap. 2). In fact, she has to succumb to Jane's fate, to *become* her double through the realization that she too has been manipulated as a pawn in Frank Churchill's game. The seriousness of Emma's assertive playfulness is made clear when she behaves rudely, making uncivil remarks at Box Hill, when she talks indiscreetly, unwittingly encouraging the advances of Mr. Elton, and when she allows her imagination to indulge in rather lewd suppositions about the possible sexual intrigues of Jane Fairfax and

a married man. In other words, Emma's imagination has led her
to the sin of being unladylike, and her complete mortification is a
prelude to submission as she becomes a friend of Jane Fairfax, at
one with her too in her realization of her own powerlessness. In this
respect, Mr. Elton's recitation of a well-known riddle seems ominous:

> My first doth affliction denote,
>   Which my second is destin'd to feel
> And my whole is the best antidote
>   That affliction to soften and heal.—   [I, chap. 9]

For if the answer is woe/man, then in the process of growing up
female Emma must be initiated into a secondary role of service and
silence.

Similarly, in *Northanger Abbey* Catherine Morland experiences "the
liberty which her imagination had dared to take" as a folly which
makes her feel that "She hated herself more than she could express"
(II, chap. 10) so that she too is reduced to "silence and sadness"
(II, chap. 15). Although Marianne Dashwood's sister had admitted
that "thirty-five and seventeen had better not have anything to do
with matrimony together" (I, chap. 8), Marianne allows herself at
the end to be given away to Colonel Brandon as a "reward" (III,
chap. 14) for his virtuous constancy. At nineteen she finds herself
"submitting to new attachments, entering on new duties" (III,
chap. 14). "With such a confederacy against her," the narrator
asks, "what else could she do?" Even Elizabeth Bennet, who had
"prided" herself on her "discernment," finds that she had never
known even herself (II, chap. 13). When "her anger was turned
against herself" (II, chap. 14), Elizabeth realizes that "she had
been blind, partial, prejudiced, absurd" (II, chap. 13). Significantly,
"she was humbled, she was grieved; she repented, though *she hardly
knew of what*" (III, chap. 8; italics ours).

All of these girls learn the necessity of curbing their tongues:
Marianne is silent when she learns submission and even when "a
thousand inquiries sprung up from her heart . . . she dared not urge
one" (III, chap. 10). When she finds that "For herself she was
humbled; but she was proud of him" (III, chap. 10), Elizabeth
Bennet displays her maturity by her modest reticence: not only does
she refrain from telling both her parents about her feelings for Mr.

Darcy, she never tells Jane about Mrs. Gardiner's letter or about her lover's role in persuading Mr. Bingley not to propose. Whereas before she had scorned Mr. Collins's imputation that ladies never say what they mean, at the end of *Pride and Prejudice* Elizabeth refuses to answer Lady Catherine and lies to her mother about the motives for that lady's visit. Furthermore, Elizabeth checks herself with Mr. Darcy, remembering "that he had yet to learn to be laughed at, and it was rather too early to begin" (III, chap. 16).

Emma also refrains from communicating with both Mrs. Elton and Jane Fairfax when she learns to behave discreetly. She manages to keep Harriet's secret even when Mr. Knightley proposes to her. "What did she say?" the narrator coyly asks. "Just what she ought, of course. A lady always does" (III, chap. 13). And at this point the novelist indicates her own ladylike discretion as she too refrains from detailing the personal scene explicitly. The polite talk of ladies, as Robin Lakoff has shown, is devised "to prevent the expression of strong statements,"[24] but such politeness commits both author and heroine alike to their resolve "of being humble and discreet and repressing imagination" (I, chap. 17). The novelist who has been fascinated with double-talk from the very beginning of her writing career sees the silences, evasions, and lies of women as an inescapable sign of their requisite sense of doubleness.

Austen's self-division—her fascination with the imagination and her anxiety that it is unfeminine—is part of her consciousness of the unique dilemma of all women, who must acquiesce in their status as objects after an adolescence in which they experience themselves as free agents. Simone de Beauvoir expresses the question asked by all Austen's heroines: "if I can accomplish my destiny only as the *Other*, how shall I give up my Ego?"[25] Like Emma, Austen's heroines are made to view their adolescent eroticism, their imaginative and physical activity, as an outgrown vitality incompatible with womanly restraint and survival: "how improperly had she been acting. . . . How inconsiderate, how indelicate, how irrational, how unfeeling, had been her conduct! What blindness, what madness, had led her on!" (III, chap. 11). The initiation into conscious acceptance of powerlessness is always mortifying, for it involves the fall from authority into the acceptance of one's status as a mere character, as well as the humiliating acknowledgment on the part of the witty sister that she must become her self-denying, quiet double. Assertion, imagination, and wit are tempting forms of self-definition which encourage each of the lively heroines to think that she can master or has mastered the world, but this is proven a dangerous illusion for women who must accept the fate of being mastered, and so the heroine learns the benefits of modesty, reticence, and patience.

If we recall Sophia's dying advice to Laura in *Love and Freindship*— "Run mad as often as you chuse; but do not faint"—it becomes clear that Austen is haunted by both these options and that she seems to feel that fainting, even if it only means playing at being dead, is a more viable solution for women who are acceptable to men only when they inhabit the glass coffin of silence, stillness, second-ariness. At the same time, however, Austen never renounces the subjectivity of what her heroines term their own "madness" until the end of each of their stories. The complementarity of the lively and the quiet sisters, moreover, suggests that these two inadequate responses to the female situation are inseparable. We have already seen that Marianne Dashwood's situation when she is betrayed by the man she considers her fiancé is quite similar to her sister's, and many critics have shown that Elinor has a great deal of sensibility, while Marianne has some sense.[26] Certainly Elizabeth and Jane Bennet, like Emma Woodhouse and Jane Fairfax, are confronted with similar dilemmas even as they eventually reach similar strategies for survival. In consistently drawing our attention to the friendship and reciprocity between sisters, Austen holds out the hope that maturity can bring women consciousness of self as subject and object.

Although all women may be, as she is, split between the conflicting desire for assertion in the world and retreat into the security of the home—speech and silence, independence and dependency—Austen implies that this psychic conflict can be resolved. Because the rela-tionship between personal identity and social role is so problematic for women, the emerging self can only survive with a sustained double vision. As Austen's admirers have always appreciated, she does write out accommodations, even when admitting their cost: since the polarities of fainting and going mad are extremes that tempt but destroy women, Austen describes how it is possible for a kind of dialectic of self-consciousness to emerge. While this aspect of female consciousness has driven many women to schizophrenia,

Austen's heroines live and flourish *because* of their contradictory projections. When the heroines are able to live Christian lives, doing unto others as they would be done, the daughters are ready to become wives. Self-consciousness liberates them from the self, enabling them to be exquisitely sensitive to the needs and responses of others. This is what distinguishes them from the comic victims of Austen's wit, who are either imprisoned in officious egoism or incapacitated by lethargic indolence: for Austen selfishness and selflessness are virtually interchangeable.

Only the mature heroines can sympathize and identify with the self-important meddlers and the somnambulant valetudinarians who abound in Austen's novels. But their maturity implies a fallen world and the continual possibility, indeed the necessity, of self-division, duplicity, and double-talk. As the narrator of *Emma* explains, "Seldom, very seldom, does complete truth belong to any human disclosure; seldom can it happen that something is not a little disguised or a little mistaken" (III, chap. 13). Using silence as a means of manipulation, passivity as a tactic to gain power, submission as a means of attaining the only control available to them, the heroines *seem* to submit as they get what they both want and need. On the one hand, this process and its accompanying sense of doubleness is psychologically and ethically beneficial, even a boon to women who are raised by it to real heroism. On the other hand, it is a painful degradation for heroines immersed or immured in what de Beauvoir would call their own "alterity."

The mortifications of Emma, Elizabeth, and Marianne are, then, the necessary accompaniment to the surrender of self-responsibility and definition. While Marianne Brandon, Elizabeth Darcy, and Emma Knightley never exist except in the slightly malevolent futurity of all happily-ever-afters, surely they would have learned the intricate gestures of subordination. And in *Mansfield Park* (1814), where Austen examines most carefully the price of doubleness, the mature author dramatizes how the psychic split so common in women can explode into full-scale fragmentation when reintegration becomes impossible. Nowhere in her fiction is the conflict between self and other portrayed with more sensitivity to the possibility of the personality fragmenting schizophrenically than in this novel in which Austen seems the most conflicted about her own talents.

Fanny Price and Mary Crawford enact what has developed into a familiar conflict in Austen's fiction. Fanny loves the country, where she lives quietly and contentedly, conservative in her tastes, revering old buildings and trees, and acquiescent in her behavior, submitting to indignities from every member of the household with patient humility. But "what was tranquillity and comfort to Fanny was tediousness and vexation to Mary" (II, chap. 11), because differences of disposition, habit, and circumstance make the latter a talented and restless girl, a harpist, a superb card player, and a witty conversationalist capable of parody and puns. In the famous play episode the two are most obviously contrasted: exemplary Fanny refuses to play a part, deeming the theatrical improper in Sir Bertram's absence, while Mary enters into the rehearsals with vivacity and anticipation of the performance precisely because it gives her the opportunity to dramatize, under the cover of the written script, her own amorous feelings toward Edmund. This use of art links Mary to Austen in a way further corroborated by biographical accounts of Austen's delight as a girl in such home theatricals. While many critics agree that Austen sets out to celebrate Fanny's responsiveness to nature,[27] in fact it is Mary who most resembles her creator in seeing "inanimate nature, with little observation; her attention was all for men and women, her talents for the light and lively" (I, chap. 8).

In spite of their antithetical responses, Mary and Fanny, like the other "sisters" in Austen's fiction, have much in common. Both are visitors in the country and virtually parentless outsiders at Mansfield Park. Both have disreputable family histories which they seek to escape in part through their contact with the Bertram household. Both are loving sisters to brothers very much in need of their counsel and support. Both are relatively poor, dependent on male relatives for financial security. While Mary rides Fanny's horse, Fanny wears what she thinks is one of Mary's necklaces. While Fanny loves to hear Mary's music, Mary consistently seeks out Fanny's advice. They are the only two young people aware that Henry is flirting outrageously with both Bertram sisters and thereby creating terrible jealousies. Both see Rushworth as the fool that he is, both are aware of the potential impropriety of the play, and both are in love with

Edmund Bertram. Indeed, each seems incomplete because she lacks precisely the qualities so fully embodied by the other: thus, Fanny seems constrained, lacking nerve and will, while Mary is insensitive to the needs and feelings of her friends; one is too silent, the other too talkative.

Perhaps Fanny does learn enough from Mary to become a true Austen heroine. Not only does she "come out" at a dance in her honor, but she does so in a state "nearly approaching high spirits" (II, chap. 10). She rejects the attempts at persuasion made by Sir Thomas and he accuses her of "wilfulness of temper, self-conceit, and . . . independence of spirit" (III, chap. 1). In defending herself against the unwelcome addresses of Henry Crawford, Fanny also speaks more, and more angrily, than she ever has before. Finally, she does liberate herself from the need for Edmund's approval, specifically when she questions his authority and becomes "vexed into displeasure, and anger, against Edmund" (III, chap. 8). Recently, two feminist critics have persuasively argued that, when Fanny refuses to marry for social advantage, she becomes the moral model for all the other characters, challenging their social system and exposing its flimsy values.[28] And certainly Fanny does become a kind of authority figure for her younger sister Susan, whom she eventually liberates from the noisy confinement of the Portsmouth household.

Yet, trapped in angelic reserve, Fanny can never assert or enliven herself except in extreme situations where she only succeeds through passive resistance. A model of domestic virtue—"dependent, helpless, friendless, neglected, forgotten" (II, chap. 7)—she resembles Snow White not only in her passivity but in her invalid deathliness, her immobility, her pale purity. And Austen is careful to show us that Fanny can only assert herself through silence, reserve, recalcitrance, and even cunning. Since, as Leo Bersani has argued, "nonbeing is the ultimate prudence in the world of *Mansfield Park*,"[29] Fanny is destined to become the next Lady Bertram, following the example of Sir Thomas's corpselike wife. With purity that seems prudish and reserve bordering on hypocrisy, Fanny is far less likeable than Austen's other heroines: as Frank Churchill comments of Jane Fairfax, "There is safety in reserve, but no attraction" (II, chap. 6).

Obedience, tears, pallor, and martyrdom are effective but not especially endearing methods of survival, in part because one senses some pride in Fanny's self-abasement.

If Fanny Price seems unable fully to actualize herself as an authentic subject, Mary Crawford fails to admit her contingency. Because of this, like the Queen who insists on telling and living her own lively stories, she is exorcised from Mansfield Park, both the place and the plot, in a manner that dramatizes Austen's obsessive anxiety over Mary's particular brand of impropriety—her audacious speech. When Mary's liberty deteriorates into license and her self-actualization into selfishness, Edmund can only defend her by claiming that "She does not *think* evil, but she speaks it—speaks it in playfulness—" and he admits this means "the mind itself was tainted" (II, chap. 9). Although Mary's only crimes do, in fact, seem to be verbal, we are told repeatedly that her mind has been "led astray and bewildered, and without any suspicion of being so; darkened, yet fancying itself light" (III, chap. 6). Because she would excuse as "folly" what both Fanny and Edmund term "evil," her *language* gives away her immodesty, her "blunted delicacy" (III, chap. 16). Edmund says in horror, "No reluctance, no horror, no feminine—shall I say? no modest loathings!" (III, chap. 16). It is, significantly, "the manner in which she spoke" (III, chap. 16) that gives the greatest offense and determines Edmund's final rejection.

When, during the episode of the theatricals, Fanny silently plays the role of the angel by refusing to play, Mary Crawford metamorphoses into a siren as she coquettishly persuades Edmund to participate in the very theatricals he initially condemned as improper. Fanny knows that in part her own reticence is caused by fear of exposing herself, but this does not stop her from feeling extremely jealous of Mary, not only because Mary is a fine actress but because she has chosen to play a part that allows her to express her otherwise silent opposition to Edmund's choice of a clerical profession. Heretical, worldly, cynical in her disdain for the institutions of the Church, Mary is a damned Eve who offers to seduce prelapsarian Edmund Bertram in the garden of the green room, when the father is away on a business trip, and she almost succeeds, at least until the absent father reappears to burn all the scripts, to repress this libidinal outbreak in paradise and call for music which "helped conceal the want of real harmony" (II, chap. 2). Since the rehearsals have brought nothing but restlessness, rivalry, vexation, pettiness, and sexual license, *Lover's Vows* illustrates Austen's belief that self-expression and artistry are dangerously attractive precisely because they liberate actors from the rules, roles, social obligations, and familial bonds of every day life.[30]

Mary's seductive allure is the same as her brother Henry's. He is the best actor, both on and off the stage, because he has the ability to be "every thing to every body" (II, chap. 13). But he can "do nothing without a mixture of evil" (II, chap. 13). Attractive precisely because of his protean ability to change himself into a number of attractive personages, Henry is an impersonator who degenerates into an imposter, not unlike Frank Churchill, who is also "acting a part or making a parade of insincere professions" (*E*, II, chap. 6). Indeed, Henry is a good representative of the kind of young man with whom each of the heroines falls briefly in love before she is finally disillusioned: Willoughby, Wickham, Frank Churchill, Henry Crawford, and Mr. Elliot are eminently agreeable because they are self-changers, self-shapers. In many respects they are attractive to the heroines because somehow they act as doubles: younger men who must learn to please, narcissists, they experience traditionally "feminine" powerlessness and they are therefore especially interested in becoming the creators of themselves.

In *Mansfield Park*, however, Austen defines this self-creating spirit as a "bewitching" (II, chap. 13) "infection" (II, chap. 1), and the epidemic restlessness represented by the Crawfords is seen as far more dangerous than Fanny's invalid passivity. Fanny's rejection of Henry represents, then, her censure of his presumptuous attempt to author his own life, his past history, and his present fictional identities. Self-divided, indulging his passions, alienated from authority, full of ambition, and seeking revenge for past injuries, the false young man verges on the Satanic. While he manages to thrive in his own fashion, finding a suitable lover or wife and generally making his fortune in the process, his way cannot be the Austen heroine's. Although his crimes are real actions while hers are purely rhetorical, she is more completely censured because her liberties more seriously defy her social role.

When her Adam refuses to taste the fruit offered by Mary Crawford,

Austen follows the example of Samuel Richardson in her favorite of his novels, *Sir Charles Grandison*, where Harriet draws a complimentary analogy between Sir Charles and Adam: the former would not have been so compliant as to taste the forbidden fruit; instead he would have left it to God to annihilate the first Eve and supply a second.[31] Just as Fanny sees through the play actor, Henry Crawford, to the role-player and hypocrite, Edmund finally recognizes Mary's playfulness as her refusal to submit to the categories of her culture, a revolt that is both attractive and immoral because it gains her the freedom to become whatever she likes, even to choose not to submit to one identity but to try out a variety of voices. For all these reasons, she has to be annihilated. But, unlike Richardson, Austen in destroying this unrepentant, imaginative, and assertive girl is demonstrating her own self-division.

In all six of Austen's novels women who are refused the means of self-definition are shown to be fatally drawn to the dangerous delights of impersonation and pretense. But Austen's profession depends on just these disguises. What else, if not impersonation, is characterization? What is plot, if not pretense? In all the novels, the narrator's voice is witty, assertive, spirited, independent, even (as D. W. Harding has shown) arrogant and nasty.[32] Poised between the subjectivity of lyric and the objectivity of drama, the novel furnishes Austen with a unique opportunity: she can create Mary Crawford's witty letters or Emma's brilliant retorts, even while rejecting them as improper; furthermore, she can reprove as indecent in a heroine what is necessary to an author. Authorship for Austen is an escape from the very restraints she imposes on her female characters. And in this respect she seems typical, for women may have contributed so significantly to narrative fiction precisely because it effectively objectifies, even as it sustains and hides, the subjectivity of the author. Put another way, in the novels Austen questions and criticizes her own aesthetic and ironic sensibilities, noting the limits and asserting the dangers of an imagination undisciplined by the rigors of art.

Using her characters to castigate the imaginative invention that informs her own novels, Austen is involved in a contradiction that, as we have seen, she approves as the only solution available to her heroines. Just as they manage to survive only by seeming to submit, she succeeds in maintaining her double consciousness in fiction that proclaims its docility and restraint even as it uncovers the delights of assertion and rebellion. Indeed the comedy of Austen's novels explores the tensions between the freedom of her art and the dependency of her characters: while they stutter and sputter and lapse into silence and even hasten to perfect felicity, she attains a woman's language that is magnificently duplicitous. In this respect, Austen serves as a paradigm of the literary ladies who would emerge so successfully and plentifully in the mid-nineteenth century, popular lady novelists like Rhoda Broughton, Charlotte Mary Yonge, Home Lee, and Mrs. Craik[33] who strenuously suppressed awareness of how their own professional work called into question traditional female roles. Deeply conservative as their content appears to be, however, it frequently retains traces of the original duplicity so manifest in its origin, even as it demonstrates their own exuberant evasion of the inescapable limits they prescribe for their model heroines.

Although Austen clearly escapes the House of Prose that confines her heroines by making her story out of their renunciation of storytelling, she also dwells in the freer prospects of Emily Dickinson's "Possibility" by identifying not only with her model heroines, but also with less obvious, nastier, more resilient and energetic female characters who enact her rebellious dissent from her culture, a dissent, as we have seen, only partially obscured by the "blotter" of her plot. Many critics have already noticed duplicity in the "happy endings" of Austen's novels in which she brings her couples to the brink of bliss in such haste, or with such unlikely coincidences, or with such sarcasm that the entire message seems undercut[34]: the implication remains that a girl without the aid of a benevolent narrator would never find a way out of either her mortifications or her parents' house.

Perhaps less obvious instances of Austen's duplicity occur in her representation of a series of extremely powerful women each of whom acts out the rebellious anger so successfully repressed by the heroine and the author. Because they so rarely appear and so infrequently speak in their own voices, these furious females remain secret presences in the plots. Not only do they play a less prominent role in the novels than their function in the plot would seem to require; buried or killed or banished at the end of the story, they seem to warrant this punishment by their very unattractiveness. Like Lady Susan, they are mothers or surrogate mothers who seek to destroy their docile children. Widows who are no longer defined by men simply because they have survived the male authorities in their lives, these women can exercise power even if they can never legitimize it; thus they seem both pushy and dangerous. Yet if their energy appears destructive and disagreeable, that is because this is the mechanism by which Austen disguises the most assertive aspect of herself as the Other. We shall see that these bitchy women enact impulses of revolt that make them doubles not only for the heroines but for their author as well.

We have seen Austen at her most conflicted in *Mansfield Park*, so perhaps it is here that we can begin to understand how she quietly yet forcefully undercuts her own moral. Probably the most obnoxious character in the book, Aunt Norris, is clearly meant to be a dark parody of Mary Crawford, revealing—as she does—how easily Mary's girlish liveliness and materialism could degenerate into meddlesome, officious penny-pinching. But, as nasty as she is repeatedly shown and said to be when she tries to manage and manipulate, to condescend to Fanny, to save herself some money, Aunt Norris is in some ways castigated for moral failures which are readily understandable, if not excusable. After all, she is living on a small, fixed income, and if she uses flattery to gain pecuniary help, her pleasures are dependent on receiving it. Like Fanny Price, Aunt Norris knows that she must please and placate Sir Thomas. Even when he gives "advice," both accept it as "the advice of absolute power" (II, chap. 18). Perhaps one reason for her implacable hatred of Fanny is that Aunt Norris sees in her a rival for Sir Thomas's protection, another helpless and useful dependent. Furthermore, like Fanny, Aunt Norris uses submission as a strategy to get her own way: acquiescing to the power in authority, she manages to talk her brother-in-law into all her schemes.

Unlike "good" Lady Bertram, Aunt Norris is an embittered, manipulative, pushy female who cannot allow other people to live their own lives. At least, this is how these sisters first strike us, until we remember that, for all her benign dignity, Lady Bertram does nothing but sit "nicely dressed on a sofa, doing some long piece of needlework, of little use and no beauty, thinking more of her pug than her children" (I, chap. 2). Indeed, the contrast between her total passivity and Aunt Norris's indiscriminate exertions recalls again the options described by Sophia in *Love and Freindship*— fainting or running mad. Like all the other "good" mothers in Austen's fiction who are passive because dead, dying, or dumb, Lady Bertram teaches the necessity of submission, the all-importance of a financially sound marriage, and the empty-headedness that goes with these values. For all her noisy bustling, Aunt Norris is a much more loving mother to Lady Bertram's daughters. If she indulges them, it is in part out of genuine affection and loyalty. And as she herself actively lives her own life and pursues her own ends, Aunt Norris quite naturally identifies with her headstrong nieces. Unlike the figure of the "good" mother, the figure of bad Aunt Norris implies that female strength, exertion, and passion are necessary for survival and pleasure.

Instead of abandoning Maria after the social disgrace of the elopement and divorce, Aunt Norris goes off to live with her as her surrogate mother. Although she is thereby punished and driven from Mansfield Park, Aunt Norris (we cannot help suspecting) is probably as relieved to have escaped the dampening effect of Sir Thomas's sober rule as he is to have rid himself of the one person who has managed to assert herself against his wishes, to evade his control. This shrew is still talking at the end of the book, untamed and presumably untameable. As if to authenticate her completely unacceptable admiration for this kind of woman, Austen constructs a plot which quite consistently finds its impetus in Aunt Norris. It is she, for instance, who decides to take Fanny from her home and bring her to Mansfield; she places Fanny in Sir Thomas's household and allocates her inferior status; she rules Mansfield in Sir Thomas's absence and allows the play to progress; she plans and executes the visit to Southerton that creates the marriage between Maria and Mr. Rushworth. Quite openly dedicated to the pursuit of pleasure and activity, especially the joy of controlling other people's lives, Aunt Norris is a parodic surrogate for the author, a suitable double whose manipulations match those of Aunt Jane.

As vilified as she is, Aunt Norris was the character most often praised and enjoyed by Jane Austen's contemporaries, to the author's delight.[35] Hers is one of the most memorable voices in *Mansfield Park*. She resembles not only the hectic, scheming Queen, stepmother to Snow White, but also the Queen of the Night in Mozart's *The Magic Flute*. Actually, all the angry dowagers in Austen's novels represent a threat to the enlightened reason of the male god who eventually wins the heroine only by banishing the forces of female sexuality, capriciousness, and loquacity. But, as in *The Magic Flute*, where the Queen of the Night is carried offstage still singing her exuberantly strenuous resistence, women like Aunt Norris are never really completely stifled. The despised Mrs. Ferrars of *Sense and Sensibility*, for example, exacts the punishment which Elinor Dashwood could not help but wish on a man who has been selfishly deceiving her for the entire novel. By tampering with the patriarchal line of inheritance, Mrs. Ferrars proves that the very forms valued by Elinor are arbitrary. But even though *Sense and Sensibility* ends with the overt message that young women like Marianne and Elinor must submit to the powerful conventions of society by finding a male protector, Mrs. Ferrars and her scheming protégée Lucy Steele prove that women can themselves become agents of repression, manipulators of conventions, and survivors.

Most of these powerful widows would agree with Lady Catherine De Bourgh in seeing "no occasion for entailing estates from the female lines" (*PP*, II, 6). Opposed to the very basis of patriarchy, the exclusive right of male inheritance, Lady Catherine quite predictably earns the vilification always allotted by the author to the representatives of matriarchal power. She is shown to be arrogant, officious, egotistical, and rude as she patronizes all the other characters in the novel. Resembling Lady Susan in her disdain for her own pale, weak, passive daughter, Lady Catherine delights in managing the affairs of others. Probably most unpleasant when she opposes Elizabeth's right to marry Darcy, she questions Elizabeth's birth and breeding by admitting that Elizabeth is "a gentleman's daughter," but demanding, "who was your mother?" (III, chap. 14).

As dreadful as she seems to be, however, Lady Catherine is herself in some ways an appropriate mother to Elizabeth because the two women are surprisingly similar. Her ladyship points this out herself when she says to Elizabeth, "You give your opinion very decidedly for so young a person" (II, chap. 6). Both speak authoritatively of matters on which neither is an authority. Both are sarcastic and certain in their assessment of people. Elizabeth describes herself to Darcy by asserting, "There is a stubbornness about me that never can bear to be frightened at the will of others" (II, chap. 8), and in this respect too she resembles Lady Catherine, whose courage is indomitable. Finally, these are the only two women in the novel capable of feeling and expressing genuine anger, although it is up to Lady Catherine to articulate the rage against entailment that Elizabeth must feel since it has so rigidly restricted her own and her sisters' lives. When Elizabeth and Lady Catherine meet in conflict, each retains her decided resolution of carrying her own purpose. In all her objections to Elizabeth's match with Darcy, Lady Catherine only articulates what Elizabeth has herself thought on the subject, that her mother is an unsuitable relation for him and her sister an even less appropriate connection. Highly incensed and unresponsive to advice, Elizabeth resembles her interlocutor; it is fitting not only that she takes the place meant for Lady Catherine's daughter when she marries Darcy, but that she also sees to it that her husband is persuaded to entertain his aunt at Pemberley. As Darcy and Elizabeth both realize, Lady Catherine has been the author of their marriage, bringing about the first proposal by furnishing the occasion and place for meetings, and the second by endeavoring to separate them when she actually communicates Elizabeth's renewed attraction to a suitor waiting for precisely such encouragement.

The vitriolic shrew is so discreetly hidden in *Emma* that she never appears at all, yet again she is the causal agent of the plot. Like her predecessors, Mrs. Churchill is a proud, arrogant, and capricious woman who uses all means, including reports of her poor health, to elicit attention and obedience from her family. In fact, only her death—which clears the way for the marriage of Frank Churchill to Jane Fairfax—convinces them that her nervous disorders were more than selfish, imaginary complaints. Actually Mrs. Churchill can be viewed as the cause of all the deceit practiced by the lovers inasmuch as their secret engagement is a response to her disapproval of the match. Thus this disagreeable women with "no more heart than a stone to people in general, and the devil of a temper" (I, chap. 14) is the "invisible presence" which, as W. J. Harvey explains, "enables Jane Austen to embody that aspect of our intuition of reality summed up by Auden—'we are lived by powers we do not understand.' "[36]

But Mrs. Churchill is more than the representative of the unpredictable contingency of reality. On the one hand, she displays an uncanny and ominous resemblance to Jane Fairfax, who will also be a penniless upstart when she marries and who is also subject to nervous headaches and fevers. Mrs. Churchill, we are told by Mr. Weston, "is as thorough a fine lady as anybody ever beheld" (II, chap. 18), so it is quite fitting that polite Jane Fairfax becomes the next Mrs. Churchill and inherits that lady's jewels. On the other hand, Mrs. Churchill seems much like Emma, who is also involved in becoming a pattern lady: selfish in their very imaginings, both have the power of having too much their own way, both are convinced of their superiority in talent, elegance of mind, fortune, and consequence, and both want to be first in society where they can enjoy assigning subservient parts to those in their company.

The model lady haunts all the characters of *Emma*, evoking "delicate plants" to Mr. Woodhouse (II, chap. 16) and the showy finery of Selena for Mrs. Elton. But it is Mrs. Churchill who illustrates the bankruptcy of the ideal, for she is not only a monitory image of what Austen's heroines could be, she is also a double of what they are already fast becoming. If Mrs. Churchill represents Austen's guilt at her own authorial control, she also reminds us that feminine propriety, reserve, and politeness can give way to bitchiness since the bitch is what the young lady's role and values imply from the beginning, built—as we have seen them to be—out of complicity, manipulation, and deceit. At the same time, however, Mrs. Churchill is herself the victim of her own ladylike silences, evasions, and lies: no one takes seriously her accounts of her own ill health, no one believes that her final illness is more than a manipulative fiction, and her death—one of the few to occur in Austen's mature fiction—is an ominous illustration of feminine vulnerability that Austen would more fully explore in her last novel.

It is not only Austen's mad matriarchs who reflect her discomfort with the glass coffin of female submission. Her last completed novel,

Persuasion (1818), focuses on an angelically quiet heroine who has given up her search for a story and has thereby effectively killed herself off. Almost as if she were reviewing the implications of her own plots, Austen explores in *Persuasion* the effects on women of submission to authority and the renunciation of one's life story. Eight years before the novel begins, Anne Elliot had been persuaded to renounce her romance with Captain Wentworth, but this decision sickened her by turning her into a nonentity. Forced into "knowing [her] own nothingness" (I, chap. 6), Anne is a "nobody with either father or sister" so her word has "no weight" (I, chap. 1). An invisible observer who tends to fade into the background, she is frequently afraid to move lest she should be seen. Having lost the "bloom" of her youth, she is but a pale vestige of what she had been and realizes that her lover "should not have known [her] again" (I, chap. 7), their relationship being "now nothing!" Anne Elliot is the ghost of her own dead self; through her, Austen presents a personality haunted with a sense of menace.

At least one reason why Anne has deteriorated into a ghostly insubstantiality is that she is a dependent female in a world symbolized by her vain and selfish aristocratic father, who inhabits the mirrored dressing room of Kellynch Hall. It is significant that *Persuasion* begins with her father's book, the *Baronetage*, which is described as "the book of books" (I, chap. 1) because it symbolizes male authority, patriarchal history in general, and her father's family history in particular. Existing in it as a first name and birth date in a family line that concludes with the male heir presumptive, William Walter Elliot, Esq., Anne has no reality until a husband's name can be affixed to her own. But Anne's name is a new one in the *Baronetage*: the history of this ancient, respectable line of heirs records "all the Marys and Elizabeths they had married" (I, chap. 1), as if calling our attention to the hopeful fact that, unlike her sisters Mary and Elizabeth, Anne may not be forced to remain a character within this "book of books." And, in fact, Anne will reject the economic and social standards represented by the *Baronetage*, deciding, by the end of her process of personal development, that not she but the Dowager Viscountess Dalrymple and her daughter the Honourable Miss Carteret are "nothing" (II, chap. 4). She will also discover that Captain Wentworth is "no longer nobody" (II, chap. 12), and, even more significantly, she will insist on her ability to seek and find "at least the comfort of telling the whole story her own way" (II, chap. 9).

But before Anne can become somebody, she must confront what being a nobody means: "I'm Nobody!" (J. 228), Emily Dickinson could occasionally avow, and certainly, by choosing not to have a story of her own, Anne seems to have decided to dwell in Dickinson's realm of "Possibility," for what Austen demonstrates through her is that the person who has not become anybody is haunted by everybody. Living in a world of her father's mirrors, Anne confronts the several selves she might have become and discovers that they all reveal the same story of the female fall from authority and autonomy.

As a motherless girl, Anne is tempted to become her own mother, although she realizes that her mother lived invisibly, unloved, within Sir Walter's house. Since Anne could marry Mr. Elliot and become the future Lady Elliot, she has to confront her mother's unhappy marriage as a potential life story not very different from that of Catherine Morland's Mrs. Tilney. At the same time, however, since serviceable Mrs. Clay is an unattached female who aspires to her mother's place in the family as her father's companion and her sister Elizabeth's intimate, Anne realizes that she could also become patient Penelope Clay, for she too understands "the art of pleasing" (I, chap. 2), of making herself useful. When Anne goes to Uppercross, moreover, she functions something like Mrs. Clay, "being too much in the secret of the complaints" of each of the tenants of both households (I, chap. 6), and trying to flatter or placate each and all into good humor. The danger exists, then, that Anne's sensitivity and selflessness could degenerate into Mrs. Clay's ingratiating, hypocritical service.

Of course, Mary Musgrove's situation is also a potential identity for Anne, since Charles had actually asked for Anne's hand in marriage before he settled on her younger sister, and since Mary resembles Anne in being one of Sir Walter's unfavored daughters. Indeed, Mary's complaint that she is "always the last of my family to be noticed" (II, chap. 6) could easily be voiced by Anne. Bitter about being nobody, Mary responds to domestic drudgery with "feminine" invalidism that is an extension of Anne's sickening self-doubt, as well as the only means at Mary's disposal of using her imagination to add some drama and importance to her life. Mary's hypochondria reminds us that Louisa Musgrove provides a kind of paradigm for all these women when she literally falls from the Cobb and suffers from a head injury resulting in exceedingly weak nerves. Because incapacitated Louisa is first attracted to Captain Wentworth and finally marries Captain Benwick, whose first attentions had been given to Anne, she too is clearly an image of what Anne might have become.

Through both Mary and Louisa, then, Austen illustrates how growing up female constitutes a fall from freedom, autonomy, and strength into debilitating, degrading, ladylike dependency. In direct contradiction to Captain Wentworth's sermon in the hedgerow, Louisa discovers that even firmness cannot save her from such a fall. Indeed, it actually precipitates it, and she discovers that her fate is not to jump from the stiles down the steep flight of seaside stairs but to read love poetry quietly in the parlor with a suitor suitably solicitous for her sensitive nerves. While Louisa's physical fall and subsequent illness reinforce Anne's belief that female assertion and impetuosity must be fatal, they also return us to the elegiac autumnal landscape that reflects Anne's sense of her own diminishment, the loss she experiences since her story is "now nothing."

Anne lives in a world of mirrors both because she could have become most of the women in the novel and, as the title suggests, because all the characters present her with their personal preferences rationalized into principles by which they attempt to persuade her. She is surrounded by other people's versions of her story and offered coercive advice by Sir Walter, Captain Wentworth, Charles Musgrove, Mrs. Musgrove, Lady Russell, and Mrs. Smith. Eventually, indeed, the very presence of another person becomes oppressive for Anne, since everyone but she is convinced that his or her version of reality is the only valid one. Only Anne has a sense of the different, if equally valid, perspectives of the various families and individuals among which she moves. Like Catherine Morland, she struggles against other people's fictional use and image of her; and finally she penetrates to the secret of patriarchy through absolutely no skill of detection on her own part. Just as Catherine blunders on the secret of the ancestral mansion to understand the arbitrary power of General Tilney, who does not mean what he says, Anne stumbles fortuitously on the secret of the heir to Kellynch Hall, William Elliot, who had married for money and was very unkind to his first wife. Mr. Elliot's "manoevres of selfishness and duplicity must ever be revolting" (II, chap. 7) to Anne, who comes to believe that "the evil" of this suitor could easily result in "irremediable mischief" (II, chap. 10).

For all of Austen's heroines, as Mr. Darcy explains, "detection could not be in [their] power, and suspicion certainly not in [their] inclination" (II, chap. 3). Yet Anne does quietly and attentively watch and listen and judge the members of her world and, as Stuart Tave has shown, she increasingly exerts herself to speak out, only gradually to discover that she is being heard.[37] Furthermore, in her pilgrimage from Kellynch Hall to Upper Cross and Lyme to Bath, the landscapes she encounters function as a kind of psychic geography of her development so that, when the withered hedgerows and tawny autumnal meadows are replaced by the invigorating breezes and flowing tides of Lyme, we are hardly surprised that Anne's bloom is restored (I, chap. 12). Similarly, when Anne gets to Bath, this woman who has heard and overheard others has trouble listening because she is filled with her own feelings, and she decides that "one half of her should not be always so much wiser than the other half, or always suspecting the other half of being worse than it was" (II, chap. 7). Therefore, in a room crowded with talking people, Anne manages to signal to Captain Wentworth her lack of interest in Mr. Elliot through her assertion that she has no pleasure in parties at her father's house. "She had spoken it," the narrator emphasizes; if "she trembled when it was done, conscious that her words were listened to" (II, chap. 10), this is because Anne has actually "never since the loss of her dear mother, known the happiness of being listened to, or encouraged" (I, chap. 6).

The fact that her mother's loss initiated her invisibility and silence is important in a book that so closely associates the heroine's felicity with her ability to articulate her sense of herself as a woman. Like Elinor Tilney, who feels that "A mother could have been always present. A mother would have been a constant friend; her influence would have been beyond all others" (*NA*, II, chap. 7), Anne misses the support of a loving female influence. It is then fitting that the powerful whispers of well-meaning Mrs. Musgrove and Mrs. Croft furnish Anne with the cover—the opportunity and the encouragement—to discuss with Captain Harville her sense of exclusion from patriarchal culture: "Men have had every advantage of us in telling their own story. . . . The pen has been in their hands" (II, chap. 11). Anne Elliot will "not allow books to prove anything" because they "were all written by men" (II, chap. 11); her contention that women love longest because their feelings are more tender directly contradicts the authorities on women's "fickleness" that Captain Harville cites. As we have already seen, her speech reminds us that the male charge of "inconstancy" is an attack on the irrepressible interiority of women who cannot be contained within the images provided by patriarchal culture. Though Anne remains inalterably inhibited by these images since she cannot express her sense of herself by "saying what should not be said" (II, chap. 11) and though she can only replace the *Baronetage* with the *Navy Lists*—a book in which women are conspicuously absent—still she is the best example of her own belief in female subjectivity. She has both deconstructed the dead selves created by all her friends to remain true to her own feelings, and she has continually reexamined and reassessed herself and her past.

Finally, Anne's fate seems to be a response to Austen's earlier stories in which girls are forced to renounce their romantic ambitions: Anne "had been forced into prudence in her youth, she learned romance as she grew older—the natural sequel of an unnatural beginning" (I, chap. 4). It is she who teaches Captain Wentworth the limits of masculine assertiveness. Placed in Anne's usual situation of silently overhearing, he discovers her true, strong feelings. Significantly, his first reponse is to drop his pen. Then, quietly, under the cover of doing some business for Captain Harville, Captain Wentworth writes her his proposal, which he can only silently hand to her before leaving the room. At work in the common sitting-room of the White Hart Inn, alert for inauspicious interruptions, using his other letter as a kind of blotter to camouflage his designs, Captain Wentworth reminds us of Austen herself. While Anne's rebirth into "a second spring of youth and beauty" (II, chap. 1) takes place within the same corrupt city that fails to fulfill its baptismal promise of purification in *Northanger Abbey*, we are led to believe that her life with this man will escape the empty elegance of Bath society.

That the sea breezes of Lyme and the watery cures of Bath have revived Anne from her ghostly passivity furnishes some evidence that naval life may be an alternative to and an escape from the corruption of the land so closely associated with patrilineal descent. Sir Walter Elliot dismisses the navy because it raises "men to honours which their fathers and grandfathers never dreamt of" (I, chap. 3). And certainly Captain Wentworth seems almost miraculously to evade the hypocrisies and inequities of a rigid class system by making money on the water. But it is also true that naval life seems to justify Sir Walter's second objection that "it cuts up a man's youth and vigour most horribly." While he is thinking in his vanity only about the rapidity with which sailors lose their looks, we are given an instance of the sea cutting up a man's youth, a singularly unprepossessing man at that: when worthless Dick Musgrove is created by Austen only to be destroyed at sea, we are further reminded of her trust in the beneficence of nature, for only her anger against the unjust adulation of sons (over daughters) can explain the otherwise gratuitous cruelty of her remarks about Mrs. Musgrove's "large fat sighings over the destiny of a son, whom alive nobody had cared for" (I, chap. 8). Significantly, this happily lost son was recognized as a fool by Captain Wentworth, whose naval success closely associates him with a vocation that does not as entirely exclude women as most landlocked vocations do: his sister, Mrs. Croft, knows that the difference between "a fine gentleman" and a navy man is that the former treats women as if they were "all fine ladies, instead of rational creatures" (I, chap. 8). She herself believes that "any reasonable woman may be perfectly happy" on board ship, as she was when she crossed the Atlantic four times and traveled to and from the East Indies, more comfortably (she admits) than when she settled at Kellynch Hall, although her husband *did* take down Sir Walter's mirrors.

Naval men like Captain Wentworth and Admiral Croft are also closely associated, as is Captain Harville, with the ability to create "ingenious contrivances and nice arrangements . . . to turn the actual space to the best possible account" (I, chap. 11), a skill not unrelated to a "profession which is, if possible, more distinguished in its domestic virtue than in its national importance" (II, chap. 12). While Austen's dowagers try to gain power by exploiting traditionally male prerogatives, the heroine of the last novel discovers an egalitarian society in which men value and participate in domestic life, while women contribute to public events, a complementary ideal that presages the emergence of an egalitarian sexual ideology.[38] No longer confined to a female community of childbearing and childrearing, activities portrayed as dreary and dangerous in both Austen's novels and her letters,[39] Anne triumphs in a marriage that represents the union of traditionally male and female spheres. If such a consummation can only be envisioned in the future, on the water, amid imminent threats of war, Austen nonetheless celebrates friendship between the sexes as her lovers progress down Bath streets with "smiles reined in and spirits dancing in private rapture" (II, chap. 11).

When Captain Wentworth accepts Anne's account of their story, he agrees with her highly ambivalent assessment of the woman who advised her to break off their engagement. Lady Russell is one of Austen's last pushy widows, but, in this novel which revises Austen's earlier endorsement of the necessity of taming the shrew, the cautionary monster is one of effacement rather than assertion. If the powerful origin of *Emma* is the psychologically coercive model of the woman as lady, in *Persuasion* Austen describes a heroine who refuses to become a lady. Anne Elliot listened to the persuasions of the powerful, wealthy, proper Lady Russell when she refrained from marrying the man she loved. But finally she rejects Lady Russell, who is shown to value rank and class over the dictates of the heart, in part because her own heart is perverted, capable of revelling "in angry pleasure, in pleased contempt" (II, chap. 1) at events sure to hurt Anne. Anne replaces this cruel stepmother with a different kind of mother surrogate, another widow, Mrs. Smith. Poor, confined, crippled by rheumatic fever, Mrs. Smith serves as an emblem of the dispossession of women in a patriarchal society, and she is, as Paul Zietlow has shown, also the embodiment of what Anne's future could have been under less fortunate circumstances.[40]

While Lady Russell persuaded Anne not to marry a poor man, Mrs. Smith explains why she should not marry a rich one. Robbed of all physical and economic liberty, with "no child . . . no relatives . . . no health . . . no possibility of moving" (II, chap. 5), Mrs. Smith is paralyzed, and, although she exerts herself to maintain good humor in her tight place, she is also maddened. She expresses her rage at the false forms of civility, specifically at the corrupt and selfish double-dealings of Mr. Elliot, the heir apparent and the epitome of patriarchal society. With fierce delight in her revengeful revelations, Mrs. Smith proclaims herself an "injured, angry woman" (II, chap. 9) and she articulates Anne's—and Austen's—unacknowledged fury at her own unnecessary and unrecognized paralysis and suffering. But although this widow is a voice of angry female revolt against the injustices of patriarchy, she is as much a resident of Bath as Lady Russell. This fashionable place for cures reminds us that society *is* sick. And Mrs. Smith participates in the moral degeneration of the place when she selfishly lies to Anne, placing her own advancement over Anne's potential marital happiness by withholding the truth about Mr. Elliot until she is quite sure Anne does not mean to marry him. Like Lady Russell, then, this other voice within Anne's psyche can also potentially victimize her.

It is Mrs. Smith's curious source of knowledge, her informant or her muse, who best reveals the corruption that has permeated and informs the social conventions of English society. A woman who nurses sick people back to health, wonderfully named nurse Rooke resembles in her absence from the novel many of Austen's most important avatars. Pictured perched on the side of a sickbed, nurse Rooke seems as much a vulture as a savior of the afflicted. Her freedom of movement in society resembles the movement of a chess piece which moves parallel to the edge of the board, thereby defining the limits of the game. And she "rooks" her patients, discovering their hidden hoards.

Providing ears and eyes for the confined Mrs. Smith, this seemingly ubiquitous, omniscient nurse is privy to all the secrets of the sickbed. She has taught Mrs. Smith how to knit, and she sells "little thread-cases, pin-cushions and cardracks" not unlike Austen's "little bit (two Inches wide) of Ivory." What she brings as part of her services are volumes furnished from the sick chamber, stories of weakness and selfishness and impatience. A historian of private life, nurse Rooke communicates in typically female fashion as a gossip engaged in the seemingly trivial, charitable office of selling feminine handcrafts to the fashionable world. This and her gossip are, of course, a disguise for her subversive interest in uncovering the sordid realities behind the decorous appearances of high life. In this regard she is a wonderful portrait of Austen herself. While seemingly unreliable, dependent (as she is) for information upon many interactions which are subject to errors of misconception and ignorance, this uniquely female historian turns out to be accurate and revolutionary as she reveals "the manoevers of selfishness and duplicity" (II, chap. 9) of one class to another. Finally, sensible nurse Rooke also resembles Austen in that, despite all her knowledge, she does not withdraw from society. Instead, acknowledging herself a member of the community she nurses, she is a "favourer of matrimony" who has her own "flying visions" of social success (II, chap. 9). Although many of Austen's female characters seem inalterably locked inside Mr. Elton's riddle, nurse Rooke resembles the successful heroines of the author's works in making the best of this tight place.

That Austen was fascinated with the sickness of her social world, especially its effect on people excluded from a life of active exertion, is probably last illustrated through the Parker sisters in *Sanditon*, where officious Diane supervises the application of six leeches a day for ten days and the extraction of a number of teeth in order to cure her disabled sister Susan's poor health. One sister representing "activity run mad" (chap. 9), the other languishing on the sofa, the two remind us of lethargic Lady Bertram, crippled Mrs. Smith, ill Jane Fairfax, fever-stricken Marianne Dashwood, the infected Crawfords, hypochondriacal Mary Musgrove, ailing Louisa Musgrove, and pale, sickly Fanny Price. But, as nurse Rooke's healing arts imply, the diseased shrews and the dying fainters define the boundaries of the state in which Austen's most successful characters usually manage to settle. A few of her heroines do evade the culturally induced idiocy and impotence that domestic confinement and female socialization seem to breed. Neither fainting into silence nor self-destructing into verbosity, Elizabeth Bennet, Emma Woodhouse, and Anne Elliot echo their creator in their duplicitous ability to speak with the tact that saves them from suicidal somnambulism on the one hand and contaminating vulgarity on the other, as they exploit the evasions and reservations of feminine gentility.

III

How Are We Fal'n?: Milton's Daughters

6 Milton's Bogey: Patriarchal Poetry and Women Readers

I say that words are men and when we spell
In alphabets we deal with living things;
With feet and thighs and breasts, fierce heads, strong wings;
Material Powers, great Bridals, Heaven and Hell.
There is a menace in the tales we tell.

                                    —Anna Hempstead Branch

Torn from your body, furbished from your rib;
I am the daughter of your skeleton,
Born of your bitter and excessive pain . . .

                                    —Elinor Wylie

Patriarchal Poetry their origin and their history their history
patriarchal poetry their origin patriarchal poetry their history
their origin patriarchal poetry their history their origin
patriarchal poetry their history patriarchal poetry their origin
patriarchal poetry their history their origin.

                                    —Gertrude Stein

Adam had a time, whether long or short, when he could wander
about on a fresh and peaceful earth. . . . But poor Eve found him
there, with all his claims upon her, the moment she looked into the
world. That is a grudge that woman has always had against the
Creator [so that some] young witches got everything they wanted
as in a catoptric image [and believed] that no woman should allow
herself to be possessed by any male but the devil. . . . this they got
from reading—in the orthodox witches' manner—the book of
Genesis backwards.

                                    —Isak Dinesen

To resurrect "the dead poet who was Shakespeare's sister," Virginia
Woolf declares in *A Room of One's Own*, literate women must "look

past Milton's bogey, for no human being should shut out the view."[1]
The perfunctory reference to Milton is curiously enigmatic, for the
allusion has had no significant development,[2] and Woolf, in the midst
of her peroration, does not stop to explain it. Yet the context in which
she places this apparently mysterious bogey is highly suggestive.
Shutting out the view, Milton's bogey cuts women off from the
spaciousness of possibility, the predominantly male landscapes of
fulfillment Woolf has been describing throughout *A Room*. Worse,
locking women into "the common sitting room" that denies them
individuality, it is a murderous phantom that, if it didn't actually
kill "Judith Shakespeare," has helped to keep her dead for hundreds
of years, over and over again separating her creative spirit from "the
body which she has so often laid down."

Nevertheless, the mystery of Woolf's phrase persists. For who (or
what) *is* Milton's bogey? Not only is the phrase enigmatic, it is
ambiguous. It may refer to Milton himself, the real patriarchal
specter or—to use Harold Bloom's critical terminology—"Covering
Cherub" who blocks the view for women poets.[3] It may refer to Adam,
who is Milton's (and God's) favored creature, and therefore also a
Covering Cherub of sorts. Or it may refer to another fictitious specter,
one more bogey created by Milton: his inferior and Satanically
inspired Eve, who has also intimidated women and blocked their
view of possibilities both real and literary. That Woolf does not
definitively indicate which of these meanings she intended suggests
that the ambiguity of her phrase may have been deliberate. Certainly
other Woolfian allusions to Milton reinforce the idea that for her,
as for most other women writers, both he and the creatures of his
imagination constitute the misogynistic essence of what Gertrude
Stein called "patriarchal poetry."

As our discussion of the metaphor of literary paternity suggested,
literary women, readers and writers alike, have long been "confused"
and intimidated by the patriarchal etiology that defines a solitary
Father God as the only creator of all things, fearing that such a
cosmic Author might be the sole legitimate model for all earthly
authors. Milton's myth of origins, summarizing a long misogynistic
tradition, clearly implied this notion to the many women writers
who directly or indirectly recorded anxieties about his paradigmatic
patriarchal poetry. A minimal list of such figures would include

Margaret Cavendish, Anne Finch, Mary Shelley, Charlotte and Emily Brontë, Emily Dickinson, Elizabeth Barrett Browning, George Eliot, Christina Rossetti, H. D., and Sylvia Plath, as well as Stein, Nin, and Woolf herself. In addition, in an effort to come to terms with the institutionalized and often elaborately metaphorical misogyny Milton's epic expresses, many of these women devised their own revisionary myths and metaphors.

Mary Shelley's *Frankenstein*, for instance, is at least in part a despairingly acquiescent "misreading" of *Paradise Lost*, with Eve-Sin apparently exorcised from the story but really translated into the monster that Milton hints she is. Emily Brontë's *Wuthering Heights*, by contrast, is a radically corrective "misreading" of Milton, a kind of Blakeian Bible of Hell, with the fall from heaven to hell transformed into a fall from a realm that conventional theology would associate with "hell" (the Heights) to a place that parodies "heaven" (the Grange). Similarly, Elizabeth Barrett Browning's "A Drama of Exile," Charlotte Brontë's *Shirley*, and Christina Rossetti's "Goblin Market" all include or imply revisionary critiques of *Paradise Lost*, while George Eliot's *Middlemarch* uses Dorothea's worship of that "affable archangel" Casaubon specifically to comment upon the disastrous relationship between Milton and his daughters. And in her undaughterly rebellion against that "Papa above" whom she also called "a God of Flint" and "Burglar! Banker—Father," Emily Dickinson, as Albert Gelpi has noted, was "passionately Byronic," and therefore, as we shall see, subtly anti-Miltonic.[4] For all these women, in other words, the question of Milton's misogyny was not in any sense an academic one.[5] On the contrary, since it was only through patriarchal poetry that they learned "their origin and their history"—learned, that is, to define themselves as misogynistic theology defined them—most of these writers read Milton with painful absorption.

Considering all this, Woolf's 1918 diary entry on *Paradise Lost*, an apparently casual summary of reactions to a belated study of that poem, may well represent all female anxieties about "Milton's bogey," and is thus worth quoting in its entirety.

Though I am not the only person in Sussex who reads Milton, I mean to write down my impressions of *Paradise Lost* while I am about it. Impressions fairly well describes the sort of thing left in my mind. I have left many riddles unread. I have slipped on too easily to taste the full flavour. However I see, and agree to some extent in believing, that this full flavour is the reward of highest scholarship. I am struck by the extreme difference between this poem and any other. It lies, I think, in the sublime aloofness and impersonality of the emotion. I have never read Cowper on the sofa, but I can imagine that the sofa is a degraded substitute for *Paradise Lost*. The substance of Milton is all made of wonderful, beautiful, and masterly descriptions of angels' bodies, battles, flights, dwelling places. He deals in horror and immensity and squalor and sublimity but never in the passions of the human heart. Has any great poem ever let in so little light upon one's own joys and sorrows? I get no help in judging life; I scarcely feel that Milton lived or knew men and women; except for the peevish personalities about marriage and the woman's duties. He was the first of the masculinists, but his disparagement rises from his own ill luck and seems even a spiteful last word in his domestic quarrels. But how smooth, strong and elaborate it all is! What poetry! I can conceive that even Shakespeare after this would seem a little troubled, personal, hot and imperfect. I can conceive that this is the essence, of which almost all other poetry is the dilution. The inexpressible fineness of the style, in which shade after shade is perceptible, would alone keep one gazing into it, long after the surface business in progress has been despatched. Deep down one catches still further combinations, rejections, felicities and masteries. Moreover, though there is nothing like Lady Macbeth's terror or Hamlet's cry, no pity or sympathy or intuition, the figures are majestic; in them is summed up much of what men thought of our place in the universe, of our duty to God, our religion.[6]

Interestingly, even the diffident first sentence of this paragraph expresses an uncharacteristic humility, even nervousness, in the presence of Milton's "sublime aloofness and impersonality." By 1918 Woolf was herself an experienced, widely published literary critic, as well as the author of one accomplished novel, with another in progress. In the preceding pages she has confidently set down judg-

ments of Christina Rossetti ("She has the natural singing power"),
Byron ("He has at least the male virtues"), Sophocles' *Electra* ("It's
not so fearfully difficult after all"), and a number of other serious
literary subjects. Yet Milton, and Milton alone, leaves her feeling
puzzled, excluded, inferior, and even a little guilty. Like Greek or
metaphysics, those other bastions of intellectual masculinity, Milton
is for Woolf a sort of inordinately complex algebraic equation, an
insoluble problem that she feels obliged—but unable—to solve ("I
have left many riddles unread"). At the same time, his *magnum opus*
seems to have little or nothing to do with her own, distinctively female
perception of things ("Has any great poem ever let in so little light
upon one's own joys and sorrows?"). Her admiration, moreover,
is cast in peculiarly vague, even abstract language ("how smooth,
strong and elaborate it all is"). And her feeling that Milton's verse
(not the dramas of her beloved, androgynous Shakespeare) must be
"the essence of which almost all other poetry is the dilution" perhaps
explains her dutiful conclusion, with its strained insistence that in
the depths of Milton's verse "is summed up much of what men
thought of our place in the universe, of our duty to God, our religion."
Our? Surely Woolf is speaking here "as a woman," to borrow one
of her own favorite phrases, and surely her conscious or unconscious
statement is clear: Milton's bogey, whatever else it may be, is
ultimately his cosmology, his vision of "what *men* thought" and his
powerful rendering of the culture myth that Woolf, like most other
literary women, sensed at the heart of Western literary patriarchy.

The story that Milton, "the first of the masculinists," most notably
tells to women is of course the story of woman's secondness, her
otherness, and how that otherness leads inexorably to her demonic
anger, her sin, her fall, and her exclusion from that garden of the
gods which is also, for her, the garden of poetry. In an extraordinarily
important and yet also extraordinarily distinctive way, therefore,
Milton is for women what Harold Bloom (who might here be para-
phrasing Woolf) calls "the great Inhibitor, the Sphinx who strangles
even strong imaginations in their cradles." In a line even more
appropriate to women, Bloom adds that "the motto to English poetry
since Milton was stated by Keats: 'life to him would be death to
me.'" [7] And interestingly, Woolf herself echoes just this line in
speaking of her father years after his death. Had Sir Leslie Stephen

lived into his nineties, she remarks, "His life would have entirely ended mine. What would have happened? No writing, no books:—inconceivable."[8] For whatever Milton is to the male imagination, to the female imagination Milton and the inhibiting Father—the Patriarch of patriarchs—are one.

For Woolf, indeed, even Milton's manuscripts are dramatically associated with male hegemony and female subordination. One of the key confrontations in *A Room* occurs when she decides to consult the manuscript of *Lycidas* in the "Oxbridge" library and is forbidden entrance by an agitated male librarian

> like a guardian angel barring the way with a flutter of black gown instead of white wings, a deprecating, silvery, kindly gentleman, who regretted in a low voice as he waved me back that ladies are only admitted to the library if accompanied by a Fellow of the College or furnished with a letter of introduction.[9]

Locked away from female contamination at the heart of "Oxbridge's" paradigmatically patriarchal library—in the very heaven of libraries, so to speak—there is a Word of power, and the Word is Milton's.

Although *A Room* merely hints at the cryptic but crucial power of the Miltonic text and its misogynistic context, Woolf clearly defined Milton as a frightening "Inhibitor" in the fictional (rather than critical) uses she made or did not make of Milton throughout her literary career. Both *Orlando* and *Between the Acts*, for instance, her two most ambitious and feminist re-visions of history, appear quite deliberately to exclude Milton from their radically transformed chronicles of literary events. Hermaphroditic Orlando meets Shakespeare the enigmatic androgyne, and effeminate Alexander Pope—but John Milton simply does not exist for him/her, just as he doesn't exist for Miss La Trobe, the revisionary historian of *Between the Acts*. As Bloom notes, one of the ways in which a poet evades anxiety is to deny even the existence of the precursor poet who is the source of anxiety.

On the other hand, when Woolf does allude to Milton in a novel, as she does in *The Voyage Out*, her reference grants him his pernicious power in its entirely. Indeed, the motto of the heroine, Rachel Vinrace, might well be Keats's "Life to him would be death to me," for twenty-four-year-old Rachel, dying of some unnamed disease mysteriously related to her sexual initiation by Terence Hewet, seems to drown in waves of Miltonic verse. "Terence was reading Milton aloud, because he said the words of Milton had substance and shape, so that it was not necessary to understand what he was saying ... [But] the words, in spite of what Terence had said, seemed to be laden with meaning, and perhaps it was for this reason that it was painful to listen to them."[10] An invocation to "Sabrina Fair," the goddess "under the glassy, cool, translucent wave," the words Terence reads from *Comus* seek the salvation of a maiden who has been turned to stone. But their effect on Rachel is very different. Heralding illness, they draw her toward a "deep pool of sticky water" murky with images derived from Woolf's own episodes of madness, and ultimately they plunge her into the darkness "at the bottom of the sea."[11] Would death to Milton, one wonders, have been life for Rachel?

Charlotte Brontë would certainly have thought so. Because Woolf was such a sophisticated literary critic, she may have been at once the most conscious and the most anxious heiress of the Miltonic culture myth. But among earlier women writers it was Brontë who seemed most aware of Milton's threatening qualities, particularly of the extent to which his influence upon women's fate might be seen as—to borrow a pun from Bloom—an unhealthy *influenza*.[12] In *Shirley* she specifically attacked the patriarchal Miltonic cosmology, within whose baleful context she saw both her female protagonists sickening, orphaned and starved by a male-dominated society. "Milton was great; but was he good?" asks Shirley Keeldar, the novel's eponymous heroine.

> [He] tried to see the first woman, but ... he saw her not. ... It was his cook that he saw; or it was Mrs. Gill, as I have seen her, making custards, in the heat of summer, in the cool dairy, with rose-trees and nasturtiums about the latticed window, preparing a cold collation for the rectors,—preserves, and "dulcet creams"—puzzled "What choice to choose for delicacy best."[13]

Shirley's allusion is to the passage in book 5 of *Paradise Lost* in which housewifely Eve, "on hospitable thoughts intent," serves Adam and his angelic guest an Edenic cold collation of fruits and nuts, berries and "dulcet creams." With its descriptions of mouth-watering seraphic banquets and its almost Victorian depiction of primordial domestic bliss, this scene is especially vulnerable to the sort of parodic wit Brontë has Shirley turn against it. But the alternative that Brontë and Shirley propose to Milton's Eve-as-little-woman is more serious and implies an even severer criticism of *Paradise Lost*'s visionary misogyny. The first woman, Shirley hypothesizes, was not an Eve, "half doll, half angel," and always potential fiend. Rather, she was a Titan, and a distinctively Promethean one at that:

> " . . . from her sprang Saturn, Hyperion, Oceanus; she bore Prometheus. . . . The first woman's breast that heaved with life on this world yielded the daring which could contend with Omnipotence: the strength which could bear a thousand years of bondage,—the vitality which could feed that vulture death through uncounted ages,—the unexhausted life and uncorrupted excellence, sisters to immortality, which . . . could conceive and bring forth a Messiah . . . I saw—I now see—a woman-Titan. . . . she reclines her bosom on the ridge of Stilbro' Moor; her mighty hands are joined beneath it. So kneeling, face to face she speaks with God. That Eve is Jehovah's daughter, as Adam was his son."

Like Woolf's concept of "Milton's bogey," this apparently bold vision of a titanic Eve is interestingly (and perhaps necessarily) ambiguous. It is possible, for instance, to read the passage as a comparatively conventional evocation of maternal Nature giving birth to *male* greatness. Because she "bore Prometheus," the first woman's breast nursed daring, strength, vitality. At the same time, however, the syntax here suggests that "the daring which could content with Omnipotence" and "the strength which could bear a thousand years of bondage" belonged, like the qualities they parallel —"the unexhausted life and uncorrupted excellence . . . which . . . could . . . bring forth a Messiah"—to the first woman herself. Not only did Shirley's Eve bring forth a Prometheus, then, she was herself a Prometheus, contending with Omnipotence and defying bondage.[14] Thus, where Milton's Eve is apparently submissive, except for one moment of disastrous rebellion in which she listens to the wrong voice, Shirley's is strong, assertive, vital. Where Milton's Eve is domestic, Shirley's is daring. Where Milton's Eve is from the first curiously hollow, as if somehow created corrupt, "in outward show / Elaborate, of inward less exact" (*PL* 8. 538–39) Shirley's is filled with "unexhausted life and uncorrupted excellence." Where Milton's Eve is a sort of divine afterthought, an almost superfluous and mostly material being created from Adam's "supernumerary" rib, Shirley's is spiritual, primary, "heaven-born." Finally, and perhaps most significantly, where Milton's Eve is usually excluded from God's sight and, at crucial moments in the history of Eden, drugged and silenced by divinely ordained sleep, Shirley's speaks "face to face" with God. We may even speculate that, supplanted by a servile and destructive specter, Shirley's Eve is the first avatar of that dead poet whom Woolf, in her re-vision of this myth, called Judith Shakespeare and who was herself condemned to death by Milton's bogey.

Besides having interesting descendants, Shirley's titanic woman has interesting ancestors. For instance, if she is herself a sort of Prometheus as well as Prometheus's mother, she is in a sense closer to Milton's Satan than to his Eve. Certainly "the daring which could contend with Omnipotence" and "the strength which could bear a thousand years of bondage" are qualities that recall not only the firm resolve of Shelley's Prometheus (or Byron's or Goethe's or Aeschylus's) but "the unconquerable will" Milton's fiend opposes to "The tyranny of Heav'n." Also, the gigantic size of Milton's fallen angel (". . . in bulk as huge / As whom the Fables name of monstrous size, / *Titanian*, or *Earth-born*" [*PL* 1. 196–98]) is repeated in the enormity of Shirley's Eve. She "reclines her bosom on the ridge of Stillbro' Moor" just as Satan lies "stretched out huge in length" in book 1 of *Paradise Lost*, and just as Blake's fallen Albion (another neo-Miltonic figure) appears with his right foot "on Dover cliffs, his heel / On Canterbury ruins; his right hand [covering] lofty Wales / His left Scotland," etc.[15] But of course Milton's Satan is himself the ancestor of all the Promethean heroes conceived by the Romantic poets who influenced Brontë. And as if to acknowledge that fact, she has Shirley remark that under her Titan woman's breast "I see her zone, purple like that horizon: through its blush shines the star of evening"—Lucifer, the "son of the morning" and the evening star, who is Satan in his unfallen state.

Milton's Satan transformed into a Promethean Eve may at first sound like a rather unlikely literary development. But even the briefest reflection on *Paradise Lost* should remind us that, despite Eve's apparent passivity and domesticity, Milton himself seems deliberately to have sketched so many parallels between her and Satan that it is hard at times for the unwary reader to distinguish the sinfulness of one from that of the other. As Stanley Fish has pointed out, for instance, Eve's temptation speech to Adam in book 9 is "a tissue of Satanic echoes," with its central argument "Look on me. / Do not believe," an exact duplicate of the anti-religious empiricism embedded in Satan's earlier temptation speech to her.[16] Moreover, where Adam falls out of uxorious "fondness," out of a self-sacrificing love for Eve which, at least to the modern reader, seems quite noble, Milton's Eve falls for exactly the same reason that Satan does: because she wants to be "as Gods," and because, like him, she is secretly dissatisfied with her place, secretly preoccupied with questions of "equality." After *his* fall, Satan makes a pseudo-libertarian speech to his fellow angels in which he asks, "Who can in reason then or right assume / Monarchy over such as live by right / His equals, if in power and splendor less, / In freedom equal?" (*PL* 5. 794–97). After *her* fall, Eve considers the possibility of keeping the fruit to herself "so to add what wants / In Female Sex, the more to draw [Adam's] Love, / And render me more equal" (*PL* 9. 821–23).

Again, just as Milton's Satan—despite his pretensions to equality with the divine—dwindles from an angel into a dreadful (though subtle) serpent, so Eve is gradually reduced from an angelic being to a monstrous and serpentine creature, listening sadly as Adam thunders, "Out of my sight, thou Serpent, that name best / Befits thee with him leagu'd, thyself as false / And hateful; nothing wants, but that thy shape, / Like his, and colour Serpentine may show / Thy inward fraud" (*PL* 10. 867–71) The enmity God sets between the woman and the serpent is thus the discord necessary to divide those who are not opposites or enemies but too much alike, too much attracted to each other. In addition, just as Satan feeds Eve with the forbidden fruit, so Eve—who is consistently associated with fruit, not only as Edenic chef but also as herself the womb or bearer of fruit—feeds the fruit to Adam. And finally, just as Satan's was a fall into generation, its first consequence being the appearance of the material world of Sin and Death, so Eve's (and not Adam's) fall completes the human entry into generation, since its consequence is the pain of birth, death's necessary opposite and mirror image. And just as Satan is humbled and enslaved by his desire for the bitter fruit, so Eve is humbled by becoming a slave not only to Adam the individual man but to Adam the archetypal man, a slave not only to her husband but, as de Beauvoir notes, to the species.[17] By contrast, Adam's fall is fortunate because, among other reasons, from the woman's point of view his punishment seems almost like a reward, as he himself suggests when he remarks that "On mee the Curse aslope / Glanc'd on the ground, with labour I must earn / My bread; what harm? Idleness had been worse . . . " (*PL* 10. 1053–55).

We must remember, however, that as Milton delineates it Eve's relationship to Satan is even richer, deeper, and more complex than these few points suggest. Her bond with the fiend is strengthened not only by the striking similarities that link her to him, but also by the ways in which she resembles Sin, his female avatar and, indeed— with the exception of Urania, who is a kind of angel in the poet's head—the only other female who graces (or, rather, disgraces) *Paradise Lost*.[18] Brontë's Shirley, whose titanic Eve is reminiscent of the Promethean aspects of Milton's devil, does not appear to have noticed this relationship, even in her bitter attack upon Milton's little woman. But we can be sure that Brontë herself, like many other female readers, did—if only unconsciously—perceive the likeness. For not only is Sin female, like Eve, she is serpentine as Satan is and as Adam tells Eve *she* is. Her body, "Woman to the waist, and fair, / But [ending] foul in many a scaly fold / Voluminous and vast, a Serpent arm'd / With mortal sting" exaggerates and parodies female anatomy just as the monstrous bodies of Spenser's Error and Duessa do (*PL* 2. 650–53). Similarly, with her fairness ironically set against foulness, Sin parodies Adam's fearful sense of the tension between Eve's "outward show / Elaborate" and her "inward less exact." Moreover, just as Eve is a secondary and contingent creation, made from Adam's rib, so Sin, Satan's "Daughter," burst from the fallen angel's brain like a grotesque subversion of the Graeco-Roman story of wise

Minerva's birth from the head of Jove. In a patriarchal Christian context the pagan goddess Wisdom may, Milton suggests, become the loathesome demoness Sin, for the intelligence of heaven is made up exclusively of "Spirits Masculine," and the woman, like her dark double, Sin, is a "fair defect / Of Nature" (*PL* 10. 890–93).

If Eve's punishment, moreover, is her condemnation to the anguish of maternity, Sin is the only model of maternity other than the "wide womb of Chaos" with which *Paradise Lost* provides her, and as a model Milton's monster conveys a hideous warning of what it means to be a "slave to the species." Birthing innumerable Hell Hounds in a dreadful cycle, Sin is endlessly devoured by her children, who continually emerge from and return to her womb, where they bark and howl unseen. Their bestial sounds remind us that to bear young is to be not spiritual but animal, a *thing* of flesh, an incomprehensible and uncomprehending body, while their ceaseless suckling presages the exhaustion that leads to death, companion of birth. And Death is indeed their sibling as well as the father who has raped (and thus fused with) his mother, Sin, in order to bring this pain into being, just as "he" will meld with Eve when in eating the apple she ends up "eating Death" (*PL* 9. 792).

Of course, Sin's pride and her vulnerability to Satan's seductive wiles make her Eve's double too. It is at Satan's behest, after all, that Sin disobeys God's commandments and opens the gates of hell to let the first cause of evil loose in the world, and this act of hers is clearly analogous to Eve's disobedient eating of the apple, with its similar consequences. Like both Eve and Satan, moreover, Sin wants to be "as Gods," to reign in a "new world of light and bliss" (*PL* 2. 867), and surely it is not insignificant that her moving but blasphemous pledge of allegiance to Satan ("Thou art my Father, thou my Author, thou / My being gav'st me; whom should I obey / But thee, whom follow?" [*PL* 2. 864–66]) foreshadows Eve's most poignant speech to Adam ("But now lead on ... with thee to go, / Is to stay here; without thee here to stay, / Is to go hence unwilling; thou to mee / Art all things under Heav'n...." [*PL* 12. 614–18]), as if in some part of himself Milton meant not to instruct the reader by contrasting two modes of obedience but to undercut even Eve's "goodness" in advance. Perhaps it is for this reason that, in the grim shade of Sin's Medusa-like snakiness, Eve's beauty, too, begins (to an experienced reader of *Paradise Lost*) to seem suspect: her golden tresses waving in wanton, wandering ringlets suggest at least a sinister potential, and it hardly helps that so keen a critic as Hazlitt thought her nakedness made her luscious as a piece of fruit.[19]

Despite Milton's well-known misogyny, however, and the highly developed philosophical tradition in which it can be placed, all these connections, parallels, and doublings among Satan, Eve, and Sin are shadowy messages, embedded in the text of *Paradise Lost*, rather than carefully illuminated overt statements. Still, for sensitive female readers brought up in the bosom of a "masculinist," patristic, neo-Manichean church, the latent as well as the manifest content of such a powerful work as *Paradise Lost* was (and is) bruisingly real. To such women the unholy trinity of Satan, Sin and Eve, diabolically mimicking the holy trinity of God, Christ, and Adam,[20] must have seemed even in the eighteenth and nineteenth centuries to illustrate that historical dispossession and degradation of the female principle which was to be imaginatively analyzed in the twentieth century by Robert Graves, among others. "The new God," Graves wrote in *The White Goddess*, speaking of the rise of the Judaic-Pythagorean tradition whose culture myth Milton recounts,

> claimed to be dominant as Alpha and Omega, the Beginning and the End, pure Holiness, pure Good, pure Logic, able to exist without the aid of woman; but it was natural to identify him with one of the original rivals of the Theme [of the *White Goddess*] and to ally the woman and the other rival permanently against him. The outcome was philosophical dualism with all the tragi-comic woes attendant on spiritual dichotomy. If the True God, the God of the Logos, was pure thought, pure good, whence came evil and error? Two separate creations had to be assumed: the true spiritual Creation and the false material Creation. In terms of the heavenly bodies, Sun and Saturn were now jointly opposed to Moon, Mars, Mercury, Jupiter and Venus. The five heavenly bodies in opposition made a strong partnership, with a woman at the beginning and a woman at the end. Jupiter and the Moon Goddess paired together as the rulers of the material World, the lovers Mars and Venus paired together as the lustful Flesh, and between the pairs stood Mercury who was the Devil,

the Cosmocrator or author of the false creation. It was these five who composed the Pythagorean *hyle*, or grove, of the five material senses; and spiritually minded men, coming to regard them as sources of error, tried to rise superior to them by pure meditation. This policy was carried to extreme lengths by the Godfearing Essenes, who formed their monkish communities within compounds topped by acacia hedges, from which all women were excluded; lived ascetically, cultivated a morbid disgust for their own natural functions and turned their eyes away from World, Flesh and Devil.[21]

Milton, who offers at least lip service to the institution of matrimony, is never so intensely misogynistic as the fanatically celibate Essenes. But a similar though more disguised misogyny obviously contributes to Adam's espousal of Right Reason as a means of transcending the worldly falsehoods propounded by Eve and Satan (and by his vision of the "Bevy of fair Women" whose wiles betrayed the "Sons of God" [*PL* 11. 582, 622]). And that the Right Reason of *Paradise Lost* did have such implications was powerfully understood by William Blake, whose fallen Urizenic Milton must reunite with his female Emanation in order to cast off his fetters and achieve imaginative wholeness. Perhaps even more important for our purposes here, in the visionary epic *Milton* Blake reveals a sure grasp of the psychohistorical effects he thought Milton's misguided "chastity" had, not only upon Milton, but upon women themselves. While Milton-as-noble-bard, for instance, ponders "the intricate mazes of Providence," Blake has his "six-fold Emanation" howl and wail, "Scatter'd thro' the deep / In torment."[22] Comprised of his three wives and three daughters, this archetypal abandoned woman knows very well that Milton's anti-feminism has deadly implications for her own character as well as for her fate. "Is this our Feminine Portion," Blake has her demand despairingly. "Are we Contraries O Milton, Thou & I / O Immortal! how were we led to War the Wars of Death [?]" And, as if to describe the moral deformity such misogyny fosters in women, she explains that "Altho' our Human Power can sustain the severe contentions ... our Sexual cannot: but flies into the [hell of] the Ulro. / Hence arose all our terrors in Eternity!"[23]

Still, although he was troubled by Milton's misogyny and was

radically opposed to the Cartesian dualism Milton's vaguely Mani-
chean cosmology anticipated, Blake did portray the author of *Paradise
Lost* as the hero—the redeemer even—of the poem that bears his
name. Beyond or behind Milton's bogey, the later poet saw, there
was a more charismatic and congenial figure, a figure that Shirley
and her author, like most other female readers, must also have
perceived, judging by the ambiguous responses to Milton recorded
by so many women. For though the epic voice of *Paradise Lost* often
sounds censorious and "masculinist" as it recounts and comments
upon Western patriarchy's central culture myth, the epic's creator
often seems to display such dramatic affinities with rebels against
the censorship of heaven that Romantic readers well might conclude
with Blake that Milton wrote "in fetters" and "was of the devil's
party without knowing it."²⁴ And so Blake, blazing a path for Shirley
and for Shelley, for Byron and for Mary Shelley, and for all the
Brontës, famously defined Satan as the real, burningly visionary
god—the Los—of *Paradise Lost*, and "God" as the rigid and death-
dealing Urizenic demon. His extraordinarily significant misreading
clarifies not only the lineage of, say, Shelley's Prometheus, but also
the ancestry of Shirley's titanic Eve. For if Eve is in so many negative
ways like Satan the serpentine tempter, why should she not also be
akin to Satan the Romantic outlaw, the character whom (Harold
Bloom reminds us) T. S. Eliot considered "Milton's curly-haired
Byronic hero"?²⁵

   That Satan is throughout much of *Paradise Lost* a handsome devil
and therefore a paradigm for the Byronic hero at his most attractive
is, of course, a point frequently made by critics of all persuasions,
including those less hostile than Eliot was to both Byron and Milton.
Indeed, Satan's Prometheanism, the indomitable will and courage
he bequeathed to characters like Shirley's Eve, almost seems to have
been created to illustrate some of the crucial features of Romanticism
in general. Refusing, like Shelley's Prometheus, to submit to the
"tyranny of Heaven," and stalking "apart in joyless revery" like
Byron's Childe Harold,²⁶ Milton's Satan is as alienated from celestial
society as any of the early nineteenth-century poets *maudit* who made
him their emblem. Accursed and self-cursing, paradoxical and mys-

tical ("Which way I fly is hell; myself am Hell . . . Evil be thou my Good" [*PL* 4. 75, 110]), he experiences the guilty double consciousness, the sense of a stupendous self capable of nameless and perhaps criminal enormities, that Byron redefined in *Manfred* and *Cain* as marks of superiority. Moreover, to the extent that the tyranny of heaven is associated with Right Reason, Satan is Romantically antirational in his exploration of the secret depths of himself and of the cosmos. He is anti-rational—and Romantic—too, in his indecorous yielding to excesses of passion, his Byronic "gestures fierce" and "mad demeanor" (*PL* 4. 128–29). At the same time, his aristocratic egalitarianism, manifested in his war against the heavenly system of primogeniture that has unjustly elevated God's "Son" above even the highest angels, suggests a Byronic (and Shelleyan and Godwinian) concern with liberty and justice for all. Thunder-scarred and worldweary, this black-browed devil would not, one feels, have been out of place at Missolonghi.

Significantly, Eve is the only character in *Paradise Lost* for whom a rebellion against the hierarchical status quo is as necessary as it is for Satan. Though he is in one sense oppressed, or at least manipulated, by God, Adam is after all to his own realm what God is to His: absolute master and guardian of the patriarchal rights of primogeniture. Eve's docile speech in book 4 emphasizes this: "My Author and Disposer, what thou bidd'st / Unargu'd I obey; so God ordains, / God is thy Law, thou mine: to know no more / Is woman's happiest knowledge and her praise" (*PL* 4. 635–38). But the dream she has shortly after speaking these words to Adam (reported in book 5) seems to reveal her true feelings about the matter in its fantasy of a Satanic flight of escape from the garden and its oppressions: "Up to the Clouds . . . I flew, and underneath beheld / The Earth outstretcht immense, a prospect wide / And various. . ." [27] (*PL* 5.86–89), a redefined prospect of happy knowledge not unlike the one Woolf imagines women viewing from their opened windows. And interestingly, brief as is the passage describing Eve's flight, it foreshadowed fantasies that would recur frequently and compellingly in the writings of both women and Romantic poets. Byron's *Cain*, for instance, disenchanted by what his author called the "politics of paradise," [28] flies through space with his seductive Lucifer like a masculine version of Milton's Eve, and though Shirley's Eve is earthbound—almost earthlike—innumerable other "Eves" of female origin have flown, fallen, surfaced, or feared to fly, as if to acknowledge in a backhanded sort of way the power of the dream Milton let Satan grant to Eve. But whether female dreams of flying escapes are derived from Miltonic or Romantic ideas, or from some collective female unconscious, is a difficult question to answer. For the connections between Satan, Romanticism, and concealed or incipient feminism are intricate and far-reaching indeed.

Certainly, if both Satan and Eve are in some sense alienated, rebellious, and therefore Byronic figures, the same is true for women writers as a class—for Shirley's creator as well as for Shirley, for Virginia Woolf as well as for "Judith Shakespeare." Dispossessed by her older brothers—the "Sons of God"—educated to submission, enjoined to silence, the woman writer, in fantasy if not in reality, must often have "stalked apart in joyless revery," like Byron's heroes, like Satan, like Prometheus. Feeling keenly the discrepancy between the angel she was supposed to be and the angry demon she knew she often was, she must have experienced the same paradoxical double consciousness of guilt and greatness that afflicts both Satan and, say, Manfred. Composing herself to saintly stillness, brooding narcissistically like Eve over her own image and like Satan over her own power, she may even have feared occasionally that like Satan—or Byron's Lara, or his Manfred—she would betray her secret fury by "gestures fierce" or a "mad demeanor." Asleep in the bower of domesticity, she would be unable to silence the Romantic/Satanic whisper— "Why sleepst thou Eve?"—with its invitation to join the visionary world of those who fly by night.

Again, though Milton goes to great lengths to associate Adam, God, Christ, and the angels with visionary prophetic powers, that visionary night-world of poetry and imagination, insofar as it is a *demonic* world, is more often subtly associated in *Paradise Lost* with Eve, Satan, and femaleness than with any of the "good" characters except the epic speaker himself. Blake, of course, saw this quite clearly. It is the main reason for the Satan-God role reversal he postulates. But his friend Mary Wollstonecraft and her Romantic female descendants must have seen it too, just as Byron and Shelley did. For though Adam is magically shown, as in a crystal ball, what the future holds, Satan and Eve are both the real dreamers of *Paradise Lost*, possessed in the Romantic sense by seductive reflections and uncontrollable imaginings of alternative lives to the point where, like Manfred or Christabel or the Keats of *The Fall of Hyperion*, they are so scorched by visionary longings they become fevers of themselves, to echo Moneta's words to Keats. But even this suffering sense of the hellish discrepancy between Satan's (or Eve's) aspiration and position is a model of aesthetic nobility to the Romantic poet and the Romantically inspired feminist. Contemplating the "lovely pair" of Adam and Eve in their cosily unfallen state, Mary Wollstonecraft confesses that she feels "an emotion similar to what we feel when children are playing or animals sporting," and on such occasions "I have, with conscious dignity, or Satanic pride, turned to hell for sublimer subjects." [29] Her deliberate, ironic confusion of "conscious dignity" and "Satanic pride," together with her reverence for the "sublime," prefigure Shelley's Titan as clearly as Shirley's titanic woman. The imagining of more "sublime" alternative lives, moreover, as Blake and Wollstonecraft also saw, reinforces the revolutionary fervor that Satan the visionary poet, like Satan the aristocratic Byronic rebel, defined for women and Romantics alike.

That the Romantic aesthetic has often been linked with visionary politics is, of course, almost a truism. From the apocalyptic revolutions of Blake and Shelley to those of Yeats and D. H. Lawrence, moreover, re-visions of the Miltonic culture myth have been associated with such repudiations of the conservative, hierarchical "politics of paradise." "In terrible majesty," Blake's Satanic Milton thunders, "Obey thou the words of the Inspired Man. / All that can be annihilated must be annihilated / That the children of Jerusalem may be saved from slavery." [30] Like him, Byron's Lucifer offers autonomy and knowledge —the prerequisites of freedom—to Cain, while Shelley's Prometheus, overthrowing the tyranny of heaven, ushers in "Life, Joy, Empire, and Victory" for all of humanity. [31] Even D. H. Lawrence's Satanic snake, emerging one hundred years later from the hellishly burning bowels of the earth, seems to be "one of the lords / Of life," an exiled king "now due to be crowned again," signalling a reborn society. [32] For in the revolutionary cosmologies of all these Romantic poets, both Satan and his other self, Lucifer ("son of the morning"), were emblematic of that liberated dawn in which it *would* be bliss to be alive.

It is not surprising, then, that women, identifying at their most rebellious with Satan, at their least with rebellious Eve, and almost all the time with the Romantic poets, should have been similarly obsessed with the apocalyptic social transformations a revision of Milton might bring about. Mary Wollstonecraft, whose *A Vindication of the Rights of Woman* often reads like an outraged commentary on *Paradise Lost*, combined a Blakeian enthusiasm for the French Revolution—at least in its early days—with her "pre-Romantic" reverence for the Satanic sublime and her feminist anger at Milton's misogyny. But complicated as it was, that complex of interrelated feelings was not hers alone. For not only have feminism and Romantic radicalism been consciously associated in the minds of many women writers, Byronically (and Satanically) rebellious visionary politics have often been used by women as metaphorical disguises for sexual politics. Thus in *Shirley* Brontë not only creates an anti-Miltonic Eve, she also uses the revolutionary anger of the frame-breaking workers with whom the novel is crucially concerned as an image for the fury of its dispossessed heroines. Similarly, as Ellen Moers has noted, English-women's factory novels (like Gaskell's *Mary Barton*) and American women's anti-slavery novels (like Stowe's *Uncle Tom's Cabin*) submerged or disguised "private, brooding, female resentment" in ostensibly disinterested examinations of larger public issues.[33] More recently, even Virginia Woolf's angrily feminist *Three Guineas* purports to have begun not primarily as a consideration of the woman question but as an almost Shelleyan dream of transforming the world—abolishing war, tyranny, ignorance, etc.—through the formation of a female "Society of Outsiders."

But of course such a society would be curiously Satanic, since in the politics of paradise the Prince of Darkness was literally the first Outsider. Even if Woolf herself did not see far enough past Milton's bogey to recognize this, a number of other women, both feminists and anti-feminists, did. In late nineteenth-century America, for instance, a well-known journal of Romantically radical politics and feminism was called *Lucifer the Light-bearer*, and in Victorian England Mrs. Rigby wrote of Charlotte Brontë's Byronic and feminist *Jane Eyre* that "the tone of mind and thought which has overthrown authority and violated every code human and divine abroad, and fostered Chartism and rebellion at home"—in other words, a Byronic,

Promethean, Satanic, and Jacobin tone of mind—"is the same which has also written *Jane Eyre*." [34]

Paradoxically, however, Brontë herself may have been less conscious of the extraordinary complex of visionary and revisionary impulses that went into *Jane Eyre* than Mrs. Rigby was, at least in part because, like many other women, she found her own anger and its intellectual consequences almost too painful to confront. Commenting on the so-called condition of women question, she told Mrs. Gaskell that there are "evils—deep-rooted in the foundation of the social system—which no efforts of ours can touch; of which we cannot complain: of which it is advisable not too often to think." Like Mary Elizabeth Coleridge, she evidently had moments in which she saw "no friend in God—in Satan's host no foes." [35] Still, despite her refusal to "complain," Brontë's unwillingness to think of social inequities was more likely a function of her anxiety about her own rebelliously Satanic impulses than a sign of blind resignation to what Yeats called "the injustice of the skies." [36]

The relationship between women writers and Milton's curly-haired Byronic hero is, however, even more complicated than we have so far suggested. And in the intricate tangle of this relationship resides still another reason for the refusal of writers like Brontë consciously to confront their obsessive interest in the impulses incarnated in the villain of *Paradise Lost*. For not only is Milton's Satan in certain crucial ways very much *like* women, he is also (as we saw in connection with Austen's glamorously Satanic anti-heroes) enormously attractive to women. Indeed, both Eliot's phrase and Byron's biography imply that he is in most ways the incarnation of worldly male sexuality, fierce, powerful, experienced, simultaneously brutal and seductive, devilish enough to overwhelm the body and yet enough a fallen angel to charm the soul. As such, however, in his relations with women he is a sort of Nietzschean *Übermensch*, giving orders and expecting homage to his "natural"—that is, masculine—superiority, as if he were God's shadow self, the id of heaven, Satanically reduplicating the politics of paradise wherever he goes. And yet, wherever he goes, women follow him, even when they refuse to follow the God whose domination he parodies. As Sylvia Plath so famously noted, "Every woman adores a Fascist, / The boot in the face, the brute / Brute heart of a brute like you." Speaking of "Daddy," Plath was of course speaking also of Satan, "a man in black with a Mein Kampf look."[37] And the masochistic phenomenon she described helps explain the unspeakable, even unthinkable sense of sin that also caused women like Woolf and Brontë to avert their eyes from their own Satanic impulses. For if Eve is Sin's as well as Satan's double, then Satan is to Eve what he is to Sin—both a lover and a daddy.

That the Romantic fascination with incest derived in part from Milton's portrayal of the Sin-Satan relationship may be true but is in a sense beside the point here. That both women and Romantic poets must have found at least an analog for their relationship to each other in Satan's incestuous affair with Sin is, however, very much to the point. Admiring, even adoring, Satan's Byronic rebelliousness, his scorn of conventional virtues, his raging energy, the woman writer may have secretly fantasized that she *was* Satan— or Cain, or Manfred, or Prometheus. But at the same time her feelings of female powerlessness manifested themselves in her conviction that the closest she could really get to being Satan was to be his creature, his tool, the witchlike daughter/mistress who sits at his right hand. Leslie Marchand recounts a revealing anecdote about Mary Shelley's stepsister, Claire Clairmont, that brilliantly illuminates this movement from self-assertive identification to masochistic self-denial. Begging Byron to criticize her half-finished novel, rebellious Claire (who was later to follow the poet to Geneva and bear his daughter Allegra) is said to have explained that he *must* read the manuscript because "the creator ought not to destroy his creature."[38]

Despite Brontë's vision of a Promethean Eve, even her *Shirley* betrays a similar sense of the difficulty of direct identification with the assertive Satanic principle, and the need for women to accept their own instrumentality, for her first ecstatic description of an active, indomitable Eve is followed by a more chastened story. In this second parable, the "first woman" passively wanders alone in an alienating landscape, wondering whether she is "thus to burn out and perish, her living light doing no good, never seen, never needed" even though "the flame of her intelligence burn[s] so vivid" and "something within her stir[s] disquieted." Instead of coming from that Promethean fire within her, however, as the first Eve's salvation implicitly did, this Eva's redemption comes through a Byronic/Satanic god of the Night called "Genius," who claims her, a "lost atom of life," as his bride. "I take from thy vision, darkness . . . I, with my presence, fill vacancy," he declares, explaining that "Unhumbled, I can take what is mine. Did I not give from the altar the very flame which lit Eva's being?"[39] Superficially, this allegorical narrative may be seen as a woman's attempt to imagine a male muse with whom she can have a sexual interaction that will parallel the male poet's congress with his female muse. But the incestuous Byronic love story in which Brontë embodies her allegorical message is more significant here than the message itself.

It suggests to begin with that, like Claire Clairemont, Brontë may have seen herself as at best a creation of male "Genius"—whether artwork or daughter is left deliberately vague—and therefore a being ultimately lacking in autonomy. Finding her ideas astonishingly close to those of an admired male (Byron, Satan, "Genius"), and accustomed to assuming that male thought is the source of all female thinking just as Adam's rib is the source of Eve's body, she supposes that he has, as it were, invented her. In addition, her autonomy is further denied even by the incestuous coupling which appears to link her to her creator and to make them equals. For, as Helene Moglen notes, the devouring ego of the Satanic-Byronic hero found the fantasy (or reality) of incest the best strategy for metaphorically annihilating the otherness—the autonomy—of the female. "In his union with [his half-sister] Augusta Leigh," Moglen points out, "Byron was in fact striving to achieve union with himself," just as Manfred expresses his solipsistic self-absorption by indulging his forbidden passion for his sister, Astarte. Similarly, the enormity of Satan's ego is manifested in the sexual cycle of his solipsistic production and reproduction of himself first as Sin and later as Death. Like Byron, he seems to be "attempting to become purely self-dependent by possessing his past in his present, affirming a more complete identity by enveloping and containing his other, complementary self. But, as Moglen goes on to remark, "to incorporate 'the other' is also after all to negate it. No space remains for the female. She can either allow herself to be devoured or she can retreat into isolation."[40]

It is not insignificant, then, that the fruit of Satan's solipsistic union with Sin is Death, just as death is the fruit of Manfred's love for

Astarte and ultimately—as we shall see—of all the incestuous neo-Satanic couplings envisioned by women writers from Mary Shelley to Sylvia Plath. To the extent that the desire to violate the incest taboo is a desire to be self-sufficient—self-begetting—it is a divinely interdicted wish to be "as Gods," like the desire for the forbidden fruit of the tree of knowledge, whose taste also meant death. For the woman writer, moreover, even the reflection that the Byronic hero is as much a creature of her mind—an incarnation of her "private, brooding, female resentments"—as she is an invention of his, offers little solace. For if in loving her he loves himself, in loving him she loves herself, and is therefore similarly condemned to the death of the soul that punishes solipsism.

But of course such a death of the soul is implied in any case by Satan's conception of his unholy creatures: Sin, Death, and Eve. As a figure of the heavenly interloper who plays the part of false "cosmocrator" in the dualistic patriarchal cosmology Milton inherited from Christian tradition, Satan is in fact a sort of artist of death, the paradigmatic master of all those perverse aesthetic techniques that pleasure the body rather than the soul, and serve the world rather than God. From the golden palace he erects at Pandemonium to his angelic impersonations in the garden and the devilish machines he engineers as part of his war against God, he practices false, fleshly, death-devoted arts (though a few of them are very much the kinds of arts a Romantic sensualist like Keats sometimes admired). As if following Milton even here, Byron makes the Satanic Manfred similarly the master of false, diabolical arts. And defining herself as the "creature" of one or the other of these irreligious artists, the woman writer would be confirmed not only in her sense that she was part of the "effeminate slackness" of the "false creation" but also in her fear that she was herself a false creator, one of the seductive "bevy of fair women" for whom the arts of language, like those of dance and music, are techniques "Bred only ... to the taste / Of lustful appetance," sinister parodies of the language of the angels and the music of the spheres (*PL* 11. 618–19). In the shadow of such a fear, even her housewifely arts would begin, like Eve's cookery—her choosing of delicacies "so contriv'd as not to mix / Tastes" (*PL* 5. 334–35)—to seem suspect, while the poetry she conceived might well appear to be a monster birth, like Satan's horrible child Death. Fallen like Anne Finch into domesticity, into the "dull mannage of a servile house"[41] as well as into the slavery of generation, she would not even have the satisfaction Manfred has of dying nobly. Rather, dwindling by degrees into an infertile drone, she might well conclude that this image of Satan and Eve as the false artists of creation was finally the most demeaning and discouraging avatar of Milton's bogey.

What would have made her perception of this last bogey even more galling, of course, would have been the magisterial calm with which Milton, as the epic speaker of *Paradise Lost*, continually calls attention to his own art, for the express purpose, so it seems, of defining himself throughout the poem as a type of the true artist, the virtuous poet who, rather than merely delighting (like Eve and Satan), delights while instructing. A prophet or priestly bard and therefore a guardian of the sacred mysteries of patriarchy, he serenely proposes to justify the ways of God to men, calls upon subservient female muses for the assistance that is his due (and in real, life upon slavish daughters for the same sort of assistance), and at the same time wars upon women with a barrage of angry words, just as God wars upon Satan. Indeed, as a figure of the true artist, God's emissary and defender on earth, Milton himself, as he appears in *Paradise Lost*, might well have seemed to female readers to be as much akin to God as they themselves were to Satan, Eve, or Sin.

Like God, for instance, Milton-as-epic-speaker creates heaven and earth (or their verbal equivalents) out of a bewildering chaos of history, legend, and philosophy. Like God, he has mental powers that penetrate to the furthest corners of the cosmos he has created, to the depths of hell and the heights of heaven, soaring with "no middle flight" toward ontological subjects "unattempted yet in Prose or Rhyme" (*PL* 1. 16). Like God, too, he knows the consequence of every action and event, his comments upon them indicating an almost divine consciousness of the simultaneity of past, present, and future. Like God, he punishes Satan, rebukes Adam and Eve, moves angels from one battle station to another, and grants all mankind glimpses of apocalyptic futurity, when a "greater Man" shall arrive to restore Paradisal bliss. And like God—like the Redeemer, like the Creator, like the Holy Ghost—he is male. Indeed, as a male poet justifying the ways of a male deity to male readers he rigorously excludes all females from the heaven of his poem, except insofar as he can beget new ideas upon their chaotic fecundity, like the Holy Spirit "brooding on the vast Abyss" and making it pregnant (*PL* 1. 21–22).

Even the blindness to which this epic speaker occasionally refers makes him appear godlike rather than handicapped. Cutting him off from "the cheerful ways" of ordinary mortals and reducing Satan's and Eve's domain of material nature to "a universal blanc," it elevates him above trivial fleshly concerns and causes "Celestial light" to "shine inward" upon him so that, like Tiresias, Homer, and God, he may see the mysteries of the spiritual world and "tell / Of things invisible to mortal sight" (*PL* 3. 55). And finally, even the syntax in which he speaks of these "things invisible" seems somehow godlike. Certainly the imposition of a Latinate sentence structure on English suggests both supreme confidence and supreme power. *Paradise Lost* is the "most remarkable Production of the world," Keats dryly decided in one of his more anti-Miltonic moments, because of the way its author forced a "northern dialect" to accommodate itself "to greek and latin inversions and intonations."[42] But not only are Greek and Latin the quintessential languages of masculine scholarship (as Virginia Woolf, for instance, never tired of noting), they are also the languages of the Church, of patristic and patriarchal ritual and theology. Imposed upon English, moreover, their periodic sentences, perhaps more than any other stylistic device in *Paradise Lost*, flaunt the poet's divine foreknowledge. When Milton begins a sentence "Him the Almighty" the reader knows perfectly well that only the poet and God know how the sentence—like the verse, the book, and the epic of humanity itself—will come out in the end.

That the Romantics perceived, admired, and occasionally identified with Milton's bardlike godliness while at the same time identifying with Satan's Promethean energy and fortitude is one of the more understandable paradoxes of literary history. Though they might sometimes have been irreligious and radically visionary with Satan, poets like Wordsworth and Shelley were after all fundamentally "masculinist" with Milton, even if they revered Mary Wollstonecraft (as Shelley did) or praised Anne Finch (as Wordsworth did). In this respect, their metaphors for the poet and "his" art are

as revealing as Milton's. Both Wordsworth and (as we have seen)
Shelley conceive of the poet as a divine ruler, an "unacknowledged
legislator" in Shelley's famous phrase and "an upholder and pre-
server" in Wordsworth's more conservative words. As such a ruler,
a sort of inspired patriarch, he is, like Milton, the guardian and
hierophant of sacred mysteries, inalterably opposed to the "idleness
and unmanly despair" of the false, effeminate creation. More, he is
a virile trumpet that calls mankind to battle, a fiercely phallic sword
that consumes its scabbard, and—most Miltonic of all—a godlike
"influence which is moved not, but moves," modeled upon Aristotle's
Unmoved Mover.[43]

No wonder then that, as Joseph Wittreich puts it, the author of
Paradise Lost was "the quintessence of everything the Romantics
most admired . . . the Knower moved by truth alone, the Doer . . .
causing divine deeds to issue forth from divine ideas, the Sayer who
translates the divine idea into poetry. . . . Thus to know Milton was
to know the answers to the indistinguishable questions—What is a
poet? What is poetry?"[44] Virginia Woolf, living in a world where
the dead female poet who was "Judith Shakespeare" had laid aside
her body so many times, made the same point in different words:
"This is the essence of which almost all other poetry is the dilution."
Such an assertion might seem jubilant if made by a man. But the
protean shadow of Milton's bogey seems to darken the page as
Woolf writes.

7 Horror's Twin:
Mary Shelley's Monstrous Eve

The nature of a Female Space is this: it shrinks the Organs
Of Life till they become Finite & Itself seems Infinite
And Satan vibrated in the immensity of the Space! Limited
To those without but Infinite to those within . . .
—William Blake

The woman writes as if the Devil was in her; and that is the only
condition under which a woman ever writes anything worth reading.
—Nathaniel Hawthorne, on Fanny Fern

I probed Retrieveless things
My Duplicate—to borrow—
A Haggard Comfort springs

From the belief that Somewhere—
Within the Clutch of Thought—
There dwells one other Creature
Of Heavenly Love—forgot—

I plucked at our Partition
As One should pry the Walls—
Between Himself—and Horror's Twin—
Within Opposing Cells—
—Emily Dickinson

What was the effect upon women writers of that complex of culture
myths summarized by Woolf as Milton's bogey? Surrounded by
"patriarchal poetry," what strategies for artistic survival were they
able to develop? The comments of writers like Brontë, Woolf, and
Wollstonecraft show that intelligent women were keenly conscious
of the problems Milton posed. But they were dizzied by them, too,

213

for the secret messages of *Paradise Lost* enclosed the poem's female
readers like a roomful of distorting mirrors. Keats's wondering
remark—"Whose head is not dizzy at the possibly [*sic*] speculations
of Satan in the serpent prison"[1]—seems to apply with even greater
force to women, imprisoned in the coil of serpentine images that
misogynistic myths and traditions constructed for them. On the
surface, however, many women writers responded equably, even
docilely to Milton and all he represented. Certainly the following
dialogue from *Middlemarch* seems to suggest a dutiful and submissive
attitude toward patriarchal poetry:

> "Could I not be preparing myself now to be more useful?"
> said Dorothea to [Casaubon], one morning, early in the time
> of courtship; "could I not learn to read Latin and Greek aloud
> to you, as Milton's daughters did to their father, without under-
> standing what they read?"
>
> "I fear that would be wearisome to you," said Mr. Casaubon
> smiling; "and, indeed, if I remember rightly, the young women
> you have mentioned regarded that exercise in unknown tongues
> as a ground for rebellion against the poet."
>
> "Yes; but in the first place they were very naughty girls, else
> they would have been proud to minister to such a father; and
> in the second place they might have studied privately and
> taught themselves to understand what they read, and then it
> would have been interesting. I hope you don't expect me to be
> naughty and stupid?"[2]

Usefulness, reading aloud, "ministering" to a wise father—all
these terms and notions reinforce Milton's concept of woman as at
best a serviceable second, a penitent Eve bearing children or pruning
branches under Adam's thoughtful guidance. Offering herself with
"ardent submissive affection" as helpmate to paternal Casaubon,
Dorothea Brooke appears as nobly free of Satanic aspirations as
George Eliot herself must have wished to be. A closer look at this
passage and at its context, however, transforms this interpretation,
revealing that with characteristic irony Eliot has found a way of
having submissive Dorothea intend, among other things, the very
opposite of what she says to Casaubon. Indeed, even the passage's
concern with Milton as father (rather than with, say, Milton as

politician or Milton as bard) tends paradoxically to sap the strength of the patriarchal associations that accrue around the name "Milton."

To take the last point first, paintings of Milton dictating to his daughters were quite popular at the end of the eighteenth century and throughout the nineteenth. One of Keats's first acts on moving into new lodgings, for instance, was to unpack his books and pin up "Haydon—Mary Queen [of] Scotts, and Milton with his daughters in a row."[3] Representing virtuous young ladies angelically ministering to their powerful father, the picture would seem to hold a mirror up to the nature of one of Western culture's fondest fantasies. At the same time, however, from a female point of view—as the *Middlemarch* passage suggests—the image of the Miltonic father *being ministered to* hints that his powers are not quite absolute, that in fact he has been reduced to a state of dependence upon his female descendents. Blinded, needing tea and sympathy as well as secretarial help, the godlike bard loses at least some of his divinity and is humanized, even (to coin a term) Samsonized. Thus, just as Charlotte Brontë implies that Jane Eyre leading blinded Rochester through the grounds of his own rural seat has found a rather Delilah-ish way of making herself not only useful to him but equal to him, so Eliot, working in the same iconographic tradition, implies that Dorothea secretly desires to make herself the equal of a Romantically weakened Casaubon: "it was not entirely out of devotion to her future husband that she wished to know Latin and Greek. . . . she had not reached that point of renunciation at which she would have been satisfied with having a wise husband: she wished, poor child, to be wise herself."[4]

But this unspoken wish to be as wise as a wise (though weak-eyed) husband is not only made possible by the dramatic situation of Milton and his daughters, it is expressed by Dorothea herself even when she seems merely to be stating her "ardent submissive affection," and it is clarified by Eliot in other passages. Milton's "naughty" daughters, Dorothea says, should have been "proud to minister to such a father." Not to "their" father, not to *any* father, but to a special father whose wisdom they might imbibe from close daily contact, as she herself hopes to imbibe Casaubon's learning. More important, she speculates that "they might have studied privately and taught themselves to understand what they read, and then it would have been interesting." They might, in other words, have refused to accept their secondary position, might have made themselves their father's equals in knowledge, might—like Dorothea— have wished to be wise themselves.

To the extent, however, that Dorothea's wish to be wise is not only a wish to be equal to her husband but also a wish to penetrate those forbidden "provinces of masculine knowledge . . . from which all truth could be seen more truly," it is a longing for intellectual self-reliance that parodies the Satanic. More, such a wish obviously subverts the self-effacing rhetoric in which it is couched ("Could I not be preparing myself now to be more useful?"), making it possible to impute to Dorothea—of all people—a sort of Satanic deviousness. And in fact, though any deviousness on her part is largely unconscious, her Satanic aspirations for power and wisdom as well as her Eve-like curiosity (itself a function of the Satanic) are clearly if guardedly defined in several places. Her desire "to arrive at the core of things," for instance, though ostensibly the result of a docile wish to "judge soundly on the duties of a Christian," is inextricably bound up with her ambitious plan to renovate her society by designing new housing for the poor. But "how could she be confident that one-room cottages were not for the glory of God," asks Eliot dryly, "when men who knew the classics appeared to conciliate indifference to the cottagers with zeal for the glory? Perhaps even Hebrew might be necessary," she notes, "at least the alphabet and a few roots—in order to arrive at the core of things" —and in order, by implication, to defeat the arguments of learned men on their own terms.[5]

In an earlier passage, in which Dorothea considers together the problems of education and architecture, Eliot makes the nature and intensity of her ambition even clearer. Indeed, in its expression of a will to be "as Gods" this passage seems almost like a direct prose translation of Eve's musings in Book 9 of *Paradise Lost*.

> "I should learn everything then [married to Casaubon]," she said to herself. . . . "It would be my duty to study that I might help him the better in his great works. There would be nothing trivial about out lives. Everyday things with us would mean the greatest things. . . . I should learn to see the truth by the same

> light as great men have seen it by. . . . I should see how it was
> possible to lead a grand life here—now—in England"[6]

Though this Eve may not yet have eaten the apple, her desire to be
both "good" and "wise," together with her longing for "a grand
life here—now," suggest that she may soon succumb to a passion
for such "intellectual food." That the food is also associated in her
mind with freedom makes the point most strongly of all. When
Dorothea fantasizes about the benefits of a marriage with Casaubon,
Eliot remarks that "the union which attracted her was one that
would deliver her from her girlish subjection to her own ignorance,
and give her the freedom of voluntary submission to a guide who
would take her along the grandest path."[7] For clearly this aspiring
scholar imagines Casaubon a connubial guide to whom secret studies
would soon make her equal, "for inferior who is free?"

Interestingly, as a guide along the grandest path Casaubon seems
at first more archangel than Adam, and even more idealized Milton
than archangel. Certainly Eliot's epigraph to chapter 3 of *Middlemarch*
("Say, goddess, what ensued, when Raphael, / The affable . . . ")
portrays the guide of Dorothea's dreams as affable archangel,
heavenly narrator, "winged messenger," and Dorothea herself as
an admiring Eve waiting to be instructed, while other passages
show him metamorphosing into a sort of God: "he thinks a whole
world of which my thought is but a poor two penny mirror."[8] And
as both instructing angel and Godlike master of the masculine
intellectual spheres, this dream-Casaubon would come close, as
Dorothea's daughterly speech implies, to being a sort of reincarnated
Milton.

Behind the dream-Casaubon, however, lurks the real Casaubon,
a point Eliot's irony stresses from the scholar's first appearance in
Middlemarch, just as—the Miltonic parallels continually invite us
to make this connection—the "real" Milton dwelt behind the carefully constructed dream image of the celestial bard. Indeed, Eliot's
real Casaubon, as opposed to Dorothea's idealized Casaubon, is in
certain respects closer to the real author of *Paradise Lost* than his
dream image is to the Miltonic epic speaker. Like Milton, after all,
Casaubon is a master of the classics and theology, those "provinces
of masculine knowledge . . . from which all truth could be seen more

truly." Like Milton's, too, his intellectual ambition is vast, ontological, almost overweening. In a sense, in fact, Casaubon's ambition
is identical with Milton's, for just as Milton's aim was to justify the
ways of God to man by learnedly retelling the central myth of
Western culture, so Casaubon's goal is to "reconcile complete knowledge with devoted piety" by producing a "key to all mythologies." [9]
It is not at all unreasonable of Dorothea, therefore, to hope that as
a dutiful daughter-wife-pupil she might be to Casaubon as Milton's
daughters were to Milton, and that her virtuous example would
criticize, by implication, the vices of her seventeenth-century precursors.

If the passionate reality of Dorothea comments upon the negative
history of Milton's daughters, however, the dull reality of Casaubon
comments even more forcefully upon history's images of Milton. For
Casaubon as the forger of a key to all myths is of course a ludicrous
caricature of Milton as sublime justifier of sublimity. Bonily self-
righteous, pedantic, humorless, he dwindles in the course of *Middlemarch* from heavenly scholar to tiresome Dryasdust to willful corpse
oppressing Dorothea even from beyond the grave, and in his carefully
articulated dissolution he is more like Milton's Satan, minus the
Byronic glamour, than he is like Milton. But his repudiation of the
guilty flesh, his barely disguised contempt for Dorothea's femininity,
his tyranny, and his dogmatism make him the parodic shadow of
the Miltonic misogynist and (at the same time) an early version of
Virginia Woolf's red-faced, ferocious "Professor von X. engaged
in writing his monumental work entitled *The Mental, Moral, and
Physical Inferiority of the Female Sex.*" [10] Uneasily wed to such a man,
ambitious Dorothea inevitably metamorphoses into the archetypal
wretched woman Blake characterized as Milton's wailing six-fold
Emanation, his three wives and three daughters gathered into a
single grieving shape. That she herself had defined the paradigm of
Milton's daughters more hopefully is no doubt an irony Eliot fully
intended.

If the story of Milton's daughters was so useful to both Eliot and
her protagonist, ambiguous iconography and all, it is even more
useful now for critics seeking to understand the relationship between

women and the cluster of misogynistic themes Milton's work brought together so brilliantly. Since the appearance of *Paradise Lost*—even, in a sense, before—all women writers have been to some extent Milton's daughters, continually wondering what their relationship to his patriarchal poetry ought to be and continually brooding upon alternative modes of daughterhood very much like those Dorothea describes. Margaret of Newcastle, for instance, seems to be trying to explain Milton's cosmos to herself in the following passage:

> ... although nature has not made women so strong of body and so clear of understanding as the ablest of men, yet she has made them fairer, softer, slenderer.... [and] has laid in tender affections, as love, piety, charity, clemency, patience, humility, and the like, which makes them nearest to resemble angels, which are the most perfect of all her works, where men by their ambitions, extortion, fury, and cruelty resemble the devil. But some women are like devils too when they are possessed with those evils, and the best of men ... are like to gods.[11]

Similarly, Anne Finch's "How are we fal'n, fal'n by mistaken rules, / And Education's more than Nature's fools?" defines the Miltonic problem of the fall as a specifically female dilemma.[12] And the Elizabethan "Jane Anger," like Milton's "naughty" daughters, inveighs against the patriarchal oppression of a proto-Miltonic cosmology in which "the gods, knowing that the minds of mankind would be aspiring, and having thoroughly viewed the wonderful virtues wherewith women are enriched, least they should provoke us to pride, and so confound us with Lucifer, they bestowed the supremacy over us to man."[13] Even before Milton had thought about women, it seems, women had thought of Milton.

Following the rise of Romanticism, however, with its simultaneous canonization of Milton *and* Satan, women writers have been undeniably Milton's daughters. More important, they have even more obviously claimed for themselves precisely the options Eliot has Dorothea explain to Casaubon: on the one hand, the option of apparently docile submission to male myths, of being "proud to minister to such a father," and on the other hand the option of secret study aimed toward the achievement of equality. In a large, metaphorical sense, these two courses of action probably define categories in which almost all writing by women can be subsumed. More narrowly—but still metaphorically—these two alternative patterns describe the main critical responses nineteenth- and twentieth-century women writers have made specifically to their readings, or misreadings, of *Paradise Lost*.

We shall argue here that the first alternative is the one Mary Shelley chooses in *Frankenstein* : to take the male culture myth of *Paradise Lost* at its full value—on its own terms, including all the analogies and parallels it implies—*and rewrite it so as to clarify its meaning*. The way of Milton's more ardently submissive daughters, it is the choice of the woman writer who, like Dorothea, strives to minister to such a father by understanding exactly what he is telling her about herself and what, therefore, he wants of her. But again, like Dorothea's ministrations, this apparently docile way of coping with Miltonic misogyny may conceal fantasies of equality that occasionally erupt in monstrous images of rage, as we shall see in considering *Frankenstein*.

Such guarded fury comes closer (though not completely) to the surface in the writing of women who choose the second alternative of Milton's daughters, the alternative of *rewriting Paradise Lost so as to make it a more accurate mirror of female experience*. This way of coping with Miltonic patriarchy is the modus operandi chosen by, for instance, Emily Brontë (in *Wuthering Heights* and elsewhere), and it is the way of the imaginary daughter who studies Greek and Latin in secret—the woman, that is, who teaches herself the language of myth, the tongue of power, so that she can reinvent herself and her own experience while seeming innocently to read to her illustrious father. We shall see that, resolutely closing their Goethe, these women often passionately reopen their Byron, using Romantic modes and manners to enact subversively feminist reinterpretations of *Paradise Lost*. Thus, though the woman writer who chooses this means of coping with her difficult heritage may express her anger more openly, she too produces a palimpsestic or encoded artwork, concealing female secrets within male-devised genres and conventions. Not only *Wuthering Heights* but more recently such female—even feminist—myths as Christina Rossetti's "Goblin Market," Virginia Woolf's *Orlando*, and Sylvia Plath's *Ariel* are works by women who have chosen this alternative. But of course the connection of such re-visions of *Paradise Lost* to the patriarchal poetry that fathered them becomes increasingly figurative in the twentieth century, an era whose women have had an unusually developed female tradition from which they can draw strength in their secret study of Milton's language. It is in earlier, lonelier works, in novels like *Frankenstein* and *Wuthering Heights*, that we can see the female imagination expressing its anxieties about *Paradise Lost* most overtly. And *Frankenstein* in particular is a fiction-alized rendition of the meaning of *Paradise Lost* to women.

Many critics have noticed that *Frankenstein* (1818) is one of the key Romantic "readings" of *Paradise Lost*.[14] Significantly, however, as a woman's reading it is most especially the story of hell: hell as a dark parody of heaven, hell's creations as monstrous imitations of heaven's creations, and hellish femaleness as a grotesque parody of heavenly maleness. But of course the divagations of the parody merely return to and reinforce the fearful reality of the original. For by parodying *Paradise Lost* in what may have begun as a secret, barely conscious attempt to subvert Milton, Shelley ended up telling, too, the central story of *Paradise Lost*, the tale of "what misery th' inabstinence of Eve / Shall bring on men."

Mary Shelley herself claims to have been continually asked "how I . . . came to think of and to dilate upon so very hideous an idea" as that of *Frankenstein*, but it is really not surprising that she should have formulated her anxieties about femaleness in such highly literary terms. For of course the nineteen-year-old girl who wrote *Frankenstein* was no ordinary nineteen-year-old but one of England's most notable literary heiresses. Indeed, as "the daughter of two persons of distinguished literary celebrity," and the wife of a third, Mary Wollstonecraft Godwin Shelley was the daughter and later the wife of some of Milton's keenest critics, so that Harold Bloom's useful conceit about the family romance of English literature is simply an accurate description of the reality of her life.[15]

In acknowledgment of this web of literary/familial relationships, critics have traditionally studied *Frankenstein* as an interesting example of Romantic myth-making, a work ancillary to such established Promethean masterpieces as Shelley's *Prometheus Unbound* and Byron's *Manfred*. ("Like almost everything else about [Mary's] life," one such critic remarks, *Frankenstein* "is an instance of genius observed and admired but not shared."[16]) Recently, however, a number of writers have noticed the connection between Mary Shelley's "waking dream" of monster-manufacture and her own experience of awakening sexuality, in particular the "horror story of Maternity" which accompanied her precipitous entrance into what Ellen Moers calls "teen-age motherhood."[17] Clearly they are articulating an increasingly uneasy sense that, despite its male protagonist and its underpinning of "masculine" philosophy, *Frankenstein* is somehow a "woman's book," if only because its author was caught up in such a maelstrom of sexuality at the time she wrote the novel.

In making their case for the work as female fantasy, though, critics like Moers have tended to evade the problems posed by what we must define as *Frankenstein*'s literariness. Yet, despite the weaknesses in those traditional readings of the novel that overlook its intensely sexual materials, it is still undeniably true that Mary Shelley's "ghost story," growing from a Keatsian (or Coleridgean) waking dream, is a Romantic novel about—among other things—Romanticism, as well as a book about books and perhaps, too, about the writers of books. Any theorist of the novel's femaleness and of its significance as, in Moers's phrase, a "birth myth" must therefore confront this self-conscious literariness. For as was only natural in "the daughter of two persons of distinguished literary celebrity," Mary Shelley explained her sexuality to herself in the context of her reading and its powerfully felt implications.

For this orphaned literary heiress, highly charged connections between femaleness and literariness must have been established early, and established specifically in relation to the controversial figure of her dead mother. As we shall see, Mary Wollstonecraft Godwin read her mother's writings over and over again as she was growing up. Perhaps more important, she undoubtedly read most of the reviews of her mother's *Posthumous Works*, reviews in which Mary Wollstonecraft was attacked as a "philosophical wanton" and a monster, while her *Vindication of the Rights of Woman* (1792) was called "A scripture, archly fram'd for propagating w[hore]s."[18] But in any case, to the "philosophical wanton's" daughter, all reading about (or of) her mother's work must have been painful, given her knowledge that that passionate feminist writer had died in giving life to *her*, to bestow upon Wollstonecraft's death from complications of childbirth the melodramatic cast it probably had for the girl herself. That Mary Shelley was conscious, moreover, of a strangely intimate relationship between her feelings toward her dead mother, her romance with a living poet, and her own sense of vocation as a reader and writer is made perfectly clear by her habit of "taking her books to Mary Wollstonecraft's grave in St. Pancras' Churchyard, there," as Muriel Spark puts it, "to pursue her studies in an atmosphere of communion with a mind greater than the second Mrs. Godwin's [and] to meet Shelley in secret." [19]

Her mother's grave: the setting seems an unusually grim, even ghoulish locale for reading, writing, or lovemaking. Yet, to a girl with Mary Shelley's background, literary activities, like sexual ones, must have been primarily extensions of the elaborate, gothic psycho-drama of her family history. If her famous diary is largely a compendium of her reading lists and Shelley's that fact does not, therefore, suggest unusual reticence on her part. Rather, it emphasizes the point that for Mary, even more than for most writers, reading a book was often an emotional as well as an intellectual event of considerable magnitude. Especially because she never knew her mother, and because her father seemed so definitively to reject her after her youthful elopement, her principal mode of self-definition—certainly in the early years of her life with Shelley, when she was writing *Frankenstein*—was through reading, and to a lesser extent through writing.

Endlessly studying her mother's works and her father's, Mary Shelley may be said to have "read" her family and to have been related to her reading, for books appear to have functioned as her surrogate parents, pages and words standing in for flesh and blood. That much of her reading was undertaken in Shelley's company, moreover, may also help explain some of this obsessiveness, for Mary's literary inheritance was obviously involved in her very literary romance and marriage. In the years just before she wrote *Frankenstein*, for instance, and those when she was engaged in composing the novel (1816–17), she studied her parents' writings, alone or together with Shelley, like a scholarly detective seeking clues to the significance of some cryptic text. [20]

To be sure, this investigation of the mysteries of literary genealogy was done in a larger context. In these same years, Mary Shelley recorded innumerable readings of contemporary gothic novels, as well as a program of study in English, French, and German literature that would do credit to a modern graduate student. But especially, in 1815, 1816, and 1817, she read the works of Milton. *Paradise Lost* (twice), *Paradise Regained, Comus, Areopagetica, Lycidas.* And what makes the extent of this reading particularly impressive is the fact that in these years, her seventeenth to her twenty-first, Mary Shelley was almost continuously pregnant, "confined," or nursing. At the same time, it is precisely the coincidence of all these disparate activities— her family studies, her initiation into adult sexuality, and her literary self-education—that makes her vision of *Paradise Lost* so significant. For her developing sense of herself as a literary creature and/or creator seems to have been inseparable from her emerging self-definition as daughter, mistress, wife, and mother. Thus she cast her birth myth— her myth of origins—in precisely those cosmogenic terms to which her parents, her husband, and indeed her whole literary culture continually alluded: the terms of *Paradise Lost*, which (as she indicates even on the title page of her novel), she saw as preceding, paralleling, and commenting upon the Greek cosmogeny of the Prometheus play her husband had just translated. It is as a female fantasy of sex and reading, then, a gothic psychodrama reflecting Mary Shelley's own sense of what we might call bibliogenesis, that *Frankenstein* is a version of the misogynistic story implicit in *Paradise Lost*.

It would be a mistake to underestimate the significance of *Frankenstein*'s title page, with its allusive subtitle ("The Modern Prometheus") and carefully pointed Miltonic epigraph ("Did I request thee, Maker, from my clay / To mould me man? Did I solicit thee / From darkness to promote me?"). But our first really serious clue to the highly literary nature of this history of a creature born outside history is its author's use of an unusually *evidentiary* technique for conveying the stories of her monster and his maker. Like a literary jigsaw puzzle, a collection of apparently random documents from whose juxtaposition the scholar-detective must infer a meaning, *Frankenstein* consists of three "concentric circles" of narration (Walton's letters, Victor Frankenstein's recital to Walton, and the monster's speech to Frankenstein), within which are embedded pockets of digression containing other miniature narratives (Frankenstein's mother's story, Elizabeth Lavenza's and Justine's stories, Felix's and Agatha's story, Safie's story), etc.[21] As we have noted, reading and assembling documentary evidence, examining it, analyzing it and researching it comprised for Shelley a crucial if voyeuristic method of exploring origins, explaining identity, understanding sexuality. Even more obviously, it was a way of researching and analyzing an emotionally unintelligible text, like *Paradise Lost*. In a sense, then, even before *Paradise Lost* as a central item on the monster's reading list becomes a literal event in *Frankenstein*, the novel's literary structure prepares us to confront Milton's patriarchal epic, both as a sort of research problem and as the framework for a complex system of allusions.

The book's dramatic situations are equally resonant. Like Mary Shelley, who was a puzzled but studious Miltonist, this novel's key characters—Walton, Frankenstein, and the monster—are obsessed with problem-solving. "I shall satiate my ardent curiosity with the sight of a part of the world never before visited," exclaims the young explorer, Walton, as he embarks like a child "on an expedition of discovery up his native river" (2, letter 1). "While my companions contemplated . . . the magnificent appearance of things," declares Frankenstein, the scientist of sexual ontology, "I delighted in investigating their causes" (22, chap. 2). "Who was I? What was I? Whence did I come?" (113–15, chap. 15) the monster reports wondering, describing endless speculations cast in Miltonic terms. All three, like Shelley herself, appear to be trying to understand their presence in a fallen world, and trying at the same time to define the nature of the lost paradise that must have existed before the fall. But unlike Adam, all three characters seem to have fallen not merely from Eden but from the earth, fallen directly into hell, like Sin, Satan, and—by implication—Eve. Thus their questionings are in some sense female, for they belong in that line of literary women's questionings of the fall into gender which goes back at least to Anne Finch's plaintive "How are we fal'n?" and forward to Sylvia Plath's horrified "I have fallen very far!"[22]

From the first, however, *Frankenstein* answers such neo-Miltonic questions mainly through explicit or implicit allusions to Milton, retelling the story of the fall not so much to protest against it as to clarify its meaning. The parallels between those two Promethean overreachers Walton and Frankenstein, for instance, have always been clear to readers. But that both characters can, therefore, be described (the way Walton describes Frankenstein) as "fallen angels" is not as frequently remarked. Yet Frankenstein himself is perceptive enough to ask Walton "Do you share my madness?" at just the moment when the young explorer remarks Satanically that "One man's life or death were but a small price to pay . . . for the dominion I [wish to] acquire" (13, letter 4). Plainly one fallen angel can recognize another. Alienated from his crew and chronically friendless, Walton tells his sister that he longs for a friend "on the wide ocean," and what he discovers in Victor Frankenstein is the fellowship of hell.

In fact, like the many other secondary narratives Mary Shelley offers in her novel, Walton's story is itself an alternative version of the myth of origins presented in *Paradise Lost*. Writing his ambitious letters home from St. Petersburgh [*sic*], Archangel, and points north, Walton moves like Satan away from the sanctity and sanity represented by his sister, his crew, and the allegorical names of the places he leaves. Like Satan, too, he seems at least in part to be exploring the frozen frontiers of hell in order to attempt a return to heaven, for the "country of eternal light" he envisions at the Pole (1, letter 1) has much in common with Milton's celestial "Fountain of Light" (*PL* 3. 375).[23] Again, like Satan's (and Eve's) aspirations, his ambition has violated a patriarchal decree: his father's "dying injunction" had forbidden him "to embark on a seafaring life." Moreover, even the icy hell where Walton encounters Frankenstein and the monster is Miltonic, for all three of these diabolical wanderers must learn, like the fallen angels of *Paradise Lost*, that "Beyond this flood a frozen Continent / Lies dark and wild . . . / Thither by harpy-footed Furies hal'd, / At certain revolutions all the damn'd / Are brought . . . From Beds of raging Fire to starve in Ice" (*PL* 2. 587–600).

Finally, another of Walton's revelations illuminates not only the likeness of his ambitions to Satan's but also the similarity of his anxieties to those of his female author. Speaking of his childhood, he reminds his sister that, because poetry had "lifted [my soul] to heaven," he had become a poet and "for one year lived in a paradise of my own creation." Then he adds ominously that "You are well-acquainted with my failure and how heavily I bore the disappointment" (2–3, letter 1). But of course, as she confesses in her introduction to *Frankenstein*, Mary Shelley, too, had spent her childhood in "waking dreams" of literature; later, both she and her poet-husband hoped she would prove herself "worthy of [her] parentage and enroll [herself] on the page of fame" (xii). In a sense, then, given the Miltonic context in which Walton's story of poetic failure is set, it seems possible that one of the anxious fantasies his narrative helps Mary Shelley covertly examine is the fearful tale of a female fall from a lost paradise of art, speech, and autonomy into a hell of sexuality, silence, and filthy materiality, "A Universe of death, which God by curse / Created evil, for evil only good, / Where all life dies, death lives, and Nature breeds, / Perverse, all monstrous, all prodigious things" (*PL* 2. 622–25).

Walton and his new friend Victor Frankenstein have considerably more in common than a Byronic (or Monk Lewis-ish) Satanism. For one thing, both are orphans, as Frankenstein's monster is and as it turns out all the major and almost all the minor characters in *Frankenstein* are, from Caroline Beaufort and Elizabeth Lavenza to Justine, Felix, Agatha, and Safie. Victor Frankenstein has not always been an orphan, though, and Shelley devotes much space to an account of his family history. Family histories, in fact, especially those of orphans, appear to fascinate her, and wherever she can include one in the narrative she does so with an obsessiveness suggesting that through the disastrous tale of the child who becomes "an orphan and a beggar" she is once more recounting the story of the fall, the expulsion from paradise, and the confrontation of hell. For Milton's Adam and Eve, after all, began as motherless orphans reared (like Shelley herself) by a stern but kindly father-god, and ended as beggars rejected by God (as she was by *God*win when she eloped). Thus Caroline Beaufort's father dies leaving her "an orphan and a beggar," and Elizabeth Lavenza also becomes "an orphan and a beggar"—the phrase is repeated (18, 20, chap. 1)—with the disappearance of her father into an Austrian dungeon. And though both girls are rescued by Alphonse Frankenstein, Victor's father, the early alienation from the patriarchal chain-of-being signalled by their orphanhood prefigures the hellish fate in store for them and their family. Later, motherless Safie and fatherless Justine enact similarly ominous anxiety fantasies about the fall of woman into orphanhood and beggary.

Beyond their orphanhood, however, a universal sense of guilt links such diverse figures as Justine, Felix, and Elizabeth, just as it will eventually link Victor, Walton, and the monster. Justine, for instance, irrationally confesses to the murder of little William, though she knows perfectly well she is innocent. Even more irrationally, Elizabeth is reported by Alphonse Frankenstein to have exclaimed "Oh, God! I have murdered my darling child!" after her first sight of the corpse of little William (57, chap. 7). Victor, too, long before he knows that the monster is actually his brother's killer, decides that his "creature" has killed William and that therefore he, the creator, is the "true murderer": "the mere presence of the idea," he notes, is "an irresistable proof of the fact" (60, chap. 7). Complicity in the murder of the child William is, it seems, another crucial component of the Original Sin shared by prominent members of the Frankenstein family.

At the same time, the likenesses among all these characters—the common alienation, the shared guilt, the orphanhood and beggary— imply relationships of redundance between them like the solipsistic relationships among artfully placed mirrors. What reinforces our sense of this hellish solipsism is the barely disguised incest at the heart of a number of the marriages and romances the novel describes. Most notably, Victor Frankenstein is slated to marry his "more than sister" Elizabeth Lavenza, whom he confesses to having always considered "a possession of my own" (21, chap. 1). But the mysterious Mrs. Saville, to whom Walton's letters are addressed, is apparently in some sense *his* more than sister, just as Caroline Beaufort was clearly a "more than" wife, in fact a daughter, to her father's friend Alphonse Frankenstein. Even relationless Justine appears to have a metaphorically incestuous relationship with the Frankensteins, since as their servant she becomes their possession and more than sister, while the female monster Victor half-constructs in Scotland will be a more than sister as well as a mate to the monster, since both have the same parent/creator.

Certainly at least some of this incest-obsession in *Frankenstein* is, as Ellen Moers remarks, the "standard" sensational matter of Romantic novels.[24] Some of it, too, even without the conventions of the gothic thriller, would be a natural subject for an impressionable young woman who had just spent several months in the company of the famously incestuous author of *Manfred*.[25] Nevertheless, the streak of incest that darkens *Frankenstein* probably owes as much to the book's Miltonic framework as it does to Mary Shelley's own life and times. In the Edenic cosiness of their childhood, for instance, Victor and Elizabeth are incestuous as Adam and Eve are, literally incestuous because they have the same creator, and figuratively so because Elizabeth is Victor's pretty plaything, the image of an angelic soul or "epipsyche" created from his own soul just as Eve is created from Adam's rib. Similarly, the incestuous relationships of Satan and Sin, and by implication of Satan and Eve, are mirrored in the incest fantasies of *Frankenstein*, including the disguised but intensely sexual waking dream in which Victor Frankenstein in effect couples with his monster by applying "the instruments of life" to its body and inducing a shudder of response (42, chap. 5). For Milton, and therefore for Mary Shelley, who was trying to understand Milton, incest was an inescapable metaphor for the solipsistic fever of self-awareness that Matthew Arnold was later to call "the dialogue of the mind with itself."[26]

If Victor Frankenstein can be likened to both Adam and Satan, however, who or what is he *really*? Here we are obliged to confront both the moral ambiguity and the symbolic slipperiness which are at the heart of all the characterizations in *Frankenstein*. In fact, it is probably these continual and complex reallocations of meaning, among characters whose histories echo and re-echo each other, that have been so bewildering to critics. Like figures in a dream, all the people in *Frankenstein* have different bodies and somehow, horribly, the same face, or worse—the same two faces. For this reason, as Muriel Spark notes, even the book's subtitle "The Modern Prometheus" is ambiguous, "for though at first Frankenstein is himself the Prometheus, the vital fire-endowing protagonist, the Monster, as soon as he is created, takes on [a different aspect of] the role."[27] Moreover, if we postulate that Mary Shelley is more concerned with Milton than she is with Aeschylus, the intertwining of meanings grows even more confusing, as the monster himself several times points out to Frankenstein, noting "I ought to be thy Adam, but I am rather the fallen angel," (84, chap. 10), then adding elsewhere that "God, in pity, made man beautiful . . . after His own image; but my form is a filthy type of yours. . . . Satan had his companions . . . but I am solitary and abhorred" (115, chap. 15). In other words, not only do Frankenstein and his monster both in one way or another enact the story of Prometheus, each is at one time or another like God (Victor as creator, the monster as his creator's "Master"), like Adam (Victor as innocent child, the monster as primordial "creature"), and like Satan (Victor as tormented overreacher, the monster as vengeful fiend).

What is the reason for this continual duplication and reduplication of roles? Most obviously, perhaps, the dreamlike shifting of fantasy figures from part to part, costume to costume, tells us that we are in fact dealing with the psychodrama or waking dream that Shelley herself suspected she had written. Beyond this, however, we would argue that the fluidity of the narrative's symbolic scheme reinforces in another way the crucial significance of the Miltonic skeleton around which Mary Shelley's hideous progeny took shape. For it becomes increasingly clear as one reads *Frankenstein* with *Paradise Lost* in mind that because the novel's author is such an inveterate student of literature, families, and sexuality, and because she is using her novel as a tool to help her make sense of her reading, *Frankenstein* is ultimately a mock *Paradise Lost* in which both Victor and his monster, together with a number of secondary characters, play all the neo-biblical parts over and over again—all except, it seems at first, the part of Eve. Not just the striking omission of any obvious Eve-figure from this "woman's book" about Milton, but also the barely concealed sexual components of the story as well as our earlier analysis of Milton's bogey should tell us, however, that for Mary Shelley the part of Eve *is* all the parts.

On the surface, Victor seems at first more Adamic than Satanic or Eve-like. His Edenic childhood is an interlude of prelapsarian innocence in which, like Adam, he is sheltered by his benevolent father as a sensitive plant might be "sheltered by the gardener, from every rougher wind" (19–20, chap. 1). When cherubic Elizabeth Lavenza joins the family, she seems as "heaven-sent" as Milton's

Eve, as much Victor's "possession" as Adam's rib is Adam's. Moreover, though he is evidently forbidden almost nothing ("My parents [were not] tyrants . . . but the agents and creators of many delights"), Victor hints to Walton that his deific father, like Adam's and Walton's, did on one occasion arbitrarily forbid him to pursue his interest in arcane knowledge. Indeed, like Eve and Satan, Victor blames his own fall at least in part on his father's apparent arbitrariness. "If . . . my father had taken the pains to explain to me that the principles of Agrippa had been entirely exploded. . . . It is even possible that the train of my ideas would never have received the fatal impulse that led to my ruin" (24–25, chap. 2). And soon after asserting this he even associates an incident in which a tree is struck by Jovian thunder bolts with his feelings about his forbidden studies.

As his researches into the "secrets of nature" become more feverish, however, and as his ambition "to explore unknown powers" grows more intense, Victor begins to metamorphose from Adam to Satan, becoming "as Gods" in his capacity of "bestowing animation upon lifeless matter," laboring like a guilty artist to complete his false creation. Finally, in his conversations with Walton he echoes Milton's fallen angel, and Marlowe's, in his frequently reiterated confession that "I bore a hell within me which nothing could extinguish" (72, chap. 8). Indeed, as the "true murderer" of innocence, here cast in the form of the child William, Victor perceives himself as a diabolical creator whose mind has involuntarily "let loose" a monstrous and "filthy demon" in much the same way that Milton's Satan's swelled head produced Sin, the disgusting monster he "let loose" upon the world. Watching a "noble war in the sky" that seems almost like an intentional reminder that we are participating in a critical rearrangement of most of the elements of *Paradise Lost*, he explains that "I considered the being whom I had cast among mankind . . . nearly in the light of my own vampire, my own spirit let loose from the grave and forced to destroy all that was dear to me" (61, chap. 7).

Even while it is the final sign and seal of Victor's transformation from Adam to Satan, however, it is perhaps the Sin-ful murder of the child William that is our first overt clue to the real nature of the bewilderingly disguised set of identity shifts and parallels Mary Shelley incorporated into *Frankenstein*. For as we saw earlier, not just Victor and the monster but also Elizabeth and Justine insist upon responsibility for the monster's misdeed. Feeling "as if I had been guilty of a crime" (41, chap. 4) even before one had been committed, Victor responds to the news of William's death with the same self-accusations that torment the two orphans. And, significantly, for all three—as well as for the monster and little William himself—one focal point of both crime and guilt is an image of that other beautiful orphan, Caroline Beaufort Frankenstein. Passing from hand to hand, pocket to pocket, the smiling miniature of Victor's "angel mother" seems a token of some secret fellowship in sin, as does Victor's post-creation nightmare of transforming a lovely, living Elizabeth, with a single magical kiss, into "the corpse of my dead mother" enveloped in a shroud made more horrible by "grave-worms crawling in the folds of the flannel" (42, chap. 5). Though it has been disguised, buried, or miniaturized, femaleness—the gender definition of mothers and daughters, orphans and beggars, monsters and false creators—is at the heart of this apparently masculine book.

Because this is so, it eventually becomes clear that though Victor Frankenstein enacts the roles of Adam and Satan like a child trying on costumes, his single most self-defining act transforms him definitively into Eve. For as both Ellen Moers and Marc Rubenstein have pointed out, after much study of the "cause of generation and life," after locking himself away from ordinary society in the tradition of such agonized mothers as Wollstonecraft's Maria, Eliot's Hetty Sorel, and Hardy's Tess, Victor Frankenstein has a baby.[28] His "pregnancy" and childbirth are obviously manifested by the existence of the paradoxically huge being who emerges from his "workshop of filthy creation," but even the descriptive language of his creation myth is suggestive: "incredible labours," "emaciated with confinement," "a passing trance," "oppressed by a slow fever," "nervous to a painful degree," "exercise and amusement would ... drive away incipient disease," "the instruments of life" (39–41, chap. 4), etc. And, like Eve's fall into guilty knowledge and painful maternity, Victor's entrance into what Blake would call the realm of "generation" is marked by a recognition of the necessary interdependence of those complementary opposites, sex and death: "To examine the causes of life, we must first have recourse to death," he observes (36, chap. 4), and in his isolated workshop of filthy creation—filthy because obscenely sexual[29]—he collects and arranges materials furnished by "the dissecting room and the slaughterhouse." Pursuing "nature to her hiding places" as Eve does in eating the apple, he learns that "the tremendous secrets of the human frame" are the interlocked secrets of sex and death, although, again like Eve, in his first mad pursuit of knowledge he knows not "eating death." But that his actual orgasmic animation of his monster-child takes place "on a dreary night in November," month of All Souls, short days, and the year's last slide toward death, merely reinforces the Miltonic and Blakean nature of his act of generation.

Even while Victor Frankenstein's self-defining procreation dramatically transforms him into an Eve-figure, however, our recognition of its implications reflects backward upon our sense of Victor-as-Satan and our earlier vision of Victor-as-Adam. Victor as Satan, we now realize, was never really the masculine, Byronic Satan of the first book of *Paradise Lost*, but always, instead, the curiously female, outcast Satan who gave birth to Sin. In his Eve-like pride ("I was surprised . . . that I alone should be reserved to discover so astonishing a secret" [37, chap. 4]), this Victor-Satan becomes "dizzy" with his creative powers, so that his monstrous pregnancy, bookishly and solipsistically conceived, reenacts as a terrible bibliogenesis the moment when, in Milton's version, Satan "dizzy swum / In darkness, while [his] head flames thick and fast / Threw forth, till on the left side op'ning wide" and Sin, Death's mother-to-be, appeared like "a Sign / Portentous" (*PL* 2: 753–61). Because he has conceived— or, rather, misconceived—his monstrous offspring by brooding upon the *wrong* books, moreover, this Victor-Satan is paradigmatic, like the falsely creative fallen angel, of the female artist, whose anxiety about her own aesthetic activity is expressed, for instance, in Mary Shelley's deferential introductory phrase about her "hideous progeny," with its plain implication that in her alienated attic workshop of filthy creation she has given birth to a deformed book, a literary abortion or miscarriage. "How [did] I, then a young girl, [come] to think of and to *dilate* upon so very hideous an idea?" is a key (if disingenuous) question she records. But we should not overlook her word play upon *dilate*, just as we should not ignore the anxious pun on the word *author* that is so deeply embedded in *Frankenstein*.

If the adult, Satanic Victor is Eve-like both in his procreation and his anxious creation, even the young, prelapsarian, and Adamic

Victor is—to risk a pun—*curiously* female, that is, Eve-like. Innocent and guided by silken threads like a Blakeian lamb in a Godwinian garden, he is consumed by "a fervent longing to penetrate the secrets of nature," a longing which—expressed in his explorations of "vaults and charnelhouses," his guilty observations of "the unhallowed damps of the grave," and his passion to understand "the structure of the human frame"—recalls the criminal female curiosity that led Psyche to lose love by gazing upon its secret face, Eve to insist upon consuming "intellectual food," and Prometheus's sister-in-law Pandora to open the forbidden box of fleshly ills. But if Victor-Adam is also Victor-Eve, what is the real significance of the episode in which, away at school and cut off from his family, he locks himself into his workshop of filthy creation and gives birth by intellectual parturition to a giant monster? Isn't it precisely at this point in the novel that he discovers he is not Adam but Eve, not Satan but Sin, not male but female? If so, it seems likely that what this crucial section of *Frankenstein* really enacts is the story of Eve's discovery not that she must fall but that, having been created female, she *is* fallen, femaleness and fallenness being essentially synonymous. For what Victor Frankenstein most importantly learns, we must remember, is that he is the "author" of the monster—for him alone is "reserved . . . so astonishing a secret"—and thus it is he who is "the true murderer," he who unleashes Sin and Death upon the world, he who dreams the primal kiss that incestuously kills both "sister" and "mother." Doomed and filthy, is he not, then, Eve instead of Adam? In fact, may not the story of the fall be, for women, the story of the discovery that one is not innocent and Adam (as one had supposed) but Eve, and fallen? Perhaps this is what Freud's cruel but metaphorically accurate concept of penis-envy really means: the girl-child's surprised discovery that she is female, hence fallen, inadequate. Certainly the almost grotesquely anxious self-analysis implicit in Victor Frankenstein's (and Mary Shelley's) multiform relationships to Eve, Adam, God, and Satan suggest as much.

The discovery that one is fallen is in a sense a discovery that one is a monster, a murderer, a being gnawed by "the never-dying worm" (72, chap. 8) and therefore capable of any horror, including but not limited to sex, death, and filthy literary creation. More, the discovery that one is fallen—self-divided, murderous, material—is the discovery that one has released a "vampire" upon the world, "forced to destroy all that [is] dear" (61, chap. 7). For this reason—because *Frankenstein* is a story of woman's fall told by, as it were, an apparently docile daughter to a censorious "father"—the monster's narrative is embedded at the heart of the novel like the secret of the fall itself. Indeed, just as Frankenstein's workshop, with its maddening, riddling answers to cosmic questions is a hidden but commanding attic womb/room where the young artist-scientist murders to dissect and to recreate, so the murderous monster's single, carefully guarded narrative commands and controls Mary Shelley's novel. Delivered at the top of Mont Blanc—like the North Pole one of the Shelley family's metaphors for the indifferently powerful source of creation and destruction—it is the story of deformed Geraldine in "Christabel," the story of the dead-alive crew in "The Ancient Mariner," the story of Eve in *Paradise Lost*, and of her degraded double Sin—all secondary or female characters to whom male authors have imperiously denied any chance of self-explanation.[30] At the same time the monster's narrative is a philosophical meditation on what it means to be born without a "soul" or a history, as well as an exploration of what it feels like to be a "filthy mass that move[s] and talk[s]," a thing, an other, a creature of the second sex. In fact, though it tends to be ignored by critics (and film-makers), whose emphasis has always fallen upon Frankenstein himself as the archetypal mad scientist, the drastic shift in point of view that the nameless monster's monologue represents probably constitutes *Frankenstein*'s most striking technical *tour de force*, just as the monster's bitter self-revelations are Mary Shelley's most impressive and original achievement.[31]

Like Victor Frankenstein, his author and superficially better self, the monster enacts in turn the roles of Adam and Satan, and even eventually hints at a sort of digression into the role of God. Like Adam, he recalls a time of primordial innocence, his days and nights in "the forest near Ingolstadt," where he ate berries, learned about heat and cold, and perceived "the boundaries of the radiant roof of light which canopied me" (88, chap. 11). Almost too quickly, however, he metamorphoses into an outcast and Satanic figure, hiding in a shepherd's hut which seems to him "as exquisite . . . a retreat as

Pandemonium . . . after . . . the lake of fire" (90, chap. 11). Later, when he secretly sets up housekeeping behind the De Laceys' pigpen, his wistful observations of the loving though exiled family and their pastoral abode("Happy, happy earth! Fit habitation for gods . . . " [100, chap. 12]) recall Satan's mingled jealousy and admiration of that "happy rural seat of various view" where Adam and Eve are emparadised by God and Milton (*PL* 4. 247). Eventually, burning the cottage and murdering William in demonic rage, he seems to become entirely Satanic: "I, like the arch-fiend, bore a hell within me" (121, chap. 16); "Inflamed by pain, I vowed eternal hatred . . . to all mankind" (126, chap. 16). At the same time, in his assertion of power over his "author," his mental conception of another creature (a female monster), and his implicit dream of founding a new, vegetarian race somewhere in "the vast wilds of South America," (131, chap. 17), he temporarily enacts the part of a God, a creator, a master, albeit a failed one.

As the monster himself points out, however, each of these Miltonic roles is a Procrustean bed into which he simply cannot fit. Where, for instance, Victor Frankenstein's childhood really was Edenic, the monster's anxious infancy is isolated and ignorant, rather than in- sulated or innocent, so that his groping arrival at self-consciousness— "I was a poor, helpless, miserable wretch; I knew and could distin- guish nothing; but feeling pain invade me on all sides, I sat down and wept" (87–88, chap. 11)—is a fiercely subversive parody of Adam's exuberant "all things smil'd, / With fragrance and with joy my heart o'erflowed. / Myself I then perus'd, and Limb by Limb / Survey'd, and sometimes went, and sometimes ran / With supple joints, as lively vigor led" (*PL* 8. 265–69). Similarly, the monster's attempts at speech ("Sometimes I wished to express my sensations in my own mode, but the uncouth and inarticulate sounds which broke from me frightened me into silence again" (88, chap. 11) parody and subvert Adam's ("To speak I tri'd, and forthwith spake, / My Tongue obey'd and readily could name / Whate'er I saw" (*PL* 8. 271–72). And of course the monster's anxiety and confusion ("What was I? The question again recurred to be answered only with groans" [106, chap. 13]) are a dark version of Adam's wondering bliss ("who I was, or where, or from what cause, / [I] Knew not. . . . [But I] feel that I am happier than I know" (*PL* 8. 270–71, 282).

Similarly, though his uncontrollable rage, his alienation, even his enormous size and superhuman physical strength bring him closer to Satan than he was to Adam, the monster puzzles over discrepancies between his situation and the fallen angel's. Though he is, for example, "in bulk as huge / As whom the Fables name of monstrous size, / *Titanian*, or *Earth-born*, that warr'd on *Jove*," and though, indeed, he is fated to war like Prometheus on Jovean Frankenstein, this demon/monster has fallen from no heaven, exercised no power of choice, and been endowed with no companions in evil. "I found myself similar yet at the same time strangely unlike to the beings concerning whom I read and to whose conversation I was a listener," he tells Frankenstein, describing his schooldays in the De Lacey pigpen (113, chap. 15). And, interestingly, his remark might well have been made by Mary Shelley herself, that "devout but nearly silent listener" (xiv) to masculine conversations who, like her hideous progeny, "continually studied and exercised [her] mind upon" such "histories" as *Paradise Lost*, Plutarch's *Lives*, and *The Sorrows of Werter* [*sic*] "whilst [her] friends were employed in their ordinary occupations" (112, chap. 15).

In fact, it is his intellectual similarity to his authoress (rather than his "author") which first suggests that Victor Frankenstein's male monster may really be a female in disguise. Certainly the books which educate him—*Werter*, Plutarch's *Lives*, and *Paradise Lost*—are not only books Mary had herself read in 1815, the year before she wrote *Frankenstein*, but they also typify just the literary categories she thought it necessary to study: the contemporary novel of sensibility, the serious history of Western civilization, and the highly cultivated epic poem. As specific works, moreover, each must have seemed to her to embody lessons a female author (or monster) must learn about a male-dominated society. Werter's story, says the monster—and he seems to be speaking for Mary Shelley—taught him about "gentle and domestic manners," and about "lofty sentiments . . . which had for their object something out of self." It functioned, in other words, as a sort of Romantic conduct book. In addition, it served as an introduction to the virtues of the proto-Byronic "Man of Feeling," for, admiring Werter and never mentioning Lotte, the monster explains to Victor that "I thought Werter himself a more divine being than I had ever . . . imagined," adding, in a line whose female

irony about male self-dramatization must surely have been intentional, "I wept [his extinction] without precisely understanding it"
(113, chap. 15).

If *Werter* introduces the monster to female modes of domesticity
and self-abnegation, as well as to the unattainable glamour of male
heroism, Plutarch's *Lives* teaches him all the masculine intricacies
of that history which his anomalous birth has denied him. Mary
Shelley, excluding herself from the household of the second Mrs.
Godwin and studying family as well as literary history on her mother's
grave, must, again, have found in her own experience an appropriate
model for the plight of a monster who, as James Rieger notes, is
especially characterized by "his unique knowledge of what it is like
to be born free of history."[32] In terms of the disguised story the novel
tells, however, this monster is not unique at all, but representative,
as Shelley may have suspected she herself was. For, as Jane Austen
has Catherine Morland suggest in *Northanger Abbey*, what is woman
but man without a history, at least without the sort of history related
in Plutarch's *Lives*? "History, real solemn history, I cannot be interested in," Catherine declares " . . . the men all so good for nothing,
and hardly any women at all—it is very tiresome" (*NA* I, chap. 14).

But of course the third and most crucial book referred to in the
miniature *Bildungsroman* of the monster's narrative is *Paradise Lost*,
an epic myth of origins which is of major importance to him, as it is
to Mary Shelley, precisely because, unlike Plutarch, it does provide
him with what appears to be a personal history. And again, even the
need for such a history draws Shelley's monster closer not only to
the realistically ignorant female defined by Jane Austen but also to
the archetypal female defined by John Milton. For, like the monster,
like Catherine Morland, and like Mary Shelley herself, Eve is characterized by her "unique knowledge of what it is like to be born free
of history," even though as the "Mother of Mankind" she is fated to
"make" history. It is to Adam, after all, that God and His angels
grant explanatory visions of past and future. At such moments of
high historical colloquy Eve tends to excuse herself with "lowliness
Majestic" (before the fall) or (after the fall) she is magically put to
sleep, calmed like a frightened animal "with gentle Dreams . . . and
all her spirits compos'd / To meek submission" (*PL* 12. 595–96).

Nevertheless, one of the most notable facts about the monster's ceaselessly anxious study of *Paradise Lost* is his failure even to mention Eve. As an insistently male monster, on the surface of his palimpsestic narrative he appears to be absorbed in Milton's epic only because, as Percy Shelley wrote in the preface to *Frankenstein* that he drafted for his wife, *Paradise Lost* "most especially" conveys "the truth of the elementary principles of human nature," and conveys that truth in the dynamic tensions developed among its male characters, Adam, Satan, and God (xvii). Yet not only the monster's uniquely ahistorical birth, his literary anxieties, and the sense his readings (like Mary's) foster that he must have been parented, if at all, by *books*; not only all these facts and traits but also his shuddering sense of deformity, his nauseating size, his namelessness, and his orphaned, motherless isolation link him with Eve and with Eve's double, Sin. Indeed, at several points in his impassioned analysis of Milton's story he seems almost on the verge of saying so, as he examines the disjunctions among Adam, Satan, and himself:

> Like Adam, I was apparently united by no link to any other being in existence; but his state was far different from mine in every other respect. He had come forth from the hands of God a perfect creature, happy and prosperous, guided by the especial care of his Creator; he was allowed to converse with and acquire knowledge from beings of a superior nature, but I was wretched, helpless, and alone. Many times I considered Satan as the fitter emblem of my condition, for often, like him, when I viewed the bliss of my protectors, the bitter gall of envy rose within me. . . . Accursed creator! Why did you form a monster so hideous that even *you* turned from me in disgust? God, in pity, made man beautiful and alluring, after his own image; but my form is a filthy type of yours, more horrid even from the very resemblance. Satan had his companions, fellow devils, to admire and encourage him, but I am solitary and abhorred. [114–15, chap. 15]

It is Eve, after all, who languishes helpless and alone, while Adam converses with superior beings, and it is Eve in whom the Satanically bitter gall of envy rises, causing her to eat the apple in the hope of adding "what wants / In Female Sex." It is Eve, moreover, to whom deathly isolation is threatened should Adam reject her, an isolation more terrible even than Satan's alienation from heaven. And finally it is Eve whose body, like her mind, is said by Milton to resemble "less / His Image who made both, and less [to express] / The character of that Dominion giv'n / O'er other Creatures ... " (*PL* 8. 543–46). In fact, to a sexually anxious reader, Eve's body might, like Sin's, seem "horrid even from [its] very resemblance" to her husband's, a "filthy" or obscene version of the human form divine.[33]

As we argued earlier, women have seen themselves (because they have been seen) as monstrous, vile, degraded creatures, second-comers, and emblems of filthy materiality, even though they have also been traditionally defined as superior spiritual beings, angels, better halves. "Woman [is] a temple built over a sewer," said the Church father Tertullian, and Milton seems to see Eve as both temple and sewer, echoing that patristic misogyny.[34] Mary Shelley's conscious or unconscious awareness of the monster woman implicit in the angel woman is perhaps clearest in the revisionary scene where her monster, as if taking his cue from Eve in *Paradise Lost* book 4, first catches sight of his own image: "I had admired the perfect forms of my cottagers ... but how was I terrified when I viewed myself in a transparent pool. At first I started back, unable to believe that it was indeed I who was reflected in the mirror; and when I became fully convinced that I was in reality the monster that I am, I was filled with the bitterest sensations of despondence and mortification" (98–99, chap. 12). In one sense, this is a corrective to Milton's blindness about Eve. Having been created second, inferior, a mere rib, how could she possibly, this passage implies, have seemed anything but monstrous to herself? In another sense, however, the scene supplements Milton's description of Eve's introduction to herself, for ironically, though her reflection in "the clear / Smooth Lake" is as beautiful as the monster's is ugly, the self-absorption that Eve's confessed passion for her own image signals is plainly meant by Milton to seem morally ugly, a hint of her potential for spiritual deformity: "There I had fixt / Mine eyes till now, and pin'd with vain desire, / Had not a voice thus warn'd me, What thou seest, / What there thou seest fair Creature is thyself ... " (*PL* 4. 465–68).

The figurative monstrosity of female narcissism is a subtle deformity, however, in comparison with the literal monstrosity many women are taught to see as characteristic of their own bodies. Adrienne Rich's twentieth-century description of "a woman in the

shape of a monster / A monster in the shape of a woman" is merely
the latest in a long line of monstrous female self-definitions that
includes the fearful images in Djuna Barnes's *Book of Repulsive Women*,
Denise Levertov's "a white sweating bull of a poet told us / our cunts
are ugly" and Sylvia Plath's "old yellow" self of the poem "In
Plaster."[35] Animal and misshapen, these emblems of self-loathing
must have descended at least in part from the distended body of
Mary Shelley's darkly parodic Eve/Sin/Monster, whose enormity
betokens not only the enormity of Victor Frankenstein's crime and
Satan's bulk but also the distentions or deformities of pregnancy
and the Swiftian sexual nausea expressed in Lemuel Gulliver's
horrified description of a Brobdignagian breast, a passage Mary
Shelley no doubt studied along with the rest of *Gulliver's Travels*
when she read the book in 1816, shortly before beginning *Frankenstein*.[36]

At the same time, just as surely as Eve's moral deformity is symbolized by the monster's physical malformation, the monster's physical
ugliness represents his social illegitimacy, his bastardy, his namelessness. Bitchy and dastardly as Shakespeare's Edmund, whose association with filthy femaleness is established not only by his devotion
to the material/maternal goddess Nature but also by his interlocking
affairs with those filthy females Goneril and Regan, Mary Shelley's
monster has also been "got" in a "dark and vicious place." Indeed,
in his vile illegitimacy he seems to incarnate that bestial "unnameable" place. And significantly, he is himself as nameless as a woman
is in patriarchal society, as nameless as unmarried, illegitimately
pregnant Mary Wollstonecraft Godwin may have felt herself to be
at the time she wrote *Frankenstein*.

"This nameless mode of naming the unnameable is rather good,"
Mary commented when she learned that it was the custom at
early dramatizations of *Frankenstein* to place a blank line next to
the name of the actor who played the part of the monster.[37] But
her pleased surprise was disingenuous, for the problem of names
and their connection with social legitimacy had been forced into
her consciousness all her life. As the sister of illegitimate and therefore
nameless Fanny Imlay, for instance, she knew what bastardy meant,
and she knew it too as the mother of a premature and illegitimate
baby girl who died at the age of two weeks without ever having

been given a name. Of course, when Fanny dramatically excised her name from her suicide note Mary learned more about the significance even of insignificant names. And as the stepsister of Mary Jane Clairmont, who defined herself as the "creature" of Lord Byron and changed her name for a while with astonishing frequency (from Mary Jane to Jane to Clara to Claire), Mary knew about the importance of names too. Perhaps most of all, though, Mary's sense of the fearful significance of legitimate and illegitimate names must have been formed by her awareness that her own name, Mary Wollstonecraft Godwin, was absolutely identical with the name of the mother who had died in giving birth to *her*. Since this was so, she may have speculated, perhaps her own monstrosity, her murderous illegitimacy, consisted in her being—like Victor Franken-stein's creation—a reanimation of the dead, a sort of galvanized corpse ironically arisen from what should have been "the cradle of life."

This implicit fantasy of the reanimation of the dead in the mon-strous and nameless body of the living returns us, however, to the matter of the monster's Satanic, Sin-ful and Eve-like moral deformity. For of course the crimes that the monster commits once he has accepted the world's definition of him as little more than a namelessly "filthy mass" all reinforce his connection with Milton's unholy trinity of Sin, Eve/Satan, and Death. The child of two authors (Victor Frankenstein and Mary Shelley) whose mothers have been stolen away by death, this motherless monster is after all made from dead bodies, from loathsome parts found around cemeteries, so that it seems only "natural" for him to continue the Blakeian cycle of despair his birth began, by bringing further death into the world. And of course he brings death, in the central actions of the novel: death to the childish innocence of little William (whose name is that of Mary Shelley's father, her half-brother, and her son, so that one can hardly decide to which male relative she may have been alluding); death to the faith and truth of allegorically named Justine; death to the legitimate artistry of the Shelleyan poet Clerval; and death to the ladylike selflessness of angelic Elizabeth. Is he acting, in his vile way, for Mary Shelley, whose elegant femininity seemed, in view of her books, so incongruous to the poet Beddoes and to literary Lord Dillon? "She has no business to be a woman by her books," noted Beddoes. And "your writing and your manners are not in accordance," Dillon told Mary herself. "I should have thought of you—if I had only read you—that you were a sort of . . . Sybil, outpouringly enthusiastic . . . but you are cool, quiet and feminine to the last degree. . . . Explain this to me." [38]

Could Mary's coolness have been made possible by the heat of her monster's rage, the strain of her decorous silence eased by the demonic abandon of her nameless monster's ritual fire dance around the cottage of his rejecting "Protectors"? Does Mary's cadaverous creature want to bring more death into the world because he has failed—like those other awful females, Eve and Sin—to win the compassion of that blind and curiously Miltonic old man, the Godlike musical patriarch De Lacey? Significantly, he is clinging to the blind man's knees, begging for recognition and help—"Do not you desert me in the hour of trial!"—when Felix, the son of the house, appears like the felicitous hero he is, and, says the monster, "with supernatural force [he] tore me from his father . . . in a transport of fury, he dashed me to the ground and struck me violently with a stick . . . my heart sank within me as with bitter sickness" (119, chap. 15). Despite everything we have been told about the monster's physical vileness, Felix's rage seems excessive in terms of the novel's overt story. But as an action in the covert plot—the tale of the blind rejection of women by misogynistic/Miltonic patriarchy —it is inevitable and appropriate. Even more psychologically appropriate is the fact that having been so definitively rejected by a world of fathers, the monster takes his revenge, first by murdering William, a male child who invokes his father's name ("My papa is a syndic—he is M. Frankenstein—he will punish you") and then by beginning a doomed search for a maternal, female principle in the harsh society that has created him.

In this connection, it begins to be plain that Eve's—and the monster's—motherlessness must have had extraordinary cultural and personal significance for Mary Shelley. "We think back through our mothers if we are women," wrote Virginia Woolf in *A Room of One's Own*.[39] But of course one of the most dramatic emblems of Eve's alienation from the masculine garden in which she finds herself is her motherlessness. Because she is made in the image of a man who is himself made in the image of a male creator, her unprecedented femininity seems merely a defective masculinity, a deformity like the monster's inhuman body.[40] In fact, as we saw, the only maternal model in *Paradise Lost* is the terrifying figure of Sin. (That Eve's punishment for *her* sin is the doom of agonized maternity—the doom of painfully becoming no longer herself but "Mother of Human Race"—appears therefore to seal the grim parallel.) But all these powerful symbols would be bound to take on personal weight and darkness for Shelley, whose only real "mother" was a tombstone— or a shelf of books—and who, like all orphans, must have feared that she had been deliberately deserted by her dead parent, or that, if she was a monster, then her hidden, underground mother must have been one too.

For all these reasons, then, the monster's attitude toward the possibility (or impossibility) of finding a mother is unusually conflicted and complex. At first, horrified by what he knows of the only "mother" he has ever had—Victor Frankenstein—he regards his parentage with loathing. Characteristically, he learns the specific details of his "conception" and "birth" (as Mary Shelley may have learned of hers) through reading, for Victor has kept a journal which records "that series of disgusting circumstances" leading "to the production of [the monster's] . . . loathsome person."[41] Later, however, the ill-fated miniature of Caroline Beaufort Frankenstein, Victor's "angel mother," momentarily "attract[s]" him. In fact, he claims it is because he is "forever deprived of the delights that such beautiful creatures could bestow" that he resolves to implicate Justine in the murder of William. His reproachful explanation is curious, though ("The crime had its source in her; be hers the punishment"), as is the sinister rape fantasy he enacts by the side of the sleeping orphan ("Awake, fairest, thy lover is near—he who would give his life but to obtain one look of affection from thine eyes" [127–28, chap. 16]). Clearly feelings of rage, terror, and sexual nausea, as well as idealizing sentiments, accrete for Mary and the monster around the maternal female image, a fact which explains the later climactic wedding-night murder of apparently innocent Elizabeth. In this fierce, Miltonic world, *Frankenstein* says, the angel woman and the monster woman alike must die, if they are not dead already. And what is to be feared above all else is the reanimation of the dead, specifically of the maternal dead. Perhaps that is why a significant pun is embedded in the crucial birth scene ("It was on a dreary night of November") that, according to Mary Shelley, rose "unbidden" from her imagination. Looking at the "demoniacal corpse to which I had so miserably given life," Victor remarks that "A *mummy* again endued with animation could not be so hideous as that wretch" (43, chap. 5). For a similarly horrific (and equally punning) statement of sexual nausea, one would have to go back to Donne's "Loves Alchymie" with its urgent, misogynistic imperative: "Hope not for minde in women; at their best / Sweetnesse and wit, they are but / *Mummy* possest."

Interestingly, the literary group at Villa Diodati received a packet of books containing, among other poems, Samuel Taylor Coleridge's recently published "Christabel," shortly before Mary had her monster-dream and began her ghost story. More influential than "Loves Alchymie"—a poem Mary may or may not have read— "Christabel"'s vision of femaleness must have been embodied for the author of *Frankenstein* not only in the witch Geraldine's withered side and consequent self-loathing ("Ah! What a stricken look was hers!") but also in her anxiety about the ghost of Christabel's dead mother ("Off, wandering mother! Peak and pine!") and in Christabel's "Woe is me / She died the hour that I was born." But even without Donne's puns or Coleridge's Romanticized male definition of deathly maternity, Mary Shelley would have absorbed a keen sense of the agony of female sexuality, and specifically of the perils of motherhood, not just from *Paradise Lost* and from her own mother's fearfully exemplary fate but also from Wollstonecraft's almost prophetically anxious writings.

Maria, or the Wrongs of Woman (1797), which Mary read in 1814 (and possibly in 1815) is about, among other "wrongs," Maria's search for her lost child, her fears that "she" (for the fantasied child is a daughter) may have been murdered by her unscrupulous father, and her attempts to reconcile herself to the child's death. In a suicide scene that Wollstonecraft drafted shortly before her own death, as her daughter must have known, Maria swallows laudanum: "her soul was calm ... nothing remained but an eager longing ... to fly ... from this hell of disappointment. Still her eyes closed not.... Her murdered child again appeared to her ... [But] 'Surely it is better to die with me, than to enter on life without a mother's care!'"[42]

Plainly, *Frankenstein*'s pained ambivalence toward mothers and mummies is in some sense a response to *Maria*'s agonized reaching—from beyond the grave, it may have seemed—toward a daughter. "Off, wandering mother! Peak and pine!" It is no wonder if Coleridge's poem gave Mary Wollstonecraft Godwin Shelley bad dreams, no wonder if she saw Milton's "Mother of Human Race" as a sorrowful monster.

Though *Frankenstein* itself began with a Coleridgean and Miltonic nightmare of filthy creation that reached its nadir in the monster's revelation of filthy femaleness, Mary Shelley, like Victor Frankenstein himself, evidently needed to distance such monstrous secrets. Sinful, motherless Eve and sinned-against, daughterless Maria, both paradigms of woman's helpless alienation in a male society, briefly emerge from the sea of male heroes and villains in which they have almost been lost, but the ice soon closes over their heads again, just as it closes around those two insane figure-skaters, Victor Frankenstein and his hideous offspring. Moving outward from the central "birth myth" to the icy perimeter on which the novel began, we find ourselves caught up once more in Walton's naive polar journey, where Frankenstein and his monster reappear as two embattled grotesques, distant and archetypal figures solipsistically drifting away from each other on separate icebergs. In Walton's scheme of things, they look again like God and Adam, Satanically conceived. But now, with our more nearly complete understanding of the bewildered and bewildering perspective Mary Shelley adopted as "Milton's daughter," we see that they were Eve and Eve all along.

Nevertheless, though Shelley did manage to still the monster's suffering and Frankenstein's and her own by transporting all three from the fires of filthy creation back to the ice and silence of the Pole, she was never entirely to abandon the sublimated rage her monster-self enacted, and never to abandon, either, the metaphysical ambitions *Frankenstein* incarnated. In *The Last Man* she introduced, as Spark points out, "a new, inhuman protagonist," PLAGUE (the name is almost always spelled entirely in capitals), who is characterized as female and who sees to it that "disaster is no longer the property of the individual but of the entire human race."[43] And of course PLAGUE's story is the one that Mary claims to have found in the Sibyl's cave, a tale of a literally female monster that was merely foreshadowed by the more subdued narrative of "The Modern Prometheus."

Interestingly, PLAGUE's story ends with a vision of last things, a vision of judgment and of paradise nihilistically restored that balances *Frankenstein's* vision of first things. With all of humanity wiped out by the monster PLAGUE, just as the entire Frankenstein family was destroyed by Victor's monster, Lionel Verney, the narrator, goes to Rome, that cradle of patriarchal civilization whose ruins had seemed so majestically emblematic to both Byron and Shelley. But where Mary's husband had written of the great city in a kind of ecstasy, his widow has her disinherited "last man" wander lawlessly about empty Rome until finally he resolves, finding "parts of a manuscript . . . scattered about," that "I also will write a book . . . [but] for whom to read?—to whom dedicated? And then with silly flourish (what so capricious and childish as despair?) I wrote,

DEDICATION

TO THE ILLUSTRIOUS DEAD

SHADOWS, ARISE, AND READ YOUR FALL!

BEHOLD THE HISTORY OF THE LAST MAN.[44]

His hostile, ironic, literary gesture illuminates not only his own career but his author's. For the annihilation of history may well be the final revenge of the monster who has been denied a true place in history: the moral is one that Mary Shelley's first hideous progeny, like Milton's Eve, seems to have understood from the beginning.

8 Looking Oppositely: Emily Brontë's Bible of Hell

Down from the waist they are Centaurs,
Though women all above:
But to the girdle do the Gods inherit,
Beneath is all the fiend's: there's hell, there's darkness,
There is the sulphurous pit. . .

—*King Lear*

It indeed appear'd to Reason as if Desire was cast out, but the Devils account is, that the Messiah fell. & formed a heaven of what he stole from the Abyss

—William Blake

A loss of something ever felt I—
The first that I could recollect
Bereft I was—of what I knew not
Too young that any should suspect

A Mourner walked among the children
I notwithstanding went about
As one bemoaning a Dominion
Itself the only Prince cast out—

Elder, Today, a session wiser
And fainter, too, as Wiseness is—
I find myself still softly searching
For my Delinquent Palaces—

And a Suspicion, like a Finger
Touches my Forehead now and then
That I am looking oppositely
For the site of the Kingdom of Heaven—
—Emily Dickinson

248

Frankenstein and *Wuthering Heights* (1847) are not usually seen as related works, except insofar as both are famous nineteenth-century literary puzzles, with Shelley's plaintive speculation about where she got so "hideous an idea" finding its counterpart in the position of Heathcliff's creator as a sort of mystery woman of literature. Still, if both Brontë and Shelley wrote enigmatic, curiously unprecedented novels, their works are puzzling in different ways: Shelley's is an enigmatic fantasy of metaphysical horror, Brontë's an enigmatic romance of metaphysical passion. Shelley produced an allusive, Romantic, and "masculine" text in which the fates of subordinate female characters seem entirely dependent upon the actions of ostensibly male heroes or anti-heroes. Brontë produced a more realistic narrative in which "the perdurable voice of the country," as Mark Schorer describes Nelly Dean, introduces us to a world where men battle for the favors of apparently high-spirited and independent women.[1]

Despite these dissimilarities, however, *Frankenstein* and *Wuthering Heights* are alike in a number of crucial ways. For one thing, both works *are* enigmatic, puzzling, even in some sense generically problematical. Moreover, in each case the mystery of the novel is associated with what seem to be its metaphysical intentions, intentions around which much critical controversy has collected. For these two "popular" novels—one a thriller, the other a romance—have convinced many readers that their charismatic surfaces conceal (far more than they reveal) complex ontological depths, elaborate structures of allusion, fierce though shadowy moral ambitions. And this point in particular is demonstrated by a simpler characteristic both works have in common. Both make use of what in connection with *Frankenstein* we called an evidentiary narrative technique, a Romantic story-telling method that emphasizes the ironic disjunctions between different perspectives on the same events as well as the ironic tensions that inhere in the relationship between surface drama and concealed authorial intention. In fact, in its use of such a technique, *Wuthering Heights* might be a deliberate copy of *Frankenstein*. Not only do the stories of both novels emerge through concentric circles of narration, both works contain significant digressions. Catherine Earnshaw's diary, Isabella's letter, Zillah's narrative, and Heathcliff's confidences to Nelly function in *Wuthering Heights* much as Alphonse

Frankenstein's letter, Justine's narrative, and Safie's history do in *Frankenstein*.

Their common concern with evidence, especially with written evidence, suggests still another way in which *Wuthering Heights* and *Frankenstein* are alike: more than most novels, both are consciously literary works, at times almost obsessively concerned with books and with reading as not only a symbolic but a dramatic—plot-forwarding—activity. Can this be because, like Shelley, Brontë was something of a literary heiress? The idea is an odd one to consider, because the four Brontë children, scribbling in Yorkshire's remote West Riding, seem as trapped on the periphery of nineteenth-century literary culture as Mary Shelley was embedded in its God-winian and Byronic center. Nevertheless, peripheral though they were, the Brontës had literary parents just as Mary Shelley did: the Reverend Patrick Brontë was in his youth the author of several books of poetry, a novel, and a collection of sermons, and Maria Branwell, the girl he married, apparently also had some literary abilities.[2] And of course, besides having obscure literary parents Emily Brontë had literary siblings, though they too were in most of her own lifetime almost as unknown as their parents.

Is it coincidental that the author of *Wuthering Heights* was the sister of the authors of *Jane Eyre* and *Agnes Grey*? Did the parents, especially the father, bequeath a frustrated drive toward literary success to their children? These are interesting though unanswerable questions, but they imply a point that is crucial in any consideration of the Brontës, just as it was important in thinking about Mary Shelley: it was the habit in the Brontë family, as in the Wollstonecraft-Godwin-Shelley family, to approach reality through the mediating agency of books, to read one's relatives, and to feel related to one's reading. Thus the transformation of three lonely yet ambitious Yorkshire governesses into the magisterially androgynous trio of Currer, Ellis, and Acton Bell was a communal act, an assertion of family identity. And significantly, even the games these writers played as children prepared them for such a literary mode of self-definition. As most Brontë admirers know, the four young inhabitants of Haworth Parsonage began producing extended narratives at an early age, and these eventually led to the authorship of a large library of minia-ture books which constitutes perhaps the most famous juvenilia in

English. Though in subject matter these works are divided into two groups—one, the history of the imaginary kingdom of Gondal, written by Emily and Anne, and the other, stories of the equally imaginary land of Angria, written by Charlotte and Branwell—all four children read and discussed all the tales, and even served as models for characters in many. Thus the Brontës' deepest feelings of kinship appear to have been expressed first in literary collaboration and private childish attempts at fictionalizing each other, and then, later, in the public collaboration the sisters undertook with the ill-fated collection of poetry that was their first "real" publication. Finally Charlotte, the last survivor of these prodigious siblings, memorialized her lost sisters in print, both in fiction and in non-fiction (*Shirley*, for instance, mythologizes Emily). Given the traditions of her family, it was no doubt inevitable that, for her, writing—not only novel-writing but the writing of prefaces to "family" works—would replace tombstone-raising, hymn-singing, maybe even weeping.[3]

That both literary activity and literary evidence were so important to the Brontës may be traced to another problem they shared with Mary Shelley. Like the anxious creator of *Frankenstein*, the authors of *Wuthering Heights*, *Jane Eyre*, and *The Tenant of Wildfell Hall* lost their mother when they were very young. Like Shelley, indeed, Emily and Anne Brontë were too young when their mother died even to know much about her except through the evidence of older survivors and perhaps through some documents. Just as *Frankenstein*, with its emphasis on orphans and beggars, is a motherless book, so all the Brontë novels betray intense feelings of motherlessness, orphanhood, destitution. And in particular the problems of literary orphanhood seem to lead in *Wuthering Heights*, as in *Frankenstein*, not only to a concern with surviving evidence but also to a fascination with the question of origins. Thus if all women writers, metaphorical orphans in patriarchal culture, seek literary answers to the questions "How are we fal'n, / Fal'n by mistaken rules . . . ?" motherless orphans like Mary Shelley and Emily Brontë almost seem to seek literal answers to that question, so passionately do their novels enact distinctive female literary obsessions.

Finally, that such a psychodramatic enactment is going on in both *Wuthering Heights* and *Frankenstein* suggests a similarity between the two novels which brings us back to the tension between dramatic surfaces and metaphysical depths with which we began this discussion. For just as one of *Frankenstein*'s most puzzling traits is the symbolic ambiguity or fluidity its characters display when they are studied closely, so one of *Wuthering Heights*'s key elements is what Leo Bersani calls its "ontological slipperiness."[4] In fact, because it is a *metaphysical* romance (just as *Frankenstein* is a *metaphysical* thriller) *Wuthering Heights* seems at times to be about forces or beings rather than people, which is no doubt one reason why some critics have thought it generically problematical, maybe not a novel at all but instead an extended exemplum, or a "prosified" verse drama. And just as all the characters in *Frankenstein* are in a sense the same two characters, so "everyone [in *Wuthering Heights*] is finally related to everyone else and, in a sense, repeated in everyone else," as if the novel, like an illustration of Freud's "Das Unheimlische," were about "the danger of being haunted by alien versions of the self."[5] But when it is created by a woman in the misogynistic context of Western literary culture, this sort of anxiously philosophical, problem-solving, myth-making narrative must—so it seems—inevitably come to grips with the countervailing stories told by patriarchal poetry, and specifically by Milton's patriarchal poetry.

Milton, Winifred Gérin tells us, was one of Patrick Brontë's favorite writers, so if Shelley was Milton's critic's daughter, Brontë was Milton's admirer's daughter.[6] By the Hegelian law of thesis/antithesis, then, it seems appropriate that Shelley chose to repeat and restate Milton's misogynistic story while Brontë chose to correct it. In fact the most serious matter *Wuthering Heights* and *Frankenstein* share is the matter of *Paradise Lost*, and their profoundest difference is in their attitude toward Milton's myth. Where Shelley was Milton's dutiful daughter, retelling his story to clarify it, Brontë was the poet's rebellious child, radically revising (and even reversing) the terms of his mythic narrative. Given the fact that Brontë never mentions either Milton or *Paradise Lost* in *Wuthering Heights*, any identification of her as Milton's daughter may at first seem eccentric or perverse. Shelley, after all, provided an overtly Miltonic framework in *Frankenstein* to reinforce our sense of her literary intentions. But despite the absence of Milton references, it eventually becomes plain that

Wuthering Heights is also a novel haunted by Milton's bogey. We may speculate, indeed, that Milton's absence is itself a presence, so painfully does Brontë's story dwell on the places and persons of his imagination.

That *Wuthering Heights* is about heaven and hell, for instance, has long been seen by critics, partly because all the narrative voices, from the beginning of Lockwood's first visit to the Heights, insist upon casting both action and description in religious terms, and partly because one of the first Catherine's major speeches to Nelly Dean raises the questions "What is heaven? Where is hell?" perhaps more urgently than any other speech in an English novel:

> "If I were in heaven, Nelly, I should be extremely miserable. . . . I dreamt once that I was there [and] that heaven did not seem to be my home, and I broke my heart with weeping to come back to earth; and the angels were so angry that they flung me out into the middle of the heath on the top of Wuthering Heights, where I woke sobbing for joy." [7]

Satan too, however—at least Satan as Milton's prototypical Byronic hero—has long been considered a participant in *Wuthering Heights*, for "that devil Heathcliff," as both demon lover and ferocious natural force, is a phenomenon critics have always studied. Isabella's "Is Mr. Heathcliff a man? If so, is he mad? And if not is he a devil?" (chap. 13) summarizes the traditional Heathcliff problem most succinctly, but Nelly's "I was inclined to believe . . . that conscience had turned his heart to an earthly hell" (chap. 33) more obviously echoes *Paradise Lost*.

Again, that *Wuthering Heights* is in some sense about a fall has frequently been suggested, though critics from Charlotte Brontë to Mark Schorer, Q. D. Leavis, and Leo Bersani have always disputed its exact nature and moral implications. Is Catherine's fall the archetypal fall of the *Bildungsroman* protagonist? Is Heathcliff's fall, his perverted "moral teething," a shadow of Catherine's? Which of the two worlds of *Wuthering Heights* (if either) does Brontë mean to represent the truly "fallen" world? These are just some of the controversies that have traditionally attended this issue. Nevertheless, that the story of *Wuthering Heights* is built around a central fall seems indisputable, so that a description of the novel as in part a *Bildungs-*

roman about a girl's passage from "innocence" to "experience" (leaving aside the precise meaning of those terms) would probably also be widely accepted. And that the fall in *Wuthering Heights* has Miltonic overtones is no doubt culturally inevitable. But even if it weren't, the Miltonic implications of the action would be clear enough from the "mad scene" in which Catherine describes herself as "an exile, and outcast . . . from what had been my world," adding "Why am I so changed? Why does my blood rush into a hell of tumult at a few words?" (chap. 12). Given the metaphysical nature of *Wuthering Heights*, Catherine's definition of herself as "an exile and outcast" inevitably suggests those trail-blazing exiles and outcasts Adam, Eve, and Satan. And her Romantic question—"Why am I so changed?"— with its desperate straining after the roots of identity, must ultimately refer back to Satan's hesitant (but equally crucial) speech to Beelzebub, as they lie stunned in the lake of fire: "If thou be'est he; But O . . . how chang'd" (*PL* 1. 84).

Of course, *Wuthering Heights* has often, also, been seen as a subversively visionary novel. Indeed, Brontë is frequently coupled with Blake as a practitioner of mystical politics. Usually, however, as if her book were written to illustrate the enigmatic religion of "No coward soul is mine," this visionary quality is related to Catherine's assertion that she is tired of "being enclosed" in "this shattered prison" of her body, and "wearying to escape into that glorious world, and to be always there" (chap. 15). Many readers define Brontë, in other words, as a ferocious pantheist/transcendentalist, worshipping the manifestations of the One in rock, tree, cloud, man and woman, while manipulating her story to bring about a Romantic *Liebestod* in which favored characters enter "the endless and shadowless hereafter." And certainly such ideas, like Blake's *Songs of Innocence*, are "something heterodox," to use Lockwood's phrase. At the same time, however, they are soothingly rather than disquietingly neo-Miltonic, like fictionalized visions of *Paradise Lost*'s luminous Father God. They are, in fact, the ideas of "steady, reasonable" Nelly Dean, whose denial of the demonic in life, along with her commitment to the angelic tranquility of death, represents only one of the visionary alternatives in *Wuthering Heights*. And, like Blake's metaphor of the lamb, Nelly's pious alternative has no real meaning for Brontë outside of the context provided by its tigerish opposite.

The tigerish opposite implied by *Wuthering Heights* emerges most dramatically when we bring all the novel's Miltonic elements together with its author's personal concerns in an attempt at a single formulation of Brontë's metaphysical intentions: the sum of this novel's visionary parts is an almost shocking revisionary whole. Heaven (or its rejection), hell, Satan, a fall, mystical politics, metaphysical romance, orphanhood, and the question of origins—disparate as some of these matters may seem, they all cohere in a rebelliously topsy-turvy retelling of Milton's and Western culture's central tale of the fall of woman and her shadow self, Satan. This fall, says Brontë, is not a fall *into* hell. It is a fall *from* "hell" into "heaven," not a fall from grace(in the religious sense) but a fall into grace(in the cultural sense). Moreover, for the heroine who falls it is the loss of Satan rather than the loss of God that signals the painful passage from innocence to experience. Emily Brontë, in other words, is not just Blakeian in "double" mystical vision, but Blakeian in a tough, radically political commitment to the belief that the state of being patriarchal Christianity calls "hell" is eternally, energetically delightful, whereas the state called "heaven" is rigidly hierarchical, Urizenic, and "kind" as a poison tree. But because she was metaphorically one of Milton's daughters, Brontë differs from Blake, that powerful son of a powerful father, in reversing the terms of Milton's Christian cosmogony for specifically feminist reasons.

Speaking of Jane Lead, a seventeenth-century Protestant mystic who was a significant precursor of Brontë's in visionary sexual politics, Catherine Smith has noted that "to study mysticism and feminism together is to learn more about the links between envisioning power and pursuing it," adding that "Idealist notions of transcendence may shape political notions of sexual equality as much as materialist or rationalist arguments do."[8] Her points are applicable to Brontë, whose revisionary mysticism is inseparable from both politics and feminism, although her emphasis is more on the loss than on the pursuit of power. Nevertheless, the feminist nature of her concern with neo-Miltonic definitions of hell and heaven, power and powerlessness, innocence and experience, has generally been overlooked by critics, many of whom, at their most biographical, tend to ask patronizing questions like "What is the matter with Emily Jane?"[9] Interestingly, however, certain women understood Brontë's feminist mythologies from the first. Speculating on the genesis of A. G. A., the fiery Byronic queen of Gondal with whose life and loves Emily Brontë was always obsessed, Fanny Ratchford noted in 1955 that while Arthur Wellesley, the emperor of Charlotte Brontë's fantasy kingdom of Angria, was "an arch-Byronic hero, for love of whom noble ladies went into romantic decline, . . . Gondal's queen was of such compelling beauty and charm as to bring all men to her feet, and of such selfish cruelty as to bring tragedy to all who loved her. . . . It was as if Emily was saying to Charlotte, 'You think the man is the dominant factor in romantic love, I'll show you it is the woman.'"[10] But of course Charlotte herself understood Emily's revisionary tendencies better than anyone. More than one hundred years before Ratchford wrote, the heroine of *Shirley*, that apotheosis of Emily "as she would have been in a happier life," speaks the English novel's first deliberately feminist criticism of Milton—"Milton did not see Eve, it was his cook that he saw"—and proposes as her alternative the Titan woman we discussed earlier, the mate of "Genius" and the potentially Satanic interlocutor of God. Some readers, including most recently the Marxist critic Terence Eagleton, have spoken scornfully of the "maundering rhetoric of *Shirley*'s embarrassing feminist mysticism."[11] But Charlotte, who was intellectually as well as physically akin to Emily, had captured the serious deliberation in her sister's vision. She knew that the author of *Wuthering Heights* was—to quote the Brontës' admirer Emily Dickinson—"looking oppositely / For the site of the Kingdom of Heaven" (J. 959).

Because Emily Brontë was looking oppositely not only for heaven (and hell) but for her own female origins, *Wuthering Heights* is one of the few authentic instances of novelistic myth-making, myth-making in the functional sense of problem-solving. Where writers from Charlotte Brontë and Henry James to James Joyce and Virginia Woolf have used mythic material to give point and structure to their novels, Emily Brontë uses the novel form to give substance—plausibility, really—to her myth. It is urgent that she do so because, as we shall see, the feminist cogency of this myth derives not only from its daring corrections of Milton but also from the fact that it is a distinctively nineteenth-century answer to the question of origins:

it is the myth of how culture came about, and specifically of how nineteenth-century society occurred, the tale of where tea-tables, sofas, crinolines, and parsonages like the one at Haworth came from.

Because it is so ambitious a myth, *Wuthering Heights* has the puzzling self-containment of a *mystery* in the old sense of that word—the sense of mystery plays and Eleusinian mysteries. Locked in by Lockwood's uncomprehending narrative, Nelly Dean's story, with its baffling duplication of names, places, events, seems endlessly to reenact itself, like some ritual that must be cyclically repeated in order to sustain (as well as explain) both nature and culture. At the same time, because it is so prosaic a myth—a myth about crinolines!—*Wuthering Heights* is not in the least portentous or self-consciously "mythic." On the contrary, like all true rituals and myths, Brontë's "cuckoo's tale" turns a practical, casual, humorous face to its audience. For as Lévi-Straus's observations suggest, true believers gossip by the prayer wheel, since that modern reverence which enjoins solemnity is simply the foster child of modern skepticism.[12]

Gossipy but unconventional true believers were rare, even in the pious nineteenth century, as Arnold's anxious meditations and Carlyle's angry sermons note. But Brontë's paradoxically matter-of-fact imaginative strength, her ability to enter a realistically freckled fantasy land, manifested itself early. One of her most famous adolescent diary papers juxtaposes a plea for culinary help from the parsonage housekeeper, Tabby—"Come Anne pilloputate"—with "The Gondals are discovering the interior of Gaaldine" and "Sally Mosely is washing in the back kitchen."[13] Significantly, no distinction is made between the heroic exploits of the fictional Gondals and Sally Mosely's real washday business. The curiously childlike voice of the diarist records all events without commentary, and this reserve suggests an implicit acquiescence in the equal "truth" of all events. Eleven years later, when the sixteen-year-old reporter of "pilloputate" has grown up and is on the edge of *Wuthering Heights*, the naive, uninflected surface of her diary papers is unchanged:

> . . . Anne and I went our first long journey by ourselves together, leaving home on the 30th of June, Monday, sleeping at York, returning to Keighley Tuesday evening . . . during our excursion we were Ronald Mcalgin, Henry Angora, Juliet Angusteena,

Rosabella Esmalden, Ella and Julian Egremont, Catharine Navarre, and Cordilia Fitzaphnold, escaping from the palaces of instruction to join the Royalists who are hard driven at present by the victorious Republicans. . . . I must hurry off now to my turning and ironing. I have plenty of work on hands, and writing, and am altogether full of business.[14]

Psychodramatic "play," this passage suggests, is an activity at once as necessary and as ordinary as housework: ironing and the exploration of alternative lives are the same kind of "business"—a perhaps uniquely female idea of which Anne Bradstreet and Emily Dickinson, those other visionary housekeepers, would have approved.

No doubt, however, it is this deep-seated tendency of Brontë's to live literally with the fantastic that accounts for much of the critical disputation about *Wuthering Heights*, especially the quarrels about the novel's genre and style. Q. D. Leavis and Arnold Kettle, for instance, insist that the work is a "sociological novel," while Mark Schorer thinks it "means to be a work of edification [about] the nature of a grand passion." Leo Bersani sees it as an ontological psychodrama, and Elliot Gose as a sort of expanded fairytale.[15] And strangely there is truth in all these apparently conflicting notions, just as it is also true that (as Robert Kiely has affirmed) "part of the distinction of *Wuthering Heights* [is] that it has no 'literary' aura about it," and true at the same time that (as we have asserted) *Wuthering Heights* is an unusually literary novel because Brontë approached reality chiefly through the mediating agency of literature.[16] In fact, Kiely's comment illuminates not only the uninflected surface of the diary papers but also the controversies about their author's novel, for Brontë is "unliterary" in being without a received sense of what the eighteenth century called literary decorum. As one of her better-known poems declares, she follows "where [her] own nature would be leading," and that nature leads her to an oddly literal—and also, therefore, unliterary—use of extraordinarily various literary works, ideas, and genres, all of which she refers back to herself, since "it vexes [her] to choose another guide."[17]

Thus *Wuthering Heights* is in one sense an elaborate gloss on the Byronic Romanticism and incest fantasy of *Manfred*, written, as Ratchford suggested, from a consciously female perspective. Heathcliff's passionate invocations of Catherine ("Come in! . . . hear me" [chap. 3] or "Be with me always—take any form—drive me mad" [chap. 16]) almost exactly echo Manfred's famous speech to Astarte ("Hear me, hear me . . . speak to me! Though it be in wrath . . . ").[18] In another way, though, *Wuthering Heights* is a prose redaction of the metaphysical storms and ontological nature/culture conflicts embodied in *King Lear*, with Heathcliff taking the part of Nature's bastard son Edmund, Edgar Linton incarnating the cultivated morality of his namesake Edgar, and the "wuthering" chaos at the Heights repeating the disorder that overwhelms Lear's kingdom when he relinquishes his patriarchal control to his diabolical daughters. But again, both poetic Byronic Romanticism and dramatic Shakespearean metaphysics are filtered through a novelistic sensibility with a surprisingly Austenian grasp of social details, so that *Wuthering Heights* seems also, in its "unliterary" way, to reiterate the feminist psychological concerns of a *Bildungsroman* Brontë may never have read: Jane Austen's *Northanger Abbey*. Catherine Earnshaw's "half savage and hardy and free" girlhood, for example, recalls the tomboy childhood of that other Catherine, Catherine Morland, and Catherine Earnshaw's fall into ladylike "grace" seems to explore the tragic underside of the anxiously comic initiation rites Catherine Morland undergoes at Bath and at Northanger Abbey.[19]

The world of *Wuthering Heights*, in other words, like the world of Brontë's diary papers, is one where what seem to be the most unlikely opposites coexist without, apparently, any consciousness on the author's part that there is anything unlikely in their coexistence. The ghosts of Byron, Shakespeare, and Jane Austen haunt the same ground. People with decent Christian names (Catherine, Nelly, Edgar, Isabella) inhabit a landscape in which also dwell people with strange animal or nature names (Hindley, Hareton, Heathcliff). Fairy-tale events out of what Mircea Eliade would call "great time" are given a local habitation and a real chronology in just that historical present Eliade defines as great time's opposite.[20] Dogs and gods (or goddesses) turn out to be not opposites but, figuratively speaking, the same words spelled in different ways. Funerals are weddings, weddings funerals. And of course, most important for our purposes here, hell is heaven, heaven hell, though the two are not separated, as Milton and literary decorum would prescribe, by vast

eons of space but by a little strip of turf, for Brontë was rebelliously
determined to walk

> ... not in old heroic traces
> And not in paths of high morality.
> And not among the half-distinguished faces,
> The clouded forms of long-past history.

On the contrary, surveying that history and its implications, she
came to the revisionary conclusion that "the earth that wakes *one*
human heart to feeling / Can centre both the worlds of Heaven and
Hell."[21]

   If we identify with Lockwood, civilized man at his most genteelly
"cooked" and literary, we cannot fail to begin Brontë's novel by
deciding that hell is a household very like Wuthering Heights.
Lockwood himself, as if wittily predicting the reversal of values that
is to be the story's central concern, at first calls the place "a perfect
misanthropist's Heaven" (chap. 1). But then what is the traditional
Miltonic or Dantesque hell if not a misanthropist's heaven, a site
that substitutes hate for love, violence for peace, death for life, and
in consequence the material for the spiritual, disorder for order?
Certainly Wuthering Heights rings all these changes on Lockwood's
first two visits. Heathcliff's first invitation to enter, for instance, is
uttered through closed teeth, and appropriately enough it seems to
his visitor to express "the sentiment 'Go to the Deuce.'" The house's
other inhabitants—Catherine II, Hareton, Joseph, and Zillah, as
we later learn—are for the most part equally hostile on both occasions,
with Joseph muttering insults, Hareton surly, and Catherine II
actually practicing (or pretending to practice) the "black arts."[22]
Their energies of hatred, moreover, are directed not only at their
uninvited guest but at each other, as Lockwood learns to his sorrow
when Catherine II suggests that Hareton should accompany him
through the storm and Hareton refuses to do so if it would please *her*.
   The general air of sour hatred that blankets the Heights, moreover,
manifests itself in a continual, aimless violence, a violence most
particularly embodied in the snarling dogs that inhabit the premises.
"In an arch under the dresser," Lockwood notes, "reposed a huge,

liver-coloured bitch pointer, surrounded by a swarm of squealing puppies; and other dogs haunted other recesses" (chap. 1). His use of *haunted* is apt, for these animals, as he later remarks, are more like "four-footed fiends" than ordinary canines, and in particular Juno, the matriarch of the "hive," seems to be a parody of Milton's grotesquely maternal Sin, with her yapping brood of hellhounds. Significantly, too, the only nonhostile creatures in this fiercely Satanic stronghold are dead: in one of a series of blackly comic blunders, Lockwood compliments Catherine II on what in his decorous way he assumes are her cats, only to learn that the "cats" are just a heap of dead rabbits. In addition, though the kitchen is separate from the central family room, "a vast oak dresser" reaching "to the very roof" of the sitting room is laden with oatcakes, guns, and raw meat: "clusters of legs of beef, mutton, and ham." Dead or raw flesh and the instruments by which living bodies may be converted into more dead flesh are such distinctive features of the room that even the piles of oatcakes and the "immense pewter dishes ... towering row after row" (chap. 1) suggest that, like hell or the land at the top of the beanstalk, Wuthering Heights is the abode of some particularly bloodthirsty giant.

The disorder that quite naturally accompanies the hatred, violence, and death that prevail at Wuthering Heights on Lockwood's first visits leads to more of the city-bred gentleman's blunders, in particular his inability to fathom the relationships among the three principal members of the household's pseudo-family—Catherine II, Hareton, and Heathcliff. First he suggests that the girl is Heathcliff's "amiable lady," then surmises that Hareton is "the favoured possessor of the beneficent fairy" (chap. 2). His phrases, like most of his assumptions, parody the sentimentality of fictions that keep women in their "place" by defining them as beneficent fairies or amiable ladies. Heathcliff, perceiving this, adds a third stereotype to the discussion: "You would intimate that [my wife's] spirit has taken the form of ministering angel," he comments with the "almost diabolical sneer" of a Satanic literary critic. But of course, though Lockwood's thinking is stereotypical, he is right to expect some familial relationship among his tea-table companions, and right too to be daunted by the hellish lack of relationship among them. For though Hareton, Heathcliff, and Catherine II are all in some sense related, the primordial schisms that

have overwhelmed the Heights with hatred and violence have divided
them from the human orderliness represented by the ties of kinship.
Thus just as Milton's hell consists of envious and (in the poet's view)
equality-mad devils jostling for position, so these inhabitants of
Wuthering Heights seem to live in chaos without the structuring
principle of heaven's hierarchical chain of being, and therefore
without the heavenly harmony God the Father's ranking of virtues,
thrones, and powers makes possible. For this reason Catherine sullenly
refuses to do anything "except what I please" (chap. 4), the servant
Zillah vociferously rebukes Hareton for laughing, and old Joseph—
whose viciously parodic religion seems here to represent a hellish
joke at heaven's expense—lets the dogs loose on Linton without
consulting his "maister," Heathcliff.

In keeping with this problem of "equality," a final and perhaps
definitive sign of the hellishness that has enveloped Wuthering
Heights at the time of Lockwood's first visits is the blinding snowfall
that temporarily imprisons the by now unwilling guest in the home
of his infernal hosts. Pathless as the kingdom of the damned, the
"billowy white ocean" of cold that surrounds Wuthering Heights
recalls the freezing polar sea on which Frankenstein, Walton, the
monster—and the Ancient Mariner—voyaged. It recalls, too, the
"deep snow and ice" of Milton's hell, "A gulf profound as that
Serbonian Bog . . . Where Armies whole have sunk" and where "by
harpy-footed" and no doubt rather Heathcliff-ish "Furies hal'd / . . .
all the damn'd / Are brought . . . to starve in Ice" (*PL* 2. 592–600).
But of course, as *King Lear* implies, hell is simply another word for
uncontrolled "nature," and here as elsewhere *Wuthering Heights*
follows *Lear*'s model.

Engulfing the Earnshaws' ancestral home and the Lintons', too,
in a blizzard of destruction, hellish nature traps and freezes everyone
in the isolation of a "perfect misanthropist's heaven." And again, as
in *Lear* this hellish nature is somehow female or associated with
femaleness, like an angry goddess shaking locks of ice and introducing
Lockwood (and his readers) to the female rage that will be a central
theme in *Wuthering Heights*. The femaleness of this "natural" hell is
suggested, too, by its likeness to the "false" material creation Robert
Graves analyzed so well in *The White Goddess*. Female nature has
risen, it seems, in a storm of protest, just as the Sin-like dog Juno

rises in a fury when Lockwood "unfortunately indulge[s] in winking and making faces" at her while musing on his heartless treatment of a "goddess" to whom he never "told" his love (chap. 1). Finally, that the storm is both hellish and female is made clearest of all by Lockwood's second visionary dream. Out of the tapping of branches, out of the wind and swirling snow, like an icy-fingered incarnation of the storm rising in protest against the patriarchal sermon of "Jabes Branderham," appears that ghostly female witch-child the *original* Catherine Earnshaw, who has now been "a waif for twenty years."

Why is Wuthering Heights so Miltonically hellish? And what happened to Catherine Earnshaw? Why has she become a demonic, storm-driven ghost? The "real" etiological story of *Wuthering Heights* begins, as Lockwood learns from his "human fixture" Nelly Dean, with a random weakening of the fabric of ordinary human society. Once upon a time, somewhere in what mythically speaking qualifies as pre-history or what Eliade calls "illo tempore," there is/was a primordial family, the Earnshaws, who trace their lineage back at least as far as the paradigmatic Renaissance inscription "1500 Hareton Earnshaw" over their "principal doorway." And one fine summer morning toward the end of the eighteenth century, the "old master" of the house decides to take a walking tour of sixty miles to Liverpool (chap. 4). His decision, like Lear's decision to divide his kingdom, is apparently quite arbitrary, one of those mystifying psychic *données* for which the fictional convention of "once upon a time" was devised. Perhaps it means, like Lear's action, that he is half-consciously beginning to prepare for death. In any case, his ritual questions to his two children—an older son and a younger daughter—and to their servant Nelly are equally stylized and arbitrary, as are the children's answers. "What shall I bring you?" the old master asks, like the fisherman to whom the flounder gave three wishes. And the children reply, as convention dictates, by requesting their heart's desires. In other words, they reveal their true selves, just as a father contemplating his own ultimate absence from their lives might have hoped they would.

Strangely enough, however, only the servant Nelly's heart's desire is sensible and conventional: she asks for (or, rather, accepts the promise of) a pocketful of apples and pears. Hindley, on the other hand, the son who is destined to be next master of the household, does not ask for a particularly masterful gift. His wish, indeed, seems frivolous in the context of the harsh world of the Heights. He asks for a fiddle, betraying both a secret, soft-hearted desire for culture and an almost decadent lack of virile purpose. Stranger still is Catherine's wish for a whip. "She could ride any horse in the stable," says Nelly, but in the fairy-tale context of this narrative that realistic explanation hardly seems to suffice,[23] for, symbolically, the small Catherine's longing for a whip seems like a powerless younger daughter's yearning for power.

Of course, as we might expect from our experience of fairy tales, at least one of the children receives the desired boon. Catherine gets her whip. She gets it figuratively—in the form of a "gypsy brat"— rather than literally, but nevertheless "it" (both whip and brat) functions just as she must unconsciously have hoped it would, smashing her rival-brother's fiddle and making a desirable third among the children in the family so as to insulate her from the pressure of her brother's domination. (That there should always have been three children in the family is clear from the way other fairytale rituals of three are observed, and also from the fact that Heathcliff is given the name of a dead son, perhaps even the true oldest son, as if he were a reincarnation of the lost child.)

Having received her deeply desired whip, Catherine now achieves, as Hillis Miller and Leo Bersani have noticed, an extraordinary fullness of being.[24] The phrase may seem pretentiously metaphysical (certainly critics like Q. D. Leavis have objected to such phrases on those grounds)[25] but in discussing the early paradise from which Catherine and Heathcliff eventually fall we are trying to describe elusive psychic states, just as we would in discussing Wordsworth's visionary childhood, Frankenstein's youth before he "learned" that he was (the creator of) a monster, or even the prelapsarian sexuality of Milton's Adam and Eve. And so, like Freud who was driven to grope among such words as *oceanic* when he tried to explain the heaven that lies about us in our infancy, we are obliged to use the paradoxical and metaphorical language of mysticism: phrases like *wholeness*, *fullness of being*, and *androgyny* come inevitably to mind.[26] All three, as we shall see, apply to Catherine, or more precisely to Catherine-Heathcliff.

In part Catherine's new wholeness results from a very practical shift in family dynamics. Heathcliff as a fantasy replacement of the dead oldest brother does in fact supplant Hindley in the old master's affections, and therefore he functions as a tool of the dispossessed younger sister whose "whip" he is. Specifically, he enables her for the first time to get possession of the kingdom of Wuthering Heights, which under her rule threatens to become, like Gondal, a queendom. In addition to this, however, Heathcliff's presence gives the girl a fullness of being that goes beyond power in household politics, because as Catherine's whip he is (and she herself recognizes this) an alternative self or double for her, a complementary addition to her being who fleshes out all her lacks the way a bandage might staunch a wound. Thus in her union with him she becomes, like Manfred in his union with his sister Astarte, a perfect androgyne. As devoid of sexual awareness as Adam and Eve were in the prelapsarian garden, she sleeps with her whip, her other half, every night in the primordial fashion of the countryside. Gifted with that innocent, unselfconscious sexual energy which Blake saw as eternal delight, she has "ways with her," according to Nelly, "such as I never saw a child take up before" (chap. 5). And if Heathcliff's is the body that does her will—strong, dark, proud, and a native speaker of "gibberish" rather than English—she herself is an "unfeminine" instance of transcendently vital spirit. For she is never docile, never submissive, never ladylike. On the contrary, her joy—and the Coleridgean word is not too strong—is in what Milton's Eve is never allowed: a tongue "always going—singing, laughing, and plaguing everybody who would not do the same," and "ready words: turning Joseph's religious curses into ridicule . . . and doing just what her father hated most" (chap. 5).

Perverse as it may seem, this paradise into which Heathcliff's advent has transformed Wuthering Heights for the young Catherine is as authentic a fantasy for women as Milton's Eden was for men, though Milton's misogynistically cowed daughters have rarely had the revisionary courage to spell out so many of the terms of their dream. Still, that the historical process does yield moments when that feminist dream of wholeness has real consequences is another point Brontë wishes us to consider, just as she wishes to convey her rueful awareness that, given the prior strength of patriarchal misogyny, those consequences may be painful as well as paradisal. Producing Heathcliff from beneath his greatcoat as if enacting a mock birth, old Mr. Earnshaw notes at once the equivocal nature of Catherine's whip: "You must e'en take it as a gift of God, though it's as dark almost as if it came from the devil" (chap. 4). His ambivalence is well-founded: strengthened by Heathcliff, Catherine becomes increasingly rebellious against the parodic patriarchal religion Joseph advocates, and thus, too, increasingly unmindful of her father's discipline. As she gains in rebellious energy, she becomes Satanically "as Gods" in her defiance of such socially constituted authority, and in the end, like a demonic Cordelia (that is, like Cordelia, Goneril, and Regan all in one) she has the last laugh at her father, answering his crucial dying question "Why canst thou not always be a good lass, Cathy?" with a defiantly honest question of her own: "Why cannot you always be a good man, Father?" (chap. 5) and then singing him, rather hostilely, "to sleep"—that is, to death.

Catherine's heaven, in other words, is very much like the place such a representative gentleman as Lockwood would call hell, for it is associated (like the hell of *King Lear*) with an ascendent self-willed female who radiates what, as Blake observed, most people consider "diabolical" energy—the creative energy of Los and Satan, the life energy of fierce, raw, uncultivated being.[27] But the ambiguity Catherine's own father perceives in his "gift of God" to the girl is also manifested in the fact that even some of the authentically hellish qualities Lockwood found at Wuthering Heights on his first two visits, especially the qualities of "hate" (i.e. defiance) and "violence" (i.e. energy), would have seemed to him to characterize the Wuthering Heights of Catherine's heavenly childhood. For Catherine, however, the defiance that might seem like hate was made possible by love (her oneness with Heathcliff) and the energy that seemed like violence was facilitated by the peace (the wholeness) of an undivided self.

Nevertheless, her personal heaven is surrounded, like Milton's Eden, by threats from what she would define as "hell." If, for instance, she had in some part of herself hoped that her father's death would ease the stress of that shadowy patriarchal yoke which was the only cloud on her heaven's horizon, Catherine was mistaken. For paradoxically old Earnshaw's passing brings with it the end to Catherine's Edenic "half savage and hardy and free" girlhood. It brings about a divided world in which the once-androgynous child is to be "laid alone" for the first time. And most important it brings about the accession to power of Hindley, by the patriarchal laws of primogeniture the real heir and thus the new father who is to introduce into the novel the proximate causes of Catherine's (and Heathcliff's) fall and subsequent decline.

Catherine's sojourn in the earthly paradise of childhood lasts for six years, according to C. P. Sanger's precisely worked-out chronology, but it takes Nelly Dean barely fifteen minutes to relate the episode.[28] Prelapsarian history, as Milton knew, is easy to summarize. Since happiness has few of the variations of despair, to be unfallen is to be static, whereas to fall is to enter the processes of time. Thus Nelly's account of Catherine's fall takes at least several hours, though it also covers six years. And as she describes it, that fall—or process of falling—begins with Hindley's marriage, an event associated for obvious reasons with the young man's inheritance of his father's power and position.

It is odd that Hindley's marriage should precipitate Catherine out of her early heaven because that event installs an adult woman in the small Heights family circle for the first time since the death of Mrs. Earnshaw four years earlier, and as conventional (or even feminist) wisdom would have it, Catherine "needs" a mother-figure to look after her, especially now that she is on the verge of adolescence. But precisely because she and Heathcliff are twelve years old and growing up, the arrival of Frances is the worst thing that could happen to her. For Frances, as Nelly's narrative indicates, is a model young lady, a creature of a species Catherine, safely sequestered in her idiosyncratic Eden, has had as little chance of encountering as Eve had of meeting a talking serpent before the time came for her to fall.

Of course, Frances is no serpent. On the contrary, light-footed and fresh-complexioned, she seems much more like a late eighteenth-century model of the Victorian angel in the house, and certainly her effect upon Hindley has been both to subdue him and to make him more ethereal. "He had grown sparer, and lost his colour, and spoke and dressed quite differently," Nelly notes (chap. 6); he even proposes to convert one room into a parlor, an amenity Wuthering Heights has never had. Hindley has in fact become a cultured man, so that in gaining a ladylike bride he has, as it were, gained the metaphorical fiddle that was his heart's desire when he was a boy.

It is no doubt inevitable that Hindley's fiddle and Catherine's whip cannot peaceably coexist. Certainly the early smashing of the fiddle by the "whip" hinted at such a problem, and so perhaps it would not be entirely frivolous to think of the troubles that now ensue for Catherine and Heathcliff as the fiddle's revenge. But even without pressing this conceit we can see that Hindley's angel/fiddle is a problematical representative of what is now introduced as the "heavenly" realm of culture. For one thing, her ladylike sweetness is only skin-deep. Leo Bersani remarks that the distinction between the children at the Heights and those at the Grange is the difference between "aggressively selfish children" and "whiningly selfish children." [29] If this is so, Frances foreshadows the children at the Grange —the children of genteel culture—since "her affection [toward Catherine] tired very soon [and] she grew peevish," at which point the now gentlemanly Hindley becomes "tyrannical" in just the way his position as the household's new *pater familias* encourages him to be. His tyranny consists, among other things, in his attempt to impose what Blake would call a Urizenic heavenly order at the heretofore anti-hierarchical Heights. The servants Nelly and Joseph, he decrees, must know their place—which is "the back kitchen"—and Heathcliff, because he is socially nobody, must be exiled from culture: deprived of "the instruction of the curate" and cast out into "the fields" (chap. 6).

Frances's peevishness, however, is not just a sign that her ladylike ways are inimical to the prelapsarian world of Catherine's childhood; it is also a sign that, as the twelve-year-old girl must perceive it, to be a lady is to be diseased. As Nelly hints, Frances is tubercular, and any mention of death causes her to act "half silly," as if in some part of herself she knows she is doomed, or as if she is already half a ghost. And she is. As a metaphor, Frances's tuberculosis means that she is in an advanced state of just that *social* "consumption" which will eventually kill Catherine, too, so that the thin and silly bride functions for the younger girl as a sort of premonition or ghost of what she herself will become.

But of course the social disease of ladyhood, with its attendant silliness or madness, is only one of the threats Frances incarnates for twelve-year-old Catherine. Another, perhaps even more sinister because harder to confront, is associated with the fact that though Catherine may well need a mother—in the sense in which Eve or Mary Shelley's monster needed a mother/model—Frances does not and cannot function as a good mother for her. The original Earnshaws were shadowy but mythically grand, like the primordial "true" parents of fairy tales (or like most parents seen through the eyes of preadolescent children). Hindley and Frances, on the other hand, the new Earnshaws, are troublesomely real though as oppressive as the step-parents in fairy tales.[30] To say that they are in some way like step-parents, however, is to say that they seem to Catherine like transformed or alien parents, and since this is as much a function of her own vision as of the older couple's behavior, we must assume that it has something to do with the changes wrought by the girl's entrance into adolescence.

Why do parents begin to seem like step-parents when their children reach puberty? The ubiquitousness of step-parents in fairy tales dealing with the crises of adolescence suggests that the phenomenon is both deepseated and widespread. One explanation—and the one that surely accounts for Catherine Earnshaw's experience—is that when the child gets old enough to become conscious of her parents as sexual beings they really do begin to seem like fiercer, perhaps even (as in the case of Hindley and Frances) younger versions of their "original" selves. Certainly they begin to be more threatening (that is, more "peevish" and "tyrannical") if only because the child's own sexual awakening disturbs them almost as much as their sexuality, now truly comprehended, bothers the child. Thus the crucial passage from Catherine's diary which Lockwood reads even before Nelly begins her narration is concerned not just with Joseph's pious oppressions but with the cause of those puritanical onslaughts, the fact that she and Heathcliff must shiver in the garret because "Hindley and his wife [are basking] downstairs before a comfortable fire . . .

kissing and talking nonsense by the hour—foolish palaver we should be ashamed of." Catherine's defensiveness is clear. She (and Heathcliff) are troubled by the billing and cooing of her "step-parents" because she understands, perhaps for the first time, the sexual nature of what a minute later she calls Hindley's "paradise on the hearth" and—worse—understands its relevance to her.

Flung into the kitchen, "where Joseph asseverated, 'owd Nick' would fetch us," Catherine and Heathcliff each seek "a separate nook to await his advent." For Catherine-and-Heathcliff—that is, Catherine and Catherine, or Catherine and her whip—have already been separated from each other, not just by tyrannical Hindley, the *deus* produced by time's *machina*, but by the emergence of Catherine's own sexuality, with all the terrors which attend that phenomenon in a puritanical and patriarchal society. And just as peevish Frances incarnates the social illness of ladyhood, so also she quite literally embodies the fearful as well as the frivolous consequences of sexuality. Her foolish if paradisaical palaver on the hearth, after all, leads straight to the death her earlier ghostliness and silliness had predicted. Her sexuality's destructiveness was even implied by the minor but vicious acts of injustice with which it was associated—arbitrarily pulling Heathcliff's hair, for instance—but the sex-death equation, with which Milton and Mary Shelley were also concerned, really surfaces when Frances's and Hindley's son, Hareton, is born. At that time, Kenneth, the lugubrious physician who functions like a medical Greek chorus throughout *Wuthering Heights*, informs Hindley that the winter will "probably finish" Frances.

To Catherine, however, it must appear that the murderous agent is not winter but sex, for as she is beginning to learn, the Miltonic testaments of her world have told woman that "thy sorrow I will greatly multiply / By thy Conception . . . " (*PL* 10. 192–95) and the maternal image of Sin birthing Death reinforces this point. That Frances's decline and death accompany Catherine's fall is metaphysically appropriate, therefore. And it is dramatically appropriate as well, for Frances's fate foreshadows the catastrophes which will follow Catherine's fall into sexuality just as surely as the appearance of Sin and Death on earth followed Eve's fall. That Frances's death also, incidentally, yields Hareton—the truest scion of the Earnshaw clan—

is also profoundly appropriate. For Hareton is, after all, a resurrected version of the original patriarch whose name is written over the great main door of the house, amid a "wilderness of shameless little boys." Thus his birth marks the beginning of the historical as well as the psychological decline and fall of that Satanic female principle which has temporarily usurped his "rightful" place at Wuthering Heights.

Catherine's fall, however, is caused by a patriarchal past and present, besides being associated with a patriarchal future. It is significant, then, that her problems begin—violently enough—when she literally falls down and is bitten by a male bulldog, a sort of guard/god from Thrushcross Grange. Though many readers overlook this point, Catherine does not *go* to the Grange when she is twelve years old. On the contrary, the Grange seizes her and "holds [her] fast," a metaphoric action which emphasizes the turbulent and in-exorable nature of the psychosexual *rites de passage Wuthering Heights* describes, just as the ferociously masculine bull/dog—as a symbolic representative of Thrushcross Grange—contrasts strikingly with the ascendancy at the Heights of the hellish female bitch goddess alter-nately referred to as "Madam" and "Juno."[31]

Realistically speaking, Catherine and Heathcliff have been driven in the direction of Thrushcross Grange by their own desire to escape not only the pietistic tortures Joseph inflicts but also, more urgently, just that sexual awareness irritatingly imposed by Hindley's romantic paradise. Neither sexuality nor its consequences can be evaded, however, and the farther the children run the closer they come to the very fate they secretly wish to avoid. Racing "from the top of the Heights to the park without stopping," they plunge from the periphery of Hindley's paradise (which was transforming their heaven into a hell) to the boundaries of a place that at first seems authentically heavenly, a place full of light and softness and color, a "splendid place carpeted with crimson ... and [with] a pure white ceiling bordered by gold, a shower of glass-drops hanging in silver chains from the centre, and shimmering with little soft tapers" (chap. 6). Looking in the window, the outcasts speculate that if they were inside such a room "we should have thought ourselves in heaven!" From the outside, at least, the Lintons' elegant haven appears paradisaical. But once the children have experienced its Urizenic interior, they know that in their terms this heaven is hell.

Because the first emissary of this heaven who greets them is the bulldog Skulker, a sort of hellhound posing as a hound of heaven, the wound this almost totemic animal inflicts upon Catherine is as symbolically suggestive as his role in the girl's forced passage from Wuthering Heights to Thrushcross Grange. Barefoot, as if to emphasize her "wild child" innocence, Catherine is exceptionally vulnerable, as a wild child must inevitably be, and when the dog is "throttled off, his huge, purple tongue hanging half a foot out of his mouth ... his pendant lips [are] streaming with bloody slaver." "Look ... how her foot bleeds," Edgar Linton exclaims, and "She may be lamed for life," his mother anxiously notes (chap. 6). Obviously such bleeding has sexual connotations, especially when it occurs in a pubescent girl. Crippling injuries to the feet are equally resonant, moreover, almost always signifying symbolic castration, as in the stories of Oedipus, Achilles, and the Fisher King. Additionally, it hardly needs to be noted that Skulker's equipment for aggression— his huge purple tongue and pendant lips, for instance—sounds extraordinarily phallic. In a Freudian sense, then, the imagery of this brief but violent episode hints that Catherine has been simultaneously catapulted into adult female sexuality *and* castrated.

How can a girl "become a woman" and be castrated (that is, desexed) at the same time? Considering how Freudian its iconographic assumptions are, the question is disingenuous, for not only in Freud's terms but in feminist terms, as Elizabeth Janeway and Juliet Mitchell have both observed, femaleness—implying "penis envy"—quite reasonably *means* castration. "No woman has been deprived of a penis; she never had one to begin with," Janeway notes, commenting on Freud's crucial "Female Sexuality" (1931).

> But she *has* been deprived of something else that men enjoy:
> namely, autonomy, freedom, and the power to control her
> destiny. By insisting, falsely, on female deprivation of the male
> organ, Freud is pointing to an actual deprivation and one of
> which he was clearly aware. In Freud's time the advantages
> enjoyed by the male sex over the inferior female were, of course,

even greater than at present, and they were also accepted to a much larger extent, as being inevitable, inescapable. Women were evident *social* castrates, and the mutilation of their potentiality as achieving human creatures was quite analogous to the physical wound.[32]

But if such things were true in Freud's time, they were even truer in Emily Brontë's. And certainly the hypothesis that Catherine Earnshaw has become in some sense a "social castrate," that she has been "lamed for life," is borne out by her treatment at Thrushcross Grange—and by the treatment of her alter ego, Heathcliff. For, assuming that she is a "young lady," the entire Linton household cossets the wounded (but still healthy) girl as if she were truly an invalid. Indeed, feeding her their alien rich food—negus and cakes from their own table—washing her feet, combing her hair, dressing her in "enormous slippers," and wheeling her about like a doll, they seem to be enacting some sinister ritual of initiation, the sort of ritual that has traditionally weakened mythic heroines from Persephone to Snow White. And because he is "a little Lascar, or an American or Spanish castaway," the Lintons banish Heathcliff from their parlor, thereby separating Catherine from the lover/brother whom she herself defines as her strongest and most necessary "self." For five weeks now, she will be at the mercy of the Grange's heavenly gentility.

To say that Thrushcross Grange is genteel or cultured and that it therefore seems "heavenly" is to say, of course, that it is the opposite of Wuthering Heights. And certainly at every point the two houses are opposed to each other, as if each in its self-assertion must absolutely deny the other's being. Like Milton and Blake, Emily Brontë thought in polarities. Thus, where Wuthering Heights is essentially a great parlorless room built around a huge central hearth, a furnace of dark energy like the fire of Los, Thrushcross Grange has a parlor notable not for heat but for light, for "a pure white ceiling bordered by gold" with "a shower of glass-drops" in the center that seems to parody the "sovran vital Lamp" (*PL* 3. 22) which illuminates Milton's heaven of Right Reason. Where Wuthering Heights, moreover, is close to being naked or "raw" in Lévi-Strauss' sense—its floors uncarpeted, most of its inhabitants barely literate, even the meat on its shelves open to inspection—Thrushcross Grange is clothed and "cooked": carpeted in crimson, bookish, feeding on cakes and tea and negus.[33] It follows from this, then, that where Wuthering Heights is functional, even its dogs working sheepdogs or hunters, Thrushcross Grange (though guarded by bulldogs) appears to be decorative or aesthetic, the home of lapdogs as well as ladies. And finally, therefore, Wuthering Heights in its stripped functional rawness is essentially anti-hierarchical and egalitarian as the aspirations of Eve and Satan, while Thrushcross Grange reproduces the hierarchical chain of being that Western culture traditionally proposes as heaven's decree.

For all these reasons, Catherine Earnshaw, together with her whip Heathcliff, has at Wuthering Heights what Emily Dickinson would call a "Barefoot-Rank."[34] But at Thrushcross Grange, clad first in enormous, crippling slippers and later in "a long cloth habit which she [is] obliged to hold up with both hands" (chap. 7) in order to walk, she seems on the verge of becoming, again in Dickinson's words, a "Lady [who] dare not lift her Veil / For fear it be dispelled" (J. 421) For in comparison to Wuthering Heights, Thrushcross Grange is, finally, the home of concealment and doubleness, a place where, as we shall see, reflections are separated from their owners like souls from bodies, so that the lady in anxiety "peers beyond her mesh— / And wishes—and denies— / Lest Interview— annul a want / That Image—satisfies." And it is here, therefore, at heaven's mercy, that Catherine Earnshaw learns "to adopt a double character without exactly intending to deceive anyone" (chap. 8).

In fact, for Catherine Earnshaw, Thrushcross Grange in those five fatal weeks becomes a Palace of Instruction, as Brontë ironically called the equivocal schools of life where her adolescent Gondals were often incarcerated. But rather than learning, like A. G. A. and her cohorts, to rule a powerful nation, Catherine must learn to rule herself, or so the Lintons and her brother decree. She must learn to repress her own impulses, must girdle her own energies with the iron stays of "reason." Having fallen into the decorous "heaven" of femaleness, Catherine must become a lady. And just as her entrance into the world of Thrushcross Grange was forced and violent, so this process by which she is obliged to accommodate herself to that world is violent and painful, an unsentimental education recorded by a practiced, almost sadistically accurate observer. For the young

Gondals, too, had had a difficult time of it in their Palace of Instruction: far from being wonderful Golden Rule days, their school days were spent mostly in dungeons and torture cells, where their elders starved them into submission or self-knowledge.

That education for Emily Brontë is almost always fearful, even agonizing, may reflect the Brontës' own traumatic experiences at the Clergy Daughters School and elsewhere.[35] But it may also reflect in a more general way the repressiveness with which the nineteenth century educated all its young ladies, strapping them to backboards and forcing them to work for hours at didactic samplers until the more high-spirited girls—the Catherine Earnshaws and Catherine Morlands—must have felt, like the inhabitants of Kafka's penal colony, that the morals and maxims of patriarchy were being embroidered on their own skins. To mention Catherine Morland here is not to digress. As we have seen, Austen did not subject her heroine to education as a gothic/Gondalian torture, except parodically. Yet even Austen's parody suggests that for a girl like Catherine Morland the school of life inevitably inspires an almost instinctive fear, just as it would for A. G. A. "Heavenly" Northanger Abbey may somehow conceal a prison cell, Catherine suspects, and she develops this notion by sensing (as Henry Tilney cannot) that the female romances she is reading are in some sense the disguised histories of her own life.

In Catherine Earnshaw's case, these points are made even more subtly than in the Gondal poems or in *Northanger Abbey*, for Catherine's education in doubleness, in ladylike decorum meaning also ladylike deceit, is marked by an actual doubling or fragmentation of her personality. Thus though it is ostensibly Catherine who is being educated, it is Heathcliff—her rebellious alter ego, her whip, her id—who is exiled to a prison cell, as if to implement delicate Isabella Linton's first horrified reaction to him: "Frightful thing! Put him in the cellar" (chap. 6). Not in the cellar but in the garret, Heathcliff is locked up and, significantly, starved, while Catherine, daintily "cutting up the wing of a goose," practices table manners below. Even more significantly, however, she too is finally unable to eat her dinner and retreats under the table cloth to weep for her imprisoned playmate. To Catherine, Heathcliff is "more myself than I am," as she later famously tells Nelly, and so his literal starvation is symbolic of her more terrible because more dangerous spiritual starvation, just as her literal wound at Thrushcross Grange is also a metaphorical deathblow to *his* health and power. For divided from each other, the once androgynous Heathcliff-and-Catherine are now conquered by the concerted forces of patriarchy, the Lintons of Thrushcross Grange acting together with Hindley and Frances, their emissaries at the Heights.

It is, appropriately enough, during this period, that Frances gives birth to Hareton, the new patriarch-to-be, and dies, having fulfilled her painful function in the book and in the world. During this period, too, Catherine's education in ladylike self-denial causes her dutifully to deny her self and decide to marry Edgar. For when she says of Heathcliff that "he's more myself than I am," she means that as her exiled self the nameless "gipsy" really does preserve in his body more of her original being than she retains: even in his deprivation he seems whole and sure, while she is now entirely absorbed in the ladylike wishing and denying Dickinson's poem describes. Thus, too, it is during this period of loss and transition that Catherine obsessively inscribes on her windowsill the crucial writing Lockwood finds, writing which announces from the first Emily Brontë's central concern with identity: "a name repeated in all kinds of characters, large and small—Catherine Earnshaw, here and there varied to Catherine Heathcliff, and then again to Catherine Linton" (chap. 3). In the light of this repeated and varied name it is no wonder, finally, that Catherine knows Heathcliff is "more myself than I am," for he has only a single name, while she has so many that she may be said in a sense to have none. Just as triumphant self-discovery is the ultimate goal of the male *Bildungsroman*, anxious self-denial, Brontë suggests, is the ultimate product of a female education. What Catherine, or any girl, must learn is that she does not know her own name, and therefore cannot know either who she is or whom she is destined to be.

It has often been argued that Catherine's anxiety and uncertainty about her own identity represents a moral failing, a fatal flaw in her character which leads to her inability to choose between Edgar and Heathcliff. Heathcliff's reproachful "Why did you betray your own heart, Cathy?" (chap. 15) represents a Blakeian form of this moral criticism, a contemptuous suggestion that "those who restrain desire do so because theirs is weak enough to be restrained." [36] The more vulgar and commonsensical attack of the Leavisites, on the other hand—the censorious notion that "maturity" means being strong enough to choose not to have your cake and eat it too—represents what Mark Kinkead-Weeks calls "the view from the Grange."[37] To talk of morality in connection with Catherine's fall—and specifically in connection with her self-deceptive decision to marry Edgar—seems pointless, however, for morality only becomes a relevant term where there are meaningful choices.

As we have seen, Catherine has no meaningful choices. Driven from Wuthering Heights to Thrushcross Grange by her brother's marriage, seized by Thrushcross Grange and held fast in the jaws of reason, education, decorum, she cannot do otherwise than as she does, must marry Edgar because there is no one else for her to marry and a lady must marry. Indeed, her self-justifying description of her love for Edgar—"I love the ground under his feet, and the air over his head, and everything he touches, and every word he says" (chap. 9)—is a bitter parody of a genteel romantic declaration which shows how effective her education has been in indoctrinating her with the literary romanticism deemed suitable for young ladies, the swooning "femininity" that identifies all energies with the charisma of fathers/lovers/husbands. Her concomitant explanation that it would "degrade" her to marry Heathcliff is an equally inevitable product of her education, for her fall into ladyhood has been accompanied by Heathcliff's reduction to an equivalent position of female powerlessness, and Catherine has learned, correctly, that if it is degrading to be a woman it is even more degrading to be *like* a woman. Just as Milton's Eve, therefore, being already fallen, had no meaningful choice despite Milton's best efforts to prove otherwise, so Catherine has no real choice. Given the patriarchal nature of culture, women must fall—that is, they are already fallen because doomed to fall.

In the shadow of this point, however, moral censorship is merely redundant, a sort of interrogative restatement of the novel's central fact. Heathcliff's Blakeian reproach is equally superfluous, except insofar as it is not moral but etiological, a question one part of Catherine asks another, like her later passionate "Why am I so changed?" For as Catherine herself perceives, social and biological forces have fiercely combined against her. God as—in W. H. Auden's words—a "Victorian papa" has hurled her from the equivocal natural paradise she calls "heaven" and He calls "hell" into His idea of "heaven" where she will break her heart with weeping to come back to the Heights. Her speculative, tentative "mad" speech to Nelly captures, finally, both the urgency and the inexorability of her fall. "Supposing at twelve years old, I had been wrenched from the Heights . . . and my all in all, as Heathcliff was at that time, and been converted at a stroke into Mrs. Linton, the lady of Thrushcross Grange, and the wife of a stranger: an exile, and outcast, thenceforth, from what had been my world." In terms of the psychodramatic action of *Wuthering Heights*, only Catherine's use of the word *supposing* is here a rhetorical strategy; the rest of her speech is absolutely accurate, and places her subsequent actions beyond good and evil, just as it suggests, in yet another Blakeian reversal of customary terms, that her madness may really be sanity.

Catherine Earnshaw Linton's decline follows Catherine Earnshaw's fall. Slow at first, it is eventually as rapid, sickening, and deadly as the course of Brontë's own consumption was to be. And the long slide toward death of the body begins with what appears to be an irreversible death of the soul—with Catherine's fatalistic acceptance of Edgar's offer and her consequent self-imprisonment in the role of "Mrs. Linton, the lady of Thrushcross Grange." It is, of course, her announcement of this decision to Nelly, overheard by Heathcliff, which leads to Heathcliff's self-exile from the Heights and thus definitively to Catherine's psychic fragmentation. And significantly, her response to the departure of her true self is a lapse into illness which both signals the beginning of her decline and foreshadows its mortal end. Her words to Nelly the morning after Heathcliff's departure are therefore symbolically as well as dramatically resonant: "Shut the window, Nelly, I'm starving!" (chap. 9).

As Dorothy van Ghent has shown, windows in *Wuthering Heights* consistently represent openings into possibility, apertures through which subversive otherness can enter, or wounds out of which respectability can escape like flowing blood.[38] It is, after all, on the window ledge that Lockwood finds Catherine's different names obsessively inscribed, as if the girl had been trying to decide which self to let in the window or in which direction she ought to fly after making her own escape down the branches of the neighboring pine. It is through the same window that the ghost of Catherine Linton extends her icy fingers to the horrified visitor. And it is a window at the Grange that Catherine, in her "madness," begs Nelly to open so that she can have one breath of the wind that "comes straight down the moor" (chap. 12). "Open the window again wide, fasten it open!" she cries, then rises and, predicting her own death, seems almost ready to start on her journey homeward up the moor. ("I could not trust her alone by the gaping lattice," Nelly comments wisely.) But besides expressing a general wish to escape from "this shattered prison" of her body, her marriage, her self, her life, Catherine's desire now to *open* the window refers specifically back to that moment three years earlier when she had chosen instead to close it, chosen to inflict on herself the imprisonment and starvation that as part of her education had been inflicted on her double, Heathcliff.

Imprisonment leads to madness, solipsism, paralysis, as Byron's *Prisoner of Chillon*, some of Brontë's Gondal poems, and countless other gothic and neo-gothic tales suggest. Starvation—both in the modern sense of malnutrition and the archaic Miltonic sense of freezing ("to starve in ice")—leads to weakness, immobility, death. During her decline, starting with both starvation and imprisonment, Catherine passes through all these grim stages of mental and physical decay. At first she seems (to Nelly anyway) merely somewhat "headstrong." Powerless without her whip, keenly conscious that she has lost the autonomy of her hardy and free girlhood, she gets her way by indulging in tantrums, wheedling, manipulating, so that Nelly's optimistic belief that she and Edgar "were really in possession of a deep and growing happiness" contrasts ironically with the housekeeper's simultaneous admission that Catherine "was never subject to depression of spirits before" the three interlocking events of Heathcliff's departure, her "perilous illness," and her marriage (chap. 10). But Heathcliff's mysterious reappearance six months after her wedding intensifies rather than cures her symptoms. For his return does not in any way suggest a healing of the wound of femaleness that was inflicted at puberty. Instead, it signals the beginning of "madness," a sort of feverish infection of the wound. Catherine's marriage to Edgar has now inexorably locked her into a social system that denies her autonomy, and thus, as psychic symbolism, Heathcliff's return represents the return of her true self's desires without the rebirth of her former powers. And desire without power, as Freud and Blake both knew, inevitably engenders disease.

If we understand all the action that takes place at Thrushcross Grange between Edgar, Catherine, and Heathcliff from the moment of Heathcliff's reappearance until the time of Catherine's death to be ultimately psychodramatic, a grotesque playing out of Catherine's emotional fragmentation on a "real" stage, then further discussion of her sometimes genteelly Victorian, sometimes fiercely Byronic decline becomes almost unnecessary, its meaning is so obvious. Edgar's autocratic hostility to Heathcliff—that is, to Catherine's desirous self, her independent will—manifests itself first in his attempt to have her entertain the returned "gipsy" or "plough-boy" in the kitchen because he doesn't belong in the parlor. But soon Edgar's hatred results in a determination to expel Healthcliff entirely from his house because he fears the effects of this demonic intruder, with all he signifies, not only upon his wife but upon his sister. His fear is justified because, as we shall see, the Satanic rebellion Heathcliff introduces into the parlors of "heaven" contains the germ of a terrible dis-ease with patriarchy that causes women like Catherine and Isabella to try to escape their imprisonment in roles and houses by running away, by starving themselves, and finally by dying.

Because Edgar is so often described as "soft," "weak," slim, fair-haired, even effeminate-looking, the specifically patriarchal nature of his feelings toward Heathcliff may not be immediately evident. Certainly many readers have been misled by his almost stylized angelic qualities to suppose that the rougher, darker Heathcliff incarnates masculinity in contrast to Linton's effeminacy. The returned Heathcliff, Nelly says, "had grown a tall, athletic, well-formed man, beside whom my master seemed quite slender and youthlike. His upright carriage suggested the idea of his having been in the army" (chap. 10). She even seems to acquiesce in his superior maleness. But her constant, reflexive use of the phrase "my master" for Edgar tells us otherwise, as do some of her other expressions. At this point in the novel, anyway, Heathcliff is always merely "Heathcliff" while Edgar is variously "Mr. Linton," "my master," "Mr. Edgar," and "the master," all phrases conveying the power and status he has independent of his physical strength.

In fact, as Milton also did, Emily Brontë demonstrates that the power of the patriarch, Edgar's power, begins with words, for heaven is populated by "*spirits* Masculine," and as above, so below. Edgar does not need a strong, conventionally masculine body, because his mastery is contained in books, wills, testaments, leases, titles, rent-rolls, documents, languages, all the paraphernalia by which patriarchal culture is transmitted from one generation to the next. Indeed, even without Nelly's designation of him as "the master," his notable bookishness would define him as a patriarch, for he rules his house from his library as if to parody that male education in Latin and Greek, privilege and prerogative, which so infuriated Milton's daughters.[39] As a figure in the psychodrama of Catherine's decline, then, he incarnates the education in young ladyhood that has commanded her to learn her "place." In Freudian terms he would no doubt be described as her superego, the internalized guardian of morality and culture, with Heathcliff, his opposite, functioning as her childish and desirous id.

But at the same time, despite Edgar's superegoistic qualities, Emily Brontë shows that his patriarchal rule, like Thrushcross Grange itself, is based on physical as well as spiritual violence. For her, as for Blake, heaven *kills*. Thus, at a word from Thrushcross Grange, Skulker is let loose, and Edgar's magistrate father cries "What prey, Robert?" to his manservant, explaining that he fears thieves because "yesterday was my rent day." Similarly, Edgar, having decided that he has "humored" Catherine long enough, calls for two strong men servants to support his authority and descends into the kitchen to evict Heathcliff. The patriarch, Brontë notes, needs words, not muscles, and Heathcliff's derisive language paradoxically suggests understanding of the true male power Edgar's "soft" exterior conceals: "Cathy, this lamb of yours threatens like a bull!" (chap. 11). Even more significant, perhaps, is the fact that when Catherine locks Edgar in alone with her and Heathcliff—once more imprisoning herself while ostensibly imprisoning the hated master—this apparently effeminate, "milk-blooded coward" frees himself by striking Heathcliff a breathtaking blow on the throat "that would have levelled a slighter man."

Edgar's victory once again recapitulates that earlier victory of Thrushcross Grange over Wuthering Heights which also meant the victory of a Urizenic "heaven" over a delightful and energetic "hell." At the same time, it seals Catherine's doom, locking her into her downward spiral of self-starvation. And in doing this it finally explains what is perhaps Nelly's most puzzling remark about the relationship between Edgar and Catherine. In chapter 8, noting that the love-struck sixteen-year-old Edgar is "doomed, and flies to his fate," the housekeeper sardonically declares that "the soft thing [Edgar] . . . possessed the power to depart [from Catherine] as much as a cat possesses the power to leave a mouse half killed or a bird half eaten." At that point in the novel her metaphor seems odd. Is not headstrong Catherine the hungry cat, and "soft" Edgar the half-eaten mouse? But in fact, as we now see, Edgar all along represented the devouring force that will gnaw and worry Catherine to death, consuming flesh and spirit together. For having fallen into "heaven," she has ultimately—to quote Sylvia Plath—"fallen / Into the stomach of indifference," a social physiology that urgently needs her not so much for herself as for her function.[40]

When we note the significance of such imagery of devouring, as well as the all-pervasive motif of self-starvation in *Wuthering Heights*, the kitchen setting of this crucial confrontation between Edgar and Heathcliff begins to seem more than coincidental. In any case, the episode is followed closely by what C. P. Sanger calls Catherine's "hunger strike" and by her famous mad scene.[41] Another line of Plath's describes the feelings of self-lessness that seem to accompany Catherine's realization that she has been reduced to a role, a function, a sort of walking costume: "I have no face, I have wanted to efface myself."[42] For the weakening of Catherine's grasp on the world is most specifically shown by her inability to recognize her own face in the mirror during the mad scene. Explaining to Nelly that she is not mad, she notes that if she were "I should believe you really *were* [a] withered hag, and I should think I *was* under Penistone Crag; and I'm conscious it's night and there are two candles on the table making the black press shine like jet." Then she adds, "It does appear odd—I see a face in it" (chap. 12). But of course, ironically, there is no "black press" in the room, only a mirror in which Catherine sees and repudiates her own image. Her fragmentation has now gone so far beyond the psychic split betokened by her division from Heathcliff that body and image (or body and soul) have separated.

Q. D. Leavis would have us believe that his apparently gothic episode, with its allusion to "dark superstitions about premonitions of death, about ghosts and primitive beliefs about the soul . . . is a proof of [Emily Brontë's] immaturity at the time of the original conception of *Wuthering Heights*." Leo Bersani, on the other hand, suggests that the scene hints at "the danger of being haunted by alien versions of the self."[43] In a sense, however, the image Catherine sees in the mirror is neither gothic nor alien—though she is alienated from it—but hideously familiar, and further proof that her madness may really equal sanity. Catherine sees in the mirror an image of who and what she has really become in the world's terms: "Mrs. Linton, the lady of Thrushcross Grange." And oddly enough, this image appears to be stored like an article of clothing, a trousseau-treasure, or again in Plath's words "a featureless, fine / Jew linen,"[44] in one of the cupboards of childhood, the black press from her old room at the Heights.

Because of this connection with childhood, part of the horror of Catherine's vision comes from the question it suggests: was the costume/face always there, waiting in a corner of the little girl's wardrobe? But to ask this question is to ask again, as Frankenstein does, whether Eve was created fallen, whether women are not Education's but "Nature's fools," doomed from the start to be exiles and outcasts despite their illusion that they are hardy and free. When Milton's Eve is for her own good led away from her own image by a superegoistic divine voice which tells her that "What there thou sees fair creature is thyself"—*merely* thyself—does she not in a sense determine Catherine Earnshaw's fall? When, substituting Adam's superior image for her own, she concedes that female "beauty is excell'd by manly grace / And wisdom" (*PL* 4. 490–91) does not her "sane" submission outline the contours of Catherine Earnshaw's rebelliously Blakeian madness? Such questions are only implicit in Catherine's mad mirror vision of herself, but it is important to see that they are implied. Once again, where Shelley clarifies Milton, showing the monster's dutiful disgust with "his" own self-image, Brontë repudiates him, showing how his teachings have doomed her protagonist to what dutiful Nelly considers an insane search for her lost true self. "I'm sure I should be myself were I once more among the heather on those hills," Catherine exclaims, meaning that only a journey back into the androgynous wholeness of childhood could heal the wound her mirror-image symbolizes, the fragmentation that began when she was separated from heather and Heathcliff, and "laid alone" in the first fateful enclosure of her oak-panelled bed. For the mirror-image is one more symbol of the cell in which Catherine has been imprisoned by herself and by society.

To escape from the horrible mirror-enclosure, then, might be to escape from all domestic enclosures, or to begin to try to escape. It is significant that in her madness Catherine tears at her pillow with her teeth, begs Nelly to open the window, and seems "to find childish diversion in pulling the feathers from the rents she [has] just made" (chap. 12). Liberating feathers from the prison where they had been reduced to objects of social utility, she imagines them reborn as the birds they once were, whole and free, and pictures them "wheeling over our heads in the middle of the moor," trying to get back to their nests. A moment later, standing by the window "careless of the frosty air," she imagines her own trip back across the moor to Wuthering Heights, noting that "it's a rough journey, and a sad heart to travel it; and we must pass by Gimmerton Kirk to go that journey! . . . But Heathcliff, if I dare you now, will you venture? . . . I won't rest till you are with me. I never will!" (chap. 12) For a "fallen" woman, trapped in the distorting mirrors of patriarchy, the journey into death is the only way out, Brontë suggests, and the *Liebestod* is not (as it would be for a male artist, like Keats or Wagner) a mystical but a practical solution. In the presence of death, after all, "The mirrors are sheeted," to quote Plath yet again.[45]

The masochism of this surrender to what A. Alvarez has called the "savage god" of suicide is plain, not only from Catherine's own words and actions but also from the many thematic parallels between her speeches and Plath's poems.[46] But of course, taken together, self-starvation or anorexia nervosa, masochism, and suicide form a complex of psychoneurotic symptoms that is almost classically associated with female feelings of powerlessness and rage. Certainly the "hunger strike" is a traditional tool of the powerless, as the history of the feminist movement (and many other movements of oppressed peoples) will attest. Anorexia nervosa, moreover, is a sort of mad corollary of the self-starvation that may be a sane strategy for survival. Clinically associated with "a distorted concept of body size"—like Catherine Earnshaw's alienated/familiar image in the mirror—it is fed by the "false sense of power that the faster derives from her starvation," and is associated, psychologists speculate, with "a struggle for control, for a sense of identity, competence, and effectiveness."

But then in a more general sense it can surely be argued that all masochistic or even suicidal behavior expresses the furious power hunger of the powerless. Catherine's whip—now meaning Heathcliff, her "love" for Heathcliff, and also, more deeply, her desire for the autonomy her union with Heathcliff represented—turns against Catherine. She whips herself because she cannot whip the world, and she must whip something. Besides, in whipping herself does she not, perhaps, torment the world? Of this she is, in her powerlessness, uncertain, and her uncertainty leads to further madness, reinforcing the vicious cycle. "O let me not be mad," she might cry, like Lear, as she tears off her own socially prescribed costumes so that she can more certainly feel the descent of the whip she herself has raised. In her rebelliousness Catherine has earlier played alternately the parts of Cordelia and of Goneril and Regan to the Lear of her father and her husband. Now, in her powerlessness, she seems to have herself become a figure like Lear, mourning her lost kingdom and suicidally surrendering herself to the blasts that come straight down the moor.

Nevertheless, though her madness and its setting echo Lear's disintegration much more than, say, Ophelia's, Catherine is different from Lear in a number of crucial ways, the most obvious being the fact that her femaleness dooms her to a function as well as a role, and threatens her, therefore, with the death Frances's fate had predicted. Critics never comment on this point, but the truth is that Catherine is pregnant during both the kitchen scene and the mad scene, and her death occurs at the time of (and ostensibly because of) her "confinement." In the light of this, her anorexia, her madness, and her masochism become even more fearsomely meaningful. Certainly, for instance, the distorted body that the anorexic imagines for herself is analogous to the distorted body that the pregnant woman really must confront. Can eating produce such a body? The question, mad as it may seem, must be inevitable. In any case, some psychoanalysts have suggested that anorexia, endemic to pubescent girls, reflects a fear of oral impregnation, to which self-starvation would be one obvious response.[47]

But even if a woman accepts, or rather concedes, that she is pregnant, an impulse toward self-starvation would seem to be an equally obvious response to the pregnant woman's inevitable fear of being monstrously inhabited, as well as to her own horror of being enslaved to the species and reduced to a tool of the life process. Excessive ("pathological") morning sickness has traditionally been interpreted as an attempt to vomit up the alien intruder, the child planted in the belly like an incubus.[48] And indeed, if the child has been fathered—as Catherine's has—by a man the woman defines as a stranger, her desire to rid herself of it seems reasonable enough. But what if she must kill herself in the process? This is another question Catherine's masochistic self-starvation implies, especially if we see it as a disguised form of morning sickness. Yet another question is more general: must motherhood, like ladyhood, kill? Is female sexuality necessarily deadly?

To the extent that she answers yes, Brontë swerves once again from Milton, though rather less radically than usual. For when she was separated from her own reflection, Eve was renamed "mother of human race," a title Milton seems to have considered honorifically life-giving despite the dreadful emblem of maternity Sin provided. Catherine's entrance into motherhood, however, darkly parodies even if it does not subvert this story. Certainly childbirth brings death to her (and eventually to Heathcliff) though at the same time it does revitalize the patriarchal order that began to fail at Wuthering Heights with her early assertions of individuality. Birth is, after all, the ultimate fragmentation the self can undergo, just as "confinement" is, for women, the ultimate pun on imprisonment. As if in recognition of this, Catherine's attempt to escape maternity does, if only unconsciously, subvert Milton. For Milton's Eve "knew not eating Death." But Brontë's does. In her refusal to be enslaved to the species, her refusal to be "mother of human race," she closes her mouth on emptiness as, in Plath's words, "on a communion tablet." It is no use, of course. She breaks apart into two Catherines—the old, mad, dead Catherine fathered by Wuthering Heights, and the new, more docile and acceptable Catherine fathered by Thrushcross Grange. But nevertheless, in her defiance Emily Brontë's Eve, like her creator, is a sort of hunger artist, a point Charlotte Brontë acknowledged when she memorialized her sister in *Shirley*, that other revisionary account of the Genesis of female hunger.[49]

Catherine's fall and her resulting decline, fragmentation, and death are the obvious subjects of the first half of *Wuthering Heights*. Not quite so obviously, the second half of the novel is concerned with the larger, social consequences of Catherine's fall, which spread out in concentric circles like rings from a stone flung into a river, and which are examined in a number of parallel stories, including some that have already been set in motion at the time of Catherine's death. Isabella, Nelly, Heathcliff, and Catherine II—in one way or another all these characters' lives parallel (or even in a sense contain) Catherine's, as if Brontë were working out a series of alternative versions of the same plot.

Isabella is perhaps the most striking of these parallel figures, for like Catherine she is a headstrong, impulsive "miss" who runs away from home at adolescence. But where Catherine's fall is both fated and unconventional, a fall "upward" from hell to heaven, Isabella's is both willful and conventional. Falling from Thrushcross Grange to Wuthering Heights, from "heaven" to "hell," in exactly the opposite direction from Catherine, Isabella patently chooses her own fate, refusing to listen to Catherine's warnings against Heathcliff and carefully evading her brother's vigilance. But then Isabella has from the first functioned as Catherine's opposite, a model of the stereotypical young lady patriarchal education is designed to produce. Thus where Catherine is a "stout hearty lass" raised in the raw heart of nature at Wuthering Heights, Isabella is slim and pale, a daughter of culture and Thrushcross Grange. Where Catherine's childhood is androgynous, moreover, as her oneness with Heathcliff implies, Isabella has borne the stamp of sexual socialization from the first, or so her early division from her brother Edgar—her future guardian and master—would suggest. When Catherine and Heathcliff first see them, after all, Isabella and Edgar are quarreling over a lapdog, a genteel (though covertly sexual) toy they cannot share. "When would you catch me wishing to have what Catherine wanted? or find us [arguing] divided by the whole room?" Heathcliff muses on the scene (chap. 6). Indeed, so much the opposite of Catherine's is Isabella's life and lineage that it is almost as if Brontë, in contriving it, were saying "Let's see what would happen if I told Catherine's story the 'right' way"—that is, with socially approved characters and situations.

As Isabella's fate suggests, however—and this is surely part of Brontë's point—the "right" beginning of the story seems almost as inevitably to lead to the wrong ending as the wrong or "subversive" beginning. Ironically, Isabella's bookish upbringing has prepared her to fall in love with (of all people) Heathcliff. Precisely because she has been taught to believe in coercive literary conventions, Isabella is victimized by the genre of romance. Mistaking appearance for reality, tall athletic Heathcliff for "an honourable soul" instead of "a fierce, pitiless wolfish man," she runs away from her cultured home in the naive belief that it will simply be replaced by another cultivated setting. But like Claire Clairmont, who enacted a similar drama in real life, she underestimates both the ferocity of the Byronic hero and the powerlessness of all women, even "ladies," in her society. Her experiences at Wuthering Heights teach her that hell really is hellish for the children of heaven: like a parody of Catherine, she starves, pines and sickens, oppressed by that Miltonic grotesque, Joseph, for she is unable to stomach the rough food of nature (or hell) just as Catherine cannot swallow the food of culture (or heaven). She does not literally die of all this, but when she escapes, giggling like a madwoman, from *her* self-imprisonment, she is so effectively banished from the novel by her brother (and Brontë) that she might as well be dead.

Would Isabella's fate have been different if she had fallen in love with someone less problematical than Heathcliff—with a man of culture, for instance, rather than a Satanic nature figure? Would she have prospered with the love of someone like her own brother, or Heathcliff's tenant, Lockwood? Her early relationship with Edgar, together with Edgar's patriarchal rigidity, hint that she would not. Even more grimly suggestive is the story Lockwood tells in chapter 1 about his romantic encounter at the seacoast. Readers will recall that the "fascinating creature" he admired was "a real goddess in my eyes, as long as she took no notice of [me]." But when she "looked a return," her lover "shrunk icily into myself . . . till finally the poor innocent was led to doubt her own senses . . . " (chap. 1). Since even the most cultivated women are powerless, women are evidently at the mercy of all men, Lockwoods and Heathcliffs alike.

Thus if literary Lockwood makes a woman into a goddess, he can unmake her at whim without suffering himself. If literary Isabella makes a man into a god or hero, however, she must suffer—may even have to die—for her mistake. Lockwood in effect kills his goddess for being human, and would no doubt do the same to Isabella. Heath-cliff, on the other hand, literally tries to kill Isabella for trying to be a goddess, an angel, a lady, and for having, therefore, a "mawkish, waxen face." Either way, Isabella must in some sense be killed, for her fate, like Catherine's, illustrates the double binds with which patriarchal society inevitably crushes the feet of runaway girls.[50] Perhaps it is to make this point even more dramatically that Brontë has Heathcliff hang Isabella's genteelly named springer, Fanny, from a "bridle hook" on the night he and Isabella elope. Just as the similarity of Isabella's and Catherine's fates suggests that "to fall" and "to fall in love" are equivalents, so the *bridle* or *bridal hook* is an apt, punning metaphor for the institution of marriage in a world where fallen women, like their general mother Eve, are (as Dickinson says) "Born—Bridalled—Shrouded—/ In a Day."[51]

Nelly Dean, of course, seems to many critics to have been put into the novel to help Emily Brontë disavow such uniformly dark intentions. "For a specimen of true benevolence and homely fidelity, look at the character of Nelly Dean," Charlotte Brontë says with what certainly appears to be conviction, trying to soften the picture of "perverse passion and passionate perversity" Victorian readers thought her sister had produced.[52] And Charlotte Brontë "rightly defended her sister against allegations of abnormality by pointing out that . . . Emily had created the wholesome, maternal Nelly Dean," comments Q. D. Leavis.[53] How wholesome and maternal *is* Nelly Dean, however? And if we agree that she is basically benevolent, of what does her benevolence consist? Problematic words like *wholesome* and *benevolent* suggest a point where we can start to trace the relationship between Nelly's history and Catherine's (or Isabella's).

To begin with, of course, Nelly is healthy and wholesome because she is a survivor, as the artist-narrator must be. Early in the novel, Lockwood refers to her as his "human fixture," and there is, indeed, a durable thinglike quality about her, as if she had outlasted the Earnshaw/Linton storms of passion like their two houses, or as if she were a wall, a door, an object of furniture meant to begin a narration in response to the conventional sigh of "Ah, if only these old walls could speak, what stories they would tell." Like a wall or fixture, moreover, Nelly has a certain impassivity, a diplomatic immunity to entangling emotions. Though she sometimes expresses strong feelings about the action, she manages to avoid taking sides—or, rather, like a wall, she is related to both sides. Consequently, as the artist must, she can go anywhere and hear everything.

At the same time, Nelly's evasions suggest ways in which her history has paralleled the lives of Catherine and Isabella, though she has rejected their commitments and thus avoided their catastrophes. Hindley, for instance, was evidently once as close to Nelly as Heathcliff was to Catherine. Indeed, like Heathcliff, Nelly seems to have been a sort of stepchild at the Heights. When old Mr. Earnshaw left on his fateful trip to Liverpool, he promised to bring back a gift of apples and pears for Nelly as well as the fiddle and whip Hindley and Catherine had asked for. Because she is only "a poor man's daughter," however, Nelly is excluded from the family, specifically by being defined as its servant. Luckily for her, therefore (or so it seems), she has avoided the incestuous/egalitarian relationship with Hindley that Catherine has with Heathcliff, and at the same time—because she is ineligible for marriage into either family—she has escaped the bridal hook of matrimony that destroys both Isabella and Catherine.

It is for these reasons, finally, that Nelly is able to tell the story of all these characters without herself becoming ensnared in it, or perhaps, more accurately, she is able (like Brontë herself) to use the act of telling the story as a strategy for protecting herself from such entrapment. "I have read more than you would fancy, Mr. Lockwood," Nelly remarks to her new master. "You could not open a book in this library that I have not looked into and got something out of also ... it is as much as you can expect of a poor man's daughter" (59). By this she means, no doubt, that in her detachment she knows about Miltonic fears of falling and Richardsonian dreams of rising, about the anxieties induced by patriarchal education and the hallucinations of genteel romance.[54] And precisely because she has such a keen literary consciousness, she is able ultimately to survive and to triumph over her sometimes unruly story. Even when Heathcliff locks her up, for example, Nelly gets out (unlike Catherine and Isabella, who are never really able to escape), and one by one the deviants who have tried to reform her tale—Catherine, Heathcliff, even Isabella—die, while Nelly survives. She survives and, as Bersani has also noted, she coerces the story into a more docile and therefore more congenial mode.[55]

To speak of coercion in connection with Nelly may seem unduly negative, certainly from the Leavisite perspective. And in support of that perspective we should note that besides being wholesome because she is a survivor, Nelly is benevolent because she is a nurse, a nurturer, a foster-mother. The gift Mr. Earnshaw promises her is as symbolically significant in this respect as Catherine's whip and Hindley's fiddle, although our later experiences of Nelly suggest that she wants the apples and pears not so much for herself as for others. For though Nelly's health suggests that she is a hearty eater, she is most often seen feeding others, carrying baskets of apples, stirring porridge, roasting meats, pouring tea. Wholesomely nurturing, she does appear to be in some sense an ideal woman, a "general mother"—if not from Emily Brontë's point of view, then from, say, Milton's. And indeed, if we look again at the crucial passage in *Shirley* where Charlotte Brontë's Shirley/Emily criticizes Milton, we find an unmistakable version of Nelly Dean. "Milton tried to see the first woman," says Shirley, "but, Cary, he saw her not. . . . It was his cook that he saw . . . puzzled 'what choice to choose for delicacy best. . . .' "

This comment explains a great deal. For if Nelly Dean is Eve as Milton's cook—Eve, that is, as Milton (but not Brontë or Shirley) would have had her—she does not pluck apples to eat them herself; she plucks them to make applesauce. And similarly, she does not tell stories to participate in them herself, to consume the emotional food they offer, but to create a moral meal, a didactic fare that will nourish future generations in docility. As Milton's cook, in fact, Nelly Dean is patriarchy's paradigmatic housekeeper, the man's woman who has traditionally been hired to keep men's houses in order by straightening out their parlors, their daughters, and their stories. "My heart invariably cleaved to the master's, in preference to Catherine's side," she herself declares (chap. 10), and she expresses her preference by acting throughout the novel as a censorious agent of patriarchy.

Catherine's self-starvation, for instance, is notably prolonged by Nelly's failure to tell "the master" what his wife is doing, though in the first place it was induced by tale-bearing on Nelly's part. All her life Catherine has had trouble stomaching the food offered by Milton's cook, and so it is no wonder that in her madness she sees Nelly as a witch "gathering elf-bolts to hurt our heifers." It is not so much that Nelly Dean is "Evil," as Q. D. Leavis scolds "an American critic" for suggesting,[56] but that she is accommodatingly manipulative, a stereotypically benevolent man's woman. As such, she would and does "hurt [the] heifers" that inhabit such an anti-Miltonic heaven of femaleness as Wuthering Heights. In fact, as Catherine's "mad" words acknowledge, there is a sense in which Nelly Dean herself is Milton's bogey, the keeper of the house who closes windows (as Nelly does throughout *Wuthering Heights*) and locks women into the common sitting room. And because Emily Brontë is not writing a revolutionary polemic but a myth of origins, she chooses to tell her story of psychogenesis ironically, through the words of the survivor who helped *make* the story—through "the perdurable voice of the country," in Schorer's apt phrase. Reading Nelly's text, we see what we have lost through the eyes of the cook who has transformed us into what we are.

But if Nelly parallels or comments upon Catherine by representing Eve as Milton's cook, while Isabella represents Catherine/Eve as a bourgeois literary lady, it may at first be hard to see how or why Heathcliff parallels Catherine at all. Though he is Catherine's alter ego, he certainly seems to be, in Bersani's words, "a non-identical double."[57] Not only is he male while she is female—implying many subtle as well as a few obvious differences, in this gender-obsessed book—but he seems to be a triumphant survivor, an insider, a power-usurper throughout most of the novel's second half, while Catherine is not only a dead failure but a wailing, outcast ghost. Heathcliff does love her and mourn her—and finally Catherine does in some sense "kill" him—but beyond such melodramatically romantic connections, what bonds unite these one-time lovers?

Perhaps we can best begin to answer this question by examining the passionate words with which Heathcliff closes his first grief-stricken speech after Catherine's death: "Oh, God! it is unutterable! I cannot live without my life! I cannot live without my soul!" (chap. 16). Like the metaphysical paradox embedded in Catherine's crucial adolescent speech to Nelly about Heathcliff ("He's more myself than I am"), these words have often been thought to be, on the one hand, emptily rhetorical, and on the other, severely mystical. But suppose we try to imagine what they might mean as descriptions of a psychological fact about the relationship between Heathcliff and Catherine. Catherine's assertion that Heathcliff was *herself* quite reasonably summarized, after all, her understanding that she was being transformed into a lady while Heathcliff retained the ferocity of her primordial half-savage self. Similarly, Heathcliff's exclamation that he cannot live without his soul may express, as a corollary of this idea, the "gypsy's" own deep sense of being Catherine's whip, and his perception that he has now become merely the soulless body of a vanished passion. But to be merely a body—a whip without a mistress—is to be a sort of monster, a fleshly thing, an object of pure animal materiality like the abortive being Victor Frankenstein created. And such a monster is indeed what Heathcliff becomes.

From the first, Heathcliff has had undeniable monster potential, as many readers have observed. Isabella's questions to Nelly—"Is Mr. Heathcliff a man? If so, is he mad? And if not is he a devil?" (chap. 13)—indicate among other things Emily Brontë's cool awareness of having created an anomalous being, a sort of "Ghoul" or "Afreet," not (as her sister half hoped) "despite" herself but for good reasons. Uniting human and animal traits, the skills of culture with the energies of nature, Heathcliff's character tests the boundaries between human and animal, nature and culture, and in doing so proposes a new definition of the demonic. What is more important for our purposes here, however, is the fact that, despite his outward masculinity, Heathcliff is somehow female in his monstrosity. Besides in a general way suggesting a set of questions about humanness, his existence therefore summarizes a number of important points about the relationship between maleness and femaleness as, say, Milton representatively defines it.

To say that Heathcliff is "female" may at first sound mad or absurd. As we noted earlier, his outward masculinity seems to be definitively demonstrated by his athletic build and military carriage, as well as by the Byronic sexual charisma that he has for ladylike Isabella. And though we saw that Edgar is truly patriarchal despite his apparent effeminacy, there is no real reason why Heathcliff should not simply represent an alternative version of masculinity, the maleness of the younger son, that paradigmatic outsider in patriarchy. To some extent, of course, this is true: Heathcliff is clearly just as male in his Satanic outcast way as Edgar in his angelically established way. But at the same time, on a deeper associative level, Heathcliff is "female"—on the level where younger sons and bastards and devils unite with women in rebelling against the tyranny of heaven, the level where orphans are female and heirs are male, where flesh is female and spirit is male, earth female, sky male, monsters female, angels male.

The sons of Urizen were born from heaven, Blake declares, but "his daughters from green herbs and cattle, / From monsters and worms of the pit." He might be describing Heathcliff, the "little dark thing" whose enigmatic ferocity suggests vegetation spirits, hell, pits, night— all the "female" irrationality of nature. Nameless as a woman, the gypsy orphan old Earnshaw brings back from the mysterious bowels of Liver/pool is clearly as illegitimate as daughters are in a patrilineal culture. He speaks, moreover, a kind of animal-like gibberish which, together with his foreign swarthiness, causes sensible Nelly to refer to him at first as an "it," implying (despite his apparent maleness) a deep inability to get his gender straight. His "it-ness" or id-ness emphasizes, too, both his snarling animal qualities—his appetites, his brutality—and his thingness. And the fact that he speaks gibberish suggests the profound alienation of the physical/natural/female realm he represents from language, culture's tool and the glory of "spirits Masculine." In even the most literal way, then, he is what Elaine Showalter calls "a woman's man," a male figure into which a female artist projects in disguised form her own anxieties about her sex and its meaning in her society.[58] Indeed, if Nelly Dean is Milton's cook, Heathcliff incarnates that unregenerate natural world which must be metaphorically cooked or spiritualized, and therefore a raw kind of femaleness that, Brontë shows, has to be exorcised if it cannot be controlled.

In most human societies the great literal and figurative chefs, from Brillat-Savarin to Milton, are males, but as Sherry Ortner has noted, everyday "cooking" (meaning such low-level conversions from nature to culture as child-rearing, pot-making, bread-baking) is done by women, who are in effect charged with the task of policing the realm they represent.[59] This point may help explain how and why Catherine Earnshaw becomes Heathcliff's "soul." After Nelly as archetypal house-keeper finishes nursing him, high-spirited Catherine takes over his education because he meets her needs for power. Their relationship works so well, however, because just as he provides her with an extra body to lessen her female vulnerability, so she fills his need for a soul, a voice, a language with which to address cultured men like Edgar. Together they constitute an autonymous and androgynous (or, more accurately, gynandrous) whole: a woman's man and a woman *for herself* in Sartre's sense, making up one complete woman.[60] So complete do they feel, in fact, that as we have seen they define their home at Wuthering Heights as a heaven, and themselves as a sort of Blakeian angel, as if sketching out the definition of an angel D. H. Lawrence would have Tom Brangwen offer seventy-five years later in *The Rainbow*:

> "If we've got to be Angels, and if there is no such thing as a man nor a woman amongst them, then ... a married couple makes one Angel.... For ... an Angel can't be less than a human being. And if it was only the soul of a man *minus* the man, then it would be less than a human being."[61]

That the world—particularly Lockwood, Edgar, and Isabella— sees the heaven of Wuthering Heights as a "hell" is further evidence of the hellish femaleness that characterizes this gynandrous body and soul. It is early evidence, too, that without his "soul" Heathcliff will become an entirely diabolical brute, a "Ghoul" or "Afreet." Speculating seriocomically that women have souls "only to make them capable of *Damnation*," John Donne articulated the traditional complex of ideas underlying this point even before Milton did. "Why hath the common opinion afforded women soules?" Donne asked. After all, he noted, women's only really "spiritual" quality is their power of speech, "for which they are beholding to their *bodily instruments*: For perchance an *Oxes* heart, or a *Goates*, or a *Foxes*, or a *Serpents* would speak just so, if it were in the *breast*, and could move that *tongue* and *jawes*."[62] Though speaking of women, he might have been defining the problem Isabella was to articulate for Emily Brontë: "Is Mr. Heathcliff *a man*? Or what is he?"

As we have already seen, when Catherine is first withdrawn from the adolescent Heathcliff, the boy becomes increasingly brutish, as if to foreshadow his eventual soullessness. Returning in her ladylike costume from Thrushcross Grange, Catherine finds her one-time "counterpart" in old clothes covered with "mire and dirt," his face and hands "dismally beclouded" by dirt that suggests his inescapable connection with the filthiness of nature. Similarly, when Catherine is dying Nelly is especially conscious that Heathcliff "gnashed . . . and foamed like a mad dog," so that she does not feel as if he is a creature of her own species (chap. 15). Still later, after his "soul's" death, it seems to her that Heathcliff howls "not like a man, but like a savage beast getting goaded to death with knives and spears" (chap. 16) His subsequent conduct, though not so overtly animal-like, is consistent with such behavior. Bastardly and dastardly, a true son of the bitch goddess Nature, throughout the second half of *Wuthering Heights* Heathcliff pursues a murderous revenge against patriarchy, a revenge most appropriately expressed by *King Lear*'s equally outcast Edmund: "Well, then, / Legitimate Edgar, I must have your land."[63] For Brontë's revisionary genius manifests itself especially in her perception of the deep connections among Shakespeare's Edmund, Milton's Satan, Mary Shelley's monster, the demon lover/animal groom figure of innumerable folktales—and Eve, the original rebellious female.

Because he unites characteristics of all these figures in a single body, Heathcliff in one way or another acts like all of them throughout the second half of *Wuthering Heights*. His general aim in this part of the novel is to wreak the revenge of nature upon culture by subverting legitimacy. Thus, like Edmund (and Edmund's female counterparts Goneril and Regan) he literally *takes* the *place* of one legitimate heir after another, supplanting both Hindley and Hareton at the Heights, and—eventually—Edgar at the Grange. Moreover, he not only replaces legitimate culture but in his rage strives like Frankenstein's monster to end it. His attempts at killing Isabella and Hindley, as well as the infanticidal tendencies expressed in his merciless abuse of his own son, indicate his desire not only to alter the ways of his world but literally to dis-continue them, to get at the heart of patriarchy by stifling the line of descent that ultimately gives culture its legitimacy. Lear's *"hysterica passio,"* his sense that he is being smothered by female nature, which has inexplicably risen against all fathers everywhere, is seriously parodied, therefore, by the suffocating womb/room of death where Heathcliff locks up his sickly son and legitimate Edgar's daughter.[64] Like Satan, whose fall was originally inspired by envy of the celestial legitimacy incarnated in the Son of God, Heathcliff steals or perverts birthrights. Like Eve and her double, Sin, he undertakes such crimes against a Urizenic heaven in order to vindicate his own worth, assert his own energy. And again, like Satan, whose hellish kingdom is a shadowy copy of God's luminous one, or like those suavely unregenerate animal grooms Mr. Fox and Bluebeard, he manages to achieve a great deal because he realizes that in order to subvert legitimacy he must first impersonate it; that is, to kill patriarchy, he must first pretend to be a patriarch.

Put another way, this simply means that Heathcliff's charismatic maleness is at least in part a result of his understanding that he must defeat on its own terms the society that has defeated him. Thus, though he began his original gynandrous life at Wuthering Heights as Catherine's whip, he begins his transformed, soulless or Satanic life there as Isabella's bridal hook. Similarly, throughout the extended maneuvers against Edgar and his daughter which occupy him for the twenty years between Isabella's departure and his own death, he impersonates a "devil daddy," stealing children like Catherine II and Linton from their rightful homes, trying to separate Milton's cook from both her story and her morality, and perverting the innocent Hareton into an artificially blackened copy of himself. His understanding of the inauthenticity of his behavior is consistently shown by his irony. Heathcliff knows perfectly well that he is not really a father in the true (patriarchal) sense of the word, if only because he has himself no *sur*name; he is simply acting like a father, and his bland, amused "I want my children about me to be sure" (chap. 29) comments upon the world he despises by sardonically mimicking it, just as Satan mimics God's logic and Edmund mimics Gloucester's astrologic.

On the one hand, therefore, as Linton's deathly father, Heathcliff, like Satan, is truly the father of death (begotten, however, not upon Sin but upon silliness), but on the other hand he is very consciously a mock father, a male version of the terrible devouring mother, whose blackly comic admonitions to Catherine II ("No more runnings away! . . . I'm come to fetch you home, and I hope you'll be a dutiful daughter, and not encourage my son to further disobedience" [chap. 29]) evoke the bleak hilarity of hell with their satire of Miltonic righteousness. Given the complexity of all this, it is no wonder Nelly considers his abode at the Heights "an oppression past explaining."

Since Heathcliff's dark energies seem so limitless, why does his vengeful project fail? Ultimately, no doubt, it fails because in stories of the war between nature and culture nature always fails. But that point is of course a tautology. Culture tells the story (that is, the story is a cultural construct) and the story is etiological: how culture triumphed over nature, where parsonages and tea-parties came from, how the lady got her skirts—and her deserts. Thus Edmund, Satan, Frankenstein's monster, Mr. Fox, Bluebeard, Eve, and Heathcliff all must fail in one way or another, if only to explain the status quo. Significantly, however, where Heathcliff's analogs are universally destroyed by forces outside themselves, Heathcliff seems to be killed, as Catherine was, by something within himself. His death from self-starvation makes his function as Catherine's almost identical double definitively clear. Interestingly, though, when we look closely at the events leading up to his death it becomes equally clear that Heathcliff is not just killed by his own despairing desire for his vanished "soul" but at least in part by another one of Catherine's parallels, the new and cultivated Catherine who has been reborn through the intervention of patriarchy in the form of Edgar Linton. It is no accident, certainly, that Catherine II's imprisonment at the Heights and her rapprochement with Hareton coincide with Heathcliff's perception that "there is a strange change approaching," with his vision of the lost Catherine, and with his development of an eating disorder very much akin to Catherine's anorexia nervosa.

If Heathcliff is Catherine's almost identical double, Catherine II really is her mother's "non-identical double." Though he has his doubles confused, Bersani does note that Nelly's "mild moralizing"

seems "suited to the younger Catherine's playful independence."[65] For where her headstrong mother genuinely struggled for autonomy, the more docile Catherine II merely plays at disobedience, taking make-believe journeys within the walls of her father's estate and dutifully surrendering her illicit (though equally make-believe) love letters at a word from Nelly. Indeed, in almost every way Catherine II differs from her fierce dead mother in being culture's child, a born lady. "It's as if Emily Brontë were telling the same story twice," Bersani observes, "and eliminating its originality the second time."[66] But though he is right that Brontë is telling the same story over again (really for the third or fourth time), she is not repudiating her own originality. Rather, through her analysis of Catherine II's successes, she is showing how society repudiated Catherine's originality.

Where, for instance, Catherine Earnshaw rebelled against her father, Catherine II is profoundly dutiful. One of her most notable adventures occurs when she runs away from Wuthering Heights to get *back* to her father, a striking contrast to the escapes of Catherine and Isabella, both of whom ran purposefully away from the world of fathers and older brothers. Because she is a dutiful daughter, moreover, Catherine II is a cook, nurse, teacher, and housekeeper. In other words, where her mother was a heedless wild child, Catherine II promises to become an ideal Victorian woman, all of whose virtues are in some sense associated with daughterhood, wifehood, motherhood. Since Nelly Dean was her foster mother, literally replacing the original Catherine, her development of these talents is not surprising. To be mothered by Milton's cook and fathered by one of his angels is to become, inevitably, culture's child. Thus Catherine II nurses Linton (even though she dislikes him), brews tea for Heathcliff, helps Nelly prepare vegetables, teaches Hareton to read, and replaces the wild blackberries at Wuthering Heights with flowers from Thrushcross Grange. Literary as her father and her aunt Isabella, she has learned the lessons of patriarchal Christianity so well that she even piously promises Heathcliff that she will forgive both him and Linton for their sins against her: "I know [Linton] has a bad nature . . . he's your son. But I'm glad I've a better to forgive it" (chap. 29). At the same time, she has a genteel (or Urizenic) feeling for rank which comes out in her early treatment of Hareton, Zillah, and others at the Heights.

Even when she stops biblically forgiving, moreover, literary modes dominate Catherine II's character. The "black arts" she tries to practice are essentially bookish—and plainly inauthentic. Indeed, if Heathcliff is merely impersonating a father at this point in the story, Catherine II is merely impersonating a witch. A real witch would threaten culture; but Catherine II's vocation is to serve it, for as her personality suggests, she is perfectly suited to (has been raised for) what Sherry Ortner defines as the crucial female function of mediating between nature and culture.[67] Thus it is she who finally restores order to both the Heights and the Grange by marrying Hareton Earnshaw, whom she has, significantly, prepared for his new mastery by teaching him to read. Through her intervention, therefore, he can at last recognize the name over the lintel at Wuthering Heights—the name Hareton Earnshaw—which is both his own name and the name of the founder of the house, the primordial patriarch.

With his almost preternatural sensitivity to threats, Heathcliff himself recognizes the danger Catherine II represents. When, offering to "forgive him," she tries to embrace him he shudders and remarks "I'd rather hug a snake!" Later, when she and Hareton have cemented their friendship, Heathcliff constantly addresses her as "witch" and "slut." In the world's terms, she is the opposite of these: she is virtually an angel in the house. But for just those reasons she *is* Urizenically dangerous to Heathcliff's Pandemonium at the Heights. Besides threatening his present position, however, Catherine II's union with Hareton reminds Heathcliff specifically of the heaven he has lost. Looking up from their books, the young couple reveal that "their eyes are precisely similar, and they are those of Catherine Earnshaw" (chap. 33). Ironically, however, the fact that Catherine's descendants "have" her eyes tells Heathcliff not so much that Catherine endures as that she is both dead and fragmented. Catherine II has only her mother's eyes, and though Hareton has more of her features, he too is conspicuously not Catherine. Thus when Edgar dies and Heathcliff opens Catherine's casket as if to free her ghost, or when Lockwood opens the window as if to admit the witch child of his nightmare, the original Catherine arises in her ghostly wholeness from the only places where she can still exist in wholeness: the cemetary, the moor, the storm, the irrational realm of those that fly by night, the realm of Satan, Eve, Sin, and Death. Outside of this realm, the ordinary world inhabited by Catherine II and Hareton is, Heathcliff now notes, merely "a dreadful collection of memoranda that [Catherine] did exist, and that I have lost her!" (chap. 33).

Finally, Catherine II's alliance with Hareton awakens Heathcliff to truths about the younger man that he had not earlier understood, and in a sense his consequent disillusionment is the last blow that sends him toward death. Throughout the second half of the novel Heathcliff has taken comfort not only in Hareton's "startling" physical likeness to Catherine, but also in the likeness of the dispossessed boy's situation to his own early exclusion from society. "Hareton seem[s] a personification of my youth, not a human being," Heathcliff tells Nelly (chap. 33). This evidently causes him to see the illiterate outcast as metaphorically the true son of his own true union with Catherine. Indeed, where he had originally dispossessed Hareton as a way of revenging himself upon Hindley, Heathcliff seems later to want to keep the boy rough and uncultivated so that he, Heathcliff, will have at least one strong natural descendant (as opposed to Linton, his false and deathly descendant). As Hareton moves into Catherine II's orbit, however, away from nature and toward culture, Heathcliff realizes the mistake he has made. Where he had supposed that Hareton's reenactment of his own youth might even somehow restore the lost Catherine, and thus the lost Catherine-Heathcliff, he now sees that Hareton's reenactment of his youth is essentially corrective, a retelling of the story the "right" way. Thus if we can call Catherine II C^2 and define Hareton as H^2, we might arrive at the following formulation of Heathcliff's problem: where C plus H equals fullness of being for both C and H, C^2 plus H^2 specifically equals a negation of both C and H. Finally, the ambiguities of Hareton's name summarize in another way Heathcliff's problem with this most puzzling Earnshaw. On the one hand, Hare/ton is a nature name, like Heathcliff. But on the other hand, Hare/ton, suggesting Heir/ton (Heir/town?) is a punning indicator of the young man's legitimacy.

It is in his triumphant legitimacy that Hareton, together with Catherine II, acts to exorcise Heathcliff from the traditionally legitimate world of the Grange and the newly legitimized world of Wuthering Heights. Fading into nature, where Catherine persists "in every cloud, in every tree," Heathcliff can no longer eat the carefully cooked human food that Nelly offers him. While Catherine II decorates Hareton's porridge with cut flowers, the older man has irreligious fantasies of dying and being unceremoniously "carried to the churchyard in the evening." "I have nearly attained *my* heaven," he tells Nelly as he fasts and fades, "and that of others is . . . uncoveted by me" (chap, 34). Then, when he dies, the boundaries between nature and culture crack for a moment, as if to let him pass through: his window swings open, the rain drives in. "Th' divil's harried off his soul," exclaims old Joseph, *Wuthering Heights'* mock Milton, falling to his knees and giving thanks "that the lawful master and the ancient stock [are] restored to their rights" (chap. 34). The illegitimate Heathcliff/Catherine have finally been re-placed in nature/hell, and replaced by Hareton and Catherine II—a proper couple—just as Nelly replaced Catherine as a proper mother for Catherine II. Quite reasonably, Nelly now observes that "The crown of all my wishes will be the union of" this new, civilized couple, and Lockwood notes of the new pair that "together, they would brave Satan and all his legions." Indeed, in both Milton's and Brontë's terms (it is the only point on which the two absolutely agree) they have already braved Satan, and they have triumphed. It is now 1802; the Heights —hell—has been converted into the Grange—heaven; and with patriarchal history redefined, renovated, restored, the nineteenth century can truly begin, complete with tea-parties, ministering angels, governesses, and parsonages.

Joseph's important remark about the restoration of the lawful master and the ancient stock, together with the dates—1801/1802— which surround Nelly's tale of a pseudo-mythic past, confirm the idea that *Wuthering Heights* is somehow etiological. More, the famous care with which Brontë worked out the details surrounding both the novel's dates and the Earnshaw-Linton lineage suggests she herself was quite conscious that she was constructing a story of origins and renewals. Having arrived at the novel's conclusion, we can now go back to its beginning, and try to summarize the basic story *Wuthering Heights* tells. Though this may not be the book's only story, it is surely a crucial one. As the names on the windowsill indicate, *Wuthering Heights* begins and ends with Catherine and her various avatars. More specifically, it studies the evolution of Catherine Earnshaw into Catherine Heathcliff and Catherine Linton, and then her return through Catherine Linton II and Catherine Heathcliff II to her "proper" role as Catherine Earnshaw II. More generally, what this evolution and de-evolution conveys is the following parodic, anti-Miltonic myth:

There was an Original Mother (Catherine), a daughter of nature whose motto might be "Thou, Nature, art my goddess; to thy law / My services are bound." But this girl fell into a decline, at least in part through eating the poisonous cooked food of culture. She fragmented herself into mad or dead selves on the one hand (Catherine, Heathcliff) and into lesser, gentler/genteeler selves on the other (Catherine II, Hareton). The fierce primordial selves disappeared into nature, the perversely hellish heaven which was their home. The more teachable and docile selves learned to read and write, and moved into the fallen cultured world of parlors and parsonages, the Miltonic heaven which, from the Original Mother's point of view, is really hell. Their passage from nature to culture was facilitated by a series of teachers, preachers, nurses, cooks, and model ladies or patriarchs (Nelly, Joseph, Frances, the Lintons), most of whom gradually disappear by the end of the story, since these lesser creations have been so well instructed that they are themselves able to become teachers or models for other generations. Indeed, so model are they that they can be identified with the founders of ancestral houses (Hareton Earnshaw, 1500) and with the original mother redefined as the patriarch's wife (Catherine Linton Heathcliff Earnshaw).

The nature/culture polarities in this Brontë myth have caused a number of critics to see it as a version of the so-called Animal Groom story, like Beauty and the Beast, or the Frog Prince. But, as Bruno Bettelheim has most recently argued, such tales usually function to help listeners and readers assimilate sexuality into consciousness and thus nature into culture (e.g., the beast is really lovable, the frog really handsome, etc.).[68] In *Wuthering Heights*, however, while culture does require nature's energy as raw material—the Grange needs the Heights, Edgar wants Catherine—society's most pressing need is to exorcise the rebelliously Satanic, irrational, and "female" representatives of nature. In this respect, Brontë's novel appears to be closer to a number of American Indian myths Lévi-Strauss recounts than it is to any of the fairy tales with which it is usually compared. In particular, it is reminiscent of an Opaye Indian tale called "The Jaguar's Wife."

In this story, a girl marries a jaguar so that she can get all the meat she wants for herself and her family. After a while, as a result of her marriage, the jaguar comes to live with the Indians, and for a time the girl's family becomes friendly with the new couple. Soon, however, a grandmother feels mistrust. "The young woman [is] gradually turning into a beast of prey.... Only her face remain[s] human ... the old woman therefore resort[s] to witchcraft and kill[s] her granddaughter." After this, the family is very frightened of the jaguar, expecting him to take revenge. And although he does not do so, he promises enigmatically that "Perhaps you will remember me in years to come," and goes off "incensed by the murder and spreading fear by his roaring; but the sound [comes] from farther and farther away."[69]

Obviously this myth is analogous to *Wuthering Heights* in a number of ways, with alien and animal-like Heathcliff paralleling the jaguar, Catherine paralleling the jaguar's wife, Nelly Dean functioning as the defensive grandmother, and Catherine II and Hareton acting like the family which inherits meat and a jaguar-free world from the departed wife. Lévi-Strauss's analysis of the story makes these likenesses even clearer, however, and in doing so it clarifies what Brontë must have seen as the grim necessities of *Wuthering Heights*.

> In order that all man's present possessions (which the jaguar has now lost) may come to him from the jaguar (who enjoyed them formerly when man was without them), there must be some agent capable of establishing a relation between them: this is where the jaguar's (human) wife fits in.
>
> But once the transfer has been accomplished (through the agency of the wife):
>
> a) The woman becomes useless, because she has served her purpose as a preliminary condition, which was the only purpose she had.
>
> b) Her survival would contradict the fundamental situation, which is characterized by a total absence of reciprocity.
>
> The jaguar's wife must therefore be eliminated.[70]

Though Lévi-Strauss does not discuss this point, we should note too that the jaguar's distant roaring hints he may return some day: obviously culture must be vigilant against nature, the superego must be ready at all times to battle the id. Similarly, the random weakening of Wuthering Heights' walls with which Brontë's novel began— symbolized by old Earnshaw's discovery of Heathcliff in Liverpool— suggests that patriarchal culture is always only precariously holding off the rebellious forces of nature. Who, after all, can say with certainty that the restored line of Hareton Earnshaw 1802 will not someday be just as vulnerable to the onslaughts of the goddess's illegitimate children as the line of Hareton Earnshaw 1500 was to Heathcliff's intrusion? And who is to say that the carving of Hareton Earnshaw 1500 was not similarly preceded by still another war between nature and culture? The fact that everyone has the same name leads inevitably to speculations like this, as though the drama itself, like its actors, simply represented a single episode in a sort of mythic infinite regress. In addition, the fact that the little shepherd boy still sees "Heathcliff and a woman" wandering the moor hints that the powerfully disruptive possibilities they represent may some day be reincarnated at Wuthering Heights.

Emily Brontë would consider such reincarnation a consummation devoutly to be wished. Though the surface Nelly Dean imposes upon Brontë's story is as dispassionately factual as the tone of "The Jaguar's Wife," the author's intention is passionately elegiac, as shown by the referential structure of *Wuthering Heights*, Catherine-Heathcliff's charisma, and the book's anti-Miltonic messages. This is yet another point Charlotte Brontë understood quite well, as we can see not only from the feminist mysticism of *Shirley* but also from the diplomatic irony of parts of her preface to *Wuthering Heights*. In *Shirley*, after all, the first woman, the true Eve, *is* nature—and she is noble and she is lost to all but a few privileged supplicants like Shirley-Emily herself, who tells Caroline (in response to an invitation to go to church) that "I will stay out here with my mother Eve, in these days called Nature. I love her—undying, mighty being! Heaven may have faded from her brow when she fell in paradise; but all that is glorious on earth shines there still." [71] And several years later Charlotte concluded her preface to *Wuthering Heights* with a discreetly qualified description of a literal heath/cliff that might also apply to *Shirley*'s titanic Eve:

... the crag took human shape; and there it stands, colossal, dark, and frowning, half statue, half rock: in the former sense, terrible and goblin-like; in the latter, almost beautiful, for its coloring is of mellow grey, and moorland moss clothes it; and heath, with its blooming bells and balmy fragrance, grows faithfully close to the giant's foot.[72]

This grandeur, Charlotte Brontë says, is what "Ellis Bell" was writing about; this is what she (rightly) thought we have lost. For like the fierce though forgotten seventeenth-century Behmenist mystic Jane Lead, Emily Brontë seems to have believed that Eve had become tragically separated from her fiery original self, and that therefore she had "lost her Virgin Eagle Body ... and so been sown into a slumbering Death, in Folly, Weakness, and Dishonor."[73]

Her slumbering death, however, was one from which Eve might still arise. Elegiac as it is, mournfully definitive as its myth of origin seems, *Wuthering Heights* is nevertheless haunted by the ghost of a lost gynandry, a primordial possibility of power now only visible to children like the ones who see Heathcliff and Catherine.

> No promised Heaven, these wild Desires
> Could all or half fulfil,
> No threatened Hell, with quenchless fire
> Subdue this quenchless will!

Emily Brontë declares in one of her poems.[74] The words may or may not be intended for a Gondalian speech, but it hardly matters, since in any case they characterize the quenchless and sardonically impious will that stalks through *Wuthering Heights*, rattling the windowpanes of ancient houses and blotting the pages of family bibles. Exorcised from the hereditary estate of the ancient stock, driven to the sinister androgyny of their *Liebestod*, Catherine and Heathcliff nevertheless linger still at the edge of the estate, as witch and goblin, Eve and Satan. Lockwood's two dreams, presented as prologues to Nelly's story, are also, then, necessary epilogues to that tale. In the first, "Jabes Branderham," Joseph's nightmare fellow, tediously thunders Miltonic curses at Lockwood, enumerating the four hundred and ninety sins of which erring nature and the quenchless will are guilty. In the second, nature, personified as the wailing witch child "Catherine

Linton," rises willfully in protest, and gentlemanly Lockwood's unexpectedly violent attack upon her indicates his terrified perception of the danger she represents.

Though she reiterated Milton's misogyny where Brontë struggled to subvert it, Mary Shelley also understood the dangerous possibilities of the outcast will. Her lost Eve became a monster, but "he" was equally destructive to the fabric of society. Later in the nineteenth century other women writers, battling Milton's bogey, would also examine the annihilation with which patriarchy threatens Eve's quenchless will, and the witchlike rage with which the female responds. George Eliot, for instance, would picture in *The Mill on the Floss* a deadly androgyny that seems like a grotesque parody of the *Liebestod* Heathcliff and Catherine achieve. "In their death" Maggie and Tom Tulliver "are not divided"—but the union they achieve is the only authentic one Eliot can imagine for them, since in life the one became an angel of renunciation, the other a captain of industry. Significantly, however, their death is caused by a flood that obliterates half the landscape of culture: female nature does and will continue to protest.

If Eliot specifically reinvents Brontë's *Liebestod*, Mary Elizabeth Coleride reimagines her witchlike nature spirit. In a poem that also reflects her anxious ambivalence about the influence of her great uncle Samuel, the author of "Christabel," Coleridge *becomes* Geraldine, Catherine Earnshaw, Lucy Gray, even Frankenstein's monster —all the wailing outcast females who haunt the graveyards of patriarchy. Speaking in "the voice that women have, who plead for their heart's desire," she cries

> I have walked a great while over the snow
> And I am not tall nor strong.
> My clothes are wet, and my teeth are set,
> And the way was hard and long.
> I have wandered over the fruitful earth,
> But I never came here before.
> Oh, lift me over the threshhold, and let me in at the door . . .

And then she reveals that "She came—and the quivering flame / Sank and died in the fire." [75]

Emily Brontë's outcast witch-child is fiercer, less dissembling than

Coleridge's, but she longs equally for the extinction of parlor fires and the rekindling of unimaginably different energies. Her creator, too, is finally the fiercest, most quenchless of Milton's daughters. Looking oppositely for the queendom of heaven, she insists, like Blake, that "I have also the Bible of Hell, which the world shall have whether they will or no." [76] And in the voice of the wind that sweeps through the newly cultivated garden at Wuthering Heights, we can hear the jaguar, like Blake's enraged Rintrah, roaring in the distance.

IV
The Spectral Selves of
Charlotte Brontë

9 A Secret, Inward Wound: *The Professor*'s Pupil

> The strong pulse of Ambition struck
>   In every vein I owned;
> At the same instant, bleeding broke
>   A secret, inward wound.
>   —Charlotte Brontë

> I saw my life branching out before me like the green fig tree in the story.
>
> From the tip of every branch, like a fat purple fig, a wonderful future beckoned and winked. One fig was a husband and a happy home and children, and another fig was a famous poet and another fig was a brilliant professor, and another fig was Ee Gee, the amazing editor. . . .
>
> I saw myself sitting in the crotch of this fig tree, starving to death, just because I couldn't make up my mind which of the figs I would choose. . . . and, as I sat there, unable to decide, the figs began to wrinkle and go black, and, one by one, they plopped to the ground at my feet.
>
>   —Sylvia Plath

> There is a pain—so utter—
> It swallows substance up—
> Then covers the Abyss with Trance—
> So Memory can step
> Around—across—upon it—
> As one within a Swoon—
> Goes safely—where an open eye—
> Would drop Him—Bone by Bone.
>   —Emily Dickinson

Charlotte Brontë was essentially a trance-writer. "All wondering why I write with my eyes shut," she commented in her Roe Head journal,[1]

and, as Winifred Gérin points out, the irregular lines of her manuscripts indicate that she did write this way, a habit Gérin suggests
she adopted "intentionally the better to sharpen the inner vision and
shut out her bodily surroundings."[2] Inner vision: the rhetoric is
Romantic, and it is Brontë's as much as Gérin's, recalling Wordsworth's "Trances of thought and mountings of the mind," as well as
Coleridge's "Close your eyes with holy dread." "All this day,"
Brontë wrote in the same journal, "I have been in a dream half
miserable and half ecstatic—miserable because I could not follow
it out uninterruptedly, and ecstatic because it shewed almost in the
vivid light of reality the ongoings of the infernal world [the childhood
fantasy world of Angria]."[3] This is assuredly Romantic. And yet,
we believe, it is distinctively female, too. For though most of Brontë's
vocabulary and many of her visions derive from the early nineteenth-
century writers in whose work her mind was steeped—Wordsworth,
Coleridge, Scott, Byron—the entranced obsessiveness with which
she worked out recurrent themes and metaphors seems to have been
determined primarily by her gender, her sense of her difficult sexual
destiny, and her anxiety about her anomalous, "orphaned" position
in the world.

That this was the case is made a little clearer by the following
passage from the same Roe Head journal entry:

> The parsing lesson was completed.... The thought came over
> me am I to spend all the best part of my life in this wretched
> bondage.... I crept up to the bed-room to be alone for the
> first time that day. Delicious was the sensation I experienced as
> I laid down on the spare bed & resigned myself to the luxury
> of twilight & solitude. The stream of thought, checked all day,
> came flowing free & calm along its channel.... the toil of the
> day, succeeded by this moment of divine leisure had acted on
> me like opium & was coiling about me a disturbed but fascinating
> spell such as I never felt before. What I imagined grew morbidly
> vivid. I remember I quite seemed to see with my bodily eyes a
> lady standing in the hall of a gentleman's house as if waiting
> for some one. It was dusk & there was the dim outline of antlers
> with a hat & a rough great-coat upon them. She had a flat
> candle-stick in her hand & seemed coming from the kitchen or

some such place. . . . As she waited I most distinctly heard the front-door open and saw the soft moonlight disclosed upon the lawn outside, and beyond the lawn at a distance I saw a town with lights twinkling through the gloaming. . . . No more. I have not time to work out the vision. At last I became aware of a heavy weight laid across me—I knew I was wide awake & that it was dark & that moreover the Ladies were now come into the room to get their curl-papers. . . . I heard them talking about me—I wanted to speak, to rise, it was impossible. . . . I must get up I thought, and did so with a start.

The interest of this passage derives in part from the fact that, as Gérin remarks, such a confession is "rare in the annals of literature for its perception of the actual creative processes at work."[4] But surely some of its "morbidly vivid" elements are even more interesting: the gloomy gentleman's house, with its threateningly sexual outlines of antlers and its rough great-coat, the mysterious lady standing in the hall, the front-door opening upon inaccessible and glamorous distances, and (in a later section) the enigmatic figure of the girl Lucy, whose "faded bloom . . . reminded me of one who might . . . be dead and buried under the . . . sod."

"I have not time to work out the vision," Brontë notes, complaining of "a heavy weight laid across me." Nevertheless, we would argue that this is the vision she worked out in most of her novels, a vision of an indeterminate, usually female figure (who has often come "from the kitchen or some such place") trapped—even buried—in the architecture of a patriarchal society, and imagining, dreaming, or actually devising escape routes, roads past walls, lawns, antlers, to the glittering town outside. In this respect, Brontë's career provides a paradigm of the ways in which, as we have suggested, many nineteenth-century women wrote obsessively, often in what could be (metaphorically) called a state of "trance," about their feelings of enclosure in "feminine" roles and patriarchal houses, and wrote, too, about their passionate desire to flee such roles or houses.

Certainly Brontë's Angrian tales use Byronic elements to articulate female fantasies of liberation into an exotic "male" landscape. Written during the novelist's adolescence—from the time she was ten until she was about twenty-two—these stories of the "infernal

world" are as Satanically revisionary in their assessment of patriarchal Miltonic moral categories as any of Charlotte's sister Emily's
Gondalian fictions were. But, as we shall show, Charlotte Brontë
was far more ambivalent than Emily about the dichotomies of
heaven and hell, angel and monster. Thus her famous "Farewell
to Angria," written when she was on the verge of *The Professor*,
was not just a farewell to juvenile fantasies; it was, more importantly,
a farewell to the Satanic rebellion that those fantasies embodied.
Repudiating Angria, Brontë was adopting more elaborate disguises,
committing herself to an oscillation between overtly "angelic" dogma
and covertly Satanic fury that would mark the whole of her professional literary career. On the surface, indeed, she would seem to
have drastically revised her own revisionary impulses in order to
follow Carlyle's advice to "Close thy *Byron*; open thy *Goethe*."
Careful readings of all four of her novels suggest, however, that she
was in a sense reading her Goethe *and* her Byron simultaneously.

We shall see, for example, that *Jane Eyre* parodies both the nightmare confessional mode of the gothic genre and the moral didacticism
of Bunyan's *Pilgrim's Progress* to tell its distinctively female story of
enclosure and escape, with a "morbidly vivid" escape dream acted
out by an apparently "gothic" lunatic who functions as the more
sedate heroine's double. Similarly, *Shirley* uses a judicious, author-
omniscient technique to tell, in the context of a seemingly balanced,
conservative history of the conflict between male frame-breakers
and male mill-owners, a "female" tale of the genesis of female
"starvation." And even *Villette*, the most obviously eccentric of
Brontë's novels, and thus the one that comes closest to openly presenting its readers with an alternative female aesthetic, disguises its
dream narrative of female burial and tentatively imagined resurrection in a complex structure of self-denying parables and severe moral
homilies. Metaphorically speaking, Satan and Gabriel, angel and
monster, nun and witch, engage in an elaborate dialogue throughout
its pages, from its deliberately obscure beginning to its consciously
ambiguous conclusion, as if to distract us from the real point. During
all this, moreover, Lucy Snowe—the novel's narrator—pretends, like
Goethe's Makarie, to be a woman with no story of her own except
that story of repression which gave Makarie (and perhaps Brontë
after her) such terrible headaches.[5]

Of course, like so many other women writers, Brontë was not always entirely conscious of the extent of her own duplicity—the extent, for instance, to which her entranced reveries about escape pervaded even her most craftsmanlike attempts at literary decorum. In her "Farewell to Angria," for instance, preparing herself to master the complexities of the "realistic" Victorian novel, she exclaimed that "I long to quit for a while the burning clime where we [she, Branwell, Emily, and Anne] have sojourned too long—its skies flame—the glow of sunset is always upon it—the mind would cease from excitement and turn now to a cooler region where the dawn breaks grey and sober, and the coming day for a time at least is subdued by clouds."[6] And yet *The Professor* (1846, pub. 1857), the pseudo-masculine *Bildungsroman* to which she turned with, in effect, eyes wide open, develops several crucial elements of the basic female enclosure-escape story. Perhaps more significant, though it appears dutifully to trace a traditional, hero-triumphant pattern, it contains figures whose characterizations seem as obsessive and involuntary as any in the earlier Angrian tales she was repudiating, figures who foreshadow the "morbidly vivid" dream actors in such later novels as *Jane Eyre* and *Villette*: a sensitive, outcast orphan girl; two inexplicably hostile brothers—one tyrannical, the other quietly revolutionary; a sinister and manipulative "stepmother"; and a Byronic ironist whose comments on the action often appear to reflect not just his own Romantic disaffection but also the narrator's—and the author's—secret, ungovernable rage, a rage which asserts itself the minute the novelist closes her eyes and feels again the "heavy weight" of her gender laid across her.

The narrator and the author are more carefully distinguished from each other in *The Professor* than in any of Brontë's other mature novels. Moreover, the use of the male narrator, as much as the book's "plain and homely" style, suggests an attempt by the female novelist to objectify her vision of the story she is telling, to disentangle personal fantasies from its plot and cool the "burning clime" of wish-fulfillment. For this reason, it is understandable that Winifred Gérin, among others, sees the male narrator as "an intrinsic demerit" in the work: Charlotte Brontë as William Crimsworth certainly lacks the apparent directness and confessional intensity of Charlotte Brontë as Jane Eyre or Charlotte Brontë as Lucy Snowe.

Curiously, however, even (or perhaps especially) this apparent objectivity of *The Professor* links it to the earlier, more obviously "entranced" Angrian tales, for those stories, too, were generally told by a male speaker, an "incurably inquisitive" avatar of the fledgling author with the significant name of *Charles* Arthur Florian Wellesley. Younger brother to the ambiguously fascinating Zamorna, Angria's sultanic/Satanic ruler, this early narrator openly fomented revolt against what he considered the insane tyranny of his sibling: "Serfs of Angria! Freeman of Verdopolis!" he exclaims in the preface to "The Spell, An Extravaganza," written when Brontë was eighteen, "I tell you that your tyrant, your Idol is mad! Yes! There are black veins of utter perversion of intellect born with him and running through his whole soul."[7] And while no such accusations are made by William Crimsworth, the sober professor, his restrained account of his own "ascent of the 'Hill of Difficulty' " indicts *his* older brother's "outrageous peculiarities" even more vigorously, though "rather by implication than assertion."[8]

Is there, then, any significant relationship between Brontë's literary male-impersonation (both in the Angrian tales and in *The Professor*) and her "female" proclivity for what we have called trance-writing? As we have seen, many women working in a male-dominated literary tradition at first attempt to resolve the ambiguities of their situation not merely by male mimicry but by some kind of metaphorical male impersonation. Similarly, trance-writing —in the sense in which we are using the phrase to describe Charlotte Brontë's simultaneous enactment and evasion of her own rebellious impulses—is clearly an attempt to allay the anxieties of female authorship. Beyond the fact that both are ways of resolving literary anxieties, however, it seems possible that trance-writing and male impersonation have even deeper connections. For one thing, the woman writer who may shrink from a consciously female appraisal of her female vulnerability in a male society can more easily make such an appraisal in her role of male impersonator. That is, by pretending to be a man, she can see herself as the crucial and powerful Other sees her. More, by impersonating a man she can gain male power, not only to punish her own forbidden fantasies